THE NEGRO AND ORGANIZED LABOR

THE NEGRO AND

One of a series of books from the research program of the

Institute of Industrial Relations, University of California

ORGANIZED LABOR

RAY MARSHALL

Professor of Economics
The University of Texas

JOHN WILEY & SONS, INC.

NEW YORK · LONDON · SYDNEY

Library of Congress Catalog Card Number: 65–15761
Printed in the United States of America

Preface

This study attempts to deal objectively and analytically with the relations between the Negro and organized labor with emphasis on the factors responsible for the evolution of union racial practices. It is based on the conviction that an understanding of these causal relationships must precede peaceful accommodations between the groups involved in the racial employment relationship. Part 1 outlines the historical development of the general relations between the labor movement and the Negro community and analyzes some of the forces influencing current relationships between the AFL-CIO and Negroes. Part 2 considers the main patterns of union racial practices; the influence of public policy on union racial practices is discussed in Part 3. My concluding observations are set forth in the final chapter. Throughout the book, generalizations are illustrated with representative examples.

The material for this study came mainly from field studies and interviews, union and civil-rights organization records, and published sources. The field studies were made between 1958 and 1964. Some of the material was collected in connection with related studies, particularly a history of organized labor in the South, which I am preparing for the Wertheim Committee at Harvard University, and a memorandum on union racial practices, which I prepared for Paul Norgren and Samuel E. Hill's *Toward Fair Employment* (New York: Columbia University Press, 1964).

In addition to the interviews, documents from the following sources were examined: the AFL and AFL-CIO Executive Council *Minutes;*

v

the CIO Executive Board *Minutes;* President Eisenhower's Committee on Government Contracts; the CIO Civil Rights Committee; the U. S. Department of Labor Library; the Harvard University Library; the Library of Congress; the University of Texas Library; the New York City Library; and the fair-employment practice commissions in New York, Michigan, Philadelphia, Ohio, Washington, San Francisco, Oregon, California, Pennsylvania, Connecticut, New Jersey, Colorado, Cleveland, Pittsburgh, and Wisconsin. Extensive use also was made of correspondence, telephone conversations, and published sources. The published works from which material was drawn are cited in the footnotes, but special mention should be made of the main studies that have been made in this field: *The Black Worker,* by Sterling D. Spero and Abram L. Harris (1930); *Black Workers and the New Unions,* by Horace R. Cayton and George Mitchell (1939), and especially *Organized Labor and the Negro,* by Herbert Northrup (1944).

This study presented some special problems of documentation. Some sources had to be obscured because governmental agencies were prohibited by law from releasing information from their files. And some interviewees gave information only in the strictest confidence. Much of the material cited in this book has very limited availability and therefore cannot readily be checked by the interested reader. I am well aware of the responsibility that these problems place upon me and have made every effort to double check sources wherever possible, especially where the data were important to the main arguments being developed. Perhaps the most serious problem in this connection was the relatively heavy reliance on interviews and personal notes for some factual material. Moreover, since union racial practices, like race relations generally, were in considerable ferment during the years material for this study was collected, some of the situations analyzed have undoubtedly changed. I attempted to minimize this problem, however, by continuing to observe the major trends and by focusing on general principles rather than particular cases and events.

In order to avoid misunderstanding, I should make it clear that this is not intended to be a general quantitative survey of various union racial practices. I have intentionally selected for study the unions and situations that illustrated particular problems. For this reason and because of problems involved in obtaining information in racial cases, I have probably given greater weight to the negative than to the positive aspects of union racial practices. It is hoped, however, that I have at least focused on the main problems and that challenges to my facts and their interpretation will correct any errors I have made.

Although requests for anonymity and the sheer numbers of people involved prohibit my listing all those who contributed to this study, some special acknowledgments must be made. I am particularly indebted to Professor Walter Galenson for suggesting that I make this study and for giving his advice and encouragement while it was being undertaken. I am grateful to Professor Galenson, Donald Slaiman, and Professors Margaret S. Gordon, Herbert R. Northrup, and Lloyd Ulman for reading the entire manuscript and making many useful suggestions. The Trade Union Project of the Fund for the Republic provided most of the financial assistance and the Research Advisory Council of the Trade Union Project (Clark Kerr, chairman, Benjamin Aaron, Daniel Bell, Walter Galenson, Paul Jacobs, Seymour M. Lipset, Philip Selznick, and W. Willard Wirtz) made many useful suggestions during the study's planning stages.

Valuable assistance was given by too many interviewees to be listed, but special acknowledgment is due: H. S. (Hank) Brown, Ted Brown, Elmer Carter, James Cook, William H. Crawford, Rev. Fred Dawkins, Ernest Delpit, Chris Dixie, Frank Evans, Roy R. Evans, Alex Fuller, George Googe, Shelton Granger, Carey Haigler, Albert J. Hayes, Ralph Helstein, Herbert Hill, Samuel Hill, John Hope II, Charles Houk, Herman D. Kenin, J. Harvey Kerns, Charles Logan, Wade Mackie, Carl Megal, William Mitch, H. L. Mitchell, Max Mont, Emanuel Muravchik, Paul Norgren, William H. Oliver, Revious Ortique, Jr., Charles Patterson, Mark Perlman, R. J. Petree, E. J. Petterson, Daniel A. Powell, A. Philip Randolph, William Rentfro, John E. Rousseau, Benjamin D. Segal, Brendan Sexton, Horace Sheffield, Boris Shishkin, Donald Slaiman, Stanton Smith, Ray Smithhart, Thomas J. Starling, Jack Stieber, Julius Thomas, Father L. J. Twomey, Emory Via, George L-P Weaver, Barney Weeks, Phil Weightman, E. H. Williams, Steve Wilson, J. C. Yeldell, and Charles Zimmerman.

In spite of numerous useful suggestions from others, I alone am responsible for the opinions and conclusions expressed in this study. It should also be noted that the individuals listed did not necessarily supply the information about their organizations used in this book.

Finally, I am indebted to the following journals and organizations for permission to use material from some of my previous publications: *Industrial Relations, Industrial and Labor Relations Review, Social Forces, Annals of the American Academy of Political and Social Sciences, Journal of Negro Education, Political Science Quarterly,*

the Industrial Relations Research Association, and Resources for the
Future. Some of the material used in this book also was presented in
my testimony before the U. S. Senate Subcommittee on Employment
and Manpower in September 1963.

RAY MARSHALL

Austin, Texas
December 1964

Contents

Contents

PART **I**

Evolution of
Negro-Union Relations

CHAPTER 1

Origin of the Negro-Union Relationship

Introduction

THE "RACE PROBLEM" IS UNDOUBTEDLY THE MOST IMPORTANT domestic problem this country faces. Surely no other issue has incited such passionate debate and no other question has so tested the nation's moral fiber or forced such a reexamination of basic principles. This study of the Negro and organized labor deals with an aspect of the "race problem" which has significant implications for many groups. The "civil rights" problem, as it is called in union circles, is one of the most important issues facing organized labor. This is so not only because of the importance for unions of gaining the political and economic support of minority groups (whose employment is growing relative to whites in traditionally unionized occupations), but also because the "race question" is an important moral issue which influences the public's opinion of unions. Negroes, of course, are more concerned with union racial practices than any other group. Indeed, Negroes benefited greatly from the close cooperation formed between

3

unions and the Negro community during the 1930's. Organized labor has provided decisive support for Negro causes and has used its economic and political power to combat racial discrimination in all its forms. However, the militant mood of the Negro community and the persistence of discrimination by some unions produced a growing conflict between Negroes and organized labor after the AFL-CIO merger in 1955. The intensity of the Negro community's feelings is reflected in public criticism of unions by Negro organizations and by the militant—and sometimes violent—demonstrations against building-trades unions in major Northern cities.

Employers find themselves caught between the forces demanding more integration and others demanding the continuation of the status quo. These pressures not only create industrial-relations problems, but sometimes disrupt business activity and result in the destruction of property. The rapidity of the changes in civil-rights tactics apparently caught many employers unprepared to deal with these problems. However, judging by the interest shown in this problem by management groups throughout the country, employers have become intensely aware of the need to understand and deal with racial labor problems. Indeed, this is rapidly becoming a specialized field in labor relations. And many similarities and differences are being discovered between labor-management relations and labor racial relations.

State, local, and federal governments have major responsibilities for the Negro-labor relationship. Since the Negro's political power has increased greatly with emigration from the rural South, government officials have been forced to pay attention to this problem. The international political implications of racial discrimination also increase the vulnerability of government officials to pressures from Negroes and civil-rights groups. And since pickets, boycotts, sit-ins, and other tactics by civil-rights organizations are likely to take place in urban areas, municipal governments have found it necessary to understand this problem and be prepared to adopt measures to cope with it. City governments have particularly important mediating roles to play which require detailed knowledge of the groups involved in these disputes.

Besides the obvious need to keep the peace and respond to political pressures, Negro concentrations confront governments at every level with serious economic problems. To the extent that Negroes have low incomes, are employed below their abilities, are not able to develop their productive potential, suffer much higher rates of unemployment, must live in inferior housing and attend inferior schools, they will constitute heavy burdens on governments in terms of welfare, police, and health costs, but will make relatively small contributions to tax revenues. Underemployment of Negroes also constitutes an important resource waste that the nation can ill afford. Moral and international political considerations aside, at a time of growing concern over shortages of skilled manpower, it is imperative that Negroes and other minorities be able to develop their skills to the limit of their potential. Moreover, programs to alleviate poverty, maintain full employment, improve education, and provide better public services invariably are forced to consider race problems.

Early Beginnings

Like most other racial problems, the Negro-union relationship had its roots in slavery and Reconstruction. Slavery not only caused the American Negro to be regarded as an inferior person, but produced other lasting effects on race relations. Stanley M. Elkins tells us, moreover, that slavery in the United States was almost unique in producing a stereotype of the Negro as "childlike, irresponsible, incapable of thought or foresight, lazy, ignorant, totally dependent upon his master, [and] happy." [1] No similar stereotype existed in Brazil and the West Indies. The difference, Elkins found, was because in the United States "individualism was unrestricted, freed from feudal limitations, aristocracy, a powerful church, monarchy—from any institution that could claim traditional authority. . . . Where the slave-master wielded absolute power, the slave became absolutely dependent." [2] In adapting the Negro to his needs, the planter established controls and customs that conditioned the attitudes and personalities of whites and blacks alike. As Dabbs put it:

When the planter bought the abstract, diagramatic African, he bought essentially a machine, a stripped-down powerhouse. Into that machine he tried to build certain gadgets. The slave was to be docile, submissive, unreflecting. In general, he was to be inferior, and therefore by various methods he was made inferior. [3]

Although the planter never was really able to reduce the slave to this ideal, the mark of inferiority became firmly stamped upon him in the minds of whites, and the Negro was forced in some degree to conform with this image in order to survive in the plantation economy.

Another element in the complex of factors molding the white workers' attitudes toward Negroes was direct and indirect competition between slaves and free workers. Although most slaves were employed in agriculture, they were also trained for a number of trades needed in the plantation economy, especially those trades connected with building. Slaves were sometimes indentured as apprentices by planters, but they were also purchased and trained by free craftsmen.[4] Collective action by white workers also was thwarted by the use of slaves. In 1846, for example, the superintendent of a South Carolina canal and railroad company recommended to his board of directors that slaves be bought to avert strikes.[5] And sometimes slaves were actually used to defeat strikes by white workers.[6] Moreover, there was mutual antipathy because "The poor white envied the slave's security and hated him for his material advantages, while the slave envied the white man's freedom and hated him for the advantages of his whiteness."[7]

In spite of its adverse effects, however, once slavery came under attack from forces outside the region, Southern whites closed ranks in support of this "peculiar institution," even though slave-holding families represented a very small proportion of the South's population.[8]

Hostility toward Negroes was not restricted to the South. Before the Civil War, anti-Negro demonstrations occurred in Philadelphia, Cincinnati, New York, and in smaller cities in Indiana, Ohio, New Jersey, and Pennsylvania. Some groups of Northern white workers feared competition from Negroes so much that they opposed emancipation. In 1860 the Pennsylvania legislature was urged to legalize slavery.[9] However, until the mass migrations out of the South during the First World War, this was not a very important problem in the non-South.

Emancipation, Reconstruction, and Redemption

Like slavery, the period of "Emancipation, Reconstruction, and Redemption" had a lasting impact on political, social, and economic institutions in the South.[10] After the Civil War, the South faced the difficult task of reconstructing an economy whose capital had been depleted by emancipation and war and reestablishing labor relations on some basis other than slavery. When the freedman's dream that the Yankees would furnish him forty acres and a mule proved unfounded, he was forced to turn to his old masters and the sharecropping system for subsistence. Under this system there was little incentive for the Negro worker to improve either his condition or that of the land he worked, since improvements accrued to the planter and not the sharecropper. Moreover, the exigencies of cotton growing were such that little food was raised, the diet was poor, the fertility of the soil was rapidly depleted, farming techniques were relatively static and required little other than brute strength from the sharecropper. The ambitious Negro's problems were also complicated by the obstacles to land ownership placed in his path; he had to find a white person who was willing to sell him land and generally had to be acceptable to whites in the area before he could buy land. Negroes tended to be frozen to agriculture because they had great difficulty improving their conditions by moving into urban areas since the rate of growth of nonagricultural industry in the South was very small until after 1880,[11] and even then the Negro was usually excluded from most of the new nonagricultural occupations except for disagreeable or low-status "Negro" jobs. The Negro's inferior education and low degree of skill also made it difficult for him to acquire good industrial jobs. Moreover, the planters and their political allies, who had once protected the Negro and saw to it that he was able to learn the rudimentary skills required of the plantation economy, now took measures to restrict his movements in order to assure a continuous supply of agricultural labor. The so-called "Black Codes" were ostensibly vagrancy laws, but had as one of their primary objectives the assurance of labor supplies for plantations. Finally, the sharecroppers were frequently in debt to the planter and thus not allowed to leave the plantation until this debt was cleared. As we shall see, the disfranchisement of the freedmen after 1890 made it virtually impossible for them to improve their conditions through political action.

It would be misleading, however, to leave the impression that the system established after the Civil War was entirely the fault of the planter. The planters themselves were impoverished by the war, which had also virtually destroyed the region's credit structure. Credit therefore was available to the planter only on very unfavorable terms from bankers or supply merchants, who frequently had virtual monopolies in their areas and charged high interest because of the risks of cotton culture. Many planters were unable to adjust to the harsh realities of this new economic milieu and were forced into various clerical occupations. Others remained as masters of declining estates.[12]

Poor whites were even worse off than the planters. Like the Negro, they were unfitted by training and inclination to meet the harsh conditions imposed by the Southern economy after the Civil War. They also had poorer lands, less credit or capital, and higher birth rates.

Their rapid multiplication during the last quarter of the nineteenth century gave rise to increasing competition for declining positions on the land. Indeed, one motive for the Ku Klux Klan movement of these years was a desire by low-class whites to remove the Negro as a competitor, especially in the renting of land.[13]

War and Reconstruction strengthened the unity of Southern whites built up before the war over the slavery question. The fact that the South was defeated only served to make Southern whites more conscious of their regional indentification. It was also natural that the South should resist the Yankee's intentions to remake the region entirely. In spite of twelve years of military occupation, Southern whites regained control of their political affairs. As C. Vann Woodward and others have emphasized,[14] the Negroes' part in the Reconstruction governments probably did not suffer too much by comparison with governments in other areas; but this is irrelevant for the formation of attitudes. Even though relatively few Negroes were elected to public office, the South remembers this as the period of "nigger domination," and for years defended its actions on the basis of preventing the Negro from "taking over." W. J. Cash, for example, refers to Reconstruction as an effort by the Yankee "tariff gang" to "establish themselves in the public trough" and to "rob, to loot, to waste the pitiful remaining substance of this people in riot." [15] Southern whites therefore were unified in their desire to regain political control of the region. Of course, the Southern whites were also unified by their common poverty-stricken plight. Poverty influenced the racial attitudes of common whites who were afraid that their economic condition and forced competition with Negroes would dislodge them from their position on next-to-the-last rung of the status ladder. The Negro was also a galling symbol of the South's recent defeat.

What has been said about the unifying experience of the Civil War and Reconstruction helps us understand the solid political front in the South for so many years. But this political tradition was not established immediately. For some time following the withdrawal of federal troops from the South, after 1877, the Negro vote was coveted by conservatives and liberals alike. According to Woodward, during the 1880's Southern Democrats and Republicans competed vigorously for the Negro vote. "The Negro voters were therefore courted, 'mistered,' and honored by Southern white politicians as never before." [16]

It even looked for a time during the 1880's and 1890's as if Southern Negroes and whites might be welded together politically and economically in the Populist movement. Ironically, however, the Populists were defeated by Negro votes controlled by conservative Democrats in the plantation belts. In order to form a movement that would emphasize economic considerations, the Populists became convinced that Negroes would have to be disfranchised. Of course, many whites favored disfranchisement because Negroes could become the balance of political power if whites split along economic lines. But once the Negro was disfranchised through white primaries, poll taxes, and other restrictions, demagogues were able to use the race issue for many years to prevent Negroes fom becoming politically significant. These demagogues were aided by the South's tradition of conformity and the one-party tradition. The Democratic Party became the Party of the South and Republicanism was equated with "treason to race, country, God and Southern womanhood." Consequently, according to Cash, the "master class . . . would go on . . . dealing with the government machinery of the South as their private property. . . ." [17]

Just as disfranchisement of Negroes did not occur immediately after the withdrawal of federal troops, it took some time for a rigid form of legal racial segregation to become the pattern in the South. Whether for fear of the return of Yankee troops or fear of the Negro vote, it was about a decade after the end of military occupation before the first segregation laws were passed. In Mississippi, Vernon L. Wharton found that saloons in Jackson served Negroes and whites at separate tables, and the governors of Louisiana and South Carolina went on record in favor of protecting the Negroes' right to vote. [18]

Complete legal segregation became the accepted way of handling the race problem in the South by 1900, however, because, among other things, of a feeling in the South that a majority of Northern whites also favored segregation and second-class citizenship for the Negro and therefore would not send the troops back South. This conviction was supported by: the segregation of the Negro in the federal army and the refusal of many Northern states to enfranchise the Negro, even though they insisted that the South do so; the prevalence of segregation in the North; the acquiescence of Northerners in the political compromise of 1877, which resulted in the withdrawal of federal troops; the use of race arguments by Northerners to support the adventures of the United States in the Pacific and Caribbean areas after 1898, making it difficult for them to counter the same arguments when used by Southerners against Negroes; and finally, a series of U. S. Supreme Court decisions between 1873 and 1898 establishing the legality of "separate but equal facilities" and denying the Negro federal protection for acts committed against him by private individuals.

By 1900, therefore, the Negro had become almost completely segregated by law or custom. He rode in separate compartments or in the back of public conveyances, went to segregated public schools, could not marry whites, was buried in segregated cemeteries, and ate in separate restaurants. Employment also was segregated and Negroes were displaced from some occupations they had formerly held, had great difficulty leaving agriculture, and were relegated to "Negro" jobs in urban areas. The jobs set aside for Negroes were usually the most disagreeable ones which whites would not take.

Where unions existed Negroes were either excluded from membership or, where they were too numerous to be excluded (longshoremen, cement finishers, plasterers, bricklayers, carpenters), they were sometimes organized into racially segregated locals. Unions did not create the pattern of occupational segregation in these years, but they were among the institutions used by whites to restrict colored workers to certain kinds of jobs or to remove them from jobs they had formerly held. Railroad unions took positive measures to remove Negroes from jobs such as locomotive firemen, building-trades unions (except for the trowel trades and common laborers, who were usually unorganized before the 1930's) generally restricted Negroes to work in Negro neighborhoods, and in manufacturing plants Negroes were restricted to certain menial jobs. Before the 1930's, Negroes and whites were rarely organized into the same unions and they almost never shared job opportunities equally.

However, discrimination by unions was relatively insignificant, as compared with the following factors, which also caused the Southern Negro to lose his relative position in the skilled trades after emancipation: Negroes lost the support of their former masters, who had had a vested interest in seeing that they practiced their trades; for the same wages employers usually preferred white workers;[19] there was a prevailing white sentiment against permitting Negroes to hold better jobs (Negroes had no better jobs in nonunion than in unionized sectors—indeed, textiles, the South's leading industry, never very well organized, was looked upon as "white" work); and finally, Negroes could not compete with white workers in a free labor market because as W. E. B. Dubois argued, "slavery trained artisans, but for the most part they were careless and inefficient. Only in exceptional cases were they first class mechanics."[20] Thus, even in the absence of unions, it is doubtful that Negroes could have competed with whites in the South.

Despite these handicaps, however, Negro craftsmen apparently fared better in the South than in the North after emancipation. In the North, where unions were stronger and there were fewer colored craftsmen, resistance to Negroes was so strong that Negro leaders advised colored workers to return to the South where the skilled crafts were still open to them.[21] In 1905 John R. Commons concluded that the plasterers, carpenters, masons, and painters unions admitted Negroes freely in the South, but that few Northern plasterers unions and almost none of the other crafts accepted Negroes.[22] E. Franklin Frazier found that except where he had broken in as a strikebreaker, the Negro in the North was confined principally to domestic and personal service occupations.[23]

The National Labor Union and the Knights of Labor

The two main labor federations formed in the immediate post-Civil War period—the National Labor Union (NLU) and the Knights of Labor (KL)—both attempted unsuccessfully to solve the race problem. Although both federations attempted to promote equalitarian policies, neither was able to overcome racial prejudices at the local level. In the NLU, however, political differences between Negroes and white union leaders made cooperation difficult. The NLU's leaders generally backed Democratic programs at a time when most Negro leaders were Republicans.

The KL program of organizing on an equal basis any person who "earns his living by labor and desires to unite with his fellowmen for their common good" also was not always translated into practice at the local level. Then, as now, it was easier for a politically oriented federation to make equalitarian pronouncements than it was for local collective-bargaining organizations to enforce those policies. The KL gained considerable publicity—adverse in the South—when a majority of the delegates to the 1886 Richmond convention withdrew from a hotel which would not permit a Negro delegate from New York to be seated. But in the South there were complaints of segregation and discrimination against Negroes.[24]

Summary and Conclusions

The mutual animosities between slaves and white workers survived Emancipation. After abortive attempts to form equalitarian unions and political movements immediately after Reconstruction, segregation and disfranchisement became the accepted pattern in the South by 1900. Where they had the power to do so, Southern unions followed the community pattern and segregated or excluded Negroes. Segregation was motivated partly by a desire to restrict good jobs to whites, but partly also because of the slavery-induced image of the Negro as an inferior person. The belief was prevalent that Negroes would "degrade" a trade or occupation. In a few cases, however, especially in the "trowel" and other trades with large numbers of colored workers, Negroes and whites were organized into the same unions. Although unions generally discriminated against Negroes, there were other factors contributing to the colored workers' economic disadvantages in the South. Outside the South, where unions were stronger and there were fewer Negroes, colored workers had fewer skilled job opportunities than in the South. Though both the National Labor Union and the Knights of Labor attempted to follow equalitarian policies, they were unable to overcome the racial prejudices of their rank-and-file members and local affiliates.

FOOTNOTES

1. Stanley M. Elkins, *Slavery*, Chicago: University of Chicago Press, 1959.
2. Introduction by Nathan Glazer, *ibid.*, pp. xii–xiii.
3. James McBride Dabbs, *The Southern Heritage*, New York: Knopf, 1959, p. 172.
4. See Marcus Jernigan, *Laboring and Dependent Classes in Colonial America*, Chicago: University of Chicago Press, 1931.
5. Kenneth Stampp, *The Peculiar Institution*, New York: Knopf, 1956, p. 427.
6. R. B. Morris, "Labor Militancy in the Old South," *Labor and Nation*, May–June 1948, p. 33.
7. Sterling D. Spero and Abram L. Harris, *The Black Worker*, New York: Columbia University Press, 1931, p. 4.
8. On the eve of the Civil War, there were only about 350,000 slave-holding families representing about 1,750,000 individuals, as compared with 4,000,000 slaves, 260,000 free Negroes (an additional 240,000 free Negroes lived outside the South), and 5,250,000 poor white farmers, artisans, laborers, and tradesmen. *Ibid.*, p. 3.
9. E. R. Turner, *The Negro in Pennsylvania*, Washington: American Historical Association, 1911, pp. 25–29; Spero and Harris, *op. cit.*, pp. 3–13.
10. Reconstruction refers to the period of federal control of the South following the Civil War (1860–1865). Redemption refers to the resurgence of white Southern control after Northern troops were withdrawn from the South in 1877.
11. U. S. Department of Labor, Bureau of Labor Statistics, *Labor in the South*, Bulletin No. 898, 1946, p. 5.
12. W. J. Cash, *The Mind of the South*, New York: Knopf, 1941, p. 107.
13. Dabbs, *op. cit.*, p. 107.

14. C. Vann Woodward, *The Burden of Southern History*, New York: Vintage Books, 1961, Ch. 5; John H. Franklin, *Reconstruction after the Civil War*, Chicago: University of Chicago Press, 1962; Gunnar Myrdal, *An American Dilemma*, New York: Harper, 1944, p. 446.
15. Cash, *op. cit.*, p. 33.
16. C. Vann Woodward, *Strange Career of Jim Crow*, New York: Oxford University Press, 1957, p. 40.
17. Cash, *op. cit.*, p. 133.
18. Vernon L. Wharton, *The Negro in Mississippi, 1877–1880*, Chapel Hill: University of North Carolina Press, 1947; George B. Tendall, *South Carolina Negroes, 1877–1880*, Chapel Hill: University of North Carolina Press, 1952.
19. John R. Commons, Ed., *Trade Unionism and Labor Problems*, New York: Ginn, 1905, Ch. 16; and L. G. Greene and C. G. Woodson, *The Negro Wage Earner*, Washington: Association for the Study of Negro Life and History, Inc., 1930, pp. 191, 232–233. For a theoretical discussion of why equalizing wages would cause Negroes to lose jobs, see Gary S. Becker, *The Economics of Discrimination*, Chicago: University of Chicago Press, 1957, Ch. 3.
20. W. E. B. Dubois, "The Negro Artisan," in Commons, *loc. cit.*
21. Charles H. Wesley, *Negro Labor in the United States*, New York: Vanguard Press, 1927, p. 112.
22. Commons, *op. cit.*, p. 364.
23. E. Franklin Frazier, *The Negro Family in the United States*, Chicago: University of Chicago Press, 1939, p. 447.
24. Spero and Harris, *op. cit.*, pp. 24, 40–45; H. M. Douty, "Early Labor Organizations in North Carolina," *South Atlantic Quarterly*, July 1935, p. 262; Frederic Meyers, "Knights of Labor in the South," *Southern Economic Journal*, April 1940; George S. Mitchell, *Textile Unionism and the South*, Chapel Hill: University of North Carolina Press, 1931, pp. 23–24; Holman Head, "Development of the Labor Movement in Alabama Prior to 1900," unpublished M.A. thesis, University of Alabama, 1954; Ruth A. Allen, *Chapters in the History of Organized Labor in Texas*, Austin: University of Texas Press, 1941, p. 174.

CHAPTER 2

The Negro and the AFL

Development of AFL Policies

FROM ITS INCEPTION THE LEADERS OF THE AMERICAN FEDERATION of Labor (AFL) had committed it to organizing workers without regard to race or religion.[1] Samuel Gompers and other AFL leaders clearly understood that if the Federation were to succeed, its self-interest dictated that the trade-union movement should not discriminate against any class of workers. Although it proclaimed an equalitarian ideology until it merged with the CIO in 1955, events and issues gradually forced the AFL to compromise and, in many instances, to abandon equality.

In tracing the evolution of the AFL's racial policies it must be remembered that in its early days the Federation was not the strongly organized force it later became. In those days many of the problems of early industrialism had not been brought under control; many employers were of the breed later designated as "robber barons"; social welfare and protective labor legislation was, for all practical purposes, nonexistent; grinding poverty was widespread; and working conditions often were unbelievably bad. In its early days, therefore, the survival of the AFL, as well as the survival of the labor movement itself, depended on how successfully the working class could be organized.

The AFL leaders wanted the union movement to become a national force that could speak for working-class interests. To accomplish this it needed to enlist large numbers of workers. It needed, above all, to draw local unions and their national and international organizations into the Federation.

Nevertheless, the Federation was reluctant to admit national and international unions whose locals excluded Negroes. At this time, Samuel Gompers, the AFL's first president, tried to carry out the open-membership, nondiscriminatory policy to which the Federation was committed. However, he soon ran into the same problems as those on which the National Labor Union and the Knights of Labor egalitarianism foundered: like its predecessors, the Federation lacked power to force its member locals to comply.

Not that the Federation lacked foresight; Gompers appears to have understood the dangers of the exclusion policy to the trade-union movement. When he refused to admit the Brotherhood of Locomotive Firemen and Enginemen to the Federation, he defended his action before the 1896 AFL convention on the ground that the Brotherhood's officers had told him that the union refused and would continue to refuse to admit Negroes because they worked for much lower wages than whites. To this specious logic Gompers replied: "this is all the greater reason why the advantages of organization should be extended to the colored man, in order that he may no longer be so utilized to antagonize our interests."²

The AFL's first significant contest with a union having a formal race bar occurred when the International Association of Machinists (IAM), first organized in Atlanta in 1888, and whose constitution excluded Negroes, asked to join the Federation. Gompers tried to persuade the Machinists to remove this restriction from their constitution at their next convention. Although he extracted a promise from the International's officials that this would be done, delegates to the Machinist's convention failed to carry out the agreement.

In an attempt to deal with the situation, the AFL Executive Council recommended that a rival union to be called "The International Machinists' Union" be organized. This proposal, which, in effect, would have committed the AFL to a system of dual unions, was rejected by a Federation committee set up to deal expressly with the proposal. The dangers of dual unionism, which splits the labor movement, posed a great dilemma for the Federation in its early days. Gompers continued his efforts to induce the Machinists to remove the offending stricture from their constitution, but his efforts were unsuccessful. In 1895—the only year in which Gompers was not president of the Federation—the Machinists were admitted to the AFL.[3] Although the IAM deleted the color clause from its constitution, it was maintained in the initiation ritual until 1948.

Ideologically, the AFL never abandoned its opposition to excluding Negroes from trade unions. The nondiscrimination, antisegregation policy was publicly voiced at conventions, for public interviews, and other formal occasions. But about 1900 Gompers appears to have surrendered to the realities of racial discrimination among the Federation's locals. Although he continued to emphasize that the better part of economic good sense was to organize workers regardless of race, creed, or color, he finally decided that it was better to organize whites and Negroes into separate, that is, segregated, locals than not to organize them at all.

Apparently, both the AFL and Gompers chose to believe that it would be easier to reform discriminatory unions *after* they were admitted to the Federation and that to keep them out would weaken the trade-union movement. In point of fact, the AFL Executive Council was virtually powerless to force its affiliates to comply with its expressed democratic principles. The Federation was a voluntary organization whose only weapon was moral pressure. Once the Federation admitted the Machinists, moreover, it could hardly refuse to accept other unions which discriminated against Negroes.

When the Order of Railway Telegraphers and the Brotherhood of Railway Trackmen were admitted to the Federation in 1899—four years after the Machinists—Gompers did not protest their anti-Negro policy. A year later the Federation adopted a policy of chartering separate federal and central Negro labor unions where, in the judgment of the Executive Council, "it [appeared] advisable and in the best interests of the trade union movement to do so." [4] After 1900 the Federation admitted many unions whose constitutions barred Negroes from membership and permitted some affiliates to change their constitutions in order to limit membership to whites.

Nevertheless, the dangers of the exclusion policy to the trade-union movement were apparent even to Southern white union organizers who were opposed to admitting Negroes because they were considered racially "inferior." Will Winn, a Columbus, Georgia, AFL organizer, wrote in the February 1898 number of the *American Federationist:*

Outside a few of the more skilled and organized trades, if a body of workmen generate sufficient temerity to ask for less hours or an advance in wages, the Goliath in command has only to utter the magical word "negroes," to drive them back into the ruts in fear and trembling for their positions. The fact of their not being organized is a sufficient comment on their submissiveness; they know that, in addition to the swarms of white men that may be "shooed" up from the farms, where five-cent cotton has played hide-and-seek with their appetites, there are hordes of negroes ready to drop the plowshares for work at almost any price in town for the sake of the education which the State gratuitously offers their children. There is hardly any sacrifice of the comforts that the negro will not willingly and cheerfully make in order to educate his children. . . .

I have myself participated in the organization of several unions that were, in time, forced to disband because their members could not procure work at a union wage in the face of negro competition. Unfortunately, there are but few unions in the South which have the negro as an active competitor that can truly lay claim to stability. . . .

However, Winn did not conclude that Negroes should be admitted to the unions. His solution was to send them all somewhere else. "Colonization would be a practical and mutually agreeable solution of the negro labor problem." Winn and other AFL leaders—including Samuel Gompers, who visited Georgia in 1894–1895—were especially concerned about the use of Negroes to defeat strikes.

Several factors account for the willingness of Negroes to act as strikebreakers in the early years of trade unionism. Perhaps of first importance was the frustration, anxiety, and resentment aroused by the discriminatory practices of white unions. The Negro's antipathy for labor organizations was fed by the belief that employers were in a better position to help him than unions. And employers like Henry Ford were willing to hire Negroes in many job categories, doubtless for altruistic reasons, but also to keep unions out of their plants. Most Negro strikebreakers were field hands just off the farms who knew next to nothing about unions. For the Negroes, moreover, strikebreaking was a gateway to economic, political, and social advantages for themselves and for their children. Their own leaders encouraged them to break strikes, sometimes because they were paid to do so, but also because they believed that paternalism was more dependable than the uncertain, if not hostile, treatment of the unions. Inevitably, the animosities and suspicion that had existed between white and Negro workers under slavery deepened. Racial bigotry was confirmed on both sides; anti-unionism among Negroes strengthened as trade unionism was increasingly identified as a white movement.

The resentment fostered among Negroes by the actions of white unionists was reinforced by anti-union Negro leaders such as Booker T. Washington. In his famous Atlanta Exposition address of 1895, Washington advised Negroes to shun politics and to acquire agricultural, mechanical, commercial, domestic, and professional skills to meet the competition of whites. Washington, deeply conservative, explained the pro-employer sentiments of Negroes as follows:

The average Negro who comes to town does not understand the necessity or advantage of a labor organization which stands between him and his employer and aims apparently to make a monopoly of the opportunity for labor. . . . [He is] more accustomed to work for persons than for wages. When he gets a job, therefore, he is inclined to consider the source from which it comes.[5]

Anti-unionism among Negroes became so strong that it carried over even to unions that admitted them. And though the extent to which Negroes were used as strikebreakers has been exaggerated, Negroes played an important role in breaking strikes in such industries as slaughtering, steel, coal and ore mining, automobiles, and railroads. White workers were also extensively employed to break strikes in these industries, but the Negroes were far more noticeable and far more resented by strikers.

The anti-unionism of Negro leaders also created resentment among AFL leaders. John Frey, secretary of the AFL Metal Trades Department said:

One reason that the trade union organization has failed to make more rapid progress among racial groups in our country is because these misleaders of their own racial groups use their influence to prevent the members of these races from becoming members of a trade-union organization.[6]

He added that Negro leaders were opposed to unions because they owed their own favored positions to employers.

However, Negroes were sometimes required to accept lower wages than whites in order to retain the jobs they won as strikebreakers. Employers preferred white workers to Negroes partly because they were prejudiced and partly because there was not a sufficient number of qualified Negroes. When unions organized Negro workers and equalized wages, Negroes frequently lost their jobs.[7]

Thus, the union racial practices of the AFL and its affiliates resulted from a rather complex set of forces, only one of which was racial prejudice. We would not, however, minimize the importance of prejudice. Even until quite recently fears were openly expressed by whites at union meetings that organizing Negroes would lead to social equality, intermarriage, and "mongrelization" of the white race. Moreover, although Gompers himself undoubtedly shared some of the racial prejudices of his generation, especially with respect to social equality, it is not at all clear that his trade-union policies were motivated by a conscious racist policy. Gompers' statements concerning Orientals might have betrayed some of his feelings toward Negroes, as some observers assume,[8] but we have no way of knowing whether or not this transfer of attitudes actually occurred. The attitudes of union leaders toward Orientals, like the opposition to unrestricted European immigration, undoubtedly rested primarily on economic considerations. But, in the case of Orientals, the economic fears were apparently reinforced by the prejudices held by most Americans.

The Chinese were "people of vice and sexual immorality who were incompatible with our moral concepts" and of "inferior social standards," reported an AFL convention committee in 1901.[9] An anti-Chinese pamphlet of the AFL, which Gompers quoted at the 1901 convention, maintained that the "Chinese as a race are cruel and treacherous."[10] Gompers' own rather violent reactions to the Chinese extended to the Japanese, as well, who, he wrote, were "as baneful to the interests of American labor and American civilization as are the Chinese. . . ."[11]

Thus, part of the opposition of the AFL to Oriental immigration was based on feelings of white racial superiority which perhaps also extended to Negroes. Just as Gompers admitted that the AFL policy of excluding Orientals was based not only on economic grounds but also involved "the larger question of racial preservation,"[12] so too he warned the Negroes that

if the colored man continued to lend himself to the work of tearing down what the white man has built up, a race hatred far worse than any ever known will result. Caucasian civilization will serve notice that its uplifting process is not to be interfered with in any way.[13]

For whatever reasons, it is clear that the Negro-AFL relations were strained considerably by the time of the First World War. It is also clear that both Negroes and union leaders considered the other side to be at fault. This is clearly evident in the following statement by Gompers to a group of Negro leaders who came to discuss this problem with the AFL Executive Council in 1917:

In many instances the conduct of colored workmen, and those who have spoken for them, has not been in asking or demanding that equal rights be accorded to them as to white workmen, but somehow conveying the idea that they are to be petted or coddled and given special consideration and special privilege. Of course that can't be done.[14]

For good measure, he added, with respect to Washington ". . . we could not get [from him] anything like an expression of hearty accord with our movement."[15] Gompers explained away the discriminatory policies of the AFL and its affiliates on the grounds that their first duty was to unionize workers.

You must have in mind the fact, gentlemen, that this is a Federation of organized workers, and is a voluntary body, that is, its existence depends upon the good will, the desire, the cooperation of the workers organized in their unions. We have all sorts of people to deal with. . . . We must maintain our Federation and we cannot always do that which we would like to do and yet maintain our Federation, which as you have said has grown into power and influence. It is because we have tried to keep abreast and perhaps a little ahead of the great mass of workers. We can't rush too far ahead and then find ourselves high and dry without a Federation, without a following, without anything of the support for the existence of which we can only continue.[16]

In summary, it can be said that Gompers at first believed that he could at least be an influence toward equalitarian union racial policies by withholding affiliation from those who failed to follow the Federation's egalitarian credo. But the pressures from some of its affiliates and applicants for affiliation forced the AFL to admit unions that excluded Negroes. Pro-employer and anti-union attitudes of influential Negro leaders encouraged Negroes to act as strikebreakers, which further weakened the ability of the Federation to restrain racist white union leadership. Gompers came to believe that although it was better for the labor movement to organize all workers regardless of race, creed, or color, it was preferable to organize white and colored workers in separate unions than not to organize them at all. Although many of the Federation's autonomous affiliated unions also practiced the most blatant forms of discrimination, the Federation itself did not surrender egalitarianism as its official ideology. This official ideology may have seemed hollow to Negroes, nevertheless it eventually helped Negro trade-union leaders to press for elimination of discrimination within the trade-union movement.

Urbanization and Social Change

Few forces have been as potent in changing race relations as the urbanization and migration of Negroes. Whereas the greatest impact of these migrations was felt during and after the Second World War, they had important influences between 1910 and 1930. As Negroes left the South, particularly around the time of the First World War, there arose an increasingly important protest movement to challenge conservative Negro leaders. Moreover, this protest and the accompanying social ferment began to seriously strain the rigid racial patterns which had been established in the South and in the unions by 1910. The increasing number, size, and importance of Northern Negro communities made it difficult for the nation's leaders to continue to ignore the Negro's plight. Indeed, the resistance to Negroes in the North, inside the labor movement and outside, made it unlikely that Negro leaders would let whites forget about the problem of discrimination—North or South.

The social ferment of this period was not sufficient to completely erode discrimination by unions, but it started some leaks in the dikes of discrimination which segregationists were never able to plug. Once Negroes became employed in competition with white workers, unions either had to lower their racial barriers or watch their working conditions deteriorate. Most discriminating unions recognized this economic fact of life but refused to adopt satisfactory solutions to it until forced to do so. Rather than accept the Negro into full membership, most unions with racial barriers adopted a series of compromises which proved unsatisfactory to unions and Negroes alike. But these compromises did bring increasing numbers of Negroes into the "house of labor" where they were able to use the AFL's sacred "trade union law" against discriminating unions.

These social changes also reflected America's growing industrialization. From having been a predominantly agricultural country, the United States was becoming an industrial power. This shift was accompanied by large-scale migration from farms to cities, into which poured largely unskilled and poorly educated workers to supplement the diminishing stream of immigrants from Europe. Among the millions of low-class workers flooding Northern cities were an increasing number of Southern Negroes, attracted to the jobs opened up by the First World War. The figures reveal a virtual transformation of the Negro population. In contrast to only 12 per cent in 1910 and 26 per cent in 1930, by 1964 over half of all American Negroes lived outside the Southern states, and in 1962, 93 per cent of employed Negroes worked outside agriculture.[17]

Northern Reaction to Negroes

The migration of Negro workers to the North created great resentment among Northern whites, especially when Negroes were transported North by employers to be used either as strikebreakers, as cheap labor, or in an effort to avert the unionization of their enterprises.

In 1917 and 1919 the tensions between the white workers and the Negroes from the South erupted into the most bitter race riots in the country's history when East St. Louis and Chicago, Illinois, became fierce racial battlegrounds. More than 10,000 Negroes were jammed into East St. Louis where most of them were brought by employers, who had paid little attention to their living conditions.[18] The immediate spark that ignited the East St. Louis riots was the use of Negroes to break a strike at the Aluminum Ore Company, but the pressures had been building up inexorably for some time before.

Similarly, the bloody 1919 race riot in Chicago grew from the influx into the city of thousands of Negroes, attracted by the employers' offer of what seemed to be high wages in the steel and slaughtering industries. For two years before the riot broke out, the unions in the packing industry had attempted, unsuccessfully, to get a contract with the employers, who consciously attempted to weaken the unions by playing on the racial antagonisms of both white and Negro workers.[19] Partly because of racial differences, further effective organization of the meat-packing industry did not occur until the CIO was formed.

It should not be inferred, however, that the labor movement's failure to organize the steel, automobile, meat-packing, rubber, and other basic industries during the period immediately following the First World War was due primarily to race conflict. Employers responded to the growth of unions during the First World War with vigorous anti-union campaigns that included the use of publicity against unions; court and other legal maneuvers, especially injunctions; importation of strikebreakers (whites as well as Negroes); blacklisting and discharging union members; labor spies to infiltrate the labor movement; strong-arm tactics to keep out organizers and break strikes; and, above all, paternalism, to keep workers contented. As a consequence, membership in AFL unions declined steadily throughout the period from a peak paper membership of some 4,700,-000 in 1920 to less than 2,100,000 in 1933. With few exceptions, only the strong craft unions in the construction, printing, and railroad industries were able to survive these setbacks. Left largely on their own, many of the Negro federal locals attached directly to the AFL were among the first unions to be destroyed during this open-shop period. Moreover, with few exceptions, like the unions in the garment industry and the coal mines (and even the United Mine Workers' membership declined drastically and was virtually eliminated in the South), the kinds of unions that survived these adverse conditions were likely to be the stronger organizations which practiced hostile discrimination against Negroes. These practices severely restricted the Negro's economic opportunities, and were the main objects of attacks from Negro leaders during the 1920's and 1930's.

The Federal Locals and Auxiliaries

The AFL's policy of chartering "federal" local unions affiliated directly with the Federation where a national union refused to admit Negroes proved quite unsatisfactory. The AFL was supposed to be the "national union" of these federal locals, but this proved to be an extremely clumsy arrangement. In 1919, for example, when the St. Louis local of the Brotherhood of Railroad Carmen sent strike ballots to its membership, it did not bother to consult the Negro car cleaners over whom it had jurisdiction. The Negro affiliates were forced to wire the Executive Council, whose members had to be polled individually, for instructions on whether or not to take a strike vote.[20] The colored federal locals not only lacked effective bargaining powers, but under the AFL constitution they could not appeal decisions of the Executive Council.

At the 1920 convention, federal locals in jurisdictions covered by the Railway Carmen, Blacksmiths, Boilermakers, and Machinists demanded that these unions either admit Negroes or that colored coach cleaners and freight handlers be permitted to form their own organization. The Railway Carmen responded to this pressure the next year by adding the following to their constitution:

On railroads where the employment of colored persons has become a permanent institution they shall be admitted to membership in separate lodges. Where these separate lodges of Negroes are organized they shall be under the jurisdiction of the nearest white local, and shall be represented in any meeting or convention where delegates may be seated, by white men.

This auxiliary arrangement was only slightly more satisfactory to Negroes, however, because it limited their ability to control their own affairs and consequently made it difficult for them to improve or protect their job conditions. The colored workers also resented their inferior status and refused to join the unions.

The unions, on the other hand, were dissatisfied because they "represented" these Negro workers but received no dues from them—a serious problem for any union. Some of these unions adopted rather crude tactics to get money from Negroes who would not join the auxiliary locals. For example, in 1929 a committee of the shop crafts (BRC, IBEW, Boilermakers, Blacksmiths, and Sheet Metal Workers) on the Southern Railway succeeded in getting a retroactive wage increase through arbitration. Since their efforts benefited all workers in the bargaining units, the award granted $40 each to 1200 colored shop-craft helpers, only thirty of whom belonged to the Negro auxiliaries. The white helpers in these crafts were union members. The shop crafts therefore

. . . decided to call upon the Local Shop Committees and Local Lodge officers at points where colored helpers are employed to call upon the 1,170 who were not members of any colored Auxiliary Locals of these crafts for $10 each. . . .

Now Brothers we want you to get busy on this *now*. Don't delay. Call upon these helpers and explain this situation to them. Tell them they will be expected to pay this $10 either before they receive their back pay or at the time it is paid. . . .

. . . If the Crafts who have colored helpers experience any trouble in collecting from them, we are going to suggest and expect that all Crafts cooperate and pull together in seeing to it that these colored helpers *all* pay their part of this bill.[21]

Negro Organizations

These discriminatory policies in the labor movement, and the antiunion attitudes which they produced in the Negro community, troubled those who felt that the labor movement could become an important means by which Negroes might improve their economic conditions. In May 1924, for example, the National Urban League asked the Executive Council to appoint a representative to help "in formulating a definite program for the advancement of the industrial status of the Negro" and in organizing Negroes, but nothing came of the request.[22] Other organizations sought to work more from within the labor movement. One of these was the National Association for the Promotion of Labor Unionism among Negroes, and Socialism, formed in 1919. Its president was Chandler Owen, a Negro intellectual, and its secretary-treasurer was A. Philip Randolph, who later became president of the sleeping car porters union. Many prominent Socialists were on its advisory board and it also was endorsed by the United Hebrew Trades, the Amalgamated Clothing Workers of America, the Workmen's Circle, and "other similar bodies." Its declared aim was to unionize Negroes, and for this purpose it asked for "appropriation from the national and international unions to be made on an annual sustaining fund," to promote "the spirit of class interest between black and white workers"; that is, to "put Negroes in unions for which they are potentially eligible."[23] Because of its Socialist orientation, it is not surprising that the National Association failed to gain the support of the AFL's conservative leaders. AFL Vice-President Frank Duffy, of the powerful Carpenters union, said of it:

I find it is backed up and supported by the radical socialistic trades of New York, and you can, therefore, realize that I am not in favor of it whatever.

We can organize the negroes along trade union lines, but positively not along party political lines.[24]

The Brotherhood of Sleeping Car Porters (BSCP)

After the failure of this effort, Randolph and his associates tried a more direct approach to their problem. They formed a union—the Brotherhood of Sleeping Car Porters—which was destined to have an influence in the Negro community and in the labor movement far out of proportion to its size.[25]

For nearly forty years Randolph, whose union was never very big and grows smaller each year, has been the symbol of the Negro fighting for recognition within the trade unions. Randolph was born in 1889 in Florida, the son of a traveling Methodist preacher. He attended high school in the South but then moved to New York City where he worked at a variety of odd jobs while attending the College of the City of New York. Later Randolph also attended Howard University.

In 1917 Randolph and Chandler Owen founded *The Messenger,* a "revolutionary and militant magazine." Originally, both men had been employed as editors of the *Hotel Messenger,* published by the Headwaiters and Sidewaiters Society of New York, but had left that magazine in a dispute over its policy. The new *Messenger* was committed to "economic radicalism" and pledged itself to be an organ of labor unionism and Socialism among Negroes, although the Socialism was of a non-Marxian variety.

Randolph was originally opposed to the American Federation of Labor which he believed was "the most wicked machine for the propagation of race prejudice in the country." Because of the AFL's policy of exclusion, Randolph's orientation was toward the organization of Negro workers into unions of their own. Late in 1917 he and Owen established the United Brotherhood of Elevator and Switchboard Operators, which had a membership of about 600 from an approximate total of 10,000 Negro operators in New York. But the Brotherhood failed to grow and its membership eventually affiliated to an AFL union.

During the early 1920's, Randolph made a number of other attempts to encourage Socialism and unionism among Negroes but most of the organizations that were created had very short lives.

In spite of these failures, however, Randolph emerged as the most articulate voice of the Negro worker and when the Brotherhood of Sleeping Car Porters (BSCP) was organized in 1925, he was chosen as its general organizer. The BSCP quickly organized a majority of the porters and was granted the right to bargain for them by the Railway Labor Board (RLB). However, the Porters were unable to get a contract because the Pullman Company continued to bargain with a company union created for this purpose. The RLB was powerless to force the company to bargain with the BSCP because the dispute did not represent a "substantial interruption of commerce." In spite of advice not to do so by William Green and other AFL leaders—who gave the Porters their "moral" support—the BSCP threatened to strike in order to cause the dispute to be sufficiently important to induce the NMB to require the company to bargain. The strike threat was a bluff, however, which the Porters were not strong enough to carry out. The BSCP lost considerable prestige in the Negro community when it was forced to "postpone" this strike. These difficulties convinced the Brotherhood's leaders that the survival of the new union depended on affiliation with the AFL.

Randolph's efforts to get a national charter from the AFL were blocked, however, by several important leaders of that organization, some of whom opposed Randolph for racial reasons and others because of his Socialist activities. But jurisdictional disputes with other unions posed the most important obstacle to the BSCP's affiliation with the AFL. Jurisdiction is jealously guarded by unions, even when they refuse to admit to membership some workers in that jurisdiction, because it gives them their membership territory and determines their success or failure, growth or decline.

Thus, the AFL Executive Council denied the BSCP's request for a charter in 1928,[26] because the Hotel and Restaurant Employees (HRE) claimed jurisdiction over the Negro sleeping car porters.[27]

In appealing the Council's decision, Randolph argued that granting a charter to his organization would serve to break down "the idea which prevails among colored workers that they do not receive the same recognition from the labor movement as white workers. It would tend to break down the idea that a barrier exists and would help to prevent Negroes from being used as strikebreakers." Randolph asserted that the HRE could not hold the allegiance of the sleeping car porters and that he was authorized to represent them

before the Railway Labor Board.   Randolph also told the Council
that a charter to the sleeping car porters would be a blow to Communism.   "They are endeavoring to impregnate the Negro mind with
Communism and while the Negro is not easily led along that way,
they are very subtle in their methods."   Since some AFL leaders
were opposed to him personally, Randolph said that he would be
willing to step aside if the Council would grant a charter.[28]

Asked by President Wharton of the International Association of
Machinists if the porters would accept white officers if they were
granted a charter, Randolph replied that the Brotherhood was entitled to manage its own affairs.   Although the porters were given
federal charters by the AFL, the BSCP continued to press for a
national charter.[29]

In 1934 Randolph again appeared before the Executive Council.
On this occasion, the BSCP's application for a charter was blocked
by the Sleeping Car Conductors (OSCC) who planned to organize
the porters into auxiliary locals because the OSCC's constitution excluded Negroes.[30]   The Conductors claimed jurisdiction over the
porters when they "ran in charge" of sleeping cars,[31] and were awarded
this jurisdiction by the AFL Executive Council.

In 1936, however, after a 1935 National Mediation Board election
awarded the BSCP sole jurisdiction over the porters,[32] and despite
protests from both the HRE and the OSCC, the Executive Council
awarded the BSCP a national charter.[33]

Following its admission to the AFL, the BSCP sought by various
tactics to eliminate racial discrimination within the labor movement.
Although some Negro workers resisted his efforts, Randolph sought
to strengthen the BSCP by gaining jurisdiction over all colored railway employees who could not get into the unions with jurisdiction
over them.   The Executive Council permitted the BSCP to expand
its jurisdiction to some of these workers.[34]   However, Randolph continued his efforts to organize all colored railway workers and became
involved in jurisdictional disputes with various other railroad unions.
Perhaps the most serious of these disputes involved the BSCP's efforts
to organize the Pullman coach cleaners and yard men who were
claimed by the powerful railroad shop crafts (Brotherhood of Railway Employees, Brotherhood of Railway Carmen, International
Brotherhood of Electrical Workers, Sheet Metal Workers, and Boilermakers) most of which had formal or informal racial restrictions.
In spite of a number of threats from the AFL (including the Executive Council's instruction that Randolph discontinue his organizing
among the workers or the Council would "be compelled to take fur-

ther action," [24, 34] a 1946 convention resolution recommending the
BSCP's suspension "unless they immediately cease . . . their raid-
ing;" [35] and further threats of suspension by the Executive Council [36]),
Randolph continued his campaign—through a "provisional committee"
—until 1948, when the Brotherhood of Railway Carmen won the
National Mediation Board election for the disputed workers. It lost
the contest with the shop crafts, but the BSCP's efforts were not
entirely in vain because competition with the BSCP was obviously a
factor in causing those unions to relax their restrictive racial policies.[37]

Their conflicts with the BSCP also demonstrated the shop crafts'
vulnerability because of their restrictive racial policies. The BSCP,
with a membership of fewer than 10,000, could successfully defy the
shop-craft organizations with over a million members because expulsion from the AFL would have lost prestige for the Federation in the
Negro community at a time when its unfavorable racial image was
causing it to lose some important contests to the Committee on (later
Congress of) Industrial Organizations (CIO), formed in 1935. Moreover, the BSCP's activities on behalf of Negro railroad workers and
Randolph's leadership in the Negro community gave him considerable
prestige among Negroes, so the shop crafts had to consider the prob-
ability that expulsion of the Porters would cause Negro railroad workers to defect to Randolph's union in large numbers.

Many social and economic forces converged during the thirties to
give Negroes more leverage in forcing changes in the racial practices
of the AFL and its affiliates. The Great Depression gave rise to the
New Deal and the urban Northern Negroes took on a new political
significance.

The AFL, which had suffered a heavy loss in membership, was
revitalized by the passage of the National Industrial Recovery Act,
section 7a, which gave workers the right to organize and bargain
collectively. Very quickly, more than a million workers joined AFL
unions or spontaneously formed unions of their own, especially in the
mass-production industries.[38]

The sharp increase in union consciousness within the mass-production industries where Negroes were employed brought with it a sharp
split within the AFL. Quite apart from the merits of the claims put
forth by the craft unions which were involved in these long and acri-
monious quarrels, the jurisdictional claims of the craft unions had
also inhibited the growth of the Federation. The steel industry remained unorganized after the disastrous strike of 1919 which had
been defeated by the employers, using every anti-union device available to them, including Negro strikebreakers. After the strike was

over, no new organizing attempt was made because the twenty-four craft unions involved could not agree on how the steel workers should be divided among them. The issue came into sharp focus at the 1935 AFL convention when delegate after delegate got up to attack the craft-union philosophy of the Federation. These delegates told of the discouragement and confusion felt by workers in mass-production industries who were refused the right to organize industrial unions because of the jurisdictional claims made upon them by the craft organizations. But these speakers lost their fight to get convention approval for industrial unionism.

Undeterred, the militant advocates of industrial organizations set themselves up as a committee within the AFL and began organizing the mass-production industries. In 1938 the AFL expelled the unions involved in the committee, but by that time it was too late; the CIO had quickly grown into thirty-two unions and its dynamic spirit was sweeping the country.

While these developments were taking place, Negro union members, led by Randolph and other BSCP leaders, were hammering away from within the labor movement at the AFL's racial practices.

In 1934 Randolph's resolution demanding expulsion of excluding unions was changed to provide for the appointment of a five-man committee to investigate conditions of colored workmen and report to the next convention.[39] The committee appointed by the AFL held open hearings in Washington,[40] produced evidence of widespread discrimination by unions, and formulated an educational and action program to harmonize union racial practices with AFL policy. AFL Vice-President George Harrison, of the BRSC, whose union excluded Negroes,[41] wanted the committee to issue a statement which would have glossed over the problem. But John Brophy of the Mine Workers prevented the report's suppression by sending a copy to Randolph, who protested the manner in which the report was handled and embodied its main provisions in a convention resolution.[42]

Randolph and other BSCP leaders introduced resolutions against discrimination at succeeding conventions.[43] Anticipating the Supreme Court's *Steele* decision [44] by four years, Randolph told the 1940 convention that it was unconstitutional for trade unions to deny Negro members of a bargaining unit their rights, and added: "The trade unions to a great extent have taken over uncritically, without examination, the capitalistic, imperialistic idea of the inferiority of the darker races and they have brought the notion into the trade union movement." [45] Randolph further criticized the AFL convention, which was being held in New Orleans, for segregating convention delegates, and pointed out that the International Longshoremen's Association had been able to hold an unsegregated convention in New Orleans.

Randolph struck a nerve that was becoming extremely sensitive in the AFL about this time when he told the Convention that he had been trying to win Negroes to the AFL and that "They are beginning to see it that way, but when they are elbowed aside and told they are not wanted, they feel rather different about it." [46]   He told the 1941 convention that even though he could not respond to President Green's request to come to Detroit and help win Negro workers at Ford away from the CIO, he could not have done any good there anyway because Negroes were asking why they should join the AFL when it could not control the racial practices of its affiliates.[47]

President Frey of the Building Trades Department reflected the sentiments of other AFL leaders who attacked Randolph during these debates when he said that it was obvious that the Negro leader had come to the convention prepared to present an indictment against the AFL because he had researched the subject so thoroughly in order to make specific accusations. He said that he would not be surprised if Randolph issued a pamphlet and distributed it in sections where it would "hurt us most in organizing colored workers." [48] Frey told the convention that the Negro owed more to the AFL than to any institution in America; that if it had not been for the AFL the BSCP could not have come into existence. He resented the fact that Randolph had no words of appreciation for the AFL and had only presented indictments against it. In Frey's judgment, the best thing that could be done for Negroes was to organize them into unions, but "It almost seems as if [Randolph] was deliberately endeavoring to inject a statement into this convention which would make our task of organizing the Negro workers ten thousand times more difficult than it has been in the past."

President Green of the AFL used this opportunity to reveal some of his thinking and to "preserve the good name and standing of the American Federation of Labor." He said that the AFL was opposed to discrimination and gave charters to Negroes where nationals would not take them in. Green made a distinction between the practices of the AFL and the practices of its affiliates, adding that it was not fair to put the name of the AFL before the public as opposed to the organization of Negroes. "That hurts me very much," he declared. He said that he would remove the officers of any federal labor union if they discriminated against Negroes.

At the Ford Motor Company elections, which the AFL had lost

to the CIO shortly before the convention, Green said he sent in colored organizers to try to organize Negroes into a federal labor union.
The race issue was raised and such Negro notables as Paul Robeson
and representatives of Negro organizations came in and attacked the
AFL as being against Negroes.

Randolph answered Green by saying that everybody knew the AFL
as such did not discriminate, but that it was hard for the public to
differentiate between the AFL and its affiliates. He pointed out, however, that the AFL had forced the freight handlers into the BRSC
where they had no right to vote.[49]

Summary and Conclusions

We may conclude this discussion of AFL racial practices in the in-
terwar period by noting some of the changes in the Federation's practices during these years. Although we must distinguish the AFL's
policies from those of its affiliates, the Federation itself issued charters to directly affiliated segregated central bodies and federal labor
unions and failed adequately to protect the interests of the federal
locals. Moreover, when Gompers was president of the AFL, some
of these white federal locals discriminated against Negroes, particularly in the South, and were not prohibited from doing so by the
Federation's leaders. After about 1939, however, the AFL seems to
have discontinued the practice of giving charters to racially segregated central labor organizations.[50]

By 1941 many of the AFL's affiliates still barred Negroes from membership, but a number of others had relaxed their complete racial restrictions in favor of auxiliary and segregated locals. Though this
was an inferior status, it was at least an indication that unions had
seen the need for admitting Negroes. Moreover, as the 1941 debates
reveal, AFL leaders apparently had become sensitive to charges of
racial discrimination. When the BSCP was first admitted to the Federation, its charges of racial discrimination were usually ignored by
AFL convention delegates. But in 1941 top AFL leaders were forced
to debate this issue at length.

The forces producing these changes included the continued movement of Negroes into jobs over which unions had jurisdiction; pressure from within the AFL from the BSCP and other Negro organizations; external pressures from the growing Negro communities in the
North; and, perhaps most important, competition among unions for
Negro membership. The BSCP provided some of this competition

but it became especially important with the upsurge of union membership associated with the New Deal and the formation of the CIO, to be discussed at greater length in the following chapter.

FOOTNOTES

1. It is not certain how many Negro delegates were present at the founding convention of the AFL in 1881, but the record reveals that none attended subsequent conventions, probably because those present at the initial gathering represented local Negro organizations affiliated with the Knights of Labor. They did not attend later conventions because of the conflict that developed between the Federation and the Knights.   At the founding convention, four colored organizations, designated as such, were represented: Cigar Makers Union at London, Ontario, Binghamton, N. Y., and Mayesville, Ky., and the Detroit Trades Council.   Negro delegates to subsequent conventions were from affiliated craft unions.
2. AFL *Convention Proceedings*, 1896, President's Report.
3. AFL *Convention Proceedings*, 1895, p. 69.
4. AFL *Convention Proceedings*, 1900, pp. xiii, 12–13.
5. Booker T. Washington, "The Negro and the Labor Unions," *Atlantic Monthly*, June 1913, p. 756.
6. John P. Frey, "Attempts to organize Negro Workers," *American Federationist*, March 1929.
7. See John R. Commons, Ed., *Trade Unionism and Labor Problems*, New York: Ginn, 1905, p. 365.
8. See Bernard Mandel, "Samuel Gompers and the Negro Workers, 1886–1914," *Journal of Negro History*, January 1955: Herbert Hill, "Labor Unions and the Negro," *Commentary*, December 1959.
9. AFL *Convention Proceedings*, 1901, pp. 154–155.
10. Samuel Gompers and Herman Gutstadt, "Meat vs. Rice, American Manhood against Asiatic Cooliesism—Which Shall Survive?," San Francisco, Calif.: Asiatic Exclusion League, 1908, p. 34.
11. American Federationist, May 1905.
12. Gompers to Senator Ellison D. Smith, May 1, 1914.
13. *American Federationist*, September 1905.
14. AFL *Executive Council Minutes*, February 10–17, 1917.
15. *Ibid.*
16. *Ibid.*, pp. 22–23.
17. Calvin B. Hoover and B. U. Ratchford, *Economic Resources and Policies of the South*, New York: Macmillan, 1951, p. 20.
18. See Gunnar Myrdal, *An American Dilemma*, New York: Harper, 1944, p. 567.
19. Chicago Commission on Racial Relations, *The Negro in Chicago*, Chicago: University of Chicago Press, 1922, pp. 67–72.
20. Telegram, Frank Morrison from Frank Duffy, August 20, 1919.   Letter, AFL Executive Council from Frank Morrison, August 14, 1919.
21. Letter from Committee of Shop Crafts to All Members and Locals Affiliated with Southern and Allied Lines Federation Employed on Southern Railway System Lines, June 19, 1929.

22. AFL *Executive Council Minutes*, May 7, 1957, pp. 7, 33.
23. *Messenger*, May–June 1919.
24. Letter, Frank Morrison from Frank Duffy, August 30, 1919.
25. Information on the BSCP came from the sources cited and interviews with A. Philip Randolph and Theodore Brown (former education director of the Brotherhood). For a history of the BSCP, see Brailsford R. Brazeal, *The Brotherhood of Sleeping Car Porters*, New York: Harper, 1946.
26. AFL *Executive Council Minutes*, April 24–May 2, 1928, pp. 4, 15–17, 81.
27. *Ibid.*, January 17–25, 1928, p. 39.
28. *Ibid.*, October 18–25, 1928, pp. 7–13.
29. AFL *Executive Council Minutes*, February 18–25, 1929, p. 29.
30. OSCC Circular, November 12, 1934.
31. *Ibid.*, August 6–17, 1934.
32. Letter, Edward Flore from A. Philip Randolph, January 15, 1936.
33. AFL *Executive Council Minutes*, January 15–29, 1936.
34. AFL *Executive Council Minutes*, January 30–February 14, 1939; "Supplementary Statement of the Question of Jurisdiction of BSCP over Train Porters"; Brief of Brakemen–Porters 21711-AFL, St. Louis; AFL *Executive Council Minutes*, January 29–February 9, 1940.
35. "Report of Railway Labor Executive Association to Assist in the Enactment of a Law to Regulate the Operation of Sleeping Cars June 15, 1940"; AFL *Executive Council Minutes*, May 19–28, 1941, pp. 46–69.
36. AFL *Convention Proceedings*, 1946, Res. 158, pp. 320, 452. AFL *Executive Council Minutes*, January 29–February 8, 1947, p. 28; August 23–27, 1948, pp. 25–26; April 21–25, 1947; May 10–14, 1948, pp. 55–58; Letters, William Green from A. Philip Randolph, March 3 and May 6, 1948.
37. *Ibid.*
38. For an excellent study of unions during these years, see Walter Galenson, *The CIO Challenge to the AFL*, Cambridge, Mass.: Harvard University Press, 1960.
39. AFL *Convention Proceedings*, 1934, pp. 330–332.
40. AFL *Executive Council Minutes*, August 5–16, 1935.
41. See Chapter 5.
42. AFL *Executive Council Minutes*, October 5, 6, 12, 21, 30, 1935, pp. 4, 5, 51, 52, 115, 116.
43. AFL *Convention Proceedings*, 1940, Res. 17, pp. 237–238, 507–511, 645, 648, 649.
44. Steele v. L. & N. R. R., 65 S ct. 226 (1944).
45. AFL *Convention Proceedings*, 1940, p, 645.
46. *Ibid.*
47. AFL *Convention Proceedings*, 1941, pp. 475–492.
48. *Ibid.*, p. 484.
49. See Chapter 5.
50. Personal interview, George Googe, AFL Southern representative, April 12, 1959.

CHAPTER 3

The Negro and the CIO

Factors Influencing CIO Racial Policies

AS NOTED IN CHAPTER 2, THE CIO WAS A PRODUCT OF BOTH THE
social unrest of the 1930's and the AFL's failure to take advantage
of this period's favorable organizing climate.   The long periods of
chronic unemployment and other hardships of the Great Depression
prepared the workers psychologically for unionization, and the New
Deal's favorable attitude toward unions gave them the legal protection to organize.   The Norris-La Guardia Act of 1932 greatly restricted
the use of injunctions against unions and made the "yellow dog" contract (by which employers had forced workers to agree not to join
unions) unenforceable in federal courts.   The anti-injunction provision of the Norris-La Guardia Act gave a particularly important psychological boost to unions, because the injunction had become a symbol of the "open shop" period of the 1920's.   Section 7a of the National Industrial Recovery Act of 1933 gave workers the "right to organize and bargain collectively through representatives of their own
choosing," and forbade any "interference, restraint or coercion by employers."   Although the NIRA was declared unconstitutional in 1935
—and had proved unenforceable even earlier—the psychological ad-

vantage of this legislation produced a burst of unionizing activity. The most notable successes were achieved by the United Mine Workers who launched whirlwind campaigns to organize almost all of the nation's miners. The ACWA and the ILGWU also experienced rapid membership increases. These successes encouraged the AFL to authorize special organizing campaigns in other basic industries. But indecisiveness and jurisdictional disputes paralyzed the Federation. This paralysis produced bitter conflicts at the 1935 AFL convention and led to the formation of the CIO. At the same time, the passage of the Wagner Act of 1935 greatly strengthened the prospects for union organizing by giving workers the right to vote for their own bargaining representatives, outlawing certain unfair labor practices used by employers to defeat unions, and creating a National Labor Relations Board with power to enforce the act. The AFL responded to the CIO's challenge by extending its membership in older jurisdictions and launching organizing drives in new fields. The Wagner Act and the AFL-CIO rivalry stimulated union organizing and had important consequences for union racial practices. This was inevitable in view of the large numbers of Negroes employed in the steel, auto, mining, packinghouse, rubber, and other mass-production industries which were the primary targets of the CIO's organizing activities.

For example, in 1933 Negroes accounted for 8.5 per cent of all iron and steel wage earners,[1] and in 1930 they constituted 16.5 per cent of the laborers in blast furnaces and steel rolling mills in the United States [2]; about 17 per cent of all semiskilled and unskilled workers in the slaughter and packinghouse industry [3]; 68 per cent of the to-bacco industry of North Carolina, Virginia, and Kentucky, where the industry was concentrated [4]; and 9.2 per cent of all the nation's coal miners.[5] Whereas only 4 per cent of the nation's automobile workers were Negroes in 1930, they constituted 12.2 per cent of the Ford Motor Company's employees.[6] These figures, however, do not adequately reveal the importance of the Negro to CIO unionizing activities because Negroes usually were a more cohesive group and occupied key positions for unionizing because they were employed in strategic companies where they previously had been used as strikebreakers.

No CIO leader better understood the importance of equalitarian racial policies for successful unionism than John L. Lewis of the United Mine Workers, who provided much of the financial support and leadership for the CIO.[7] Relative geographic isolation from the social influences of the larger community and common economic and occupational hardships minimized racial differences among coal miners. The only special adjustments made by the UMW to accommodate its Southern organizing activities during the 1930's was the practice of having white presidents, Negro vice-presidents, and white secretary-treasurers in its Alabama locals. This practice was copied by the Steelworkers and others (who were organized by men with UMW backgrounds) in the Birmingham area. This is not to argue, of course, that the UMW overcame all racial differences among its members in the South. That union encountered considerable opposition from segregationists inside and outside the unions in Alabama. And relations betwen Negroes and whites were on a relatively formal basis with segregated seating in the union halls.[8] Nevertheless, the UMW adopted relatively equalitarian policies from its earliest days and its leaders carried these policies with them into the CIO.

Ideological factors also played a part in the CIO's racial policies. Generally, the CIO attracted younger, more idealistic leaders who had a broader social outlook than the AFL's older, more conservative leaders. Moreover, many Communists were active in CIO unions during its early days. The Communists have almost always adopted equalitarian racial policies, though they too have had trouble enforcing these policies at the local level. Although many argue that the Communists are really not sincere in the equalitarian positions—because they have refused to support Negro causes (the FEPC during the Second World War, for example), when it was not in the interest of the Soviet Union for them to do so, and frequently intentionally created race trouble by adopting policies they knew whites would not accept—Communists nevertheless were unquestionably a force for equalitarianism in the CIO. By raising the race issue to gain Negro support, the Communists forced white union leaders to pay more attention to racial matters.

The CIO's industrial structure was also more conducive to equalitarianism than the AFL's craft unions. Industrial unions seek to organize all workers hired by the employer, whereas craft unions frequently determine whom he hires. Craft organizations restrict membership in order to control the supply of labor, and these restrictions have applied to whites as well as Negroes. Since they have control of entry into labor markets, craft unions have been able to bar Negroes from membership. Industrial unions, on the other hand, have relatively little direct control over the labor supply.

The CIO was also younger than the AFL and, other things equal, the long-run trend in race relations is such that younger organizations will normally have the more equalitarian policies. When most AFL unions were formed it would have been considered as bad taste to admit Negroes to equal membership as it does to exclude them today.

Finally, the CIO needed the Negro's support for its broader political programs. Although the AFL's political objectives had broadened some from its early policy of opposing almost all social legislation, by the time the CIO was formed the political objectives of most of its affiliates still were more narrowly restricted to matters which did not require extensive political support. The CIO sought improved minimum wages, unemployment insurance, and social-security legislation which appealed to all low-income groups, including Negroes.

United Packinghouse Workers

The importance of equalitarian measures in union organizing was demonstrated by the Packinghouse Workers' experiences, but could be extended to almost all of the other unorganized mass-production industries organized by the CIO. Indeed, there is a remarkable similarity in the racial aspects of these experiences.

Like many other low-wage or undesirable occupations, in 1935 many packinghouse jobs were held by Negroes or immigrants. Indeed, the ethnic composition of stockyard and packinghouse occupations is a fairly accurate indicator of the waves of immigration to this country and the migration of Negroes from the South.[9] Negroes were first employed by the Chicago packinghouses as strikebreakers during an 1894 sympathy strike for Eugene Debs. Although most of the Negroes lost their jobs when the strike ended, this experience demonstrated to management the value of the Southern reservoir of unskilled black labor.

As a result, leaders of the Amalgamated Meat Cutters Union (AMC), formed in 1896, saw the need for, and adopted, an egalitarian racial policy. Such were the promanagement, anti-union attitudes of Negro leaders, however, that until the 1930's, few Negroes would join the Meat Cutters. The Amalgamated called a strike in 1904, which again was defeated by Negro strikebreakers from the South. Another wave of Negroes swept into the Chicago packinghouses during the Second World War to take the places of immigrants who left this industry for better jobs opened up by the war. By 1920 fully one-fifth of Chicago packinghouse workers were Negroes; a proportion which had probably increased to 30 per cent in the larger companies by 1928.[10]

Although the AMC stepped up its efforts to enroll Negroes after the First World War, the union's organizing drive was opposed by the Chicago Urban League, Negro churches, and the companies. The AMC's racial difficulties also were exacerbated by the antipathies generated by the terrible 1919 Chicago race riots. A 1921 strike was defeated after nine weeks of bitter fighting, partly because of large-scale importation of Negroes from the South. As a result, unionism virtually disappeared from the industry until the New Deal period.

In the fall of 1937, however, the Packinghouse Workers Organizing Committee-CIO (PWOC), under the direction of UMW officials, succeeded in organizing many Negro and white packinghouse workers. There can be little doubt that the PWOC's successes stemmed in large measure from the CIO's favorable racial image, though the Supreme Court's validation of the Wagner Act and support from the Catholic Church and former AFL leaders in the industry also played a part. Many Negroes participated in the PWOC drive, and one of them, who became assistant national director of the PWOC, explained:

Now the union is the biggest force toward brotherhood. National prejudice melts away when people see men and women of all nationalities standing together bravely and winning better conditions for all.[11]

Although the PWOC organized only part of the Swift and Wilson chains, it became fairly well entrenched in two of the other "big four" —Armour and Cudahy—and was sufficiently strong in 1943 that the CIO transformed it into the United Packinghouse Workers Union (UPWA).[12] There apparently was never any question in the minds of the UPWA's founders that the union would follow equalitarian racial policies. The history of labor relations in the industry served better than a thousand pages of logic to demonstrate the necessity of racial unity in building a strong union. But the CIO's relative successes required a virtual transformation of Negro attitudes toward unions. And this transformation, like CIO organizing, was by no means accidental or automatic.

Early CIO-Negro Community Relations

In view of the importance of Negro support for its organizational and political objectives, the CIO adopted many programs to gain a favorable image among Negroes. These programs included financial contributions to organizations like the NAACP and Negro churches and newspapers, the adoption of equalitarian racial resolutions, the use of Negroes to organize in Negro communities, the creation of the Committee to Abolish Racial Discrimination, and interlocking officials between unions and such organizations as the NAACP and the National Urban League.

Before the CIO was formed, national NAACP leaders were very skeptical of the AFL's organizing activities because, according to Roy Wilkins, then the Association's assistant secretary, "We strongly suspect, although we cannot prove, the AF of L unions have attempted to use Section 7-A [of the National Recovery Act] to drive Negroes out of occupations . . ." [13] Wilkins added that

It is not easy for an Association which knows so intimately the raw deals that have been given Negro labor by the AF of L to get out and shout from the housetops to Negro workers urging them to affiliate. At the same time we realize that affiliation would be best for all concerned provided one did not have just as great a battle after getting in the union as one had on the outside. [14]

With the formation of the CIO, however, the NAACP realized that Negroes had an opportunity to ally themselves with a new, different, and perhaps powerful labor movement and consequently actively supported the new organization. In September 1936, for example, *Crisis*, the official organ of the NAACP, proposed that Negroes join the CIO if it followed the racial policies of the United Mine Workers. *Crisis* also sought to overcome Negro opposition to the CIO by declaring:

In this struggle of labor to organize and win the right of collective bargaining, it is fitting that the Negro workers be represented in the front line trenches. . . . They have everything to gain and nothing to lose by affiliation with the CIO and if they fight now, side by side with their fellow workers, when the time comes to divide up the benefits they can demand their share. [15]

However, Negro leaders who had formed close working relations with employers like Henry Ford in Detroit did not easily surrender the advantages of these alliances for the uncertain benefits to be derived from an emerging power center. Negroes constituted 12.2 per cent of Ford's work force shortly before the Second World War. [16] Ford had consciously cultivated the Negro community, which he encouraged to vote no-union and Republican. As a result, many NAACP branches at first opposed CIO as well as AFL unions, local branches in Chicago, Indianapolis, and Detroit being particularly outspoken in their opposition. [17] At the NAACP's 1936 annual conference in Detroit, several Negro ministers who had received financial support from

Ford objected to including labor representatives (especially UAW President Homer Martin) on the program. The conference finally adopted a resolution which suggested to

Negro workers that they go into no labor organization blindly but that they instead appraise critically the motives and practices of all labor unions and that they bear their full share of activity and responsibility in building of a more just and more intelligent labor union.[18]

Concerning this conference, *Crisis* argued that "to have held a national conference and ignored discussion of the biggest labor movement in a quarter century would have been a farce deserving nationwide condemnation." [19]

The National Urban League (NUL) also established close working relations with the CIO. The NUL had sought to form a better relationship with the AFL as early as 1919, but the latter organization gave the League little active help or encouragement in these efforts. Moreover, several of the NUL's local affiliates had reputations as strikebreaking organizations. During the ferment of the New Deal days, the League urged Negroes, through Negro Workers Councils, to join unions. It stated that Negroes should ". . . seek union membership and maintain it, even when their presence was undesired by white officers or members of a local union." [20] The Urban League also warned labor leaders "that a continuance of racial discrimination would create a racist Frankenstein down the road."

Although the Urban League's activities were obviously more favorable to the CIO than to the AFL, the League renewed its efforts to work with the latter. For example, President Green's statement to the 1941 AFL convention that the NUL and other Negro organizations had intervened on the side of the CIO in a number of representative elections, drew a denial from the League's industrial relations secretary, who countered with a proposal that the AFL set up machinery to abolish discrimination. NUL officials also assured the AFL that open support of the CIO was contrary to League policy. Green asked Urban League officials to send a memorandum outlining a plan to promote closer relations between the AFL and the Negro community. The League's industrial secretary sent plans for the establishment of such a committee,[21] but this proposal was rejected by Green as "impractical and inadvisable." [22]

The relationship between the CIO and the Negro community proved mutually beneficial. The NAACP actively campaigned for CIO unions and Walter White, NAACP executive secretary, personally aided the United Automobile Workers' drive to organize the Ford

Motor Company. White's activities on behalf of the UAW probably helped avert a potential race riot by persuading the large number of Negroes in the plant not to act as strikebreakers in the 1941 strike to organize that company.[23] During this strike the Detroit branch of the NAACP Youth Councils distributed leaflets and several hundred of the approximately 1000 Negroes who remained in the plant left after White appealed to them from a sound truck.[24] For their part union leaders gave financial support to the NAACP and actively participated in its affairs. John L. Lewis addressed the Association's 1940 convention, and Philip Murray (president of the Steelworkers and the CIO) and Walter Reuther (president of the Auto Workers and Murray's successor as president of the CIO) became members of the NAACP Board of Directors. Unions also actively supported civil-rights legislation, prompting Thurgood Marshall, the NAACP's chief legal adviser, to declare that "The program of the CIO has become a Bill of Rights for Negro labor in America." [25] After the Supreme Court desegregation decision of May 1954, the CIO reported that although "the NAACP has taken the leadership in forging the law into an instrument of social precision to accomplish its objectives, the CIO has always been closely associated with the NAACP and other likeminded groups in this struggle." [26] The loyalty of the Negro community was of great advantage to the CIO and the Democratic Party in the 1948 national election. Walter White told the 1948 CIO convention, after President Truman had been elected with Negro-labor support, that

. . . the results would have been impossible for the Negro without labor, or for labor without the Negro vote. It was the job done by organized labor which narrowed the margin between the two major parties to the point where the Negro vote could be decisive.[27]

White pointed out that the Democrats had won because of 78 electoral votes in California, Illinois, and Ohio in which the Negro vote had been decisive.[28] The NAACP's support also helped unions prevent the passage of "right-to-work" laws in those industrial states with heavy Negro concentrations.

Impact of CIO Competition on AFL Racial Practices

There can also be little question that the CIO's equalitarian position was a factor in causing the AFL to abandon its discriminatory practices and to try to project a more favorable image. For example, in its competition with the CIO during the Southern organizing drives launched in 1946, AFL officers in the North and South emphasized the Federation's equalitarian racial position.

After the steel, auto, rubber, and meat-packing industries were organized, the South became the most important reservoir of unorganized workers in the United States. And the AFL realized as fully as the CIO that hegemony in the American labor movement could well depend on victory in the South's petroleum, textile, chemical, garment, lumber, tobacco, and woodworking industries. It was also clear by 1946 that the CIO had already used its favorable racial image to advantage in winning many of the mass-production industries from the AFL. Moreover, both the AFL and the CIO were concerned about the anti-union attitudes of Southern politicians which produced a flood of anti-union legislation in the South after 1944 and threatened labor's national political objectives.[29]

In 1946, therefore, both the AFL and the CIO launched major organizing drives in the South. The CIO drive, known as "Operation Dixie," lasted until 1953, whereas the AFL campaign lasted only a little over a year. Both campaigns were launched with fanfare, and it soon became obvious that the race issue was important. Philip Murray told the CIO Executive Board that the Southern organizing drive "was a civil rights program . . . which not only encompassed the organization of workers into unions . . . but the freedom of Southern workers from economic and political bondage, the institution of policies designed to exclude all types of racial and other forms of discrimination."[30]

The AFL drive was launched at a conference in Asheville, North Carolina, in May 1946. George Meany, then secretary-treasurer of the AFL, set the tone for the AFL campaign when he told the conference:

Let there be no pussyfooting on the race issue. The American Federation of Labor is determined to bring into the fold of real free trade unionism all American workers of the South—white and black, Gentile and Jew, Protestant and Catholic. The American Federation of Labor has consistently opposed the racial and religious prejudice in all its conventions for long years past. It stands on the same solid conviction today—in the South, in the North and in every other area of the country.[31]

In closing the conference, President Green said:

I hope and trust that the workers of the South regardless of race, creed and color will respond and become a member of the American Federation of Labor . . . refuse to be led or misled by appeals to your prejudice. We have within our great movement one national union, a great effective national union, composed exclusively of colored workers, all the railroad porters operating on every Pullman car in the United States are members of that wonderful colored organization. We chartered that union, we are proud of their affiliation and all the economic support of the American Federation of Labor, its seven million members stand with that organization every minute, every hour and every day. Now my friends the doors of our movement are open to all. Do not allow political appeals and prejudice to influence you in your decision . . . we are determined in this modern day to wipe out of our movement if any exist, any attempt to discriminate against any man because of his race, color or nationality.[32]

The AFL's national officers were not alone in their belief that the race issue would be important in these organizing campaigns. The Southern Organizing Campaign Policy Board, made up of the most outstanding AFL labor leaders in the South, met in June 1946 to map strategy for the campaign. The Policy Board was "unanimous and emphatic" on the need and importance for special attention to Negroes, and called for elimination of the "few remaining handicaps and discriminations" against Negroes in the AFL.

Seventeen of the 117 AFL organizers for the AFL's Southern Organizing Committee were Negroes, and others were added later. International unions with large Negro memberships, or with large Negro potentials, brought in extra Negro organizers for the Southern drive, and AFL organizers of both races were available for special work among Negroes. The Policy Board meeting emphasized the need for "equal employment opportunity for the Negro worker and full participation in American Federation of Labor Unionism." [33]

However, the AFL's unfavorable racial image was not easily overcome and several elections in the early days of the campaign were lost because Negroes voted for the CIO. In 1946 one of the most important of these election victories established a CIO "beachhead" in Mississippi when the workers of the Masonite Corporation, the state's largest plant, swung to the CIO.[34]

After this defeat the AFL redoubled its efforts among Negroes. It circulated a pamphlet among Negro workers called "Pie in the Sky?" [35] which claimed that the CIO unions offered the Negro "pie in the sky . . . with little chance of delivery," whereas the AFL "does not offer you words but results." As to claims of discrimination leveled against the AFL, the pamphlet said:

There are only a half dozen small AFL unions with no Negro members. But a check of these unions shows that employer employment practice— not union discrimination—is the reason. If the Air Line Pilots Association has no colored members, it is no more the union's fault than it is the fault of the Brotherhood of Sleeping Car Porters that they have no white members.

The pamphlet failed to add, of course, that Negroes were frequently barred from membership by formal means even when employers hired them. The pamphlet also claimed that more workers in CIO than AFL unions were involved in strikes against Negro employment during the war and that the number of such unions involved was about evenly divided between them. A factor of some significance at this time was the AFL's claim, in this pamphlet, that:

Out of 36 [CIO] International Unions, 21 are dominated by leaders who follow the Communist Party line. It is a well-known fact that Moscow has given orders to its American Fifth Columnists to give special attention to spreading unrest and dissension among American Negroes. If you fall for this you are Dictator Joe Stalin's prize suckers.

AFL organizers charged that few CIO unions other than "Communist dominated" organizations had high-ranking Negro officers.

The AFL conducted two surveys of Negro membership and found that of 650,000 Negro members in the AFL, 450,000 were in the South. "In other words, the AFL has many more Negro members in the South than the CIO has both Negro and white members in the South." The AFL declared that:

The separate local is rapidly disappearing but is still found in the South. They were often necessary when local, state laws and community tradition made even the hiring of a hall for a mixed meeting impossible. Curiously enough where they still exist it is more often the Negro members who desire separate locals. Negro workers in the South sometimes feel that if they are a minority in numbers in a union they will not have the best opportunity to participate and control their affairs.

The pamphlet also contained statements from AFL Negro unionists and detailed some of the more important cases of discrimination against Negroes by CIO unions. This pamphlet was designed primarily for the Southern campaign, but was also used against the CIO on the West Coast.

Both the AFL and the CIO encountered racial difficulties in their efforts to organize Southern workers. To attempt to organize Negro workers, first, was to risk alienating the whites. The temptation to sign up Negro workers first was strong because where Negro community leaders were pro-union colored workers were more easily organized than whites. Organizers interested in rapid results, or who catered to the prejudices of the workers involved, frequently created lasting problems for the organizations. AFL organizers complained that the CIO, by catering excessively to Negro workers, made it impossible to organize the whites. But both the AFL and the CIO frequently used similar tactics in concrete organizing situations. A few CIO unions permitted segregation where it was considered a prerequisite to unionization. Generally, however, CIO unions refused to permit segregated locals in the South. These internal union problems in the South following the AFL-CIO merger and the racial turmoil following the U. S. Supreme Court's 1954 school desegregation decision will be discussed at length in Chapter 8.

Nature of CIO Racial Problems

Although the CIO was generally more favorably regarded by Negroes, especially in the North, it would be misleading to give the impression that the CIO automatically followed equalitarian policies and got Negro support while all AFL locals discriminated and were shunned by Negroes. As we have seen, some CIO locals barred Negroes from membership and others permitted segregated locals. Moreover, Negroes either segregated themselves, or were segregated by whites, in most of the "integrated" CIO unions in the South; in some places racially segregated facilities were maintained in CIO headquarters and segregated CIO political affairs meetings were held. Indeed, CIO President Philip Murray was infuriated shortly before his death in 1952 when he addressed a segregated audience of the Steelworkers (of which he was the national president) in Alabama; when the crowd spilled out of the union hall into the street, union officials gave policemen orders to maintain segregation in the street!

Perhaps the most serious problems for Negroes in CIO unions were the racially segregated jobs in most of the basic industries. These seniority arrangements were primarily the responsibility of the employers and local customs, of course, but few unions did anything actively to break down job segregation at the plant level. Indeed, as we shall see later, much of the resistance to job desegregation during the 1950's and 1960's came from local industrial-union members. Nor was this problem restricted to the South, because in the North CIO members struck during the Second World War when Negroes were hired or upgraded into formerly all-white organizations.[36] It should be noted, however, that the CIO's national affiliates almost invariably joined the employers in putting down these racial strikes.

In some cases CIO unions even lost bargaining rights to AFL unions at least partly because of racial reasons. For instance, the CIO Steelworkers lost the Ingalls Company in Birmingham in 1941 to the AFL Iron Workers because the CIO union had done nothing for the Negro third of the company's work force. Under the CIO, Negroes were denied promotion and their ability to participate in union affairs was limited, but after the AFL won bargaining rights, it proceeded to reclassify and upgrade Negro-held jobs, won a large increase for colored workers, and placed Negroes on contract grievance committees.[37] In longshoring and the building trades, where the AFL had many more Negro members (usually in segregated locals) than the CIO in the South, the CIO was unable to shake the loyalty of the Negro workers to the AFL. In longshoring, for example, Negroes dominated general longshoring positions in the ports of the Gulf and South Atlantic, and in 1938, when the International Longshoremen and Warehousemen used the CIO's favorable racial image in a raid on the key Mobile and New Orleans ports, it got less than one-fourth of the votes in the NLRB election. It should be conceded, however, that Negro loyalty to AFL unions in the South was due in some measure to the protection of vested economic interests of Negro union leaders. Furthermore, there was a perceptible difference in the Negroes' reaction in unorganized situations as compared with places where the AFL was already entrenched when the CIO was formed. In the former, the CIO's favorable image in Negro communities almost always gained it the Negroes' support, whereas the latter situations were usually structured in the AFL's favor. However, whether the AFL or the CIO retained Negro support during raids depended on how the incumbents had treated their colored members.

CIO Civil Rights Committee's Relations with Negro Community

The CIO unquestionably enjoyed a much more favorable reputation in the Negro community than the AFL, but there is evidence that this reputation was beginning to fade by the time of the AFL-CIO merger in 1955. This fact was most obvious in the activities of the CIO Civil Rights Committee (CRC) which was established as the Committee to Abolish Racial Discrimination in 1942, and which helped the CIO gain a favorable image in the Negro community. (This committee will be referred to as the CRC, even though it had other official names.) The CRC was opposed by many international unions which either gave it only symbolic support or ignored it entirely; some international leaders considered it to be Communist inspired, despite the fact that the committee was vigorously anti-Communist and actually functioned in part as an organization to fight Communists in other organizations and in the Negro community. Other CIO leaders (including the head of the United Mine Workers)

argued that the CRC and similar committees in Auto, Rubber, Packinghouse, Electrical, Steelworkers, and other unions [38] were unnecessary because they would merely serve to "smother" rather than solve
problems; it was also argued that racial problems should be handled
through the regular internal union machinery, which had more power
to solve these problems. Moreover, it was feared that special civil-
rights programs would split the labor movement along racial lines.

Although the Committee served to help various internationals with
their racial problems, it was clear from the outset that the CRC was
to be primarily a public-relations organization with advisory powers
on racial matters. Members of the committee like Willard Townsend,
president of the virtually all-Negro United Transport Service Employees, wrote articles for influential Negro papers like the *Pittsburgh
Courier*. It was also clear that the organization had no power or accepted procedures for handling racial cases, but sought "to move in
on a racial situation as it occurred" to prevent unfavorable publicity,
especially during organizing campaigns.[39]

The CRC encountered difficulties with the Negro press from the
start, but the most serious trouble came after the Second World War
when the Committee was criticized for being a purely symbolic organization with no power. In 1949, for instance, an influential writer
for the *Pittsburgh Courier* charged that the Committee had done little or nothing to overcome discrimination in the Negro community.
This writer said that in Pittsburgh and other Northern cities the Negro had not experienced "high labor standards" and had "been sys-
tematically denied upgrading because of contract clauses which set
up discriminatory job line classifications in various plants." [40] The
committee should have been abolished, according to the *Courier*
writer, because it

is serving no useful purpose to CIO union members and hasn't even proved
itself to be of nominal nuisance value. It is nice window dressing for the
organization . . . but in its present form is doing its union and the liberal
forces of this country a distinct disservice.

This writer suggested that a new committee of elected members be
established so that it would be free from the pressures of various
union leaders. "Such a program would do much to end the spectacle
made by certain CIO officials of color who now hold their offices on
a 'puppet' basis."

The *Courier* writer continued his attacks on the Civil Rights Committee and its Negro members in later editions. Concerning the performance of two of the Committee's members, including its Negro
director, at the 1949 UAW convention, he declared that "about the

only thing missing from the show was a pair of handkerchiefs wrapped around each of the gentlemen's expansive brows." [41]

The *CIO News* and the Committee's members issued public statements attacking the *Courier* writer and calling him a "Black Pegler" because he had tried to "smear CIO leaders." [42] But the Negro writer answered that the *CIO News* was smearing "a consistently friendly writer, simply because he found it good and appropriate to criticize certain individuals or practices in the CIO with which honest differences arose from time to time." [43]

Although it is difficult to tell how accurately the *Courier* writer reflected the thinking of the Negro community, these and other attacks on the Civil Rights Committee caused its members to discuss their public image at the September 1949 meeting, at which Willard Townsend concluded that the Committee was "recognized not as a committee to do something, but more like a symbol." [44] Townsend was disturbed because of the CIO's declining reputation among Negroes; he was especially concerned that Negroes in the South were supporting the Communist-dominated Mine, Mill and Smelter Workers in preference to the CIO Steelworkers. Another Negro member of the Committee reported that the "Negro community is saying the [CRC] is yes men for the CIO," and they "jump us for being Uncle Toms for the CIO." [45] The CRC's members also agreed that the Committee's main problem was its lack of power. The CIO found that its international unions could sometimes be about as autonomous as those in the AFL and that it was difficult for a civil-rights committee to halt discrimination in a local or international union without the support of the latter. The Committee's only power over local organizations and internationals was moral suasion and expulsion. Moral suasion could be supplemented by publicizing discriminatory practices, but the Civil Rights Committee rejected this because, as Chairman James B. Carey of the Electrical Workers argued, publicity "would injure all unions." Some of the Committee members recommended revoking charters of discriminating unions, but the majority of the Committee refused to adopt this position on the grounds that it would not solve the problem.

Summary and Conclusions

Thus, although there was growing disenchantment with the CIO in the Negro community by the time of the AFL-CIO merger in 1955, we must conclude that the upsurge in unionism in the 1930's and during the Second World War greatly increased the number of Negro union members and that, by the time of the merger, the main Negro organizations in the United States were still basically pro-union, that Negro-labor political alliances showed little signs of splitting, and that Negroes had more strength within the unions than ever before. Precise Negro union-membership figures are not available, but there were probably at least 1.5 million Negro unionists at the time of the merger. Between 1926 and 1928, there were an estimated 61,000 Negroes in the AFL.[46] Another estimate put 45,000 Negroes in the AFL in 1930 and another 11,000 in independent unions.[47] There were an estimated 600,000 Negro union members in 1940, and 1,250,000 at the peak of employment during the Second World War.[48] At the time of the merger, Negro union membership probably represented a larger proportion of potential membership than was true of whites, but Negroes were concentrated in relatively few unions.[49]

It should not be inferred from the previous discussion that the CIO did not in fact attempt to pursue equalitarian racial practices. Indeed, we have suggested that the CIO was forced to adopt such policies if it hoped to organize the basic industries where large numbers of Negroes were concentrated. It was also seen that the CIO's policies were influenced by those of the UMW which had learned long before 1935 that the increasingly important Southern coal mines could not be organized on other than an equalitarian basis. Other factors influencing the CIO's policies were that the CIO was younger than the AFL, the competition within the CIO between Communists and non-Communists, and the broader social outlook of its leaders.

FOOTNOTES

1. C. G. Daugherty, *Economics of the Iron and Steel Industry*, cited by Horace Cayton and George Mitchell, *Black Workers and the New Unions*, Chapel Hill: University of North Carolina Press, 1939, p. 11.
2. 1930 Census, Vol. IV, *Population: Occupations by State.*
3. Census figures cited by *ibid.*, p. 457.
4. 1930 Census cited by Herbert Northrup, *Organized Labor and the Negro*, New York: Harper, 1944, p. 105.
5. Census figures cited by *ibid.*, p. 154.
6. Lloyd H. Bailer, "The Negro Automobile Worker," *Journal of Political Economy*, October 1943, p. 461.
7. UMW *Convention Proceedings*, 1942, p. 189.
8. Cayton and Mitchell, *op. cit.*, Ch. 18.
9. Information on the UPWA's antidiscrimination program came from personal interviews with observers and members in Louisiana, Tennessee, Georgia, Texas, Washington, D. C., Chicago, New York, and Detroit. John Hope II directed a very thorough study of the UPWA's racial practices, published as *Equality of Opportunity, a Union Approach to Fair Employment*, Washington, D. C.: Public Affairs Press, 1956. The historical development of unions

in the packinghouse industry is taken mainly from John R. Commons, "Labor Conditions in Meat Packing and the Recent Strike," *Quarterly Journal of Economics*, November 1904; Alma Herbst, *The Negro in the Slaughtering and Meat Packing Industry in Chicago*, Boston: Houghton Mifflin, 1932; The Chicago Commission of Race Relations, *The Negro in Chicago*, University of Chicago Press, 1932; St. Claire Drake and Horace R. Cayton, *The Black Metropolis*, New York: Harcourt, Brace, 1945; Sterling P. Spero and Abram L. Harris, *The Black Worker*, New York: Columbia University Press, 1931; Horace R. Cayton and George S. Mitchell, *Black Workers and the New Unions*, Chapel Hill: University of North Carolina Press, 1939, Section 2; and Theodore V. Purcell, *The Worker Speaks His Mind on Company and Union*, Cambridge, Mass.: Harvard University Press, 1954, Ch. 3.

10. See Paul S. Taylor, *Mexican Labor in the United States*, Berkeley: University of California Press, 1932, p. 46.
11. Quoted by Purcell, *op. cit.*, p. 54.
12. See Walter Galenson, *The CIO Challenge to the AFL*, Cambridge, Mass.: Harvard University Press, 1960, Ch. 10.
13. Letter to Horace Cayton, October 30, 1934, quoted by Cayton and Mitchell, *op. cit.*, pp. 413–414.
14. *Ibid.*
15. *Crisis*, July 1936, p. 209.
16. Bailer, *op. cit.*, p. 415.
17. Cayton and Mitchell, *op. cit.*, pp. 414–415.
18. *Crisis*, August 1937, p. 246.
19. *Ibid.*, p. 241.
20. *National Urban League and Organized Labor*, pamphlet, n.d.
21. Letter to William Green from Julius Thomas, January 14, 1944.
22. AFL *Executive Council Minutes*, May 1–9, 1944.
23. Irving Howe and B. J. Widick, *The UAW and Walter Reuther*, New York: Random House, 1949, p. 218; Galenson, *op. cit.*, pp. 180–181.
24. NAACP *Annual Report*, 1941, p. 31; see also Northrup, *op. cit.*, pp. 192–196.
25. CIO *Convention Proceedings*, 1952, p. 367.
26. *Ibid.*, 1948, p. 251.
27. *Ibid.*, 1948, p. 348.
28. *Ibid.*
29. See my "Some Factors Influencing the Growth of Unions in the South," *Proceedings* of the Industrial Relations Research Association, 1960.
30. CIO *Executive Board Minutes*, August 30, 31, and September 1, 1948, pp. 15–17.
31. Asheville *Conference Proceedings*, AFL-CIO Library, Washington, D. C.
32. *Ibid.*
33. *Minutes of the Southern Organizing Campaign Policy Board Meeting*, June 3–6, 1946; George Googe, "The Southern Campaign," Report to the AFL Executive Council, August 1946.
34. Personal interview, George Googe, director of the AFL Southern organizing campaign, April 11, 1959.
35. Copy in AFL-CIO Library, Washington, D. C., and in the writer's possession.
36. For example, in December 1944, over 1000 white employees at the Pullman Standard Car Manufacturing Company in Chicago struck to prevent the promotion to gang leader of a Negro pipe fitter. Both management and the United Steelworkers' leadership opposed this strike. Another Steelworkers'

plant was struck in East St. Louis, Illinois, when a Negro was promoted to crane operator. The union again backed the Negro and the strike was broken. In 1944 at Harvey, Illinois, 300 white workers struck for four days for segregated toilets. In Cincinnati, Ohio, 15,000 white workers represented by the UAW struck to prevent the promotion of seven Negroes. The UAW supported the company and the strike was broken. The UAW had to put down a number of strikes by its white members in Detroit against the hiring and upgrading of Negroes during the Second World War. (Cases in the files of the CIO Civil Rights Committee.)

37. "Negroes War," *Fortune*, June 1942.
38. The Eleventh Constitutional Convention of the CIO in 1950 adopted a resolution "That each CIO affiliate create a Civil Rights Committee, or Department on Fair Practices within its respective organization." Thereafter, the following organizations established such machinery: Amalgamated Clothing Workers; Communications Workers; International Union of Electrical Workers; United Furniture Workers; United Gas, Coke and Chemical Workers; American Newspaper Guild; Oil Workers; United Paperworkers of America; Retail, Wholesale and Department Store Union; United Shoe Workers of America; Transport Workers Union of America; and International Woodworkers of America. Many of these organizations had already established committees by 1950, but they had not assigned specific responsibilities for their day-to-day operation. (Report of the Director, Committee to Abolish Discrimination, November 18, 1950; Committee to Abolish Discrimination, *Minutes*, May 25, 1943, and October 25, 1949; Committee to Abolish Discrimination, *Report*, November 1946; Committee to Abolish Discrimination, *Minutes*, May 12, 1945.)
39. CIO *Executive Board Minutes*, August 30, 31, and September 1, 1948; Committee to Abolish Discrimination, *Minutes*, August 16, 1946.
40. *Pittsburgh Courier*, August 29, 1949.
41. *Ibid.*, July 16, 1949.
42. *CIO News*, August 8, 1949.
43. *Pittsburgh Courier*, August 29, 1949.
44. Committee to Abolish Discrimination, *Minutes*, September 8, 1949.
45. *Ibid.*
46. Ira de A. Reid, *Negro Membership in Labor Unions*, New York: National Urban League, 1930.
47. Abram L. Harris, *The Negro Worker*, New York: Conference for Progressive Labor Action, 1930.
48. Jessie P. Guzman, *The Negro Year Book*, Tuskegee Institute, Alabama, 1947; see also George F. McCrary, "The Labor Movement, 1944–1945," in Florence Murray, ed., *The Negro Handbook*, New York: Current Books, 1947, p. 109.
49. The following table gives Negro union membership in 1945, as estimated by the Labor Research Association (*Labor Fact Book*, No. 7, 1945, pp. 73–74) and by McCrary. (George F. McCrary, "The Labor Movement, 1944–1945" in Florence Murray, Ed., *The Negro Handbook*, New York: Current Books, 1947, p. 109.) The figures in the table reveal that the CIO had approximately 394,500 in the unions listed if we use the more complete figures of the Labor Research Association, whereas the AFL unions listed had 299,000 if we use the LRA's figures, plus 38,000 as the estimate for the Hotel and Restaurant Employees and McCrary's estimate of 5000 for the United Automobile Workers AFL.

Estimated Negro Union Membership, Selected Unions, 1945

	Negro Membership	
Union	Labor Research Assn. (1945)	McCrary (Dec. 1945)
Congress of Industrial Organizations		
United Steelworkers	95,000	85,000
United Auto Workers	90,000	100,000
Marine and Shipbuilding Workers	40,000	16,000
United Electrical Workers	40,000	10,000
United Packinghouse Workers	22,500	25,000
Mine, Mill and Smelter Workers	20,000	6,000
Amalgamated Clothing Workers	15,000	15,000
United Federal Workers	10,000	6,000
United Transport Service	10,000	12,000
National Maritime Union	8,500	2,000
Textile Workers	6,500	
Food, Tobacco and Allied Workers	6,000	10,500
International Longshoremen and Warehousemen	13,000	3,000
Retail, Wholesale and Department Store Employees	6,000	
Furniture Workers	6,000	
Farm Equipment Workers	3,000	6,000
American Federation of Labor		
Hod Carriers and Common Laborers	55,000	55,000
Hotel and Restaurant Employees	35,000–40,000	9,000
Building Service Employees	35,000	10,000
Maintenance of Way Employees	25,000	5,000
Amalgamated Meat Cutters	25,000	
Railway and Steamship Clerks	12,000	12,000
Teamsters	15,000	12,000
Boilermakers (Jan. 1944)	14,000	18,000
Longshoremen's Assn.	10,000	16,000
Ladies Garment Workers	14,000	10,000
Tobacco Workers	9,100	
Sleeping Car Porters	12,000	8,500
American Federation of Musicians	10,000	4,500
Brotherhood of Railway Carmen	4,500	
United Automobile Workers		5,000
Carpenters and Joiners	3,000	3,000
Bricklayers	3,000	3,000
Pressmen	3,000	
Cement, Lime and Gypsum	3,000	
Pulp, Sulphite and Paper Mill	2,000	
Painters	1,500	
Cigar Makers	500	

CHAPTER 4

The Negro and the AFL-CIO

The Changing Mood of the Negro Community

THE 1955 AFL-CIO MERGER CAME AT A TIME OF MOMENTOUS, IF not revolutionary, changes in American race relations. The Negro protest movement was undergoing a rapid change from legal agitation by a relatively few Negro leaders to a mass movement with many militant and competing leaders. In order to even partly understand the growing militancy of the Negro mood, we must try to see how Negro leaders view their history in America.[1] As noted earlier, after 1900 the Southern Negro was virtually frozen to agriculture and certain menial nonagricultural jobs, into which he was trapped by a vicious cycle of discrimination, low incomes, large families, ignorance, and lack of incentives. Even under these conditions, however, Negroes seem to have had hope that a better day lay ahead. True, the hope held out by the Yankees during Reconstruction proved disappointing, but leaders like Booker T. Washington assured Negroes that political and social equality could be deferred until hard work, industrial education, and alliances with employers improved their economic position relative to whites. Some improvement was possible, but most

Negroes found only limited escape through strikebreaking and industrial education.

More "radical" Northern Negro leaders like W. E. B. DuBois and the founders of the NAACP, formed in 1909, were radical only when compared with Washington and his supporters, because in its early years the Association was really a "black bourgeois" organization, led by middle-class Negroes and whites, which promised the Negro salvation through legal action. Washington and the NAACP also were challenged by various escapist movements which taught that Negroes should separate themselves physically from white America because they would never achieve complete acceptance.

Outside the rural South,[2] the Negro found new hope in his increased political and economic power and the liberal white union and political leaders who were willing to champion his cause. There were also the Communists, who offered him salvation through "self-determination"—a scheme to give Negroes control of the black belt of the South, a crescent of counties stretching from Virginia to Texas which had Negro majorities in 1930. This scheme was too ridiculous to gain much support among Negroes, though it was not officially abandoned until 1959. The CIO also gave Negroes hope that unionism might offer a means to equality, but, as discussed earlier, by the time of the AFL-CIO merger some Negroes apparently were becoming disappointed with the CIO.[3]

As will be discussed at greater length in Chapter 7, the Negro's economic condition, which had improved markedly during the Second World War, became more acute during the recessions after 1949 because of the higher unemployment rates among Negroes, who were concentrated in jobs most likely to be abolished by automation and recessions. Moreover, Negroes soon realized that state antidiscrimination laws were not as effective in changing job patterns as many had hoped; even though these laws covered virtually the entire nonwhite population outside the South in 1964, we shall see that Negroes' median income actually deteriorated relative to whites.

During the time between Reconstruction and the Second World War, the hopes of many Southern Negroes were kept alive by the belief that their conditions could be improved if they crossed over to the promised land beyond Mason and Dixon's line. Although many Negroes were able to improve their positions, for many others these hopes were dashed by the realities of this land, which turned out to contain job, housing, and school segregation, poverty, inordinately high rates of unemployment, slums, narcotics, and discrimination untempered by even the slightest traces of *noblesse oblige*. The political freedom found by the Negro in the North did little to allay his disillusionment. Indeed, his condition made him easy prey to Negro demagogues who, having learned their lessons well from generations of Southern politicians, were very effective at inciting the Negro's hatred for whites in general and greatly oversimplifying the causes of this trouble.

Although these deferred and disappointed hopes lessened the Negro's faith in white people, a number of developments strengthened his ability to solve his own problems, especially his increased political power and the Supreme Court's decisions confirming equality in all public areas of American society. The international importance of racial discrimination also strengthened the Negro by making American politicians more vulnerable to racial protest. At the same time, the growth of nationalism in Africa gave Negroes new racial pride; the example of these African nations undoubtedly made Negroes more determined to press harder for their own rights.

Against this background, the Negro's militant mood becomes more comprehensible. Now that Negroes have moved to their last bastion of hope in the North and many apparently have found that wanting, they exhibit a variety of reactions ranging from resignation to desperate militancy and escape from the white man's world through black nationalism. In spite of this mood, however, the militancy of the Negro community undoubtedly also reflects the progress that has been made as well as the obstacles to that progress, because protest is more likely to come from people who have gained the freedom to protest than from people who are totally oppressed. Indeed, a major problem for public policy is that irresponsible and extremist groups can easily capitalize on the Negro's militant mood to engage in acts of violence which could harden white resistance to the civil-rights movement.

AFL-CIO Civil-Rights Program

Partly as a result of the influence of the mood of the Negro community and the prevailing attitude on race relations, and partly because of organized activity by Negro unionists led by A. Philip Randolph, the AFL-CIO adopted a relatively strong civil-rights program. The Federation's constitution listed among its objectives: "To encourage all workers without regard to race, creed, color, national origin or ancestry to share equally in the full benefits of union organization." In order to help the Executive Council "bring about at the earliest possible date the effective implementation of the principle . . . of nondiscrimination," the AFL-CIO's constitution provided for a Civil Rights Committee (CRC). Day-to-day administration is carried out by a Civil Rights Department.

Although Randolph was not at all pleased with the AFL-CIO's failure to impose definite sanctions against discriminating unions,[4] he nevertheless termed the civil-rights program of the merged Federation a "step forward."[5] When Michael Quill of the CIO Transport Workers Union wanted assurances before voting for the merger that the civil-rights program would be implemented, Reuther said, "These are not just words. These will be deeds."[6] Reuther's views were shared by James B. Carey of the International Union of Electrical Workers, who had been chairman of the CIO Civil Rights Committee. Carey said civil rights had been "high on the agenda of the basic principles that concerned the AFL-CIO Unity Committee during its negotiations."[7] Negro suspicions were also allayed by the election of two Negro vice-presidents—Philip Randolph and Willard Townsend of the CIO United Transport Service Employees—and the fact that Carey, who was highly regarded in the Negro community, was made chairman of the Civil Rights Committee.[8]

However, a number of features of the merger caused Negroes to become increasingly skeptical of the Federation's civil-rights program. Some Negro leaders noted that unions could be expelled for corruption and Communism but not for civil-rights violations.[9] This skepticism was strengthened during the first year of the CRC's operations when Carey resigned as chairman because, among other things, he thought the Committee was not moving fast enough.[10] Carey was replaced by Charles Zimmerman, vice-president of the International Ladies' Garment Workers Union. As a result, the NAACP declared that

The Civil Rights Committee of the AFL-CIO is the only standing committee in the Federation whose chairman is not a member of the Federation's Executive Council and/or the president of an international union. The rigid protocol of the national labor federation indicates that such a person is not in a position to impose a policy upon an international or local union but must confine himself to issuing declarations and to exercising such persuasion as he can muster. More often than not, his efforts are fruitless.[11]

Zimmerman had long been a leader in the civil-rights activities of the Jewish Labor Committee, which, as we shall see, also came under attack by Negroes after the merger. Criticism by Negroes caused Zimmerman to resign in 1961 and, after some difficulty getting another chairman, Meany appointed AFL-CIO Secretary-Treasurer William F. Schnitzler.

Relations between the AFL-CIO and the Negro community were also influenced by the fact that two-thirds of the official positions of the merged organization, including the presidency, went to the AFL, which was never able to overcome its unfavorable image in the Negro community and which never had close relations with organizations like the NAACP and the NUL. Furthermore, the AFL-CIO Executive Council admitted two unions—the Brotherhood of Locomotive Firemen (BLF) and the Brotherhood of Railroad Trainmen (BRT)—to the merged organization even though they still had race bars in their constitutions. Only A. Philip Randolph, the Executive Council's only Negro member after the death of Willard Townsend, voted against the admission of these organizations on racial grounds.[12] White leaders apparently gave little thought to this problem and those who did were persuaded that it was better to take the unions in and seek to change their practices from "within the house of Labor." But Negro leaders could hardly believe that such CIO civil-rights stalwarts as James Carey and Walter Reuther had voted for the admission of organizations with constitutional race bars. Negro-labor relations were also exacerbated by a number of widely publicized cases of discrimination against Negroes by local unions in cities (Cleveland, Detroit, Philadelphia, San Francisco, Milwaukee, Los Angeles, Hartford, New York, and Washington, D. C.) with large Negro concentrations. The Negro community was particularly incensed at the vigorous defense of discrimination by these unions before fair-employment-practices commissions, in the courts, and before such organizations as the AFL-CIO Civil Rights Committee and the federal contract committees. At a time of increasing unemployment among Negroes, there was a growing conviction that union discrimination in apprenticeship training and upgrading within plants was at least partly responsible for the economic plight of Negro workers.

The NAACP

These developments also put a strain on the working relations formed between the NAACP and the labor movement since the 1930's. The Association's victories in the school desegregation cases increased its prestige in the Negro community, but the changes taking place in race relations made it difficult for it to continue to work closely with organizations (like the AFL-CIO) considered to be discriminatory by increasing numbers of Negroes. The Association's position of leadership also made it possible for it to rely more on Negroes and less on unions and liberal whites for financial support. Moreover, the NAACP gained membership because of the attacks on it in the South. At the same time, however, the Association was being challenged in the Negro community by younger and more militant leadership. Internally, the NAACP sought to become less bureaucratic by constitutional changes in 1947 and 1962 which permitted greater membership participation in the election of its board of directors. Finally, racial sentiment in the Negro community was such that whites were becoming less important in the leadership of the NAACP and other civil-rights organizations.[13]

These developments made it inevitable that the NAACP would become increasingly critical of unions.[14] In December 1958, NAACP Labor Secretary Herbert Hill, in a memorandum to Boris Shishkin, then the director of the AFL-CIO Civil Rights Department, filed complaints against locals of the International Brotherhood of Electrical Workers; Railroad Telegraphers; Plumbers and Pipefitters; Maintenance of Way Employees; Painters, Decorators and Paperhangers; Railway Carmen; Railway Clerks; Boilermakers and Blacksmiths; Pulp, Sulphite and Paper Mill Workers; Sheet Metal Workers; Carpenters and Joiners; and the Paper Makers and Paper Workers. Hill charged that the discriminatory practices of these unions seriously threatened the economic status of Negroes.[15]

The NAACP charged the AFL-CIO unions with: (1) excluding Negroes by constitutional provision and tacit consent; (2) discriminating against Negroes on job referrals; (3) maintaining separate lines of promotion which limited Negroes to menial jobs; [16] and (4) maintaining segregated or auxiliary locals.

In the South, the NAACP charged:

The leaders of some international unions . . . in seeking to avoid conflict over racial issues are permitting racist elements to gain control of local union operations. Direct observation indicates that in many instances union shop stewards and business agents openly solicit funds and support for the White Citizens Councils and in Front Royal, Virginia, a local affiliated to the Textile Workers Union of America has provided space in the union's building for classes to be conducted by the private school corporation.[17]

Both Hill and Roy Wilkins, NAACP executive secretary, called on the AFL-CIO Civil Rights Department in 1959 to change its method of handling complaints. Hill's memorandum stated:

It is totally inadequate for the Civil Rights Department to proceed from individual random complaints which often take years to resolve if ever.

What is clearly necessary is a direct frontal attack against segregation and discrimination within trade unions conducted on a systematic basis by the AFL-CIO. Obviously a policy has meaning only to the degree that it is enforced, otherwise one must conclude that it is simply a matter of empty ritual.[18]

In assessing the performance of the AFL-CIO five years after the merger, the NAACP's Labor Department noted that "the national labor movement has failed to eliminate the broad pattern of racial discrimination and segregation in many important affiliated unions." [19]

The responses of union leaders to these charges were not uniform, but were generally indignant. When questioned by the writer, the presidents of most of the unions under specific attack denied the charges or denied responsibility for the conditions outlined in Hill's memorandum. Most of them pointed to changes in their constitutions to prove that they did not discriminate. The president of one railroad union denied Hill's charge that his union maintained segregated lodges. He said his union had white, Negro, and mixed lodges because in some instances all the employees were of one race, and in others work jurisdictions determined the groupings.[20] The union, according to its president, had no voice in the hiring policies of the railroads. The president of another railroad union denied every allegation in Hill's memo.[21] He said that the union changed its constitution "many years ago" and had never discriminated or denied equal seniority and job rights to Negro workers. The president of still another railroad union said the NAACP charges against his brotherhood were incorrect because his organization had eliminated the word "white" from its constitution at the 1952 convention. He said this was not a "live" subject in the union because of nearly 65,000 members he was sure only about half a dozen were colored. Few Negroes, he said, had been interested in working in his craft.[22]

Other union leaders, such as the president of an industrial union with segregated locals throughout the South, expressed considerable resentment at the NAACP accusations.[23] The gist of his defense was that the economic status of Negroes under his jurisdiction had improved greatly, although Negroes were still in the most menial jobs. He also admitted that

In some instances we have had to issue separate charters for Negro workers. However, wherever it is possible, we organize Negro workers and white workers under the same charter. We sometimes find that we have to issue separate charters to white workers because the maintenance workers want their own locals. Would you call this segregation? Our International Union does not like to issue separate charters for maintenance and production workers. We do not like to have to, at times, issue separate charters to Negro workers. *We are forced to handle these practical problems in a realistic manner. We cannot overcome age-old prejudice in a few years time.* [Emphasis added.]

The replies of the union presidents minimized the extent of the discriminatory practices within their organizations and emphasized what their unions had gained for Negroes even where Negro members are clearly being discriminated against. The arguments implied that bad as things were they could have been worse. They also pointed out that the autonomy of their locals made it difficult for the international to enforce equalitarian policies. Most of those unions claiming never to have discriminated against Negroes were among those with histories of formal and informal exclusion and auxiliary and segregated locals, to be discussed in Part 2.

AFL-CIO leaders were equally disturbed by the NAACP charges. The Federation leadership treated the NAACP allegations as unfounded and unfair on the grounds that the labor movement "has done more for the Negro, with all its shortcomings, than any other group. No other organization, such as the National Association of Manufacturers and the Chamber of Commerce of the United States, have civil rights committees," according to Charles Zimmerman, then chairman of the AFL-CIO Civil Rights Committee.[24]

Zimmerman accused the NAACP of frequently acting without investigation and airing its grievances in the press before talking things over with the unions involved. According to Zimmerman, what was needed was not denunciation of the labor movement and demagogy, but united action of all civil-rights forces. The CRC chairman also pointed out that a decade ago there had been a dozen unions with exclusion clauses whereas then there were only two. He said that the NAACP failed to understand that the AFL-CIO, a voluntary organization, had no power to compel a local organization to adhere to its egalitarian policies. The main function of the Civil Rights Committee, he added, was education.[25]

Other AFL-CIO leaders echoed these sentiments, and all were opposed to expelling discriminatory unions and splintering the labor movement. When reminded during an interview with the writer that expulsion had been used by the labor movement to handle the problems of Communism and corruption, a member of the AFL-CIO Executive Council replied:

If there was any indication that the Teamsters were progressing as much as the leaders of the railroad unions they would not have been expelled. . . . We recommend against expelling because there are indications of progress and we feel that discrimination will be formally and practically eliminated in the near future. Other alternatives would defeat Negro objectives. The NAACP appears shortsighted, in fact contradictory. If we expelled unions or mandated a certain date upon which they would be out of the federation if they did not change their policies, there would be no chance of changing discrimination in these unions. . . . If my union had been expelled because those who wanted change were not successful I doubt we would have changed our policies. The NAACP is unfair to those organizations who want change by making it more difficult to accomplish this. The NAACP has made mistakes by not working with sincere elements in the labor movement; then they could accomplish more.

Although many union leaders consider Herbert Hill's attacks on the AFL-CIO and some of its affiliates to have been inaccurate and irresponsible, Hill claims that he started making his public attacks only after unsuccessfully attempting to work within the trade-union movement for two years after the merger. But, in a personal interview with the writer, Donald Slaiman, director of the AFL-CIO Civil Rights Department, replied: "For Herbert Hill to say that he stopped cooperating with the labor movement because he could not get results is nonsense. If the civil-rights movement had stopped after two years we would never have had the Civil Rights Act. Besides, Hill neglects the fact that the unions made much progress in civil rights during the first two years after the merger." Although Hill's attacks on the AFL-CIO and its affiliates have alienated him from many union leaders, this alienation seems to have been more of a personal rupture than a basic organizational schism between the NAACP and the unions, in spite of the fact that the NAACP openly supported Hill.

Although the dispute between the NAACP and the AFL-CIO became entangled with the conflicts between Negro and white unionists and the NAACP and Jewish labor leaders, to be discussed next, relations between the NAACP and the AFL-CIO apparently have improved since 1960. The NAACP filed no more complaints with the AFL-CIO Civil Rights Department between 1958 and 1964. Moreover, personality clashes undoubtedly caused the public to exaggerate the extent of the differences between the two organizations. Although other factors discussed in Chapter 12 were at work, the improvement in relations between the NAACP and the AFL-CIO apparently was caused in part by the silencing, resignation, or removal of some of the key personalities in the 1958–1960 disputes.

Postmerger Relations between Negro and White Union Leaders

Although the AFL-CIO's dispute with the NAACP's labor secretary was the most vitriolic aspect of the Negro-union rift following the merger, the conflict was not confined to these charges and counter-charges. Negro union leaders also became more outspoken in their criticism of unions, not only because they became aware of the extent of union discrimination after the NAACP's attacks and the prosecutions of unions by state and local civil-rights organizations, but also because the status of Negro trade unionists declined as the Negro community became more disenchanted with unions. In order to counter this decline and combat union discrimination, colored unionists also became more militant.

Negroes emphasized that they were demanding, not begging, white union leaders for their rights; as a Philadelphia Negro leader put it:

We've got to stop Uncle Tomming it. The spotlight is on racial integration and we've got to move while we have the opportunity. If we have to hurt our friends, then we will just have to hurt them. I consider myself to be one of the new breed of Negroes. I'm not begging at the back door for scraps, but knocking on the front door for my rights.[26]

The relations between Negro and white unionists were symbolized by those between George Meany and A. Philip Randolph, the recognized spokesman for Negro unionists. Randolph's position of leadership was due not only to his long and tireless fight for fair treatment of Negroes by unions and in the larger society, but also to the fact that his leadership in the virtually all-Negro Brotherhood of Sleeping Car Porters made him much more independent of whites than other Negro union leaders.

The most significant exchange between Meany and Randolph came at the 1959 AFL-CIO convention. The first debate involved a resolution by Randolph and other BSCP delegates calling for the expulsion of the BRT and BLF unless the latter removed their race bars within six months after the convention. George Meany and all but two other white delegates supported a subcommittee report which noted that the BRT and the BLF had "failed to carry out their pledge to the AFL-CIO Executive Council, made by them at the time of their admission to comply with the civil rights policy of the AFL-CIO," but, instead of establishing a time limit, recommended that the Executive Council be authorized to get compliance "at the earliest possible date." Meany argued that a time limitation would strengthen those within the railroad unions who wanted to keep the color bars.

The race question was raised a second time at the convention when Randolph unsuccessfully opposed the admission to the Federation of the International Longshoremen's Association (ILA) on the ground that the latter discriminated against Negroes in New York. Meany said that Randolph had never brought the charges against the Longshoremen to the attention of the Executive Council or to the subcommittee studying the ILA's admission. Meany implied that the BSCP's president was seeking publicity and said he thought it was time Randolph ". . . got on the team, joined the labor movement, and became part and parcel of the AFL-CIO. To come at this late date, where he has this audience . . . to come up with this material, I don't think that's playing the game. . . ." [27]

But the most heated conflict between Meany and Randolph came over the BSCP's resolution which would have required that segregated locals "be liquidated and eliminated" by AFL-CIO affiliates. The BSCP delegates argued that segregated locals usually deprived Negroes of equal employment opportunities and were no more defensible because their members wanted them than it was to "maintain unions under Communist domination and corrupt influences on the ground the members of said unions desired to keep them." [28] Meany replied heatedly to Randolph: "Is this your idea of a democratic process, that you don't care what the Negro members think? You don't care if they want to maintain the union they have had for so many years? I would like an answer to that." When Randolph answered "yes," Meany responded angrily: "That's not my policy. I am for the democratic rights of the Negro members. Who in the hell appointed you as guardian of the Negro members in America? You talk about tolerance!" [29]

The 1959 AFL-CIO convention debates had important consequences for subsequent relations between the Federation and the Negro community. Although Randolph, Meany, and a majority of white union leaders apparently paid little attention to Meany's statements, they were reported with indignation in the Negro press.[30]

Feelings in the Negro community were such that pressure was put on the Urban League to deny Meany its 1960 Opportunity Day award. Meany, on the other hand, attempted to overcome the impression that he was either mad at Randolph or a racist. In his speech accepting the Urban League award, the AFL-CIO president pledged:

I cannot speak for the managers of private industry, nor can I vouch for the courage, the sincerity and the ability with which the leaders of our Government will do their part in eliminating discrimination. But I can give you this assurance without reservation—the trade union movement will fulfill its responsibility to the Negro workers of this country.

That is not merely a rhetorical pledge. It has the full backing of the official policy of the AFL-CIO, unanimously adopted at our last convention.[31]

Meany emphasized that the 1959 convention had adopted this policy unanimously, and

That is extremely significant, because the history of our labor movement shows that the most effective way of obtaining compliance in a voluntary organization is through unanimous agreement on policy. The record proves that the unanimous policy of today becomes the established fact of tomorrow.

Meany also observed:

I think the record proves we have come a long way. Many of our older unions were born and grew up in an earlier and less enlightened period. They reflected the attitudes of their communities—prejudice based on ignorance. Discrimination was not only accepted; it was respectable. It is a measure of our progress that where discrimination still survives in the labor movement, it is a bootleg product, sneaked in by subterfuge. Even those who practice discrimination know that its days are numbered.

Relations between the AFL-CIO and Randolph fluctuated after this, but seem to have reached an equilibrium of cordiality by the time of the 1963 AFL-CIO convention. In 1960 Randolph and other Negro union leaders formed the Negro-American Labor Council (NALC) which sought, among other things, to fight discrimination from within the labor movement. In 1961 Randolph submitted a document to the AFL-CIO Executive Council, which, according to one AFL-CIO official, "contained a number of charges of discrimination, some general analysis and some programatic material." [32] A subcommittee of the Executive Council appointed by Meany to study Randolph's charges brought back a report which was regarded as a "censure" of Randolph by many newspapers.[33] In October 1961 the Executive Council adopted the subcommittee report which criticized Randolph for causing "the gap that has developed between organized labor and the Negro community." The report denied Randolph's charges that the AFL-CIO was lax in enforcing its racial policies, accused his BSCP of discriminating against whites, and rejected his proposals that the AFL-CIO adopt a system of penalties against discriminating unions. Voluntary compliance with the principles of equal rights, the Council said, would produce a more successful solution to this problem. George Meany said Randolph's attacks on the Federation had made the AFL-CIO's civil-rights program less effective than it should be. Randolph, according to Meany, had

In the last few years . . . become the mouthpiece of the radical few, not the leader as in the past. I resent the fact that he doesn't defend the labor movement. I have admiration for his fight to help his own people, but I also feel he has an obligation to the trade union movement. He's a union man as well as a Negro.[34]

Randolph answered the Executive Council's report by accusing the AFL-CIO of "moral paralysis, pessimism, defeatism and cynicism." [35] Randolph called the Executive Council subcommittee's report an effort to "brainwash the public into accepting a 'whitewash of labor's do-little civil rights record.' " [36]

Following this conflict, however, relations between Randolph and the AFL-CIO seem to have improved markedly. During the 1961 convention, the "censure" report was referred back to the Executive Council and "buried." [37] Meany also met for two hours with an eighteen-man delegation from the NALC to discuss plans to have the Federation take action against discrimination and heal the breach between Meany and Randolph.

The rapprochement apparently succeeded. The 1961 convention strengthened its compliance procedures and adopted a resolution calling for the end of discrimination in all areas, including the labor movement. In what was interpreted as official recognition, Meany accepted an invitation to speak at the NALC's Third Annual Convention in 1962. Meany told the Negro leaders that he had not thought the NALC necessary when it was first formed, "But I respect your motives and share your objectives." [38] Meany explained that he had refused earlier invitations because "Frankly I didn't think I would help solve our problem by going. I probably would have spoken what was on my mind and that might not have been in the interest of a peaceful solution of our troubles." [39]

Randolph told the 1962 NALC delegates that "We are going to maintain our alliance." To emphasize his point, the Negro leader opposed a move by the NALC's New York affiliate to participate in an attack against the International Ladies' Garment Workers Union by Herbert Hill and a subcommittee of the House Committee on Labor and Education, to be discussed later. Randolph said that "It is not the function of the NALC to become the ally of any Congressional committee of politicians to help train its guns of investigation through harassment and persecution against the ILGWU, the union of our fellow workers, brothers and sisters." [40] Randolph's defense of the ILGWU was particularly important because union leaders regarded Herbert Hill's attack on that organization, which had acquired a good reputation for racial practices, as politically inspired. The attacks on the ILGWU and the NAACP's unsuccessful [41] efforts to decertify an Atlanta local of the Steelworkers, an international which also had a favorable reputation for racial practices, prompted particularly strong responses from George Meany and Walter Reuther. Reuther told the 1962 NALC convention that "unfair, unfounded, indiscriminate attacks would help no one." George Meany asked the convention what contribution was made to the cause of equal opportunity by spreading "outright falsehoods, by attempting to smear" the ILGWU whose civil-rights record "shines like a beacon in the history of human progress." Meany assured the NALC delegates that the AFL-CIO was making more progress "than you know about or than I am free to tell you." Some NALC delegates sought unsuccessfully to win the organization's approval of the NAACP's decertification policy, but Randolph told the convention: "I am glad we had the wisdom to reject the doctrine of decertification of unions. . . . When you decertify a union, brother, you are at the mercy of your employer." However, the NALC adopted a resolution supporting the NAACP with the declaration that "this Convention views any attacks on the NAACP as ultimately attacks on all of us who support the NAACP." [42]

Negro Labor Organizations

The formation of Negro labor organizations following the AFL-CIO merger was by no means a new development. Unaffiliated Negro unions have a long history, for instance, on the railroads, in longshoring, and in other occupations where Negroes were numerous or were excluded from regular labor organizations. Moreover, the leaders of some of these Negro unions have been instrumental in the formation of organizations for special purposes; for example, the BSCP has established special organizations to save locomotive firemen's jobs, to overcome the Negro community's hostility to unions, to organize Negro railroad workers, and to march on Washington to get jobs for Negroes during the Second World War. Negroes have also formed "clubs" within unions or plants to promote their interests. There have also been informal Negro "caucuses" in international unions to promote and protect Negro interests through internal political pressures. These "clubs" are usually informally organized and are frequently aided by outside sources like the NAACP, the Urban League, Negro lawyers, ministers, respected leaders of political parties.

Ideological influences

A number of Negro labor organizations have been instigated by left-wing groups. For example, Socialists were instrumental in the formation of the Brotherhood of Sleeping Car Porters in 1925. After

the failure of earlier attempts, Randolph and other New York Socialists formed the Negro Labor Committee in 1935 to promote unionism
among Negroes. The NLC's slogan was "Black and White Workers
Unite," and explained race conflict largely in terms of the class struggle. Both Negro and white workers had been enslaved, lynched, and
terrorized, according to NLC leaders, who felt that: "The Negro question is part of the labor question. The one cannot be solved without
the other, and a genuine cooperative commonwealth offers the only
practical solution. Once we get rid of human exploitation the Negro
problem will soon disappear." [43] By 1946 the NLC claimed to have
transformed "Harlem from a community of scabs to a community of
labor conscious workers." [44]

The Communists have also instigated or backed a number of Negro
labor organizations. They promoted the American Negro Labor Committee (ANLC) in 1925 to overcome Negro hostility to unions. The
ANLC failed, however, because of vigorous opposition from prominent Negro and white leaders. The Communists infiltrated and ultimately gained control of the National Negro Congress (NNC) formed
at Chicago in 1936 to embrace Negro unions and other organizations.
The sponsors of the NNC were a group of non-Communist Negroes,
including Philip Randolph, who were driven away from the organization by 1940 when it became clear that it was Communist controlled. After the Second World War the Communists promoted a
number of Negro labor organizations in Harlem,[45] Chicago, Seattle,
Cleveland, Washington, D. C., Boston, Newark, and Detroit [46]

In order to extend and maintain their support among Negro trade
unionists after they were expelled from the CIO, the Communists
formed a National Negro Labor Council (NNLC) in Cincinnati in
October 1951.[47] Anti-Communists countered the NNLC by reactivat-
ing the Negro Labor Committee and calling it the Negro Labor Com-
mittee-U.S.A. (NLC-USA). However, the NNLC was not a serious
enough threat to the anti-Communists to overcome conflicts within
the NLC-USA between AFL and CIO Negro leaders, a rivalry with
the CIO Civil Rights Committee, and other internal political differences. The NLC-USA became virtually inactive after the CIO withdrew its support in January 1953. The NAACP denounced the NNLC
as being Communist dominated and forbade its members to cooperate
with the unions supporting that organization.[48]

The Communists gave their approval to the civil-rights program
adopted by the AFL-CIO, calling it "one of the truly historic events
in the long struggle to cement the Negro-Labor alliance in our country. . . ."[49]

Developments after the AFL-CIO merger

Just before the AFL-CIO merger, Negro unionists met for the purpose of securing the election of Negroes to the AFL-CIO Executive Council and getting the merged federation to adopt a strong civil-rights position. One of these premerger groups was the National Trade Union Conference for Racial Justice led by A. Philip Randolph. In Detroit, Negro leaders, especially from UAW locals 599 and 600, held an Emergency Mass Conference on Issues Affecting Negro Labor in the New Merged Labor Organizations.

The Trade Union Leadership Conference. After the merger, Negro labor groups in the larger metropolitan areas formed or reactivated organizations to promote the interests of Negroes locally. One of these organizations was the Trade Union Leadership Conference (TULC) formed by a group of Detroit Negro unionists in 1957. Most of the founders were from the UAW but in 1960 there were about as many Negroes from other unions in the TULC as from the UAW. The TULC sought to direct the power of the labor movement into broad civil-rights activities and ". . . to interpret the Negro community to the labor movement and the labor movement to the Negro community." [50]

The specific purposes of the TULC were to: (1) help eliminate discrimination in the labor movement with "pinpoint accuracy" by making factual surveys of the areas in which these practices exist; (2) insist on "carefully planned clean-up jobs by the international unions beginning with the most important places . . . the employment offices"; [51] (3) get Negroes elected to international executive boards; (4) work to get Negroes to support their unions; and (5) promote various community civil-rights objectives.

Provision was made in the TULC constitution for a board of directors controlled by charter members. According to Horace Sheffield, UAW international representative and a founder of the TULC, this provision was adopted in order to demonstrate that Negroes can organize to solve their own problems and to prevent ideological influences from disrupting the organization. [52]

Although the TULC's leaders considered the UAW to be among the more enlightened unions in the field of race relations, they were nevertheless critical of that organization for a number of reasons, particularly the absence of Negroes from the international's executive board; [53] the feeling that white union officers excluded Negroes from their intimate social gatherings where important decisions were made; discrimination against Negroes in the UAW skilled-trades apprentice-

ship program; and the ineffectiveness of the International's Fair Practices and Anti-Discrimination Department—which TULC leaders
thought was mainly "ceremonial and symbolic." [54]   The Negro leaders
also felt that their importance in the UAW had diminished after 1946
with Walter Reuther's victory over his internal opposition.   In the
days when the Communists were stronger and only a minority of
Negroes supported Reuther, Negro votes were more important.

In spite of these grievances, however, some Negro unionists opposed the TULC for fear it would produce racial polarizations within
unions.   In a 1959 election in the huge Ford Local 600 for the office
of recording secretary, for instance, a Negro incumbent was defeated
in a campaign, which before it was over

. . . was being fought almost entirely on racial lines.   Some of the incidents which took place in the plant and at the polling booths were a dis-
grace.

Tensions were built up where previously none existed and the sores still
are festering.[55]

TULC officers argued that their organization was ". . . in no way
an issue" in the Ford elections and

We do know that in many local unions where officers and committeemen
carry preferential seniority, there was a considerable increase in the number of candidates.   Unquestionably, the harsh economic situation has made
these positions more attractive because of the job security they offered . . .
[and] the Negro officeholder, in many of these situations, would normally
be considered the easiest target.   The TULC is only slightly more than
two years old.   We have been active union members for many years and
we can say that throughout all of these years wherever and whenever an
unscrupulous candidate for a union office felt that racebaiting the Negro
would pay off, he racebaited.   This obviously, therefore, is no new phe-
nomenon that the TULC's presence has brought into being. . . .[56]

TULC leaders asserted that Negroes who refused to take an independent position were:

. . . hopelessly out of step with the times and totally incapable of making
an honest appraisal of the situation as it exists.   [They] are suggesting that
the Negro should continue to be tractable and content with his lot because
the "other folks" in their "good wisdom and charity" will see that he is
provided for.   This is the old "plantation philosophy" and . . . another
aspect of our program has to do with the matter of isolating the few remaining "Toms," in this area, who are either incapable of rehabilitation or
else refuse to be rehabilitated.   We have already rendered most of them
ineffective and in the one or two instances that apparently escaped our
notice, this urgent job shall get our top priority.

The TULC's "militancy" was not limited to action against Negroes. They particularly resented AFL-CIO President Meany's outburst at Philip Randolph during the 1959 AFL-CIO convention. The TULC dispatched a letter to Meany

. . . to clear you up on the matter that seemed so vexing to you [who appointed Randolph as guardian of all the Negroes in America]. . . . The mistake you made is that Brother Randolph was not appointed to this high position. Brother Randolph was accorded this position by the acclamation of the Negro people in recognition of his having devoted almost half a century of his life "in freedom's cause." [57]

The TULC told Meany they objected to attacks on the NAACP by Charles Zimmerman.

We don't know whether Brother Zimmerman was enunciating what is now the official attitude of the AFL-CIO towards the NAACP. However, if you have issued any disclaimers to this attitude, as expressed by Brother Zimmerman, they have certainly escaped our attention. We feel that it is of vital importance that you do not miscalculate our feelings as they relate to the NAACP. As Negro trade unionists, we stand squarely behind and with the NAACP and will fight for it against any and all of its adversaries with all of the strength that God has given us. We feel confident that Brother Zimmerman would do the same thing for the Jewish Labor Committee and we would applaud him for it.[58]

The TULC also told Meany that it was "in wholehearted approval of the NAACP's memorandum to . . . the AFL-CIO Civil Rights Department, under date of December 4, 1958, 'charging racial discrimination and segregation by unions affiliated to the AFL-CIO.' " [59]

The TULC's 2500 members (in 1961) in the Detroit area had engaged in political action; contributed financially to various civil-rights activities and to political candidates; worked to improve Detroit public schools; established contacts in the Polish-, Jewish-, and Spanish-speaking communities; helped Negroes in the Hod Carriers and Common Laborers local union replace "unfriendly" white officers with Negroes and more sympathetic whites; and served as a model for the Negro-American Labor Council and similar organizations in other Northern cities.

The Negro-American Labor Council (NALC). The immediate impetus to the formation of the Negro-American Labor Council as the central organization of local groups like the TULC came at the Cleveland NAACP convention in 1958. Negro unionists at this meeting were aroused over the growing criticism of unions by the Negro community; some of those present were sufficiently dissatisfied with the

AFL-CIO civil-rights program that they even suggested supporting the "right-to-work" laws then under consideration in many states. The majority opposed this suggestion, however, on the ground that it would damage the labor movement and really would not solve the Negroes' problems.

It was decided that a national Negro organization was needed, and a planning session to launch such an organization was held under Randolph's leadership immediately after the 1959 NAACP convention in New York. The conference had no official connection with the NAACP, however, and only about half of the 53 Negro unionists in attendance had attended the NAACP convention.

Randolph set the stage for the conference of Negro unionists in his speech to the 1959 NAACP convention by calling for the formation of "a national Negro Labor Committee comparable to the Jewish Labor Committee . . . to fight and work to implement the civil rights program of the AFL-CIO, every member of which should be a member of the National Association for the Advancement of Colored People." Randolph advocated that the members of the Negro Labor Committee "should come only from the Negro members of the national and international unions." He said the committee's purpose "should be both to secure membership of Negro workers in the unions and employment and promotion on the job as well as participation in the executive, administrative, and staff areas of the union." [60]

Following the NAACP convention, Randolph outlined a program for Negro unionists.[61] The first objective, he thought, should be to secure compliance by international unions with the AFL-CIO civil-rights program by thoroughly investigating every case of discrimination, "to be followed, if the complaint is found valid, by the necessary action by the president of the AFL-CIO to bring about compliance for the elimination of said discrimination." Second, besides the education of union members and the wide publicity which must be given the civil-rights program, Randolph proposed annual regional civil-rights seminars, attended by union officials at all levels, "for the purpose of making evident and clear the policy position of the AFL-CIO on civil rights and its importance and value to labor."

But Randolph did not think these seminars would be enough. "There is need for a massive attack upon discrimination by the highest and most authentic voice of American labor, the President and Executive Council of the AFL-CIO, which can be profoundly effective in creating the climate and mood for the cause of civil rights among workers and the public."

The fewness of Negroes who have positions of responsibility and power within the labor movement is not due entirely to discrimination, according to Randolph, but

to a spirit of unconcern, indifference, apathy, and a lack of understanding on the part of too large a number of Negro trade unionists of the great significance and value of the trade union movement to all workers. . . . Negro trade unionists must be willing to struggle, sacrifice, and suffer with their fellow workers, including going to jail, to win the demand of the union.

Negroes cannot accomplish these objectives without a Negro labor organization, according to Randolph, because the AFL-CIO "must be moved to take action consistently and continuously" but "it is only possible to move an organization with another organization."

Randolph's previous attempts to form Negro labor organizations failed, he said, because they relied too much on white union leaders for support and frequently whites "could not be counted on when the chips were down." Therefore, Randolph thought the new organization should be financed by Negroes, making it possible to take a position completely independent of white unionists.

The issue of excluding whites was debated at length in the period between the New York meeting and the founding convention of NALC in May 1960. One Negro, who is vice-president of his international union, told the writer: "I am opposed to segregation in any form, but if it takes this to destroy the 'handkerchief heads' then I am for it." Others opposed the organization because of this feature, declaring that Negroes either had to be for integration or opposed to it and that it was dangerous to assume that the end justifies the means. As a result of these debates, the NALC did not restrict its membership to Negroes and has some white members. A. Philip Randolph told the NALC's founding convention:

While the Negro-American Labor Council rejects black nationalism as a doctrine and practice of racial separatism, it recognizes the fact that history has placed upon the Negro and the Negro alone, the basic responsibility to complete the uncompleted Civil War revolution through keeping the fires of freedom burning in the civil rights revolution.

It is, of course, too early to evaluate the NALC and its probable future. Internal difficulties caused it to decline from 10,000 to 4500 members during its first two years. Moreover, it was felt that Negroes refused to participate in the organization because their white bosses opposed it. But this difficulty apparently has been overcome because George Meany spoke at the NALC's 1962 convention and other top AFL-CIO leaders spoke at this and subsequent NALC conventions.

But the NALC has many other problems: many Negroes are in unions outside the AFL-CIO. This leads to suspicions concerning the motives of the Federation's critics, especially those in unions that were expelled from the AFL-CIO for Communism or corruption. In spite of Randolph's efforts to minimize their influence, Communists are reported to be active in some NALC affiliates. Some Negro unionists resented the NALC's tactics of threatening to expose as "Uncle Toms" those who disagree with its methods and procedures. Probably half of the 1.5 million Negro unionists in the United States are in the South where the NALC apparently has little support. There is some concern that the NALC follows "black nationalist" tactics that will produce racial splits within unions. Finally, some critics argue that the NALC has neither the staff nor the program to launch a significant antidiscrimination program.

In spite of these difficulties, the NALC could do much to promote and protect Negro interests within the labor movement and to interpret the labor movement and the Negro community to each other. The organization could activate Negroes within their organizations, serve as a valuable source of information on union racial practices, gain Negro support for unions with equalitarian racial practices, serve as a training ground for Negro leadership within the trade-union movement, and bring constant moral and political pressure within the AFL-CIO to overcome discriminatory practices.

Negro-Jewish Differences

Another aspect of the Negro-labor split is what some observers consider to be a growing conflict between Jews and Negroes. This conflict is disturbing to civil-rights advocates because Jews traditionally have given financial and moral support to Negro causes. Jewish-led unions like the Amalgamated Clothing Workers and the International Ladies' Garment Workers Union have been regarded as among the most progressive unions with respect to civil rights. Jewish unions also maintain the Jewish Labor Committee (JLC), with field offices in several major cities, to promote equalitarian racial policies and perform certain advisory and fact-finding services for the AFL-CIO. Since it is made up of representatives from unions, not all of whom are Jews, the JLC has had a close working relationship with the AFL-CIO. It was perhaps inevitable that the differences between the NAACP and the AFL-CIO should affect NAACP-JLC relations.

JLC representatives were likely to take the AFL-CIO's side in these conflicts. Jewish union leaders felt that the NAACP was more interested in making headlines and getting a reputation for militancy than in attempting to solve underlying problems. The NAACP, on the other hand, suspected that the JLC representatives were mainly interested in "window dressing" and "covering up" the labor movement's discriminatory practices.

The conflict between the NAACP and the JLC was given public expression in a series of exchanges between officials of the two organizations in various public media.[62] In 1959, for example, NAACP Labor Secretary Herbert Hill wrote an article in *Commentary* attacking unions,[63] which a JLC representative claimed "gives a distorted image of the relations of the labor movement to obtain civil rights for our Negro minority. It builds up a picture of extreme basic antagonisms between minorities and the labor movement, and is replete with inaccuracies and exaggeration which suggest that there is zeal to prove a one-sided thesis."[64] Hill responded that the Jewish labor "organizations would do well if they ceased to apologize for the racists in the American labor movement, and instead of attempting to create a desirable public image for the AFL-CIO, joined with Negro workers and with the NAACP in directly attacking the broad pattern of racial discrimination."[65]

The NAACP-JLC conflict received wide attention in the Negro community as a result of an article written by Harold L. Keith, managing editor of the *Pittsburgh Courier*. Keith wrote that "Negro and Jewish labor leaders are on the 'brink' of outright war between themselves with the civil-rights issue spread out before them as a prospective field of battle."[66] Keith gave the following reasons for the differences between Jewish and Negro leaders: the failure of the AFL-CIO Civil Rights Committee to move against discrimination; the "reckless effort" by certain staff members of the JLC to "assume the primary role" of leadership in the labor movement's civil-rights sphere of activity; the "paternalistic and missionary" attitude toward Negroes adopted by some Jews; in the ILGWU, "Negro members . . . don't fare so well in occupying official staff positions; and the Jewish Labor Committee exists primarily for 500,000 Jewish workers while there were over a million dues paying Negroes."

Keith's article drew protests from NAACP Executive Secretary Roy Wilkins, the National Urban League's Lester Granger, Emanuel Muravchik, field secretary of the JLC, and A. Philip Randolph. Wilkins pointed out that the ILGWU had worked closely with the NAACP over the years and accused Keith of trying to "stir up intergroup strife on the lowest level by inventing a 'Jewish-Negro' conflict." [67] Wilkins concluded:

It must be understood that all organized bodies have their primary and secondary purposes. The primary purpose of the NAACP is to combat discrimination against Negroes. The primary purpose of labor organizations is to protect the wages, hours, and working conditions of its members. Civil rights activity for them is desirable but must be secondary. Inevitably these differences in emphasis will produce tensions in greater or less degree. [68]

Lester Granger called the *Courier* article ". . . a thinly veiled bit of encouragement to the anti-Semitism that now and then crops up among Negro elements along the eastern seaboard," and, with respect to the attacks on the ILGWU, said,

. . . if the American labor movement 25 years ago had stood even with the garment workers in racial policies and had advanced as far as they have in the past quarter-century, there would be a labor movement today that could set an example in every area of American interest. And when that does come about, Jews in the labor movement will be able to claim a big share of the credit. [69]

Randolph also protested the *Courier* article, declaring that "war over civil rights between Negro and Jewish labor leaders . . . is utterably unthinkable." [70] Randolph argued that, although differences between Negro and Jewish labor leaders are "well-nigh inevitable," JLC leaders Muravchik and Zimmerman "have never failed to lend cooperation morally and financially" and that their "antiracial discrimination position cannot be questioned."

These denials and affirmations by prominent Negro and Jewish leaders, however, did not silence the conflict. In 1962, when the NAACP's labor secretary attempted to testify before a House Education and Labor Subcommittee investigating the extent of "discrimination, exploitation and corruption in the garment industry and union," he was interrupted repeatedly by committee members who objected that his testimony was "opinions, conclusions, and characterizations." [71] At the end of his statement Congressman James Roosevelt moved that Hill's entire statement be submitted for editing to the subcommittee's chief counsel and stripped of material offensive to the committee. Hill's statement was later read into the *Congressional Record*. [72] The statement was also circulated by the NAACP and published in the liberal *New Politics*. [73] ILGWU officials felt that the attacks on it were politically inspired because the chairman of the investigating subcommittee was opposed for reelection by the ILGWU-backed Lib-

eral Party. Moreover, they objected to Hill's dual role as advisor to
the subcommittee and NAACP labor secretary.

ILGWU Director of Politics, Education, and Training, Gus Tyler,
answered Hill by challenging his facts and their interpretation.[74] Tyler said that Local 89, one of the locals cited as discriminatory by
Hill, was made up of Italians because the "local was created at a time
when dressmakers' Local 22 conducted its meetings in Yiddish, because the members could not speak English." [75] Tyler termed Hill's
charge that ILGWU Locals 60 and 10 were "lily white" a pure fabri-
cation.   Hill answered that Tyler had not refuted his charges that
Negroes and Puerto Ricans were "concentrated in low-paid job classifications, with very little employment mobility," and that ". . . there
is a direct connection between the permanent condition of semipov-
erty experienced by these workers and discriminatory racial practices." [76] However, in his rebuttal Hill said:

At no time did I charge the ILGWU with discriminatory practices ema-
nating from a conscious racist ideology. What I have argued is that the
social fact of discrimination is rooted in the ILGWU today because of the
interaction of the old union leadership with the changing social composition of the membership and the nature of the industry.   Given the rapidly
increasing number of Negroes and Puerto Ricans in the garment industry
in New York, they have a unique status within the union which the all-
white top leadership clearly sees as a growing threat to its monopoly of
control.[77]

Hill, himself a Jew, also thought it incredible that his charges should
be interpreted as "anti-Semitic" and that "an ILGWU staff member
. . . together with other union representatives went to several Congressmen and other public officials and 'explained' that Hill was a
Communist stirring up racial strife, an anti-Semite, etc." [78] Hill asserted that *The Jewish Daily Forward* [79] "regards all criticisms of the
ILGWU as an act of anti-Semitism." [80]

Among the reasons given by Hill for his attack on the ILGWU, in
spite of its "progressive" reputation, were: the ILGWU is a very important union which "affects the economic welfare and dignity of hundred [sic] of thousands of Negro and Puerto Rican men, women and
children in New York"; "Most of the major breakthroughs in the past
decade made by Negro workers in the 'old line' AFL-controlled craft
occupations as well as in industrial union jurisdictions are the direct
result of NAACP exposure and pressure"; the ILGWU "passes fine
resolutions on civil rights and contributes to worthy causes" but really
cannot qualify as a "progressive" union in the sense of "militancy, internal democracy and social vision"; the ILGWU leadership does not

have the capacity "to admit that anything at all is wrong," but their "obsessive" concern about their "public image" increases the possibility that the pressures applied by the NAACP might have "salutary effects." [81]

The NAACP fully supported Hill in his conflicts with the JLC and the ILGWU. In a letter to Emanuel Muravchik, for instance, Roy Wilkins, "responding to a Jewish Labor Committee attack on the Association," defended Hill against the charge of anti-Semitism.[82] The NAACP Board of Directors called on the Special Subcommittee of the House Committee on Education and Labor to "pursue a vigorous and thoroughgoing investigation of racial discrimination within the" ILGWU. The resolution restated Hill's charges against ILGWU, and concluded that "The union cannot live on its past glories. It must face the reality of its present practices and move to eradicate inequalities."

The dispute between the ILGWU and the NAACP also involved a case filed with the New York State Commission for Human Rights (CHR). The case, filed with the CHR April 4, 1961, alleged that a Negro, Ernest Holmes, was denied membership in ILGWU Local 10 because of his color. According to the joint stipulation of May 17, 1963, which settled the case, Holmes had voluntarily sought to withdraw this case on February 7, 1963—three months before the public hearing—and said the union had offered him help which he refused because he already had a better job. He later lost that job and continued the case to get whatever help the union could give him. On June 28, 1963, a CHR investigating commissioner found "probable cause" to credit the charge against Local 10, which was erroneously interpreted by some as a finding of guilty. According to the investigating commissioner, probable cause was found because the local failed to cooperate in the investigation.[83] The union said it refused to cooperate because it was angered by what it regarded as unfair charges.[84] On May 15, 1963, when the case finally went to a hearing, approximately two hundred Spanish-speaking and Negro members of Local 10 appeared, reportedly prepared to testify on the union's behalf. The ILGWU argued that the complainant had been denied admission to Local 10 not because of his color but because he was not a qualified cutter. After three days of hearings, the charge against the ILGWU was withdrawn on the basis of a joint stipulation under which the union agreed

In line with its oft asserted and regular policy . . . against discrimination . . . that it will, on the same basis as it applies to all other applicants for admission to membership exercise its good offices in assisting the complainant to become a qualified cutter and to gain admission to membership in this union.

The ILGWU, however, called upon the governor or the legislature of New York state to investigate ". . . the conduct in this instance of the commission's chairman, investigating commissioner and chief counsel." [85]   The ILGWU considered this case an attempt to smear the union because of the obvious lack of qualifications of the complainant and what union leaders considered to be procedural irregularities.

The NAACP's attacks on the ILGWU and other unions evoked vigorous response from union leaders and others concerned with this problem.   Charles Zimmerman resigned from the NAACP Legal Defense Fund.[86]   George Meany sent a letter to the NAACP in which he said the "campaign of systematic falsehood and distortion makes re-establishment of unity in fighting civil rights difficult." [87]   Walter Reuther announced that ". . . unfair, unfounded, indiscriminate attacks would help no one," though he denied rumors that he was considering resigning from the NAACP Board of Directors.[88]

It seems clear that, although there might be some anti-Semitism among rank-and-file Negro members, the difficulties among Negro and Jewish leaders are due primarily to personality clashes and differences in the priority assigned civil-rights matters.   There is, moreover, apparently a growing conviction by Negroes that whites really cannot presume to speak for Negroes, because not even Jews experience discrimination with the intensity of the Negro.   Some Negro leaders express the sentiment, moreover, that the Jew has now been accepted into the mainstream of American society, whereas the Negro is still fighting to get in.   This does not mean, however, that Negro leaders do not see the need for cooperation with Jewish civil-rights efforts or that they do not understand that Jews have helped them in the past.[89] Whitney Young, executive secretary of the National Urban League, told Jews they should quit mouthing platitudes and give support to Negroes.[90]   Jews, he said, should not use the excuse of growing anti-Semitism among Negroes.   Although, Young added, "the Jewish storekeeper had become a symbol for anti-white feelings . . . when the chips are down, if there is a political struggle with the WASP [white Anglo-Saxon Protestant] and the Jewish person, the Negro knows his best interests are with the Jewish people."

We do not have enough information to pass on the merits of the NAACP-ILGWU conflict, but it seems obvious that if there is a case against the ILGWU it is not so much against racial discrimination as against bureaucracy and over differences about appropriate economic policy (that is, should the ILGWU fight to raise wages in New York which would accelerate the flight of the industry to lower wage areas of the South?).

The implication in the ILGWU and in many other unions is that Negroes should be represented in union offices according to their numbers in the unions. But such quota systems raise difficult questions. For example, how are we to find out how many Negroes there are in a union? The NAACP argues that there are over 100,000 Negroes and Puerto Ricans in the ILGWU, but how do we know? How many of these are Negroes and how many Puerto Ricans and other minority groups? [91] Should Negroes and Puerto Ricans be represented in proportion to their numbers, or can Puerto Ricans represent Negroes or Negroes represent Puerto Ricans?

Conclusions on Negro-Labor Differences

What will happen to the Negro-labor split? The writer would guess that it will continue, but will probably become less intense because Negro leaders realize their dependence on the labor movement and discriminating unions will be subjected to increasing regulation by the federal government, the courts, and the AFL-CIO. The most intransigent unions will change their practices when their sources of power are threatened by these regulations, by demonstrations and other pressures from the Negro community, and by alienation of public opinion. Trends in all these directions are clearly perceptible at the present time.

Furthermore, although there has been some estrangement of Negroes from the labor movement, there appears to be little likelihood that many Negro union members will leave their unions or try to form all-Negro organizations for bargaining purposes. Negro union membership is concentrated in unions controlled by whites, and there is little chance that Negro organizations could operate effectively on purely racial bases. Negro unionists understand the AFL-CIO's power limitations better than the Negro community. They also realize that Negro workers have gained considerable job protection from unions and that they have legal rights to jobs with unions that they would not have on an unorganized basis.[92] In short, Negro unionists appear to believe that the best chance for solution to their problems is not to secede, but to exert maximum pressures within the mainstream of the labor movement.

Negro leaders outside the labor movement have also noted the similarity between the tradition of the civil rights and labor movements and the common objectives that continue to bind them together despite their differences. For instance, Rev. Martin Luther King told the 1962 UAW convention:

There are more ties of kinship between labor and the Negro people than tradition. . . . [L]abor needs a wage-hour bill. . . . Negroes need the same measures, even more desperately. . . . Labor needs housing legislation . . . Negroes need housing legislated also. Labor needs an adequate old-age medical bill and so do Negroes. . . . What labor needs, Negroes need; and simple logic therefore puts us side by side in the struggle for all elements in a decent standard of living.[93]

This is not to argue, however, that the unions' unfavorable image in the Negro community has not hurt organizing among unorganized Negroes. There are some cases in which Negro organizations are apparently going back to the pre-CIO attitudes toward Negro strikebreakers. It was reported in 1962, for instance, that "Things are so bad that an NAACP chapter in New Haven, Connecticut, refused to counsel Negroes against engaging in strikebreaking."[94] The NAACP also reports that some NLRB elections have been lost by unions in the South because they failed to get the Negroes' support.[95]

Finally, although the Negro-labor political alliance has also been subjected to the strains in the conflict between the NAACP and the AFL-CIO, there is little indication that Negro voters have turned away from labor candidates and issues, except for some splits in the South.[96] On the whole, moreover, there is little evidence that Negroes will switch back to the Republicans in the South or in the nation. Negroes and unions realize that both would be weakened if the Negro vote returned to the Republican camp and unions refused to back civil-rights legislation. This explains why unions have furnished decisive support for the various state antidiscrimination laws and why Negro leaders like Randolph and organizations like the NAACP have vigorously opposed the growing support for "right-to-work" laws in the Negro community.[97]

The racial unrest in the United States during the summer of 1963 inevitably influenced Negro-union relations. As we have noted elsewhere,[98] Negro protest organizations sought by direct action in a number of major cities to get Negroes employed in the building trades. Racial demonstrations also injected a sense of urgency into the federal government's antidiscrimination activities.

There also is evidence that this increased sense of urgency has spurred unions to action. In response to President Kennedy's pleas [99] that unions and other elements in American society face up to the grave issues at stake, George Meany appointed a special committee of high-ranking union leaders to work in local communities "to wipe out discrimination wherever it exists." [100] To carry out the work of the committee and action programs, a special staff was appointed by local AFL-CIO central labor unions in cooperation with other community organizations launched in Cincinnati, Denver, Boston, Oakland, Houston, Milwaukee, Greensboro, N. C., San Francisco, Memphis, and the District of Columbia.

That the new AFL-CIO program promised to be more than "window dressing" was indicated by the 1963 AFL-CIO convention, which contrasted markedly with the two previous conventions. George Meany had had a heated exchange with Philip Randolph in 1959 and had personally endorsed the Executive Council's "censure" of him in 1961, but in 1963 he referred to him as "our own Phil Randolph." Randolph was selected to lead the discussion of civil rights at the convention, the first time he had ever been given an official role in connection with civil rights at an AFL-CIO convention. Moreover, for the first time in the Federation's history, civil rights was given priority over all other topics considered. The report by Civil Rights Committee Chairman William Schnitzler also suggested that the AFL-CIO had definitely assigned high priority to civil-rights matters and that significant changes were being made. Particularly important progress seems to have been made in the elimination of segregated locals. After the convention, the Civil Rights Department was greatly strengthened by the appointment of Donald Slaiman as full-time director and the authorization of additional staff for the department.

FOOTNOTES

1. For a good example of how firmly Negro leaders' attitudes are rooted in history, see "Today's Civil Rights Revolution," an address by A. Philip Randolph before the Fifth Constitutional Convention, Industrial Union Department AFL-CIO, November 8, 1963.
2. The South's proportion of the nation's nonwhites declined from 88% in 1910 to 85% in 1920 and 74% in 1930; in 1940, 73% of the nation's nonwhites lived in the former Confederate states plus Kentucky and Oklahoma, as compared with only 51% in 1960. Since this trend has continued and since a large proportion of nonwhites in the South are Negroes, it seems safe to conclude that today less than half of the Negroes in the United States reside in the South.
3. See my "Unions and the Negro Community," *Industrial and Labor Relations Review,* January 1963.

4. AFL-CIO *Convention Proceedings*, 1955, pp. 363, 387.
5. *Chicago Defender*, February 19, 1955.
6. AFL-CIO *Convention Proceedings*, 1955, pp. 305–308.
7. *Ibid.*
8. *Pittsburgh Courier*, December 17, 1955.
9. *Chicago Defender*, December 3, 1955.
10. Personal interview, April 1959; see also *Chicago Defender*, June 1, 1957; *Fortune*, March 11, 1959.
11. National Association for the Advancement of Colored People, Labor Department, "Racism within Organized Labor: A Report of Five Years of the AFL-CIO, 1955–1960," mimeographed, pp. 2–3.
12. AFL-CIO, *Executive Council Minutes*, December 5 and 9, 1955, pp. 11–12.
13. August Meier, "Negro Protest Movements and Organizations," *Journal of Negro Education*, Fall 1963, p. 437.
14. See *Crisis*, July 1957.
15. Memorandum to Boris Shiskin, Director, Civil Rights Department AFL-CIO from Herbert Hill, Labor Secretary, NAACP, December 4, 1958.
16. NAACP *Annual Report* for 1958, p. 53.
17. Report to the NAACP Annual Meeting by the Labor Secretary, January 5, 1959.
18. *Ibid.*
19. NAACP, "Racism within Organized Labor," *op. cit.*
20. Letter to the writer, August 14, 1959.
21. Letter to the writer, August 5, 1959.
22. Letter to the writer, August 26, 1959.
23. Letter to the writer, August 17, 1959.
24. Personal interview, April 17, 1959.
25. *Business Week*, January 10, 1959.
26. Quoted in *Greater Philadelphia Magazine*, February 1963.
27. AFL-CIO Third Constitutional Convention, *Proceedings, Fifth Day*, pp. 47–69.
28. *Ibid.*, p. 130.
29. This version of Meany's reply is taken from the writer's personal notes. The official version printed in the *Proceedings* is substantially the same, but reads: "Who appointed you as guardian. . . ."
30. See, for example, *Baltimore Afro-American*, October 24, 1959; *Pittsburgh Courier*, October 10, 1959.
31. AFL-CIO press release, March 26, 1960.
32. Letter to the writer, April 30, 1962.
33. See, for example, *New York Times*, November 12, 1962.
34. *Jet*, November 16, 1961, pp. 16–20.
35. *New York Times*, November 12, 1961.
36. *Ibid.*
37. Letter to the writer from AFL-CIO official, April 30, 1962.
38. *New York Times*, November 12, 1962.
39. Statement in *Jet*, November 16, 1961, p. 21.
40. Reported by Tom Brooks, "The Negro's Place at Labor's Table," *The Reporter*, December 6, 1962, p. 39.
41. NLRB release, April 9, 1963.
42. *New York Times*, November 12, 1962; *AFL-CIO News*, November 17, 1962.

43. Frank R. Crosswaith and Alfred Baker Lewis, *Black and White Unite for True Freedom,* New York: Negro Labor News Service, n.d., p. 43.
44. Negro Labor Committee, *Ten Year Report,* 1946.
45. Norman Ross, "The Struggle for the Negro-Labor Alliance," *Political Affairs,* June 1949, p. 79.
46. See John Williamson, "Trade-Union Tasks for the Struggle for Peace, Jobs, and Negro Rights," *Political Affairs,* November 1950, p. 37.
47. Pettis Perry, "The Third Annual Convention of the National Negro Labor Council," *Political Affairs,* February 1954, p. 4.
48. *New York Times,* July 4, 1954; see also *ibid.,* October 19, 1951, p. 14.
49. Edward E. Strong, "Developments in the Negro-Labor Alliance," *Political Affairs,* February 1956, p. 35.
50. TULC leaflet, "Do You Have the Time?" No date.
51. *Ibid.*
52. Personal interview, Detroit, January 15, 1960.
53. Although the struggle within the UAW over a Negro on the Executive Board initially was a political issue, it came to symbolize the Negro unionists' discontent with the Reuther administration. This was a major issue at the 1943 convention, when the Communists supported a position for Negroes on the Board and the Reuther faction opposed such a move as "discrimination in reverse" (UAW *Convention Proceedings,* 1943, p. 383). The 1946 convention compromised this debate by creating a Fair Practices and Anti-Discrimination Department supported by a special fund of 1% per month per member. The question of a Negro on the Executive Board was debated at subsequent conventions, however, and in 1962 a Negro was elected when his opponents declined to run.
54. The UAW established a Fair Practices and Anti-Discrimination Department in 1946; a constitutional provision provided 1% per member per month for its expenses. By 1961, 38 of the AFL-CIO's 132 affiliated internationals had civil-rights committees. ("Roster of Civil Rights Committees of National International Unions Affiliated with the AFL-CIO," October 1961, Civil Rights Department, AFL-CIO.) Besides the UAW, other relatively active civil-rights committees were established by the United Rubber Workers (URW), the International Union of Electrical Workers (IUEW), the United Steelworkers (USA), and the United Packinghouse Workers (UPWA). The URW, the UPWA, the UAW, the Retail Wholesale and Department Store Employees (RWDSU), and the USA have full-time staffs to carry out their programs.

Some unions have refused to establish special civil-rights machinery on the grounds that racial problems can better be handled by the regular union power structure. Examples of unions taking this position are the United Mine Workers, the International Longshoremen and Warehousemen's Union, and the International Association of Machinists. Indeed, some of these organizations contend that creating special committees is a sure way to see that racial problems do not get solved because decisions must be made within the regular power channels. Another argument against these committees is that there is no special need for them because questions of discrimination are not purely racial and therefore can be handled with regular internal union appeals procedures. Other critics argue that the committees are merely "window dressing" created to gain good public images in Negro communities; since they cannot really be effective, these critics hold, the committees must of necessity cause the labor movement to lose more good will in the long run than they create for it. Critics likewise contend that special committees lose prestige as being "Negro" committees and invite attacks as "race" organizations.

Proponents of the committees argue, on the other hand, that the committees at least symbolize the union's good intentions. In addition, it is argued that race relations require special expertise, and must therefore be handled by union staff people with special training. Some Negro leaders also argue that these committees should be staffed with Negroes because Negro problems cannot be effectively handled by whites.

Whatever the merits of these arguments, the writer reached several conclusions about internal union civil-rights committees from his study of their procedures:

1. For whatever reason, the committees seem to be largely inactive in most local unions.

2. There is also a tendency for Negroes to circumvent civil-rights committees and file racial grievances with regular union officers, indicating that they do not have much faith in the committees' ability to handle these problems.

3. Because these organizations have lost prestige in the Negro community, many Negro unionists refuse to serve on them.

4. The committee staffs in national headquarters have served valuable research needs on racial practices and have been valuable as public relations agencies in many areas.

5. There is no evidence that unions with civil-rights committees have more equalitarian policies than unions without them.

55. Jack Crellin, "The Labor Front," *Detroit Times*, August 5, 1959.
56. Letter to UAW Negro representative from the Executive Committee, TULC, July 5, 1959.
57. Letter to George Meany from Willie Baxter, Vice-President and Director of Civil Rights, TULC, October 1, 1959.
58. *Ibid.*
59. *Ibid.*
60. A. Philip Randolph, "The Civil Rights Revolution and Labor," address at NAACP Convention, The Coliseum, New York City, July 15, 1959.
61. Personal interview with A. Philip Randolph, July 20, 1959.
62. ILGWU, *General Executive Board Reports*, 1959, p. 203.
63. See Herbert Hill, "Labor Unions and the Negro," *Commentary*, December 1957.
64. Letter to the editor of *Commentary* from Emanuel Muravchik, February 1960.
65. Letter to the editor of *Commentary* from Herbert Hill, February 24, 1960.
66. *Pittsburgh Courier*, December 12, 1959.
67. Letter from Roy Wilkins to Harold L. Keith, *Pittsburgh Courier*, December 17, 1959.
68. *Ibid.*
69. *Amsterdam News*, December 19, 1959.
70. Letter to *Pittsburgh Courier*, January 2, 1960.
71. *New York Times*, August 19, 1962.
72. *Congressional Record*, January 31, 1963, pp. 1496–1499.

73. Herbert Hill, "The ILGWU Today—The Decay of a Labor Union," *New Politics,* Vol. 1, No. 4, p. 6.

74. Gus Tyler, "The Truth about the ILGWU," *New Politics,* Vol. 2, No. 1, p. 6; Herbert Hill, "The ILGWU—Fact and Fiction, A Reply to Gus Tyler," *New Politics,* Vol. 2, No. 2, p. 7.

75. Tyler, "The Truth about the ILGWU," *loc. cit.*

76. Hill, "The ILGWU—Fact and Fiction," *loc. cit.*

77. *Ibid.,* pp. 8–9.

78. *Ibid.,* p. 26.

79. *Ibid.;* in a footnote Hill cites the *Jewish Daily Forward,* December 10 and August 22, 1962.

80. Hill, "The ILGWU—Fact and Fiction," p. 26.

81. *Ibid.,* pp. 26–27.

82. Letter from Roy Wilkins to Emanuel Muravchik, October 31, 1962, cited by Hill in *ibid.,* p. 27.

83. *New York Times,* July 2, 1963.

84. Letter to the writer, March 17, 1964; *Justice,* June 1, 1963, p. 1.

85. *Justice* (official paper of the ILG), June 1, 1963, p. 12.

86. *New York Times,* October 12, 1962.

87. *AFL-CIO News,* December 1, 1962.

88. *Time,* November 2, 1962; *New York Times,* October 19, 1962, and November 11 and 12, 1962.

89. See, for example, the statement by Roy Wilkins, *American Judaism,* Winter 1963, reported in *New York Times,* April 5, 1963.

90. *New York Times,* November 22, 1963.

91. Lester Granger estimates, for instance, that "American Negroes" constitute "about 12% of the garment workers' strength" in New York City; he guesses that there are in the ILGWU "100,000 Spanish or African or Spanish and African background out of a total membership of 450,000" and that in New York City there are some 25,000 Negroes and 40,000 Puerto Ricans. "Manhattan and Beyond," *Amsterdam News,* December 8, 1962.

92. See Chapter 10.

93. Martin Luther King, Jr., "That Scaffold Sways the Future," *Labor Today,* Spring 1962, p. 12.

94. Brooks, "The Negro's Place at Labor's Table," *op. cit.,* p. 39.

95. NAACP, "Racism within Organized Labor," *op. cit.,* pp. 3–4.

96. See Chapter 8.

97. See Herbert Hill, " 'Right to Work' Laws and the Negro Worker," *The Crisis,* July 1957. "Randolph Urges Negroes to Repudiate " 'Work' Law," *AFL-CIO News,* February 22, 1964, p. 11.

98. See Chapters 9 and 10.

99. Letter to President Kennedy from George Meany, July 22, 1963.

100. Donald Slaiman, "Labor's Task Forces," *American Federationist,* March 1964.

PART II

Union Racial Practices
and Problems

CHAPTER 5

Formal Exclusion, Auxiliaries, and Segregated Locals

IF UNIONS COULD BE ARRANGED ALONG A CONTINUUM ACCORDING TO their racial practices, organizations that would not accept Negroes could be placed on one end and those with perfectly equalitarian practices at the other, with various degrees of discrimination represented by the organizations along the continuum. As might be expected, in reality very few unions are to be found at either extreme. Almost no unions have completely equalitarian policies in the sense that they pay no attention whatsoever to their members' or potential members' racial composition. A number of organizations bar Negroes from membership, but the tactics used to accomplish this vary considerably. In classifying union racial practices, moreover, it is necessary to distinguish the practices of federations, national or international (unions are called "international" if they have foreign affiliates) unions, and locals.

Although it is not possible to obtain the necessary information to classify union racial practices according to precise degrees of discrimination, there have been certain discernible trends and patterns.

The trend has been toward more equalitarian racial practices. Many unions have moved through a series of stages beginning with formal exclusion and followed by auxiliary locals for Negroes, segregated locals, and finally the elimination of segregated locals. These practices will be discussed in this chapter. Unions have also adopted various informal policies and procedures that restrict or promote the Negro's job opportunities; these will be discussed in succeeding chapters. Because they are the main economic units in the labor movement and their practices differ considerably from the more politically oriented federations discussed in Part 1, the racial practices of international unions and their local affiliates will be discussed in this chapter.

Formal Exclusion

The number of national unions with formal race restrictions in their constitutions or rituals declined markedly between 1930 and 1963, when the last AFL-CIO affiliate removed its race bar. In 1930, for example, there were perhaps twenty-seven unions with formal race bars, though the exact number is not certain.[1] By 1943 mergers and changing racial practices had reduced the number of restrictive unions to about fourteen, eight of which were AFL affiliates.[2] The unaffiliated organizations listed by Northrup as having formal race bars in 1943 were Brotherhood of Locomotive Engineers (BLE); Brotherhood of Locomotive Firemen (BLF); Brotherhood of Railroad Trainmen (BRT); Railroad Yardmasters of America (RYA); Railroad Yardmasters of North America (RYNA); Order of Railway Conductors (ORC); and the American Train Dispatchers Association (ATDA). In 1949 there were at least nine unions with formal race bars, one of which (ORT) was a member of the AFL. The Order of Railroad Telegraphers (ORT) removed its race bar in 1952. After the AFL-CIO merger in 1955 there would have been no major national affiliates with race bars if the BRT and BLF had not been admitted to the merged federation. The BRT removed its race bar in 1960, leaving only the ORC, the BLE, and the BLF with formal restrictions. When the BLF removed its ban in 1963, for the first time since 1895 when the IAM was admitted to the AFL, the major American labor federation had no affiliates with formal race bars.

It will be noted that almost all of the national unions with formal race bars were associated with the transportation industry except the Wire Weavers Protective Association (WWPA).[3] Indeed, even Eugene Debs' American Railway Union excluded Negroes from membership. The reasons for discrimination on the railroads are not clear, but probably include: (1) Many of these organizations were formed in the South or border states (Machinists, Maintenance of Way Employees, Blacksmiths, and Railway Clerks) and sought to acquire status for railroad workers who had sometimes incurred bad reputations because of their migratory nature. Their constitutions frequently restricted membership to white men of "good moral character, temperate habits" [4] or "white born, of good moral character, sober and industrious." [5] When these organizations were formed, they undoubtedly considered that their "status" would have been jeopardized by admitting Negroes, who were considered to be "inferior" people. These constitutional provisions are obviously based on the idea of white "superiority and competence." [6]

(2) Early railroad unions were fraternal and social organizations for men who spent many nights together away from home; they were formed at a time when it was not considered proper to have social relations with Negroes.

(3) Many of these organizations started as insurance societies at a time when the transportation business was considered too risky for many insurance companies, which also regarded Negroes as poorer risks than whites.

The forces that caused unions to abandon exclusion by formal means, or to adopt more subtle forms, will be analyzed at greater length later, but may be summarized as follows: expansion of Negro employment in jurisdictions covered by these unions, especially during the First and Second World Wars; competition between unions for Negro votes in representation elections; embarrassment of exclusionist union leaders at conventions and in the press by criticism from Negro and white union leaders, especially the moral castigations from within the AFL by the Negro leaders of the Brotherhood of Sleeping Car Porters; action by such governmental agencies as the wartime and state FEP committees; and fear of the loss of exclusive bargaining rights, union shop provisions, or other legal privileges under the Railway Labor Act or the Taft-Hartley Act. The experiences of the Boilermakers, Machinists, and Railway Clerks unions illustrate these factors.

Brotherhood of Railway Clerks (BRSC)

In 1899 the BRSC's founders, following the pattern of other railroad unions, included a "white only" clause in the union's constitution.[7] The first crack in the BRSC's racial barrier came during the

First World War when the Clerks expanded their jurisdiction to take in freighthandlers, many of whom were Negroes. Since the BRSC would not admit Negroes, the colored freighthandlers were organized into federal locals attached directly to the AFL. This arrangement proved unsatisfactory to both the BRSC and the colored workers because the Clerks lost dues and the freighthandlers got inadequate representation. The Negroes asked either for a separate charter as a national freighthandlers union or to be admitted to the Clerks, but the BRSC refused in its 1922 convention to admit Negroes and blocked their efforts to get a separate national charter.[8] Many of the Negro federal locals were too weak to survive the open shop movement of the 1920's.

With the upsurge in union organization during the 1930's, the Railway Clerks again became interested in organizing the Negro freighthandlers into federal locals. But since both the Negroes and the international union continued to be dissatisfied with this arrangement, the BRSC Executive Council was authorized by its 1939 convention to organize Negroes into auxiliary locals represented by white officers. Despite the Negroes' bitter protests to both the AFL Executive Council and the 1940 AFL convention, they again were denied a national charter and were transferred to the BRSC. This action was taken after BRSC President George Harrison assured the AFL Executive Council that the previous convention of his union had taken action "for the affiliation of these workers with full rights and privileges."[9] After the Negroes protested the auxiliary status to which they were being assigned without their consent, President William Green told the 1940 AFL convention that "these men will be members of the Brotherhood of Railway Clerks and fully entitled to enjoy the rights and privileges of the Brotherhood of Railway Clerks."[10] These promises were not kept, however, and the Negroes were relegated to auxiliaries which remained in effect until after the New York law against discrimination was passed in 1945. Although the Negro freighthandlers would have liked more representation and better opportunities for upgrading than provided by this auxiliary arrangement, it must be conceded they seem to have benefited economically from the BRSC's representation.[11]

In 1946 after the New York State Commission Against Discrimination (SCAD) informed the Clerks and other railroad unions that auxiliaries and constitutional color bars violated the New York law, George Harrison appointed a committee which included prominent Southern members who recommended to the 1947 BRSC convention that the race bar be removed. However, the delegates to this convention were assured by BRSC officers that the elimination of the word "white" from the constitution and the substitution of Brotherhood charters for the auxiliary charters would really change very little because the local lodges would continue to determine their own membership qualifications and could refuse to accept traveling delegates.[12]   The proponents of this change were able to overcome the heated objections of some Southern delegates to even this limited lowering of the race barrier by arguing that the BRSC was not only being denounced as an un-American union, causing it to be disadvantaged in representation elections, but was also liable to prosecution under the FEP laws and might lose bargaining rights under the Railway Labor Act.   President Harrison's statement was particularly revealing.   He told the convention that for nineteen years he had been embarrassed at AFL conventions because delegates pointed out that his union discriminated, and that his embarrassment was intensified as the number of unions with formal racial bars diminished.   Moreover, Harrison said, the Clerks' legal position had become tenuous since the 1944 *Steele* decision [13] imposed upon unions the duty of fair representation.   After Harrison's assurances that these formal changes were really not going to change things very much, the delegates voted to strike the word "white" from their constitution.   Negroes were then advised that they could join the white lodges, and by June 1950 a SCAD investigator found only four auxiliary BRSC lodges left in New York and New Jersey.   The legal status of the BRSC's auxiliary lodges was also weakened by the 1951 amendment to the Railway Labor Act permitting the union shop.   After this amendment the BRSC was eager to have Negroes join, but could not use union-shop provisions to require them to do so if they did not have equal conditions of membership.   After the auxiliary locals were abolished, many BRSC locals (150) continued to be virtually all-Negro, but in 1964 the Clerks had less than 50 segregated locals and these were being eliminated by attacks from many quarters, including state fair-employment laws and the federal government-contract committees.   The BRSC has argued that the all-Negro lodges resulted from employer hiring practices and happened to be all-Negro because locals are organized along jurisdictional lines.   However, the foregoing discussion of the BRSC's racial policies casts some doubt on this argument.

Boilermakers

The Boilermakers, like the BRSC and other railroad unions, had a racial bar in its constitution from its inception.   In 1908 after de-

bating whether to leave the racial bar in their constitution or to transfer it to the ritual, as the Machinists had done in 1895 as a condition
of admission to the AFL, the Boilermakers decided to leave the bar
in their constitution.   In 1937, however, some Southerners wanted
to remove the bar, not because they wanted to "defend the Negro"
but because the lower wages paid unorganized Negroes threatened
union conditions.   Accordingly, in 1937, the Boilermakers took the
first step toward eliminating the racial bar by giving the Executive
Committee authority to establish auxiliary lodges for Negroes if they
were needed.   These auxiliary locals were subordinate to white lodges
and could not send delegates to conventions.   In short, the Negroes
could organize social affairs and discussion groups, but had little
power to change their conditions within the union or to bargain with
employers.

The Executive Committee was forced to use the auxiliary device
during the early days of the Second World War when Negroes flocked
to the coasts to take jobs in shipyards.   The Boilermakers' initial reaction to these colored workers was to restrict them to menial occupations.   But the Negroes naturally protested this treatment, and various
AFL officials, including President Green, urged the Boilermakers to
alter their practices.   The union then attempted to force the Negroes
to join auxiliary locals.

The showdown on the auxiliaries came when the Boilermakers attempted to use their closed-shop agreements to have Negroes discharged for refusing to join the colored locals.   The colored workers
then turned to various governmental agencies for help, including the
NLRB, the FEPC, and the courts.   The FEPC held hearings, found
the auxiliaries discriminatory, and ordered the union and the companies to cease and desist.[14]   But the race issue was an important
internal political issue for the Boilermakers, and so the international
officers, who were up for reelection the following month, refused to
obey the FEPC's order.   The Boilermakers' president, Charles Mac-
Gowen, told FEPC Chairman Malcolm Ross that he would attempt
to solve the race problem after the union elections.[15]

While the Boilermakers, like most other unions, defied the FEPC's
directives, the Committee's actions focused attention on the union
and caused President Roosevelt to urge the international's officers and
AFL President Green to end discrimination in the union.[16]   While
the NLRB refused to make a direct ruling against the auxiliary,[17] the
California Supreme Court decided, in a number of cases, that the
union could not enforce the closed shop against members of the
auxiliary locals.[18]   After these decisions several shipyards announced

that they would no longer discharge Negroes for refusing to join the auxiliaries. Faced with this possible loss of revenue and economic control, the Boilermakers' Executive Committee authorized the elimination of auxiliary locals. As late as 1959, however, there remained twelve auxiliary Boilermakers' lodges with a total of 266 members, The union reported resistance to integration from the leaders of the auxiliary lodges.[19]

International Association of Machinists

The International Association of Machinists (IAM) barred Negroes formally from 1888, when the International was founded in Atlanta, until the bar was removed in 1948. The forces changing the IAM's practices were similar to those eroding the race bars in the BRSC and the Boilermakers, so a summary of the main turning points in the Machinists' policies is sufficient for our purposes: the race bar was transferred from the constitution to the ritual as a condition of admission to the AFL in 1895; the IAM lost some of its Southern character as it spread from Georgia into the non-South; the racial bar limited the Machinists' expansion and increasingly embarrassed its officers; the growth of Negro employment in the railroad shops, over which the IAM had jurisdiction, during and after the First World War, caused the IAM to urge the AFL to organize Negroes into federal locals attached directly to the Federation; competition between the IAM with the United Automobile Workers-CIO for membership in the aircraft industry during and after the Second World War caused many IAM officials to take more equalitarian positions; charges were filed against the IAM with the wartime FEPC;[20] the International's leaders were embarrassed by a discussion of their racial practices in the U. S. Senate;[21] IAM officers also were concerned because the race bar was being cited by unions—especially the Teamsters—as grounds for the NLRB to deny the Machinists the right to represent Negroes;[22] and finally, the IAM was afraid it might lose bargaining rights because of the state FEP laws and Taft-Hartley Law. The extent to which the IAM's official position has changed can be seen by contrasting the attitude of the union's president in 1890, who urged that Negroes not be admitted because they were "cheap men and thieves,"[23] with the following statement in 1955 from IAM President Al Hayes:

As an organization whose membership is open to all in our jurisdiction . . . dedicated to the economic wellbeing of its membership, we cannot brook inferior service to some of our members because of the color of their skin, the country of their ancestors, or the church at which they worship.[24]

As was true of the Railway Clerks and the Boilermakers, the main racial trouble confronting the IAM after 1948 involved its segregated locals, to be considered in the next section. The IAM's position with respect to these lodges in 1964 was "to merge them with other lodges wherever this is practical and feasible. A local lodge, under the Constitution, is an autonomous body, and the Grand Lodge (International) cannot force a merger unless the membership is in agreement with the merger. In each instance where a segregated lodge exists, attempts have been made to initiate mergers. . . ."[25]

Auxiliary and Segregated Locals

As we have seen, a number of international unions which did not bar Negroes from membership restricted them to auxiliary locals. This arrangement was usually adopted in lieu of formal exclusion and was sometimes the next stage following the elimination of formal restrictions. As illustrated by the IAM, the BRSC, and the Boilermakers, however, an intermediate stage between outright exclusion and auxiliary locals frequently was the organization of federal locals for Negroes. Sometimes, however, this intermediate stage was skipped altogether and auxiliaries were fused with exclusion. In 1930, for example, the AFRW and the BRC had auxiliary locals even though their constitutions contained race bars.[26]

We also discussed the pressures that caused the auxiliaries to be abolished, but we should also note the Landrum-Griffin Act of 1959 which made it possible for Negro employees to bring action to abolish auxiliary locals. A few auxiliaries remained in 1959, but had become relatively unimportant by that date.

Segregated locals [27] are theoretically different from auxiliaries in that the segregated locals have equal status and separate charters. This distinction is often more theoretical than real, however, because the whites might in fact bargain for the Negro locals. Moreover, white locals and employers sometimes take measures affecting Negroes in segregated locals without even consulting the colored workers.[28]

It is also common to refer to locals as "segregated" when they in fact have mixed memberships. In cities with large Negro populations, building-trades locals were established in Negro areas, but many of these later took in some white members. This pattern was followed, for example, by locals of the Carpenters, International Longshoremen's Association, Bricklayers, Musicians, Hod Carriers and Common Laborers, and Painters. In Washington, D. C., for example, the previously segregated Negro local had about 10 per cent white membership in 1964 and the "white" local had about 200 Negroes. Sometimes the locals were in occupations—like hod carriers and common laborers —which were traditionally "Negro" jobs but into which whites moved during depressions or when wages or working conditions in those occupations improved. Of course, some jobs, like sleeping car porters, "red caps," laborers, freighthandlers, cotton warehouse and compress workers, fertilizer workers, and some chemical operations are held almost exclusively by Negroes in many places, so the unions tend to be all-Negro. Although segregated locals have existed throughout the country, most of these have been in the South and sometimes were insisted upon by the Negroes as a condition for joining the unions. Segregation also was imposed by local laws against integrated meetings. Even where there were no segregation laws, community pressures frequently required segregation. Indeed, about the only union with a long history in the South which did not establish segregated locals was the United Mine Workers, whose members were isolated and relatively impervious to community pressure. Even so, UMW frequently was attacked in the South because of its integrated meetings.

There are, however, actually relatively few segregated locals if by this we mean that there are separate unions in the same plant or craft. A few unions almost invariably were segregated in the South—the Carpenters, the Longshoremen, Paper Makers, the Pulp Sulphite Workers, the Brotherhood of Railway Clerks, the Tobacco Workers, and the Musicians—but CIO international unions rarely had more than two or three segregated locals. Even unions like the Tobacco Workers (TWIU), with predominantly Southern memberships, adopted a policy after 1946 of not forming new segregated locals. By July 1964, however, the TWIU had merged all of its segregated locals except those at Durham, N. C., and efforts were being made to merge those locals. Other unions, like the Bricklayers, have a relatively small number of segregated locals in the South; only twenty-five of the Bricklayers' 168 Southern locals were segregated in 1960, and some of these (Atlanta and Jacksonville) had been merged by 1964. A survey by the Jewish Labor Committee in 1957 found that of 110 locals from thirty-two internationals, two-thirds had Negro membership, but that two-fifths of the biracial unions had less than 10 per cent Negro membership. Figures for unions affiliated with various state federations of labor yield similar conclusions; of 1500 locals in Texas, with 290,000 members in 1957, only fifteen, with 10,000 members, were all-Negro and nine of these were segregated; and of twenty-two locals affiliated with the Montgomery, Alabama, Central Labor Union, with 13,000 members, six were all-Negro and three of these were auxiliaries. In Tennessee, of 650 locals affiliated with the AFL-CIO in 1958, 425 were integrated, 200 were all-white and twenty-five all-Negro; there were about 700 locals affiliated with the Tennessee State Labor Council, so the racial composition of only 50 locals was unknown. Finally, in September 1963, the AFL Civil Rights Committee reported that only 172 of its 55,000 locals were segregated.

Segregated local unions have encountered increasing opposition from Negro and civil-rights groups since the Second World War. The Negro community is convinced that segregated unions like other forms of segregation contribute to the Negro's economic disadvantages and should therefore be abolished. Consequently, those Negro union leaders who favored segregation as a means of preserving the advantages of union leadership and giving Negroes some control over their own affairs find themselves out of harmony with the mainstream of Negro opinion. The Negro community's opposition to segregated locals is perhaps instinctively hardened by the alacrity with which some white labor leaders seize upon Negro opposition to merger as a justification for segregation.

In truth, however, there was apparently very little opposition to integration by white union leaders, especially where the government or some other outside force could be blamed for the change. International union leaders apparently were less opposed to integration per se than afraid of the problems involved in merging long-established local unions. Union leaders were naturally fearful of opposition from rank-and-file whites, but this rarely seems to have been a very difficult problem, though a few unions—National Association of Letter Carriers (NALC) and the American Federation of Teachers (AFT)—have lost Southern locals who refused to obey ultimatums to integrate. However, though some general tendencies seem to be supported by the evidence, it is not possible to lay down hard-and-fast principles for white reactions to integration. A key factor seems to be the proportion of Negro to white membership in the locals. Almost invariably, North or South, whites have resisted integration when they would be in the minority in the merged organizations. Indeed, even some locals in unions like the United Packinghouse Workers and the United Automobile Workers, which have relatively equalitarian policies, have tended to become almost all-Negro in attendance at union functions when Negroes were in the majority.[29] White opposition also will be great either where whites expect to lose their relative seniority positions in integrated rosters, or where Negroes will acquire previously all-white jobs. This, for example, was a problem in the tobacco, aircraft, and paper industries in the South when the federal government caused the integration of seniority rosters and local unions. Finally, where groups like the Ku Klux Klan or White Citizens Councils raise the issue, white members are likely to resist integration—at least publicly.

Some problems in merging locals affect Negroes and whites alike. The attitudes of Negro and white rank-and-file members are likely to be shaped, for example, by their interpretation of the economic advantages and disadvantages of integration. In some occupations (longshoremen, bricklayers, and musicians in the South) Negroes feel that their economic conditions will not be improved by integration. Indeed, there is even some apprehension that Negro job opportunities might actually deteriorate if integration destroys protected markets. Negroes and whites will also be concerned with the disposition of union property. In a Tennessee Boilermakers' merger, for instance, the Negroes spent all of their money on an elaborate party before merging with the white local. Similarly, a white local of the Oil, Chemical, and Atomic Workers in Texas distributed some $80,000 in its strike fund among its members before merging with the Negro local. Initially, the most successful mergers of Musicians, Longshoremen, Tobacco Workers, and Machinists seem to have required that Negroes, who will usually be in a minority, be given some official positions in the merged organizations. Although such special treatment for Negroes signifies that the groups really are not "integrated," union officials consider these important first steps toward integration. That these arrangements are considered temporary is suggested by the fact that they are rarely formalized or stated as official policy.

Just as the white workers usually will be concerned about community reaction to integration, Negro workers must be concerned about the prevailing attitudes of the Negro community. Indeed, one of the most important forces against segregated locals has been the mood of the Negro community, translated into political power and reinforced by moral condemnations of segregation by the nation's opinion makers. These pressures have put the Negro leader of a segregated local in the position of being ostracized by the Negro community if he resists integration. However, some Negro union leaders in the South have buttressed their traditional economic arguments against integration with the contentions that Negroes can better promote the civil-rights movement through segregated locals. In New

Orleans, for instance, an ILA Negro local owns several business establishments, operates a political organization, and conducts a school to teach Negroes how to register and vote. Negro leaders of this local oppose integration because, they argue, it would restrict their civil-rights activities.

These general propositions can be illustrated by the experiences of several international unions.

International Longshoremen's Association (ILA)

ILA locals in the South have maintained rigid systems of job and union segregation, and Negroes frequently complain of complete exclusion from sections of New York, Philadelphia, Boston, and other Northern piers.[30] On the Gulf ports there are segregated general longshoremen's locals, and share-the-work agreements have controlled job allocations since the Civil War. Moreover, in the South and the non-South, the better clerks and checkers jobs usually are controlled by whites, whose locals almost invariably bar Negroes from membership. Negroes have retained their general longshore jobs on Southern docks partly because colored longshoremen provide dependable supplies of labor in this sometimes heavy, uncertain, and disagreeable work. Moreover, employers say Negroes are "better suited" than whites for some longshoring jobs. Even the most prejudiced hiring agents are afraid to discriminate against Negroes because discriminating employers are easily boycotted.

In exchange for the racial job-sharing arrangements, Negro leaders have supported the ILA in bargaining with employers and against the organizing efforts of the International Longshoremen and Warehousemen's Union. These mutually beneficial arrangements have produced some powerful Negro ILA leaders, and for years Negro vice-presidents from the South have held important positions in the ILA's power structure. These Negro leaders naturally are likely to resist any changes that threaten their positions.

The ILA's racial division of labor may be illustrated by the composition of that union's New Orleans membership. In 1962 there were approximately 7000 ILA members in New Orleans—1900 whites and 5100 Negroes. Each race controlled four locals, all of which were represented in a joint council, and all locals had concurrent jurisdiction except 375 white clerks and checkers and 1200 Negro freight car unloaders. There is little doubt that the Negroes' superior numbers give them considerable power in the joint council.[31]

Building trades

The Negro bricklayers, plasterers, cement finishers, and roofers are usually integrated in the South, and Negro workers have also been able to retain these jobs because they have sufficiently large supplies of labor to furnish the entire requirements of contractors who might be boycotted by whites.[32]   Indeed, these workers, like the longshoremen, frequently have better employment opportunities in the South than in the non-South, where they are sometimes discriminated against by white unions.   The Bricklayers had about twenty-five segregated locals in the South in 1962, but were also integrated in some places. In New Orleans and Baton Rouge, Louisiana, for instance, the Negroes constituted about 80 per cent of the membership in each local in 1962. In New Orleans all of the Bricklayers' officers were Negroes, whereas in Baton Rouge they had a white business agent.   It has been common practice for some Negro or virtually all Negro unions to have white officers as "contact" men where employers refuse to deal with Negro officers.

Except for the so-called "trowel trades," however, Negro building-trades workers have sometimes been unhappy with segregation because they have inadequate job opportunities.   For example, several Negro locals of the United Brotherhood of Carpenters and Joiners (UBCJ) in the South have virtually atrophied because they could not get adequate job opportunities.   Complaints against the Carpenters are not restricted, however, to the South, because Negroes in New York City complain of having been segregated into Local 1888, which has inferior job opportunities to the traditionally "white" unions.[33] Now, however, Local 1888 is not restricted to Negroes and all other New York Carpenters locals have Negro members.   In cities such as Memphis, New Orleans, and Atlanta, white Carpenters locals have refused to work with Negro union members.   In many Southern cities Negro carpenters locals have survived in some cases by insisting upon quota systems on federal projects.   In other cases, the small Negro locals are restricted to house work in the Negro sections and the business agents sometimes act as contractors.

District councils are supposed to be set up where there are several carpenters locals in the same area, but Negro leaders complain that the district councils frequently ignored the Negro locals.   In Homestead, Florida, for instance, Negro carpenters complained to the PCGC that contractors on an air force base recruited carpenters exclusively through the white local.   Moreover, the carpenters locals in Dade

County had a "gentlemen's agreement" that Negroes would get work in the Negro community and whites would work in the white community; but the Negro local complained that the white local took the best jobs in both the Negro and white communities. The white business agent told an investigator that white carpenters would not work in the same crews with Negroes, but said whole crews of Negroes might work in separate buildings. The PCGC recommended that the companies be advised that they could not use the union agreement as an excuse for discrimination and that George Meany's help be solicited in getting equal opportunities for Negro carpenters. The lack of job opportunities for Negro carpenters locals is perhaps due in part to employer preferences, but there is ample evidence that white carpenters have actively prevented the employment of Negroes.

The UBCJ announced in 1963 that segregated locals and other forms of racial discrimination would be abolished in that union, and in March 1964 a UBCJ official told the writer, "In the past three years some eleven segregated Local Unions have been merged or disbanded." [34] It was also reported that six of these locals had been eliminated in the year preceding July 1963.[35] With respect to the economic effects of segregation, the UBCJ's general treasurer, who handles all matters pertaining to discrimination for the Carpenters' Executive Board, felt that

both whites and colored have suffered. The Negroes suffered because they lacked the strength and perhaps the know-how to make gains they might be entitled to. But the whites have been held back even more, because they have had a low-wage competitive factor working against them. In spite of Hell or high water, the lowest wages form the lowest common denominator that affects all wages. This is the main reason why we oppose segregation in any form.[36]

The Painters' experiences with segregated locals have been similar to the Carpenters'. In Atlanta, for example, the white Painters local had about 675 members in 1962, whereas the Negroes had about fourteen members who were able to survive in part because of racial quota systems on federal projects. Throughout the South, Negro painters and carpenters are largely nonunion and work on houses, posing a constant threat to the standards of unionized whites. Some Negro painters have refused to join the union because they could get adequate jobs on a nonunion basis. The threat posed to union conditions caused the 1954 Painters' convention in Seattle to adopt a resolution calling on white locals not to discriminate against Negroes. That convention also adopted a policy that no more segregated locals would be established.

The American Federation of Musicians (AFM)

As late as 1960 the AFM probably had more segregated locals scattered throughout the United States than any union except the Railway Clerks. Like other unions already discussed, the AFM at first organized Negroes into auxiliary locals. When James C. Petrillo became president of the AFM in 1940, he granted equal status to the twelve remaining Negro auxiliaries. There remained, however, many segregated locals because Petrillo had a policy of creating separate locals when fifty Negroes "requested their own charter and could meet the charter requirements." [37]

After the Second World War, however, increasing Negro opposition to segregation caused this policy to change. Sometimes Negro opposition was because of inadequate job opportunities—especially work with symphony orchestras.[38] But the greatest opposition within the AFM seems to have come from a few Negro leaders who opposed segregation on principle. Leadership for this opposition was provided by a Los Angeles Negro local, which merged with a white local in 1953 after the Negroes threatened a law suit. Negro representatives from this local also introduced a resolution at the 1957 AFM convention calling for the elimination of segregated locals. Segregation violated the AFM's constitution, according to this resolution, because of a provision that there could be only one local in an area. Furthermore, the resolution held, "The continued maintenance in our Federation of locals limited to persons of any one racial or ethnic group is contrary to good morals and tends to degrade all members of our Federation, and impose[s] an improper stigma and burden upon members of our Federation." [39]

It appeared, however, that the vast majority of Negro delegates to the 1957 convention opposed this antisegregation resolution. Fifty-seven delegates from thirty-nine of the Federation's forty-seven colored locals presented a petition opposing the merger resolution because "of the financial aspect involved with some of the larger colored locals, who have spent many years of hard work to attain their present status in the Federation. . . . Under no circumstances should a merger be forced upon us but should rather be accomplished by mutual agreement between parties concerned." [40] Only four Negro delegates from two locals opposed this petition. After the 1957 convention, Petrillo had all of the members of the AFM's colored locals vote on the merger resolution. Forty of the locals voted against merger, five in favor of it, and two did not vote.[41]

This matter was not settled by the 1957 convention, however, because the AFM's policies were subjected to increasing external pressures. The Los Angeles Negroes filed a complaint against the AFM with the AFL-CIO Civil Rights Committee (CRC) in 1958. The CRC did nothing about the case, however, apparently because Petrillo's defense of the union's racial policies satisfied the AFL-CIO. Petrillo wrote George Meany that ". . . since the colored musicians are in the minority and so represent the weaker group within our union, it is my policy to let their wishes control. It is my fond hope and earnest belief that this approach will in a peaceful and effective way, best achieve the goal of integration." [42]

One would judge from his debates with A. Philip Randolph at the 1959 AFL-CIO convention that at that time Meany's position on segregated locals was essentially the same as Petrillo's. [43]

Herman Kenin, Petrillo's successor as president of the AFM, at first continued Petrillo's policies. However, the passage of state anti-discrimination legislation and the changed national racial climate, especially after 1962, apparently caused the Federation to assign greater urgency to the problem of eliminating segregated locals. According to Mr. Kenin, "A changing National climate . . . is aiding [the AFM's leaders] somewhat in the tedious, difficult and time-consuming procedures that become necessary to the protection of job and property rights of merged minorities." [44] By the end of 1962 the Federation had merged all of its locals west of Omaha and in 1963 delivered an ultimatum for its Chicago affiliates to merge by March 1, 1964. Before then, however, some fifty Negroes had joined the white local in Chicago after their local refused to merge. In March 1964 the AFM had about thirty all-Negro locals.

Conclusions

Although the number of segregated locals is declining, they are not likely to disappear completely for many years. Several international unions, such as the Machinists, the Bricklayers, Longshoremen, Paper Makers, and various railroad unions, have policies encouraging merger but, respecting local autonomy, apparently will not employ sanctions to enforce mergers. Similarly, although the 1959 AFL-CIO convention adopted a policy against segregated locals, no sanctions were imposed for violations of that policy. Finally, the PCEEO and the NLRB apparently are moving to cripple segregated locals, but the courts and many state civil-rights commissions have refused to compel mergers of separate locals if whites and Negroes can transfer freely into either local. In these circumstances, and barring new legal measures against segregation, the resistance from Negroes and whites will be sufficient to perpetuate some segregated locals for many years.

The most important forces tending to eliminate segregated locals have been: prevailing moral sentiment against segregation; opposition from the Negro community as contrasted with Negro union members; some state FEP laws; and finally the Kennedy and Johnson administrations' policy of not permitting segregated locals to bargain for government employees and strongly discouraging them among federal contractors. Moreover, almost all international unions have signed pledges with the PCEEO agreeing to abolish discrimination, including segregated locals, within their unions.

We should note, however, that to call a local "integrated" might not mean very much. It might mean that one or two Negroes belong to the organization but never participate other than by paying dues. Those few Negroes might be janitors in the plant or they might have been admitted to the local or plant as "tokens" to prove the absence of discrimination. "Integration" might mean that Negroes are members of the industrial union and if they attend meetings they segregate themselves or are segregated by whites. In other cases, like some Woodworkers' locals, Negroes and whites ostensibly are integrated, but actually meet at different times.

FOOTNOTES

1. Abram L. Harris, in *The Negro Worker* (New York: Conference for Progressive Labor Action, 1930, p. 8), listed the following AFL unions with formal race bars in 1930:
    1. Brotherhood of Railway Carmen (BRC)
    2. The Switchmen's Union of North America (SNA)
    3. The Order of Sleeping Car Conductors (OSCC)
    4. The (International) National Organization of Masters, Mates and Pilots of North America (MMP)
    5. The Railway Mail Association (RMA)
    6. American Wire Weavers Protective Association (WWPA)
    7. Commercial Telegraphers (CT)
    8. The Boilermakers, Iron Shipbuilders and Helpers Union (BIS)
    9. The International Association of Machinists (IAM)
    10. The Order of Railway (Railroad) Telegraphers (ORT)
    11. Brotherhood of Railway and Steamship Clerks (BRSC)

    Harris listed the following unaffiliated unions as having race bars in 1930:
    1. American Federation of Express Workers (AFEW)
    2. American Federation of Railway Workers (AFRW)
    3. Brotherhood of Railway Station Employees and Clerks (BRSEC)
    4. [American] Train Dispatchers [Association] (ATDA)

    5. Railroad Yard Masters of America (RYA)
    6. Neptune Association (NA)
    7. Brotherhood of Locomotive Engineers (BLE)
    8. Brotherhood [Order] of Railway Conductors (ORC)
    9. Brotherhood of Locomotive Firemen and Enginemen (BLF)
    10. Brotherhood of Railroad Trainmen (BRT)
    11. Order of Railway Telegraphers (ORT)
    12. Brotherhood of Dining Car Conductors (BDC)
    13. Order of Railway Expressmen (ORE)

Harris said that there were 26 unions with racial bars, 10 of which were AFL affiliates, though he listed only 24 unions, 11 of which were AFL affiliates. The U. S. Department of Labor, Bureau of Labor Statistics, in its 1926 *Handbook of American Trade Unions,* listed the following unions with race bars: BDC, AFRW, ORE, AFREW, BRSEC, RYA, the Railroad Yard Masters of North America (RYNA), NA, BRT, ORC, BLE, and BLFE. In addition, Spero and Harris (*The Black Worker,* New York: Columbia University Press, 1930, p. 57) listed the following AFL organizations with race bars in 1929, which also probably had race bars in 1926: BRC, SNA, BRSC, CT, OSCC, ORT, MMP, RMA, WWPA, BIS, and the IAM. Between 1926 and 1930, however, the ORE and the AFEW returned to the BRSC, and in 1929 the BRSE no longer limited membership to whites. Thus, Spero and Harris concluded ". . . in 1930 there are nine unions affiliated with the Federation and ten unaffiliated unions whose constitutions debar Negro members." (*Ibid.,* p. 58.) In addition, an AFL affiliate, the Sheet Metal Workers' International Association (SMW), was reported by the New York State Commission on Human Rights in 1964 to have barred Negroes from membership for the previous 76 years of its existence and to have had a constitutional race bar until 1946. (*New York Times,* March 4, 1964.) It appears, however, that the SMW's bar was not absolute, but restricted Negroes to auxiliary locals governed by whites.

2. IAM, SNA, MMP, ORT, RMA, WWPA, and the Airline Pilots Association (ALPA). See Herbert Northrup, *Organized Labor and the Negro,* New York: Harper, 1944, p. 3. The unaffiliated organizations listed by Northrup in 1943 were: BLE, BLFE, BRT, RYA, RYNA, ORC, ATDA. The SMW also had a race bar in 1943. (*New York Times,* March 5, 1964.)

3. The WWPA had 431 members in 6 locals in 1957 before it merged with the Paper Makers.

4. BLE *Constitution* of June–July 1956, as amended September 1960, Section 28.

5. BLFE *Constitution,* July–August 1959, as amended January 8, 1960.

6. See Mark Perlman, *The Machinists,* Cambridge, Mass.: Harvard University Press, 1961.

7. Harry Henig, *The Brotherhood of Railway Clerks,* New York: Columbia University Press, 1937.

8. See AFL *Convention Proceedings,* 1919, Resolution 118; 1930, p. 308; and 1922 Executive Council's Report.

9. AFL *Executive Council Minutes,* September 30, October 10, 1940, p. 133.

10. AFL *Convention Proceedings,* 1940, p. 649.

11. Northrup, *op. cit.,* p. 85.

12. BRSC *Convention Proceedings,* 1947, pp. 63, 117, 173.

13. See Chapter 1.

14. FEPC *Final Report,* p. 20.
15. Malcolm Ross, *All Manner of Men,* New York: Reynal and Hitchcock, 1947, p. 147.
16. Robert Weaver, *Negro Labor,* New York: Harcourt, Brace, 1946, pp. 228–29.
17. See Chapter 1.
18. See James v. Marinship 25 Calif. 2d 721, 1944.
19. Letter to the writer from Charles W. Jones, Director of Research and Education, IBBISBBFH, November 20, 1959.
20. IAM *Executive Council Minutes,* Sept. 21–26, 1925; Dec. 3–12, 1940; Dec. 1–13, 1941; July 18–24, 1941; and June 26–31, 1942.
21. *Congressional Record,* 78th Congress, 1st Session, Vol. 89, No. 65.
22. Texas Motor Freight Lines, Hearing Case No. 16-R-2223, April 9, 1943, pp. 32–33.
23. *Monthly Machinists Journal,* Vol. II, 1890, p. 34.
24. "The Truth about Color in the IAM," speech to the annual conference of the National Urban League, Philadelphia, 1955.
25. Letter to the writer from Vernon E. Jirekowiz, IAM Director of Research, February 24, 1964.
26. Other organizations establishing auxiliary locals for Negroes included the Blacksmiths and Boilermakers; the Motion Picture Operators; the National Rural Letter Carriers; the National Federation of Rural Letter Carriers; the Maintenance of Way Employees; the Sheet Metal Workers Alliance; the Brotherhood of Railway Clerks; the American Federation of Musicians; the Rural Letter Carriers Association; the International Association of Machinists; and the Seafarers International Union. All of these organizations except the American Federation of Railroad Workers and the Rural Letter Carriers were affiliated with the AFL.
27. Although the list is not complete, the following international unions have or have had segregated locals: Brotherhood of Maintenance of Way Employees (BMWE); Brotherhood of Painters, Decorators and Paperhangers of America (BPDP); Brotherhood of Railway Carmen of America (BRC); Brotherhood of Railway and Steamship Clerks, Freight Handlers, Express and Station Employees (BRSC); Iron Workers; International Brotherhood of Boilermakers, Iron Ship Builders, Blacksmiths, Forgers and Helpers (BIS); International Union of Pulp, Sulphite and Paper Mill Workers (PPS); Aluminum Workers; Sheet Metal Workers International Association (SMW); United Brotherhood of Carpenters and Joiners of America (UBCJ); International Brotherhood of Teamsters, Chauffeurs and Warehousemen; United Brotherhood of Paper Makers and Paperworkers (UPP); the National Federation of Rural Letter Carriers (independent); International Chemical Workers (ICW); American Federation of Musicians (AFM); American Federation of Teachers (AFT); National Association of Letter Carriers (NALC); International Association of Machinists (IAM); Tobacco Workers International Union (TWIU); the Bricklayers, Masons and Plasterers (BMP); the Journeyman Barbers International Union; the Oil, Chemical and Atomic Workers (OCAW); State, County and Municipal Workers; the Textile Workers Union (TWU); the United Textile Workers (UTWA); the International Longshoremen's Association (ILA); the Molders; the Glass and Ceramic Workers; the Amalgamated Clothing Workers (ACWA); and the International Ladies' Garment Workers Union (ILGWU).

28. See my "Independent Unions in the Southern Petroleum Refining Industry —the Esso Experience," *Labor Law Journal*, September 1961.

29. See Chapter 8.

30. See Chapter 11.

31. See *New Orleans Item*, June 5, 1959, when a Negro leader opposed a strike threatened by a white official.

32. The Washington, D. C., and Richmond, Va., white locals of the BMP refused to permit Negro locals before 1903, but at Charleston the Negroes were granted a charter because they were "too numerous to be ignored" since they did not regulate apprenticeship. In 1903 the BMP amended its constitution to permit the Executive Board to issue separate charters to Negroes where whites would not accept them. Harry Bates, *Bricklayers Century of Progress*, BMP, 1955, p. 122.

33. See *New York Times*, September 15, 1963.

34. Letter to the writer from Peter E. Terzick, UBCJ General Treasurer, March 4, 1964.

35. *New York Times*, July 2, 1963.

36. Letter to the writer, March 4, 1964.

37. Letter to George Meany from James C. Petrillo, April 8, 1958.

38. See Nat Hentoff, "The Strange Case of the Missing Musicians," *The Reporter*, May 28, 1959.

39. Sixteenth Annual Convention of the American Federation of Musicians, *Proceedings*, p. 82.

40. *Ibid.*

41. Petrillo to Meany, April 8, 1958.

42. *Ibid.*

43. See Chapter 3.

44. Letter to the writer, March 4, 1964.

CHAPTER 6

Informal Exclusion

THE DECLINE IN FORMAL EXCLUSION BY INTERNATIONAL UNIONS does not mean that discrimination has declined by the same degree, of course, because of local variations from these policies. Locals of internationals with race bars sometimes accepted Negroes, and the locals of some international unions that do not have formal race bars have barred Negroes by informal means. The variety of ways in which this is done include agreements not to sponsor Negroes for membership; refusal to admit Negroes into apprenticeship programs; refusal to accept applications from Negroes, or simply ignoring their applications; general "understandings" to vote against Negroes if they are proposed (for example, as few as three members of some railroad lodges have barred applicants for membership); using examinations to refuse Negroes journeyman status which either are not given to whites or are rigged so that Negroes cannot pass them; exerting political pressure on governmental licensing agencies to see to it that Negroes fail the tests; and restricting membership to sons, nephews, or other relatives of members.

Building Trades

Because of the absence of Negroes from these unions, as well as a number of well-publicized cases of their having vigorously refused to accept Negroes, there has been much agitation by civil-rights groups against building-trades unions. Negro participation in various trades would be about equal to the Negro proportion of the total population —roughly 10 per cent—if purely random factors determined Negroes' occupational distribution. Of course, as we shall see, discrimination by unions is only one of the factors causing Negroes to be under- or overrepresented in various occupations.

Whatever is responsible for the pattern, there is no question that Negroes tend to be concentrated in certain building trades and that this pattern differs only in degree between different sections of the country. Figures on the number and proportion of Negroes in the building trades are not available for 1960, but 1950 census figures revealed that Negroes constituted relatively high proportions of cement finishers (26.1 per cent); brickmasons, stonemasons, tile setters (10.9 per cent); paperhangers (11.1 per cent); structural metal workers (7.2 per cent); and roofers and slaters (6.94 per cent). The lowest proportions of Negroes were found among tool and die makers (.3 per cent); sheet metal workers (.84 per cent); electricians (1.0 per cent); machinists and millwrights (2.0 per cent); cabinet makers (2.4 per cent); and carpenters (3.9 per cent).

The craft locals of the IBEW and the Plumbers and Pipe Fitters have a rather consistent pattern of discrimination throughout the United States, but other building-trades unions also are prominent in the list of unions against whom charges of racial discrimination are rather common. The following unions have had records of discrimination dating back at least thirty years: Granite Workers; Flint Glass Workers, the craft unions in the printing trades; IBEW; Plumbers; Structural Iron Workers; and Asbestos Workers. In addition, charges of discrimination against locals of the following organizations have been frequently made by various civil-rights organizations: Brewery Workers; Bricklayers, Masons, and Plasterers; Plasterers and Cement Masons; United Brotherhood of Carpenters and Joiners; International Association of Sheet Metal Workers; Elevator Constructors; and the Motion Picture Operators. Some of these latter unions, like the Bricklayers, Masons, and Plasterers, and the Plasterers and Cement Masons, are in occupations with relatively large Negro memberships. The unions in the so-called "trowel trades" have many Negro members in integrated or virtually all-Negro locals in the South, but there have been charges of discrimination in many places in the non-South where Negroes have lower proportions of union membership than in the South. Other organizations, such as the International Union of Operating Engineers, have reputations for barring Negroes in such places as Denver, San Francisco, and Los Angeles, but have been regarded as among the best construction unions in Washington, D. C. The Operating Engineers also have many Negro members in the South. Similarly, the Teamsters have integrated their locals in such Southern cities as Atlanta and New Orleans, are generally regarded as discriminatory on the West Coast, especially in the brewery and dairy industries, but again are regarded as one of the least discriminatory unions in St. Louis.[1] The Bricklayers have also acquired a good racial reputation in most places, but in 1957 Local 8 of that organization in Milwaukee accepted two Negro members only after extensive publicity, legal action, and a threat of expulsion from the international union. In most places in the South, even where the Bricklayers have segregated locals, that organization is regarded as one of the best building-trades unions with respect to its treatment of Negro members; indeed, as early as 1905 the Bricklayers' constitution imposed a $100 fine on any member who discriminated against a fellow member because of race.

Electricians

In 1950, according to U. S. Census figures, Negroes accounted for only 1 per cent of the electricians in the United States. There were 9360 electrical apprentices, only 90 of whom were Negroes.[2] IBEW industrial locals had many colored members, but construction locals rarely accepted Negroes. IBEW craft locals permitted Negro contractors to operate in some cases if they confined their operations to Negro neighborhoods. These same locals, however, prevented Negro electricians from working outside Negro neighborhoods. Indeed, IBEW locals have actually picketed Negro electricians when they tried to work outside the areas restricted to them, even though those locals adamantly refused to admit Negroes to membership. IBEW locals are able to enforce their rules against Negroes because they control the supply of skilled electricians, and because other skilled union members refuse to work with nonunion men. Since electricians must usually be licensed, the unions sometimes strengthen their grip on the supply of labor by controlling the licensing boards. IBEW construction locals that accepted Negroes to membership before 1950 were clearly exceptional, though subsequent pressures have forced locals in Washington, D. C., Hartford, Conn., Detroit, and Cleveland to accept Negro members. The main pre-1950 exceptions were in New York, Chicago, and Los Angeles. There were also a few Negro members of IBEW construction locals in Texas, South Carolina, and Florida in 1964, but in no other place in the South as far as the writer could determine.

In Boston, "There seems to be a tacit understanding that nonunion Negro electricians can operate within certain areas of high Negro residence without interference." [3]

A 1958 survey by the National Urban League revealed no Negroes in craft locals of the IBEW in the following cities: Akron, O.; Anderson, Ind.; Columbus, O.; Denver, Colo.; Flint, Mich.; Jacksonville, Fla.; Kansas City, Mo.; Massilon, O.; New Orleans, La.; Oklahoma City, Okla.; San Francisco, Calif.; Tampa, Fla.; Warren, O.; and Washington, D. C. The League's survey revealed that fifteen Negroes had applied for membership in the Gary IBEW Local 697, but none were accepted; these electricians worked for a Negro contractor who had to pay 1 per cent of wages to the union's Employee Benefit Fund. The Negro electricians were considering affiliation with an independent union in order to be able to work with skilled union craftsmen on commercial projects. There were twenty-five Negro electricians in Washington in 1960, none of whom were in the union; there were also thirty-five to forty Negro youngsters who would like to have been admitted to the IBEW's electrical apprenticeship program. In Louisiana, electrical licensing was by the cities and there were Negro electricians (usually trained in Negro colleges) in New Orleans, Baton Rouge, Lake Charles, Ruston, and Minden in 1962, but none of them were union members. In Atlanta the IBEW local excluded Negroes, though there were two licensed Negro electricians in 1962, one with ten employees and the other with five; these men had been trying to get into the IBEW for years. A 1964 U. S. Civil Rights Commission study found no Negroes in any IBEW local in Memphis, Nashville, Chattanooga, Knoxville, or Jackson, Tennessee.[4] There were no Negroes in the IBEW craft local in Philadelphia in 1964. According to a 1963 report from Florida: "While at present, there are 2 Negro electricians in Miami, and there have been, all told, 11 Negro journeymen in (IBEW) Local 349, they are dealt with separately by R. T. Callahan, Business Agent of . . . Local . . . 349." [5]

An examination of the racial practices of IBEW Local 38 in Cleveland, Ohio, will give a better understanding of the problems involved in breaking a strong local union's racial barriers. Local 38 defied concerted efforts by Negro electricians to get into the union over a period of forty years. Like many craft locals, Local 38's power was based on its control of the supply of skilled workers and the craft-union tradition that union men will not work with nonunion men in their own or other crafts. Indeed, an electrical contractor had great difficulty operating in Cleveland without Local 38's approval, an arrangement which was apparently quite acceptable to those contractors already approved by the Union. Local 38's constitution required electrical contractors to be "certified" by the local in order to hire union electricians, and in order to be certified a contractor was required to serve two years as a journeyman—which normally meant he must have been a member of the union for two years. Since Negroes were barred from Local 38 and could not work on union jobs, they could not get certified by the union. Negroes could operate as contractors if they passed a city licensing examination, but since they could not hire union electricians, they were restricted to nonunion work—usually in Negro neighborhoods.

Negroes in Cleveland started agitating in 1917 to break Local 38's restrictions on their economic opportunities. In 1947 Negro electricians formed a club which solicited the aid of international union officers, including IBEW President Dan Tracy and Vice-President (now President) Gordon Freeman. These early efforts ended in failure, however, when a business agent who was disposed to help the Negro electricians drowned in Lake Erie, and Dan Tracy, who had promised to do what he could to get Negroes admitted to the union, retired as president of the IBEW. These failures caused Negroes to turn to legal action as a means of changing the union's practices.

In 1955 charges were filed against Local 38 before Cleveland's Community Relations Board (CRB) which found the local guilty of racial discrimination, but, in spite of widespread adverse publicity and the efforts of Mayor Anthony Celebrezze (later Secretary of Health, Education, and Welfare), the union steadfastly refused to admit a Negro to membership. After the union ignored the CRB's ruling, the case was referred to the AFL-CIO Civil Rights Department and the President's Committee on Government Contracts. This case went to the formal hearing stage of the AFL-CIO Civil Rights Committee, after CRC Chairman James B. Carey and AFL-CIO President George Meany failed to get the local to relent. Finally, Local 38 admitted three Negroes to membership on the last day of June

1957, after President Meany told the local to admit the Negroes by July 1 or lose its charter. The local showed its continued defiance, however, by refusing to admit the man who filed the complaint with the Community Relations Board. Significantly, by July 1964 Local 38 had taken in no more journeymen, Negro or white, and the three Negroes admitted in 1957 were the first journeymen admitted in twelve years.

President Meany, the international union, the AFL-CIO Civil Rights Committee, the PCGC, and other agencies encountered even greater obstacles in getting Negroes admitted to IBEW Local 26 in Washington, D. C. Despite the efforts of President Freeman and IBEW Secretary Joseph Keenan, who served on the AFL-CIO Civil Rights Committee, AFL-CIO officers admitted in December 1958 that all their efforts to break the local's racial barrier had failed. Even before the AFL-CIO Civil Rights Committee gave up on this case, however, President Meany had attempted a novel approach to this embarrassing problem: he offered to recruit nonunion Negro electricians if the PCGC would require the government contractor on a public-housing project to hire them. Although these developments focused public attention on the building trades and caused many high-ranking building-trades officials to pledge to the PCGC that they would take measures to "do everything within (their) power to immediately correct any incidents of discrimination in employment or in apprenticeship," [6] none of these officials had sufficient economic power to break the local's resistance. As in Cleveland, Local 26's strength lay mainly in its control of the supply of skilled electricians, so President Meany and various civil-rights organizations were almost completely unsuccessful in recruiting Negro electricians. However, after the electrical needs of other federal projects in the Washington area were projected and plans were made to secure needed electricians from other areas, Local 26 issued a work permit to a Negro journeyman and in July 1964 was reported to have had twelve Negro apprentices.[7]

Connecticut adopted an approach to IBEW Local 35 in Hartford that proved effective. The first case to go to public hearing before the Connecticut Civil Rights Commission (CCRC) involved Local 35's refusal to admit qualified Negroes to membership. Local 35 argued that it did not violate the law because it discriminated against all races! The Civil Rights Commission was not impressed by the union's argument, however, and ordered it to admit the Negroes. The union defied the CCRC and the force of public opinion by voting to reject the Negro applicants, despite a court order to accept them, but it quickly capitulated when it was fined $2,000 and $500 for each week it remained in contempt of court.[8]

Plumbers

The Plumbers' racial practices closely parallel those of the IBEW locals. Locals of both organizations have successfully used licensing and inspection arrangements to restrict entry into their crafts. A 1958 survey by the National Urban League found that Plumbers locals had no Negroes in twenty of the twenty-three cities surveyed and the others had only token Negro membership.[9]

These practices are typical of others related to the writer during his field interviews throughout the United States. Indeed, locals of the Plumbers, like those of the IBEW, seem to restrict Negroes to certain kinds of work and will picket Negroes when they come out of these areas, even though they refuse to accept them as members.

Moreover, as with the electricians, licensing laws have been used to bar Negroes from the plumbing trade. In Baltimore, for example, Negroes were excluded from apprenticeship programs, so they could not qualify to take the examination. Nine Negroes in that city formed a club to study to pass the state licensing examinations and take other legal means to get Negroes licensed as plumbers in Maryland. These Negro plumbers started trying to get licensed in 1941, but at first were prohibited from taking the examination because they could not get two master plumbers to recommend them. In 1942 the Negroes succeeded in having this provision waived, but all six Negroes who were permitted to take the examination failed, though one of those taking the examination had made a grade of 90 per cent on a U. S. Civil Service examination for plumbers and pipefitters; the Negroes failed the examination again in 1943, 1946, and 1947, though they were never permitted to see their test papers. In 1949, after legislative investigations and adverse publicity, the Plumbing Board was completely reorganized and a Negro passed the journeyman test. Now, however, he encountered a new roadblock in his efforts to work as a plumber on equal terms with whites, because no white master plumber would employ him. The colored plumber solved this difficulty by forming a partnership with a retired white master plumber who had dropped out of the trade because of illness. No Negro had passed the examination to become a master plumber, permitting them to take in apprentices. In 1953 a resolution was passed in the Maryland Senate, asking the State Board of Plumbing Commissioners to explain the evidence of discrimination against plumbers in that state.

Investigation at that time disclosed that of 3200 licensed plumbers in Maryland, there were only two Negroes. It was then agreed to hold the masters' examination with senators present and though no Negroes passed in 1953, two colored plumbers succeeded in passing the examination in 1956. Similarly, a Negro passed the Colorado plumber's examination in 1950 only after a civil-rights official took the matter up with state authorities.

The 1964 Bronx Plumbers' case indicates some of the complexities involved in getting Negroes hired on construction projects, even under the most favorable conditions, as well as the difficulties in proving conclusively the existence of racial discrimination in the building trades. This case ultimately involved President Lyndon Johnson, Mayor Robert Wagner of New York City, as well as top civil-rights and labor leaders. AFL-CIO President Meany had more than the usual interest in this case because he had been a member of Plumbers Local 2, the local involved, for almost fifty years.

The Bronx Plumbers' case started early in 1964 when the New York City Commission for Human Rights (CHR) sought to get employers with public contracts to hire nonunion Negroes and Puerto Ricans in trades where unions had reputations for barring these workers on racial grounds. One of the earliest employers contacted by the Commission, a plumbing contractor on the $25 million Terminal Market project, agreed to hire Negro and Puerto Rican applicants when he expanded his work force in April 1964. The contractor was afraid of losing a $1,410,000 plumbing contract he had on the project. The Taft-Hartley Act prohibited him from maintaining a closed-shop agreement with the union, but the plumbing contractor had traditionally given preference in hiring to members of Local 2. Apparently fearing trouble with the union, the employer went to Local 2's leaders, who told him that he had a legal right to hire the nonunion workers. As is frequently the case with craft locals, political factionalism complicated the position of Local 2's leaders.

Three Puerto Ricans and one Negro went to work on the project April 29, and 41 white plumbers left the job after challenging the union status of the four new workers. Although other crafts continued to work during the dispute—which lasted almost three weeks—the entire project ultimately would have been halted by the Plumbers' walkout because concrete could not be poured until the plumbing was done and other jobs would be held up until the concrete work was completed.

In spite of racial epithets hurled by a few white union members during this dispute, and the general assumption by the press and civil-rights leaders that the union men were striking for racial reasons, the union's leaders pointed out that the local had twenty active Negro members and three Negro apprentices in its membership of approximately 4100. Moreover, four of five nonwhite youths referred to the local for apprenticeship training as a result of racial demonstrations during the summer of 1963 were being processed for admission along with four other minority youths referred from other sources.

After behind-the-scenes maneuvering by national and local civil-rights, union, and political leaders—and a blockade of Local 2's offices by the East River and Bronx chapters of the Congress of Racial Equality—a settlement was reached on May 18. The local's leaders agreed to expedite, and the four nonunion men agreed to take, the standard test given applicants for membership in the union. The nonunion men at first had refused to take the tests on the grounds that they violated the closed-shop provisions of the Taft-Hartley Law. After they were assured that the tests would be fair and that outside observers and interpreters could be present, the men took and failed the tests. One of the Puerto Ricans, the Urban League of Greater New York, and the National Association of Puerto Rican Affairs later filed charges with the NLRB alleging that the union had caused the plumbing contractor to discriminate against these workers because they were not union members. Civil-rights representatives agreed that the tests were fair and the union agreed to permit the men to take the tests again in ninety days. But, although four Negroes were among nine applicants who passed the necessary tests to become journeymen members of the union (thereby giving the local 20 Negro members of a total membership of 4100) in August 1964, the men involved in the May walkout did not take the tests. One of the Puerto Ricans and a Negro refused to take the test in August 1964 because the Union would not again permit outside observation and evaluation.

Union leaders considered the workers' failure of the tests to be a vindication of their position and Mayor Wagner made it clear that the CHR was never again to act as an employment agency for minority workers. He said that henceforth minority workers would be referred to the union, which promised to consider all applications fairly. George Meany and other union leaders hailed the Bronx Plumbers settlement as a possible pattern for other union racial disputes.

International unions

We should note the distinction between the policies of international and local unions. Both the United Association of Journeymen and Apprentices of the Plumbing and Pipefitting Industry (UA) and the IBEW have become concerned about the adverse publicity they are receiving, which has caused their actions to be carefully scrutinized by civil-rights and government agencies and which jeopardizes their control of apprenticeship and job referral procedures. The UA established a committee in 1959 to study charges of racial discrimination against its locals, and in 1962 the international union included a non-discrimination clause in its national agreement covering large contractors. Similarly, the 1958 IBEW convention adopted a "Resolution on Civil Rights," which resolved that it was the "enduring goal of our Brotherhood to assure to all workers their full share in the benefits of union organization without regard to race, creed, color or national origin." [10] Although there is frequently a vast difference between resolutions and practices, at least the international officers are moving—or being forced to move—toward more equalitarian policies.

1963 demonstrations

Although the absence of Negroes from these occupations is due to a host of other factors, discrimination by building-trades unions has been too well documented to be successfully denied by even the most vigorous defenders of those unions. Indeed, the admission of discrimination has frequently been made by ex-plumber George Meany himself.[11]

The Negro community's smoldering resentment against racial discrimination by building-trades unions produced a number of demonstrations at construction sites in several major cities during the spring and summer of 1963. The building trades were logical targets for these more militant measures, not only because these unions had acquired unfavorable images in the Negro community, but also because their work was frequently on government projects, conspicuous, and in Negro neighborhoods.

Almost simultaneously, therefore, building projects in Philadelphia, New York, and other cities were subjected to picketing, lay-downs, and sit-ins, devices which had already been tested by civil-rights groups in the South and, ironically, by the unions themselves. The earliest demonstrations appear to have occurred in Philadelphia, where NAACP pickets halted work on an $18 million building project in May.[12] There were a number of injuries in Philadelphia when police attempted to escort workmen through demonstrators on a school construction site. Some Negroes among those workers being escorted to the construction site were photographed and the president of the Philadelphia branch of the NAACP declared that they would be "ostracized by the Negro community." [13] The Philadelphia unions agreed to admit Negro apprentices only after the mayor halted work on the school project. The unions against whom these demonstrations were primarily directed—the Electricians, Plumbers, and Steamfitters —had been under attack from civil-rights groups and the Philadelphia Human Relations Commission for some time. Indeed, members of the Philadelphia AFL-CIO even ". . . testified before the Commission giving evidence of discriminatory practices in membership, rules and apprenticeship programs." [14] Of course, the building trades argued that "they do not discriminate on account of race, creed, or color; that their membership rules are of old standing and were not directed to keep out any particular section of the population . . . faced with unemployment . . . they are not willing to give nonunion Negroes super-seniority over unemployed white union members." [15] However, the Philadelphia Sheet Metal Workers have adopted what appears to be a completely nondiscriminatory method of selecting apprentices. There is no "father-son" clause, tests are announced in advance and are administered by the public schools. In one group, there were 302 applicants to the program, 55 of whom were Negroes. Of these, 32 Negroes of 190 eligible took the test. Seven Negroes and 95 whites passed the test.

In New York hundreds of demonstrators were arrested as various civil-rights groups halted work on state and city construction projects for as long as four months. In one project alone—the $23.5 million Harlem Hospital—the City of New York incurred costs of between $800 and $900 a day while the project was closed by pickets, and by early August the demonstrations are reported to have cost the city over $250,000 for overtime payments to police.[16] A ministers' group in Brooklyn succeeded in halting work on the Downstate Medical Center in Brooklyn,[17] and sit-ins protesting building-trades discrimination were conducted at the New York governor's and mayor's offices and in the city hall at Newark, New Jersey.[18] There also were scores of injuries and arrests during demonstrations in Brooklyn; Elizabeth, Paterson, and Newark, New Jersey; Detroit; Chicago; and other cities.[19]

In most of these situations, there were several civil-rights organizations with conflicting tactics and demands. In New York six major civil-rights groups [20] sought to present a united front by forming the Joint Committee on Equal Employment Opportunity (JCEEO), but there were several other competing groups, including the Greater New

York Coordinating Committee for Equal Opportunity, the Blue Ribbon Organization for Equal Opportunity Now, and the Ministers Committee on Job Opportunities for Brooklyn. These groups demonstrated independently of the JCEEO, and asked that Negroes be assigned quotas of the jobs on construction projects. The JCEEO, for example, asked that unions admit all qualified Negro and Puerto Rican journeymen to the unions and open apprenticeship programs to Negroes and Puerto Ricans at twice their proportion in the City's population "because the unemployment rate of these groups is twice that of white workers and because the historical exclusion of nonwhites from these trades has created an imbalance that needs correction." [21]

City and state officials usually responded to these demonstrations by closing the projects and attempting to get the building-trades unions to accept more Negroes. Mayor Wagner appointed a so-called "action panel" to seek a solution to the problem, but its recommendations were rejected by both the Negroes and the unions.[22] The Building and Construction Trades Council (BCTC) announced that it would not discriminate but would not lower its standards to accommodate anyone and would not accept "dictation by outside groups." The unions said they would launch their own program to get nonwhite journeymen and apprentices and threatened to "start picketing ourselves" if demonstrators stopped union members from going to work.[23] Union leaders also thought the demonstrations unfair to them because there were usually a number of Negroes on the picketed projects.[24]

After the action panel's recommendations were rejected, Mayor Wagner launched a program to recruit Negroes and Puerto Ricans for construction jobs by opening some twenty recruiting stations throughout the city; the Brooklyn ministers group, who seem to have had the support of Governor Rockefeller, opened four competing offices. Indeed, one of the mayor's stations was opened in the same building where the Brooklyn ministers had been recruiting.[25]

Political pressure also apparently was focused directly on some of the unions with poor reputations among Negroes. For example, it was reported that Plumbers Local 1, whose jurisdiction covered Brooklyn and Queens, agreed to "work out a procedure for identifying qualified minority apprentices." This agreement came "after meetings with various subcommittees of the Democratic Executive Council." Local 1 denied that minorities would be "jumped over whites" but said that the waiting list would be "mixed in at the top of the list." The union had six Negroes among its 3000 members, but all of the Negroes held "B" cards which permitted them to work on alterations at $3.25 an hour, whereas those with "A" cards worked on new construction at $5.15 an hour.[26]

The results of these recruiting drives proved disappointing to all concerned. After about a month, Mayor Wagner announced that the drive had resulted in only 2600 applications for jobs or union apprenticeship training, 60 per cent of which were from Negroes, 37 per cent from Puerto Ricans, and 3 per cent from people not included in the program.[27] The Brooklyn ministers' group had received about 1000 applications and a BCTC screening committee had referred only about 100 applicants to various unions.[28] Three months later it was reported that only 3121 had applied, and of these 1003 were not seeking apprentice or journeyman status, but were looking for positions as typists, printers, diamond cutters, elevator operators, janitors, and other jobs outside the building field. Only 849 of the applicants met minimum standards for journeymen or apprentices, and 167 of these were rejected for various reasons. Of the 682 remaining applicants, 537 qualified as apprentices and 109 as journeymen and were referred to local unions. The unions accepted 111 of the applicants, rejected two, and 28 failed to appear. A spokesman from the Referral Committee of the Building Industry noted that "We fully expect that all qualified applicants will be accepted consistent with job opportunities and openings in apprentice programs." [29] He also claimed that the report tended to show that the charges of discrimination against the building-trades unions was unjustified. "We had been led to believe," he said, "that there were thousands who couldn't gain admittance into the building trades unions. As a committee we felt that the numbers who came forward were small and that those qualified were even smaller in number." [30] A spokesman for the JCEEO branded the committee's report "an obvious and transparent attempt to blame the Negro community for a broad pattern of racial discrimination that characterizes the AFL-CIO building trades unions in this city." [31] The Brooklyn ministers' group also voiced their disappointment with efforts to get more building-trades jobs for Negroes. The ministers criticized city, state, industry, and union representatives for failing to take vigorous action "in opening union membership to nonwhite persons." [32] The ministers reported that of over 2000 applicants, only 31 workers had actually received jobs.[33]

An investigation of the building industry by the New York City Commission on Human Rights during these demonstrations found "a pattern of exclusion in a substantial portion of the building and construction industry which effectively bars nonwhites from participating in this area of the city's economic life." [34]   The CHR placed responsibility for this discrimination on employers, who "turned over the right to hire to others, notably to the trade unions under collective bargaining agreements with builders," and the unions, which imposed "almost insurmountable barriers" to nonwhites seeking union membership in a substantial number of the construction trades unions." [35] The Commission noted that "whenever the employer had control over hiring some nonwhites were employed. But in those trades where contractors traditionally relied upon the locals for referrals, nonwhites were effectively excluded from construction trades employment." Nonwhite journeymen were found by the CHR to face the union barriers of sponsorship requirements, discrimination in referrals, and priority given to out-of-town workers. Apprentices faced obstacles in the historical "for white only" clauses, "father-son" clauses, sponsorship requirements, withholding of apprenticeship information, restrictive recommendations, and apprenticeship-journeyman ratios.[36] The Commission's findings on Negro membership in various New York building trades unions are shown in Table 6-1.

While these developments were taking place, civil-rights groups in Cleveland adopted a more orderly and perhaps more important strategy to get Negroes into building-trades unions in that city. Of course, the Cleveland officials were influenced by repugnance at the demonstrations in other communities. Moreover, as we have seen, the effort to get Negroes into the Cleveland building-trades unions had been going on for some time. But the militant mood of the Negro community affected Cleveland no less than New York, Philadelphia, Chicago, and other places. And Cleveland Negroes generally considered construction unions to be among the worst anti-Negro organizations in the city.

However, a number of factors caused the Cleveland experience to be different from New York. Perhaps most important was the leadership of Cleveland's mayor, Ralph S. Locher, who had been involved (as law officer) in the earlier efforts to get Negroes admitted to IBEW Local 38 and who therefore already had some experience in dealing with union racial practices. Indeed, Locher felt that one of the difficulties in 1963 was that "more Negro apprentices weren't encouraged to enter the crafts," after the 1957 settlement; the mayor argued that if they had, "we wouldn't have this problem today." [37]   Moreover, Cleveland officials were particularly concerned about the possible adverse effects of racial demonstrations. "I have seen this picketing in New York," Mayor Locher said, "and I do not want it to happen here." [38]

Table 6-1

Racial Breakdown in Union Membership and Apprenticeship Programs, Selected Construction Unions, New York City, 1963

Union	Total Membership	Negro Members	Negro Apprentices	
Local 1, Elevator Constructors	2,300	3 maybe	No program	(*)
Local 1, Plumbers	3,000	9 (b) (nonconstruction)	2 in training (none completed)	(*)
Local 2, Plumbers and Steamfitters	4,100 total 3,800 A—Construction 300 B—Jobbing	16 approximately (A or B unknown)	2 or 3 in training (none completed)	(†)
Operating Engineers, Local 14, 14-B	1,600–1,750	23–50	No program	(**)
Local 15, A, B, C, D	4,500	8% approximately	Program pending approval of Board of Education	(**)
Local 28, Sheetmetal Workers	3,300	None	None	(†*)
Local 40, Ornamental Bridge, etc.	1,050	None (10% Indians)	None—0 in training 1 on waiting list	(**)
Local 46, Metallic Lathers Union	1,600–1,750	131 (via sister locals)	1 in training (1 on waiting list)	(*)
Local 60, Plasterers and Masons	2,080	300	None completed 5	(†*)
Local 638, Steamfitters	6,800 Total 4,000 Construction 2,800 Service	None 200 (via organizing in past couple years)	6 in training (none completed)	(**)
Carpenters and Joiners, 42 locals	34,000	5,000	In predominantly Negro locals	(†)

* Extracted from Hearing proceedings.
† Extracted from Report of New York State Advisory Committee to the U. S. Commission of Civil Rights on Discrimination in the Building Trades, August 1, 1963.
Source: New York City Commission on Human Rights, *Bias in the Building Trades: An Interim Report to the Mayor*, 1963, pp. 39–40.

Cleveland civil-rights organizations not only presented a relatively solid front through the United Freedom Movement (UFM) but also presented specific and clear-cut demands to city officials and unions. This contrasts vividly with the dissension within the civil-rights movements in and around New York.

The role of various international unions in the Cleveland experience is not clear, but it appeared for a while that the main union involved, the UA, would use sanctions against its Cleveland affiliate, and though the international apparently backed down after being defied by its Cleveland local, the sanctions threatened were plausible enough to have at least given pause to the local's leaders. At the request of Mayor Locher, a high-ranking official of the U. S. Department of Labor who was highly regarded by building-trades unionists, and Donald Slaiman, assistant director (later director) of the AFL-CIO Civil Rights Department also were involved in the Cleveland negotiations.

Although the Cleveland settlement was reached without the violence that occurred in other places, and probably has greater potential for gaining Negro entry into unions, we do not mean to imply that there was no difficulty in Cleveland or that that settlement was not reached without trouble. But let us take a closer look at the events in Cleveland.

In July 1963 the UFM announced that it would picket the Mall, a city building project, unless three Negro electricians and two Negro plumbers were hired.[39] This threat led to negotiations by representatives of the AFL-CIO, the UFM, the Community Relations Board (CRB), the U. S. Department of Labor, and the unions and contractors. During the first series of negotiations, the IBEW said that it had only two Negro electricians (of 1400 members) so would not be able to supply the UFM's demands (though it later turned out that three Negroes were members of the local).[40] The Plumbers (who had no Negroes in a local of 1300 members) were considering the applications of six Negro journeymen and a master plumber, but their applications were being delayed by procedural problems. Mayor Locher felt that Negroes should be hired on the project because it was being built with public funds. When the first negotiations failed to produce satisfactory results, the UFM announced that it would place 1000 pickets at all entrances to the Mall project, and seek to have city and federal funds withdrawn from the apprenticeship training programs of all discriminating unions. After this threat the IBEW agreed to accept two Negro apprentices on the Mall project, and the Plumbers agreed to accept two Negro journeymen and to process other Negro applications in its regular manner.[41] All parties expressed dissatisfaction with this compromise, but it was generally considered to have ended the conflict.[42]

The matter was far from settled, however, because rank-and-file union members still had to be reckoned with. When two Negro plumbers (who were described as "house plumbers") were hired on the Mall project, eleven Plumbers union members walked off the job, and were followed by forty-four pipe fitters and asbestos workers. However, 200 union members stayed on the job when they were told by their leaders that this dispute was none of their business.[43] A general organizer for the UA came to Cleveland and announced that the whole thing was a mistake, and had occurred mainly because the contractor had not given the workers sufficient notice that the Negroes were being hired. However, the Plumbers local later voted to declare a "holiday" to begin Monday, July 29, obviously to protest the hiring of the Negro workers on the Mall project. The Plumbers' general organizer announced that "There'll be no holiday—nor any other day—it's not being recognized. Any union plumber taking it takes it on his own, and he may be fired." [44] Only 700 of the city's 1400 plumbers went to work on Monday and the boycott of the Mall project continued thereafter. Faced with this obvious defiance by the local union, the general organizer announced that the international had "no problem" and that it was up to the contractor to "move the situation." Company and union representatives suggested that the dispute be settled by making the two Negroes apprentices instead of journeymen, but the UFM objected, since the July 20 agreement called for two journeymen. The UFM renewed its threat to picket the Mall project.

The local Plumbers' leaders naturally denied that their actions were dictated by racial bias. The local's secretary-treasurer claimed that membership was open to all who qualified and that six Negro applications were being processed. The union had to carefully screen applicants, he argued, because "We believe that eventually every plumber will get into the home, and it is for the protection of the general public that we require character reference." [45] Another local official said that the Negroes' lack of union membership was the main issue in the "holiday," because no "self-respecting union man would work alongside nonunion men. The fact that the two men were Negroes had nothing to do with it." [46] The Plumbers' general organizer felt that the whole thing was caused by a "few rabble-rousers" in the union who had persuaded the others. He felt that the chief issue was international intervention in a local matter; in his opinion, the holiday's main purpose was "to express a little dissatisfaction." [47]   A spokesman for the plumbing contractor being boycotted thought the "holiday" represented increasing disenchantment by the union's rank-and-file against the union leaders who were urging them to return to work.[48]

After lengthy negotiations, the dispute was settled on August 4, 1963, by representatives of the United Freedom Movement, Plumbers Local 55, the company, the City of Cleveland, John F. Henning, Under Secretary of Labor, and Donald Slaiman, Civil Rights Department, AFL-CIO. The terms of this agreement are sufficiently important to be quoted in full:

1. Local 55 agrees to sign labor contracts with the Negro Plumbing contractors and as of the date of the signing of the contract by the contractors and the union, *all Negro journeymen who are employed by such contractors will be admitted to membership in Local 55 as journeymen, upon successful passage of the journeyman's examination given by the Examining Board of Local 55;* and all apprentices who are employed by such contractors will be admitted as apprentices upon successful passage of the apprentice examination given by the Joint Apprentice Committee in accordance with the Constitution of the United Association of Journeymen and Apprentices.

   In the event an applicant for status as a journeyman feels that the examination given to qualify him for such status was unfairly administered or graded, *a review committee composed of a nominee of the U. S. Department of Labor, a nominee of the* United Association International Union of Journeymen and Apprentices, and a third member nominated by the United Freedom Movement shall have the right to review the administration and grading of the examination.
2. It is further agreed that a part of the Mall Construction job relating to plumbing will be sublet to a Negro contractor who will employ Messrs. Hilliard and Baker [the Negro plumbers involved in the dispute] as journeymen plumbers and Messrs. Hilliard and Baker in turn will be *admitted to membership in Local 55 in accordance with the Constitution* of the United Association of Journeymen and Apprentices.
3. Local Union 55 agrees that the Apprenticeship Training Program will be open to Negro applicants on the same basis as all other apprentices starting with the acceptance of applications on August 7, 1963.
4. The foregoing agreement was entered into in the presence of a representative of the Negro Plumbing Contractors who agreed to undertake the obligation required of the Negro Plumbing Contractors. [Emphasis added.]

The Cleveland agreement was suggested as a model for other settlements by Herbert Hill, NAACP labor secretary, who called it "the most significant breakthrough that we have had anywhere in the country." [49]   It was generally recognized that this compact not only resolved the immediate conflict of the plumbers on the Mall project, but also opened up the possibility of a large influx of Negroes into the union. It is particularly noteworthy that the Negroes who were rejected could appeal to an outside agency. On August 15, Local 55 admitted a Negro contractor with his four journeymen and two apprentices.

The Plumbers' settlement was no sooner announced, however, than efforts to get a Negro into the local Sheet Metal Workers Union again threatened to close the Mall project. When fourteen white sheet metal workers refused to work with a newly hired Negro, the contractor let him stay in a company trailer on the project, and the local's executive board ordered the sheet metal workers back to work.[50] The UFM again threatened to picket the project, but, in an apparently stormy meeting, was persuaded by a Negro trade unionist—who was also labor advisor to the UFM—and another UFM leader to wait until the local had a chance to act on the Negro's application.[51] When the Negro was considered by the union at its September meeting, however, he was denied membership on the ground that he had not passed the examination. The UFM, however, did not protest the union's action and apparently considered the Negro's failure legitimate.

The 1963 experiences suggest several conclusions. First, although civil-rights organizations are able to draw public attention to racial discrimination through these demonstrations, they also involve some dangers, the most important of which is that they might lead to violence, especially where union members feel that they are being unjustly accused. Moreover, these experiences indicate that negotiations will be more effective if the objectives sought are specific and clear. There is also a danger in a proliferation of demonstrating organizations, each seeking to impress the Negro community that it is more militant than the others. Demonstrations can provide bases for negotiations, but effective negotiations presuppose organizations on both sides with power to speak for and bind their constituents. There was a marked contrast between the United Freedom Movement in Cleveland and the numerous organizations in New York and New Jersey. In Cleveland the more disciplined UFM produced jobs for Negroes through negotiations with less difficulty. In New York negotiations were impossible because no organization spoke for Negroes. This problem was solved in industrial relations through the representation elections supervised by the National Labor Relations Board. It might not be feasible to provide similar machinery for Negroes, but there is an obvious need for unity among civil-rights groups during demonstrations. There also is room for competition among civil-rights groups, but the contests should be judged on such relevant standards as who can achieve specific objectives and not, as is presently too often the case, on the basis of which organization can make the most noise and claim the most credit for the few successful breakthroughs that do occur.

Summary and Conclusions

Before we examine the impact of unions and other factors on economic opportunities for Negroes, several conclusions concerning unions that bar Negroes from membership by informal means should be noted.

1. Racial exclusion by informal means is not restricted to any particular geographic area. Though restriction is undoubtedly more rigid in the South, there are some unions that have more Negro members in the South than some other places: the trowel trades, Longshoremen, Teamsters, Roofers, Hod Carriers and Common Laborers, and Hotel and Restaurant Employees. These trades have been practiced by Negroes in the South because they have been traditionally regarded as "Negro work" and because Negroes have sufficient supplies of labor to protect their interest and to protect employers who might be boycotted by whites. These occupations also have relatively old and stable techniques, making it difficult for unions to exclude Negroes by monopolizing the latest technology, as they have in electricity and plumbing. It has been common practice in some industries and occupations in the South for Negroes to be displaced when operations are mechanized.

2. Some of the craft unions have had equalitarian racial policies and some industrial unions have refused to admit Negroes, but as a rule the unions that practice exclusion are craft organizations. Craft locals have the ability to exclude Negroes from membership and from the trade if they can control the labor supply. Industrial unions, on the other hand, organize workers after they are hired. In addition, craft unions at the local level consider it to their advantage to exclude workers, whereas industrial unions consider it to their advantage to organize extensively.

3. These factors, however, are not sufficient to identify the general character of excluding unions. We have already noted some of these factors as they relate to formal exclusion by railroad unions, but there are other considerations. Because of the equalitarian trend in race

relations, older unions, other things being equal, seem more likely to exclude minorities than new unions. When the employer determines the hiring policy and therefore decides whether Negroes are to be hired, Negroes are likely to be excluded from such jobs as plumbing, milk delivering, and electrical work, which require home deliveries or repairs; apparently there have been widespread "understandings" that Negro males should not be permitted to work on jobs where they are likely to come in contact with the public. Whites are also likely to attempt to exclude Negroes from certain status jobs. And, in some cases, exclusion is directed against all except a particular nationality group; it has been common practice in the building trades and some garment unions, for instance, for locals to be restricted to a particular nationality group.

4. The foregoing evidence demonstrates widespread racial discrimination, but it should be emphasized that racial restrictions by the building-trades unions are not due entirely to racial reasons. Craft unionists are likely to have strong feelings of property rights in their crafts and their unions. They feel that these property rights have been won through years of training and fighting to build and strengthen unions. Any encroachment on either their jobs or their traditional union practices are likely to be resented—whether the encroachment comes from the international union, governments, or civil-rights organizations. There seems to be a pervasive belief among building-trades unionists that civil-rights groups are striving for special treatment for Negroes at the expense of the unions' members. Many craft union members have strong depression-created fears of unemployment; these fears are reinforced by the casual nature of the construction industry. In short, much of what appears to be discrimination by building-trades unions is in reality resentment at outside pressures. In these circumstances, discrimination is obviously also a factor, but union members are less likely to be motivated by racial prejudices than determination to win the contest against outside interference.

FOOTNOTES

1. Arnold M. Rose, *Union Solidarity,* Minneapolis: University of Minnesota Press, 1952, Ch. 5.
2. See the Appendix to Chapter 7, Tables A-4 and A-5.
3. Otis Finley, "Labor at the Crossroads in Race Relations," statement to the Fifteenth Convention of the Massachusetts and Rhode Island Association of Electrical Workers, Boston, October 2, 1959.
4. U. S. Commission on Civil Rights, *Reports on Apprenticeship,* January 1964, p. 140.

5. *Ibid.*, p. 59.
6. Joint wire from the Building and Construction Trades Department, AFL-CIO, to Richard Nixon, George Meany, and James Mitchell, February 26, 1960.
7. Report by the Commissioners' Council on Human Relations, Washington, D. C., 1963; personal interview with Donald Slaiman, director, AFL-CIO Civil Rights Department, July 30, 1964.
8. Connecticut Supplement, 125–7; *Connecticut Law Journal*, October 7, 1952, p. 2; IBEW Local 35 v. Commission on Civil Rights, Conn. Supreme Court of Errors, October Term, 1953. IBEW Local 35 v. Commission on Civil Rights, Superior Court, Hartford County, Conn., File No. 90352, March 26, 1954.
9. The following are typical comments from various cities concerning the Plumbers' racial practices:

    Akron, O.: "Because there are no Negro members in the union and because we know of Negroes having been refused journeyman and apprenticeship status, we consider the practices of the union unfavorable."

    Anderson, Ind.: "No Negro members. Apprenticeship opportunities not available to Negro youth."

    Cincinnati, O.: "The plumbers are exclusively all (with negligible exceptions) white. Since there are a fair number of Negroes doing the skilled jobs for non-union contracting firms, and since many union contractors accept Negroes for the common labor jobs, it seems unlikely that all union contractors adamantly refuse to hire Negroes for any skilled classification. It seems more reasonable to assume that the Plumbers union has consciously and systematically excluded Negroes."

    Columbus, O.: "Negroes are excluded from membership. The transfer cards of Negroes coming into the Columbus area are not honored. Apprenticeship programs not open to Negroes."

    Tampa, Fla.: "Strongly anti-Negro throughout the South. No Negro membership likely unless change in policy."

    San Francisco, Calif.: "Outstanding resistance by some unions have made it virtually impossible to place Negroes in certain categories of craft union skill. The Plumbers Union is one of the worst offenders."

    Pittsburgh, Pa.: "No Negro membership. There are approximately 20 Negro journeymen plumbers in Pittsburgh who work primarily for small Negro contractors."

    Portland, Ore.: "Since the passage of the Oregon State law against discrimination and the filing of complaints against some of the unions, there has been a relaxing of resistance to minority membership. However, some are still persistently trying to evade the law, particularly the Plumbers and Pipefitters."
10. National and local craft unions have different interests with respect to organizing; nationals gain power by expansion whereas locals gain power by exclusion and controlling the supply of labor.
11. See, for example, speech delivered to the Sixth National Legislative Conference of the Building and Construction Trades Department of the AFL-CIO, Washington, D. C., March 14, 1960; the N. Y. State Commission Against Discrimination, "Apprentices, Skilled Craftsmen and the Negro: An Analysis," 1960; Ben D. Segal, "The Practices of Craft Unions in Washington, D. C., with Respect to Minority Groups," in *Civil Rights in the National Capital*, Washington National Association of Intergroup Relations Officials, November

1959, p. 35; Memo to the writer from David Sawyer, executive director of the Commissioners' Council on Human Relations, Washington, D. C., June 3, 1959; Herman D. Bloch, "Craft Unions—a Link in the Circle of Negro Discrimination," *Phylon*, Fourth Quarter, 1958; "Craft Unions and the Negro in Historical Perspective," *Journal of Negro History*, January 1958; Herbert Northrup, *Organized Labor and the Negro*, New York: Harper, 1944, Ch. 2; National Planning Association, Committee on the South, *Negro Employment in the South*, New York, 1955; Herbert Hill, "Organized Labor and the Negro Wage Earner," *New Politics*, Winter 1962, and "Labor Unions and the Negro," *Commentary*, December 1959; National Urban League, "Negroes and the Building Trades Unions," New York, Industrial Relations Department, mimeo, n.d.; U. S. Commission on Civil Rights, Reports on Apprenticeship, January 1964; New York City Commission on Human Rights, *Bias in the Building Industry, An Interim Report to the Mayor*, December 13, 1963.

12. *New York Times*, May 16, 1963.
13. *Ibid.*, May 30, 1963.
14. Daniel Neifeld, "Civil Rights: Philadelphia," *Labor Today*, August–September, 1963, p. 18.
15. *Ibid.*
16. *Cleveland Plain Dealer*, August 8, 1963.
17. *New York Times*, August 13, 1963.
18. *Ibid.*, August 7, 1963.
19. *Ibid.*, June 30, 1963; July 10, 20, 25, and 30; August 13 and 15, 1963.
20. NAACP, Urban League, Association of Catholic Trade Unionists, Workers Defense League, Congress of Racial Equality, and the Negro-American Labor Council.
21. *New York Times*, July 8, 1963.
22. *Ibid.*, July 13, 1963.
23. *Ibid.*, July 18, 1963.
24. *Ibid.*, July 4 and 17, and November 14, 1963.
25. *Ibid.*, August 20, 1963.
26. *Ibid.*, June 21, 1963.
27. *Ibid.*, September 14, 1963.
28. *Ibid.*
29. *Ibid.*, December 19, 1963.
30. *Ibid.*
31. *Ibid.*, December 20, 1963.
32. *Ibid.*, January 30, 1964.
33. *Ibid.*
34. N. Y. City Commission on Human Rights, *Bias in the Building Industry, An Interim Report to the Mayor*, December 13, 1963, p. 10.
35. *Ibid.*, pp. 11–12.
36. *Ibid.*, pp. 12–16.
37. *Cleveland Press*, July 18, 1963.
38. *Cleveland Plain Dealer*, July 19, 1963; see also *Plain Dealer* editorial, July 22, 1963.
39. *Cleveland Press*, July 30, 1963.
40. *Cleveland Plain Dealer*, July 30, 1963.
41. *Ibid.*, July 21, 1963.
42. *Ibid.*

43. *Ibid.*, July 24, 1963.
44. *Ibid.*, July 28, 1963.
45. *Ibid.*, July 29, 1963.
46. *Ibid.*
47. *Ibid.*, July 28, 1963.
48. *Ibid.*, July 31, 1963.
49. *New York Times*, August 9, 1963.
50. *Cleveland Plain Dealer*, August 8, 1963.
51. *Ibid.*, August 20, 1963.

CHAPTER 7

Some Factors Influencing
Negro Job Opportunities

IT SHOULD NOT BE CONCLUDED FROM OUR EMPHASIS ON DISCRIMI-
nation that unions are mainly responsible for the Negro's economic
disadvantages or that they have done nothing to help him. Although
it would greatly enhance our knowledge of this problem if we knew
precisely how important discrimination (by unions or employers) was
relative to the complex of forces responsible for the Negro's condition, it unfortunately is not possible to completely disentangle individual factors from the constellation influencing the Negro's welfare.
In this chapter, however, we shall at least attempt to deduce some
of the more important elements in this constellation in order to even
approximate the union's relation to the whole. We shall first examine
the evidence with respect to the Negro's occupational status, and then
discuss some of the factors responsible for that status.[1] As we have
done with previous topics, general propositions will be illustrated with
specific cases.

Racial Employment Patterns

It is relatively easy to describe racial employment patterns because the overwhelming weight of evidence shows that Negroes are concentrated disproportionately in unskilled, menial jobs, are rarely promoted to supervisory positions over whites, and occupy skilled jobs mainly in Negro communities or occupations traditionally reserved for Negroes. Moreover, although Negroes improved their occupational positions between 1940 and 1960, they still had a long way to go to approximate the white patterns. Furthermore, improvements in racial employment patterns through shifts to better jobs have shown remarkable rigidity through time and differ geographically only in degree.[2]

Factors Influencing Negro Employment Patterns

These general facts concerning Negro employment are scarcely subject to debate, but the complex of interrelated factors producing these patterns makes it less clear why Negroes occupy inferior occupational positions. An important impediment to the Negro's ability to acquire skilled jobs is undoubtedly his easy identification and the image of inferiority stamped upon him by slavery. Not having worked in a variety of skilled, technical operations, Negroes have become stereotyped for certain jobs by employers, white workers, and even themselves. Since the Negro is regarded by many whites as an inferior person, those who would perpetuate the feeling of superiority for their crafts or occupations often seek to bar Negroes. Nor is this factor peculiar to the South. A New York study, for example, discovered that whites suddenly found the jobs they had been doing onerous and degrading when Negroes were hired for them.[3]

Negroes are also restricted in their employment opportunities by a host of cultural and social factors. Since Negroes usually live in segregated neighborhoods, and are more likely to be dominated by their mothers and other female relatives because of the absence of fathers from a large number of Negro homes, they rarely learn about jobs with few or no Negroes in them, and they apply for the kinds of jobs they know they can get. Aspirations are conditioned by one's associates, so few Negroes are motivated to try for skilled jobs.[4] And since nepotism and amicism play such important roles in job opportunities, Negroes tend to be restricted to the jobs they already hold.

Education and training

Negroes are also inadequately prepared through education and training to compete on an equal basis with whites. The educational level of nonwhites is improving,[5] but it still lags behind the level for whites by almost three years.[6] Only 15.6 per cent of nonwhites had four years of high school or college in 1960 as compared with 32.5 per cent for whites.[7] Levels of formal education do not tell the whole story, however, because Negroes have usually had inferior education, and actual levels of education generally bear little relationship to ability.[8]

Vocational and apprentice training

Negroes have also had inadequate vocational and apprenticeship training as compared with whites. Even while they are in vocational schools, moreover, Negroes are usually at a disadvantage because they have relatively less formal education than whites.[9]

In addition, vocational school training frequently perpetuates Negroes in traditional occupations. The usual practice in the South, for instance, has been to have segregated vocational schools where Negroes are trained only for occupations they have traditionally held. There are, however, some excellent vocational training schools in the South associated with Negro colleges, but the graduates of these schools usually are unable to acquire additional apprenticeship training to become journeymen. These schools also offer limited opportunities because they are only open to high-school graduates, a qualification that bars most Negroes in the South.

Civil-rights organizations have given considerable attention in recent years to apprenticeship training as a means of upgrading Negroes. Attention has been focused on this type of training by the fewness of Negroes in such programs and the decline in the unskilled and semiskilled jobs in which these workers have been concentrated. Negroes can reduce their rate of unemployment relative to whites by moving into skilled categories which have lower rates of unemployment,[10] though in the short run their higher rates of unemployment cannot be entirely eliminated by upgrading, because Negroes have higher rates of unemployment at every occupational level.[11]

Negro leaders are also motivated to seek greater apprenticeship training for Negro youths by the belief that this training is probably going to be increasingly important for the expanding skilled trades

of the future.[12]   Vocational training has rarely given students sufficient practical and theoretical training to equip them to become well-
rounded craftsmen.   Apprenticeship also has important advantages
over other means of acquiring skilled trades (armed forces, "picking-
it-up," and upgrading within plants); and assumes greater importance
as technological innovations increase the need for well-trained craftsmen.   Around 1960, however, apprenticeship training furnished only
about 70,000 to 80,000 of the 500,000 skilled craftsmen needed each
year.[13]   Although apprenticeships have been a relatively small source
of skilled workers generally, they have been very important to the
construction industry.[14]   Even so, it is estimated that apprenticeship
training will furnish a relatively small proportion of the projected
needs of skilled building tradesmen by 1970 unless something is done
to improve apprenticeship policies and increase the number of apprentices.[15]   Probably, therefore, Negro leaders have placed far too
much emphasis on apprenticeship training as a means of providing
jobs for Negroes.   Reforms in vocational, technical, and general education are quantitatively much more important.

For whatever reasons, relatively few Negroes have participated in
apprentice training.   In New York, for example, of 10,111 apprentices
in 1950 only 152 were nonwhite; in 1959 only 2 per cent of 15,000
New York apprentices were nonwhite.[16]   A Connecticut survey of
graduates of programs registered with the State Apprenticeship Committee between September 1952 and June 1954 could identify only
eight Negroes among 1509 graduates.   Even though a precise count
of Negro apprentices was not possible, partly because of the unco-
operative attitude of the State Apprenticeship Council, this study concluded that ". . . it seems fairly conclusive the Negroes possess decidedly limited opportunities for acquiring training in certain of the
highly skilled trades." [17]

The more recent evidence indicates some improvement in Negro
apprenticeship opportunities, but many programs still have no Negro
participants.   For example, a 1963 survey of apprentices in the District of Columbia found no Negro apprentices in the Asbestos Workers, Painters, Stone Masons, Lathers, Photoengravers, Glaziers, Web
Pressmen, or Tile Setters joint programs.   However, Negroes were
participating in the District of Columbia International Brotherhood
of Electrical Workers, Pipefitters, and Plumbers programs from which
they had previously been excluded; these programs had nine, four,
and seven Negro apprentices respectively in October 1963.   Negro
apprentices were also participating in a number of other joint programs from which they had not recently been excluded.   The Car-

penters had only five Negroes of 312 apprentices, but took in about 25 Negroes after July 1963. Typographical Local 101 had 50 Negroes of 228 apprentices, the Operating Engineers had 18 Negroes of 95. Ten of 40 apprentices in the Bindery Workers' program and 10 of 21 in the Cement Masons' program were Negroes. The Bricklayers had only 11 apprentices but five of these were Negroes. All other programs had fewer than five Negro apprentices in July 1963.[18] The most notable gain by Negro apprentices in an IBEW local was the admission of 140 Negroes and 60 Puerto Ricans in a group of some 1000 apprentices admitted in 1962 to Local 3 in New York.[19] Another potentially very important innovation for Negro participation in apprenticeship programs is the establishment of the statewide California Plan for Equal Employment Opportunity, which was instigated in 1959 by the California AFL-CIO's Civil Rights Committee. Various state and federal agencies concerned with apprenticeship participated in the California plan which has established apprenticeship information centers and aims to actively encourage Negroes and other minorities to enter apprenticeship programs. Although it is too early to evaluate the California program, it caused a decided relative increase in Negro apprentices. They were still only 2.2 per cent of the total in that state in 1962.[20] The Urban League and other groups have also set up apprenticeship information centers in Washington, D. C., Philadelphia, Baltimore, Boston, Cincinnati, and Chicago.[21] And in June 1964, Secretary of Labor Willard Wirtz announced plans to establish a network of youth opportunity centers in 105 cities.

In spite of modest improvements, therefore, Negro participation in apprenticeship programs continued to be very low. In Connecticut, Negroes constituted only 0.6 per cent of apprentices in 1950 and 0.7 per cent in 1960.[22] Moreover, the advisory committees to the U. S. Commission on Civil Rights in Florida, New York, Maryland, Tennessee, New Jersey, and Wisconsin reported relatively few Negroes in apprenticeship programs in those states.[23]

How are we to account for the Negro's lack of participation in apprenticeship programs? The answer to this question is far from clear, but some of the more important factors include:

1. Union exclusion. Most apprenticeship programs in the building trades, for example, are jointly administered by unions and employers, though unions frequently in fact control the programs.[24] It might be argued that unions do not limit the total number of apprentices because nonunion employers indenture no more apprentices than union employers,[25] but it cannot be denied that unions limit the total number of Negro apprentices. The union's motives for restricting appren-

tices are the same as the motives for formal or informal exclusion discussed earlier.   Indeed, control of apprenticeship is one important device for restricting entry.

2. Cultural factors.   As already noted, few Negroes apply for apprenticeship training, probably because of a general belief that they will be excluded, but also because many Negroes who could qualify for this training are more interested in the professions.   After all of these factors are accounted for, however, the evidence from every section of the country supports the conclusion that Negroes have been denied apprenticeship training solely because of their race.   Since 1961 a few unions have actively sought qualified Negro applicants, which is perhaps the best way for some craft unions to take affirmative action to improve the employment opportunities for Negroes.

3. General economic conditions.   Since fixed ratios of apprentices to journeymen are common, there are limited opportunities for apprentices when journeymen are unemployed.   There is also greater resistance to Negroes entering the skilled trades when white craftsmen are unemployed.   Paradoxically, though, when conditions improve many Negroes (and whites) drop out of (or refuse to enter) apprenticeship training because there are more lucrative alternatives that require less rigorous or lengthy training.   Apprentices are characteristically paid 50 per cent of journeyman wages, an important deterrent to nonwhites who have lower incomes than whites and perhaps cannot receive support from their families; indeed, minority youths frequently must help support their families.[26]

4. Management attitudes.   Before apprentices can be indentured, they must normally get jobs.   Management attitudes therefore condition the extent to which Negroes will be barred from apprenticeship training.   This is particularly true of the majority of apprenticeship training programs in plants, which are typically controlled exclusively by management.

In-plant training

Many workers also acquire greater skill through on-the-job training programs of varying degrees of formality.   Here again, however, few Negroes participate in upgrading programs leading to the more highly skilled and supervisory or management positions (see the appendix to this chapter).   Since it is frequently assumed that Negroes will not be promoted to skilled or managerial positions, management has hired Negroes who are generally unqualified for promotion.   This, as we shall see, was an important obstacle to the upgrading of Negroes in those Southern plants that reduced the formal barriers to upgrading after 1950.

Management policies are important determinants of the extent to which Negroes are promoted within plants because management controls promotion. There is, moreover, ample evidence that management is prejudiced against using Negroes in skilled and supervisory categories.[27] The prevailing management attitude seems to be that Negroes are not suited for skilled jobs or that customers or white workers will react unfavorably to the upgrading of Negroes. It goes without saying that it is unfair and false to apply these stereotypes to individual Negro workers. Although there is some ground for the fear of white worker reaction, the evidence seems conclusive that a firm management position on upgrading will usually prevent overt reaction from white workers, especially where management's policies are supported by the local or international union. It takes a very strong local union to defy both the international and the employer. It is sometimes argued that employers have no status reasons to oppose upgrading because top management's status is not threatened by promoting Negroes. This is only partly true, however, because in the South management representatives frequently fear the loss of status in the community if they take unpopular racial action.

Management has historically preferred Negro workers for certain kinds of jobs or for certain of their attributes. Since there is a tendency for whites to leave undesirable jobs when economic conditions improve, management has found that Negroes are more dependable in these occupations because they are "locked in" by limited occupational mobility. Moreover, many managers believe that Negroes are "better suited" than whites for hot, disagreeable work requiring great physical strength. Some Southern employers also have expressed preferences for Negroes for certain kinds of cargo unloading because they have better "rhythm." Moreover, employers have historically been willing to hire Negroes in preference to whites because of racial wage differentials and because Negroes were considered to be safeguards against unionism. The great transformation wrought by the New Deal, the CIO, and the Second World War eliminated this factor, however, because it virtually abolished racial wage differentials and changed the anti-union attitudes of important Negro leaders.

Management prejudices may be reinforced or counteracted by other factors. One such force is general market conditions, as indicated by the fact that Negroes have made their greatest occupational gains during the labor shortages accompanying the First and Second World Wars. The general pattern seems to be that when white males are not available, white women will be hired if they can do the work and are available, then Negro men and women will be hired in that order.[28]

The supply of labor is important because management will be more willing to hire Negroes in particular categories when enough colored craftsmen are available to do the work if whites quit (which they will rarely do in industrial jobs) or boycott particular employers (which is relatively easy to do in construction work). Moreover, the knowledge that there are enough Negroes to do the work will usually deter whites who might otherwise be inclined to leave good jobs.[29] In other cases where the jobs are less desirable, the introduction of Negroes has caused whites to quit and be replaced by Negroes, but employers are willing to risk losing white employees if there are sufficient Negroes to take their places.[30] Thus, if the employer has some other reason to hire or promote Negroes, like wartime labor shortages, pressure from the Negro community or governmental agencies, he will be inclined to do so if the supply of Negroes is adequate.

Employers' policies also have been changed by pressures from the government or Negro groups. It can be expected, moreover, that Negroes will continue to use their political power to overcome their economic disadvantages. The FEP laws together with the various government contract committees have undoubtedly caused upgrading of Negroes by employers who would not have done so in the absence of these measures. Several leading American economists have argued that "The industrial society *tends* to be an open society, inconsistent with the assignment of managers or workers to occupations or to jobs by traditional caste or *racial groups*, ..."[31] And another well-known University of Chicago economist thinks it "a striking historical fact that the development of capitalism has been accompanied by a major reduction in the extent to which particular . . . racial groups . . . have operated under special handicaps in respect to their economic activities. . . ."[32] Our analysis suggests, however, that if capitalism, industrialism, or the market *tended* to eliminate discrimination, they either worked with amazingly slow speed or we did not have these phenomena. The error in the argument that capitalists *tend* to be rational and therefore ignore race is the failure to consider that other forces (white worker reaction, community pressures, and so on) might make it just as "rational" for the employer to continue his racial discrimination unless other forces (government, Negro groups, for example) make it "rational" for him not to discriminate. Moreover, the evidence also suggests that many employers have prejudices which are not "rational." Our analysis suggests that racial discrimination in employment is part of a vicious cycle that responds to market conditions only under the most unusual conditions—such as war—and then only slowly.

The level of employment is an important factor influencing the Negro's ability to move up the occupational ladder, but it has had different effects at different stages. During periods of labor shortage, management appears increasingly willing to face the opposition of white employees and customers by upgrading Negroes. On the other hand, the activities of the federal contract committees, which threaten to deny government contracts to discriminating firms, suggest that management is probably more vulnerable to economic sanctions during recessions when the consequences of losing federal contracts are greatest. This has been an important factor behind the desegregation of seniority lines in the petroleum refining, rubber, paper, automobile, steel, and other industries in the South since 1954.

A number of factors influence the employer's vulnerability to pressures for equal treatment of Negroes. As will be seen below, where government contracts are important, employers have responded to governmental pressures for equal employment policies. Moreover, consumer-oriented employers are much more likely than those in basic industries like steel to respond to boycotts and other direct pressures from civil-rights groups. Employers also are more likely to adopt equalitarian employment policies where pressures are brought simultaneously on all employers in the industry. If the policies of all firms are changed at the same time, there is less likelihood of counterboycotts by whites. The extent to which a company is involved in local community affairs will also influence its racial policies. Merchants are more likely than raw material-oriented industries (like steel) to be concerned about the impact of racial violence on the economic development of an area.

It should also be noted that employer policies can change more rapidly than those of unions because companies are not democratic organizations.

Finally, it should be observed that employers are much more important than unions in the economic power structures of most communities, especially in the South. It is for this reason that business interests have been able to put an end to racial strife in many areas of the South. For whatever reasons, there is a noticeable tendency for management groups in every section of the country to reexamine and come to grips with their racial problems.

The influence of unions

Unions have had relatively more effect on the ability of Negroes to acquire skills on the railroads and in the construction trades than in industrial jobs. Since unions are normally strong enough in the former occupations to control upgrading, they have blocked the advancement of Negroes.[33] And where unions control the supply of labor and maintain de facto closed-shop conditions, they have been able to deny Negroes employment in the skilled trades by barring them from membership.

However, though craft locals have the ability to deny Negroes employment or to restrict their employment to certain areas, we have seen that statistics on the proportion of Negroes in various building trades fails to disclose any correlation with union growth, probably because the differences are qualitative and the impact of unions has not been to displace Negroes from occupations as much as it has been to displace them from the better jobs within those occupations.[34]

Unions also have been partly responsible for perpetuating employment segregation by maintaining segregated seniority rosters which restrict Negroes to certain menial jobs. This has been an important problem for industrial unions, but job segregation is more rigid where separate seniority rosters by crafts are formalized by having different unions in each craft, as is true, for instance, among longshoremen and on the railroads. Separate seniority rosters for Negroes and whites rarely are written into the contracts, but might be based on "informal" understandings that Negroes and whites will move into different jobs and that Negroes will never get jobs that will place them in supervisory positions over whites. Even those few firms following "equal employment" policies in the South have almost never promoted Negroes to positions over whites.

It would be a mistake, however, to conclude that unions caused segregated rosters, because racial divisions of labor existed long before unions were significant in the South. Indeed, the virtually unorganized Southern textile industry has had relatively few Negroes and rigid racial segregation. Almost without exception, moreover, those firms which have desegregated their lines of progression in the South are unionized. The impact of the union would appear to be to restrict the variety of work Negroes have been permitted to perform and to formalize existing lines of progression. The union can be accused of discrimination, however, where it fails to apply contracts equally and permits "informal" discriminatory practices to continue in violation of the contract.

It would likewise be a mistake to conclude that the impact of unions on Negro employment opportunities has been entirely negative. We have noted that unions have made it possible for Negroes to hold their positions in some industries by introducing the principle of seniority. Moreover, the existence of unions gives Negroes legal rights to equal treatment that they would not have if unions were not in the plants. For example, when a union is certified as bargaining agent by either the National Labor Relations Board or the National Mediation Board, it acquires the duty to represent all workers in the bargaining unit fairly, and the employer becomes jointly liable with the union for this duty.[35] A few unions have also actively sought to get Negroes hired and upgraded, and about one-fifth of the major contracts in effect in 1961 contained specific bars against discrimination.[36] Outstanding in this connection have been the United Packinghouse Workers, who have followed equalitarian policies more vigorously in the South than perhaps any other union. The Packinghouse Workers have not only worked to desegregate jobs and facilities within plants, but have taken other measures, including insistence upon nondiscrimination clauses in contracts, to get Negroes hired into a variety of jobs which were previously all white. A number of other unions, including the International Union of Electrical Workers; the Retail, Wholesale, and Department Store Union; the United Auto Workers; and the United Rubber Workers, have taken measures to protect Negro interests.

Unions have also improved the employment opportunities of minorities by promoting FEP legislation, and have been instrumental in causing the abolition of racial wage differentials, partly because the basic logic of the union must be the "common rule," but also for moral reasons. Perhaps the most important agency for removing racial wage differentials was the War Labor Board, but key cases were brought by such organizations as the Mine, Mill and Smelter Workers and the Oil Workers International Union.[37] Moreover, to the extent that unions have promoted wage leveling, they have benefited Negroes, who were concentrated in the lower-paying jobs.[38]

Taking unions as a whole, however, we must conclude that few of them have done much to improve the Negro's job conditions and opportunities where this was not incidental to such general objectives as wage equalization and wage leveling. This is partly because most union leaders at the local level frequently have seen no compelling reason to adopt equalitarian policies and most of those at the national and federation levels have lacked the power or incentive to actively promote the Negro's economic welfare, in the sense of actively encouraging Negroes to enter apprenticeship programs, as IBEW Local 3 did in New York, or actively opposing racial discrimination by employers as the UPWA, the UAW, the RWDSU, and a few other unions have done. Of course, some union leaders think it would be political suicide for them to take such affirmative measures, and perhaps it would. On the other hand, these leaders could make greater efforts to show the rank-and-file members the dangers to the labor movement of continued racial discrimination. Not only do wages suffer in some cases (painters and carpenters) where Negroes are forced to work for lower wages, but discrimination tends to weaken unions by dividing workers along racial lines. At a time when the labor movement seems to need vigorous leadership, it suffers when able leaders are held back through segregation or discrimination. And at a time when total union membership has been declining, the proportion of Negroes has been increasing relative to whites in the blue-collar occupations which are usually more highly unionized (see Chapter 7, Table A-7). Those crafts which have been able to insulate themselves through restrictions on Negro entry into the trades probably have a false sense of security. As we shall see in Part 3, these restrictive practices, which have legitimate trade-union reasons for existing, are being threatened by government regulation precisely because of these abuses. Much of the labor movement, the Negro community, and the federal government are likely to close ranks against these unions which are discrediting the entire labor movement.

We do not mean to imply, however, either that FEP legislation alone can solve the problem of equal employment opportunities for Negroes, or that it has had an appreciable effect on racial employment patterns. But legislation has established a framework that makes it easier for equalitarian procedures to be enforced. Because of the complexity and intractability of the factors responsible for racial employment patterns, effective changes will require the cooperation, and sometimes the conflict, of a variety of groups, including organizations of the aggrieved individuals, outside pressure groups and fact-finding organizations, governments, employers, and the regular internal union power structure. Any appreciable improvement in Negro employment levels must also require heroic efforts by the Negro community to prepare Negroes for better jobs if and when the racial barriers are lowered, as well as sincere efforts by all parties involved to affirmatively improve Negro job opportunities. These propositions can be illustrated by the Southern petroleum refining industry's experience with Negro employment.

Segregated Seniority Rosters: The Petroleum Refining Cases

One of the most important developments in racial labor relations since the Second World War has been the movement to eliminate segregated seniority rosters in industrial plants. Indeed, this movement started in the North during the Second World War and gained momentum in the South in the postwar period primarily because of legal pressures brought by the Negroes, especially through the NAACP. Although it is not possible to discuss all these experiences, an analysis of the Southern petroleum refining industry affords some insights into this problem.[39] The rubber, aircraft, pulp and paper, steel, and tobacco industries, however, have had similar racial employment patterns and experiences.

Besides the general agitation for racial equality during and after the Second World War, the factors which stimulated efforts to eliminate separate lines of progression in petroleum refining included the following. The industry was concentrated in the Southwest where patterns of racial segregation were less rigid than in the Southeast. Negroes were induced to take action because jobs in the industry were regarded as good and carried high pay relative to others available to Negroes. The kinds of jobs held by Negroes were being eroded by technological changes. The federal government was a major customer for most of the companies, making the threat of contract revocation serious for the highly competitive oil refineries. Finally, the main union in this industry, the Oil, Chemical and Atomic Workers (which succeeded the Oil Workers International Union, OWIU, in 1955) had taken an equalitarian racial position. Besides the opposition of white workers, the main unfavorable factor to the advancement of Negroes in the industry during this period was the decline in nontechnical employment.[40]

Racial employment patterns in Southwest petroleum refineries were similar to those of other industrial concerns in the area. Negroes traditionally were hired for the lowest-paid jobs, which were generally classified as "laborer" regardless of the kind of work done, and were commonly segregated into labor departments from which there was no advancement. To be sure, Negroes sometimes had such skilled jobs as are customarily held by Negroes in the area; it was not uncommon, for instance, to find Negro bricklayers in the refineries. In most of the refineries, especially in East Texas and Louisiana, cafeterias, rest rooms, drinking fountains, and other facilities commonly were segregated.

The pattern of job segregation symbolizes racial inferiority and denies advancement opportunities to Negroes, but it is not entirely without benefit for the colored workers involved. Informal job agreements sometimes protect Negro jobs from encroachment by whites and provide colored workers with more jobs than they might otherwise have. Given the racial preferences of employers and white workers, Negroes might not have obtained jobs in the refineries if it had not been done on a segregated basis. For instance, there is an almost negligible percentage of Negro workers in petroleum refineries outside the South.[41] Besides being barred from advancement, the forces that restricted Negroes to the lowest jobs in the refineries also caused them to be more subject to technological unemployment than white workers in other job categories.[42] Negroes also were disadvantaged by the sentiment among white workers that mechanized jobs are automatically "white" jobs.

The first significant breach in job discrimination in petroleum refining came during the Second World War, when the War Labor Board (WLB) ruled against racial wage differentials in that industry. When dispute cases came to the War Labor Board, it adopted a policy of ordering equal treatment of Negro, Mexican, and white workers, but it refused to order nondiscrimination clauses in contracts. In a case involving the Southport Refinery at Texas City, Texas, for instance, the WLB directed the company to institute a reclassification system and grant wage increases to its Negro employees which would "place them on a basis of economic parity with the white workers in the same classifications." [43]

Sporadic efforts to solve the oil industry's racial problems continued after the war, but it was not until around 1953 and the creation of President Eisenhower's Committee on Government Contracts that a sustained effort was made to eliminate segregated lines of progression in several major oil refineries. The PCGC was involved in most of these cases, but the Negro workers also used court action as a means of eliminating job segregation.

Gulf at Port Arthur

One of the most important of these cases involved the Gulf refinery at Port Arthur, Texas, and Local 23 of the OWIU. Local 23 represented the white workers at Gulf and the nearby Texaco refinery, and

Negroes were represented by Local 254, an all-Negro local. These locals had been organized originally in 1918 and reorganized in 1935, at which time the Negroes made segregation a condition of their affiliation with the OWIU. Locals 23 and 254 were jointly certified by the National Labor Relations Board as bargaining agent for the workers at Gulf in 1943; the OWIU could not have won the representation election without the support of the 1000 Negro workers because the union won by 1629 to 1096. The locals bargained with Gulf through a joint bargaining committee made up of representatives from each local. Before 1953, when Negroes elected to bid on previously all-white jobs, relations between the white and Negro union members at Gulf had been relatively peaceful. Local leaders attribute this condition to the fact that the international representative who organized the plant in 1935 was careful to teach the white workers the need for racial cooperation.

In 1953 Negro workers decided to break the informal "gentlemen's agreement" on the racial division of labor by bidding on previously all-white jobs. White union leaders at first sought to have the Negroes withdraw their bids, but, when the latter refused, told the company to honor the contract. Gulf managers said they did not care who did the work so long as it was done, so, after assuring themselves that the union leaders were willing to stand behind the company if trouble developed with the white rank-and-file, they moved a number of Negroes into jobs formerly held by whites.

Meanwhile Negro and white leaders agreed that since jobs were integrated, segregated groups within the bargaining unit were no longer necessary. They accordingly elected a bargaining committee by majority vote; since the whites had a majority, the new bargaining committee excluded Negroes entirely and negotiated a new contract effective April 17, 1954, which froze labor (Negro) and operating-mechanical jobs.

The Negroes decided to counter this discriminatory contract with court action against Local 23 for damages and a declaratory judgment alleging a violation of the duty of fair representation. The international union incurred the enmity of many white workers in Port Arthur by joining this suit *amicus curiae* on the side of its Negro members. After three years of litigation, it was ruled that the local was guilty of failure to represent fairly, but by the time a decision was finally reached in 1958, this matter had become moot because a new contract signed March 14, 1956, eliminated the separate lines of progression. Actually, Negroes had been given additional jobs despite the 1954 contract. The damage suit was continued, however, but the Negroes were denied damages on the grounds that no actual damages could be proved.[44]

By the time negotiations started on the 1956 agreement, white leaders were convinced that the preservation of the union required the adoption of equal job opportunities for Negroes, in spite of vigorous opposition by some whites. The Oil Workers faced pressures from all sides as white craftsmen sought to splinter off from the OWIU and get certified as separate bargaining units in order to prevent Negroes from moving into their jobs. The craftsmen were thwarted, however, by the no-raiding agreements between unions and seniority arrangements which would have required seceding craftsmen to enter the labor pool when they were laid off.

Thus, by the time of the 1956 negotiations, the local union's main threats came from the nondiscrimination clause in the company's federal contract and the Negroes' lawsuit. The main area in dispute was therefore not whether lines of progression would be integrated but under what conditions and how qualifications and seniority would be balanced. Management wanted to insure that top operators with long experience would not be displaced by senior Negro employees with limited experience. But Negroes wanted to advance on the basis of plant seniority (which included time in the Labor Division) instead of seniority in a particular line of progression.

The 1956 contract provided that Negroes with high-school diplomas could move out of the Labor Division into the line of progression for skilled jobs on the basis of a qualifying test which could be repeated every six months. It also provided that promotions would be made on the basis of seniority, provided the worker had served at least six months in the next lower classification to the one for which he was bidding, and provided further that management could decide, after a thirty-day trial, whether or not the employee was qualified.

The upgrading program adopted by Gulf and the OCAW made it possible for a number of Negroes to be promoted immediately. By 1958, 48 Negroes had moved into jobs previously reserved for whites and by 1959 the number of Negroes holding previously "white" jobs had increased to 78. Indeed, at one time when 60 jobs opened up, Negroes were able to get 40 of them, causing unrest among whites, some of whom started an unsuccessful movement to change the system that permitted Negroes to take the tests every six months until they were passed. More Negroes would probably have moved up at Gulf if there had not been shrinking employment in the company.[45]

Other cases

While these events were taking place at Gulf, the Negro workers at other refineries were taking similar action. At Shell in Houston, Texas, for instance, where OCAW Local 365 had bargaining rights, an agreement between the union, the PCGC, the company, and the Negroes opened all jobs on the basis of high-school diplomas and qualifications tests. This system lowered the formal barriers to Negro advancement, but it had little practical effect because very few of the 250 Negro employees had high-school diplomas.

The Oil Workers International Union became sufficiently concerned about the legal action taken against its locals at Port Arthur and other places to consult the CIO Civil Rights Committee for advice.[46] The international was in a difficult position because it did not have a majority of the industry organized and because all the lawsuits and PCGC complaints had been filed against its locals and not against its rivals—several strong independent unions, the Operating Engineers, Metal Trades Councils, Chemical Workers, and others. International officers wanted to minimize the internal breach caused by these suits, but at the same time they recognized the justice of the Negroes' case and joined them as a friend of the court against their own locals. Since about one-third of the international's membership was located in the South, mainly in Local 23 at Port Arthur, international officers were concerned that their support of the Negroes might provoke a rebellion in the South.

The Oil Workers' organizational and financial weaknesses caused that union to avoid an open break with recalcitrant locals while pushing them toward its policies with the aid of moral suasion and outside pressures. For example, the international permitted segregated locals, which it opposed in principle, at Port Arthur and Beaumont, Texas, until 1963.

After the Oil Workers complained about the absence of legal action against its rivals, the NAACP filed a number of suits with the PCGC against companies represented by other unions. In April 1955 complaints were filed against Esso at Baton Rouge, Louisiana, represented by an independent union with segregated sections; Cities Service[47] at Lake Charles, Louisiana, and the Lion Oil Company at El Dorado, Arkansas, represented by Metal Trades Councils; and Union Carbide Chemicals at Texas City, Texas, represented by the Operating Engineers. Complaints also were filed with the PCGC against a number of other companies and unions in the industry, including the Texas

Company at Port Arthur, and Magnolia at Beaumont, Texas, represented by the OCAW; and Humble at Baytown, Texas, represented by an independent union.

Management voluntarily integrated seniority rosters at the Sinclair refinery in Houston after attending a Dallas PCGC conference in May 1955. Moreover, Sinclair seems to have actively increased Negro employment at its Houston refinery while total employment was declining: in 1957 the company had 1917 employees and 235 Negroes, in 1958, 1901 and 262, and in 1959, 344 of 1873. Moreover, Sinclair had a Negro technician, two Negro supervisors, 47 Negroes in skilled and 74 in semiskilled positions. A February 1956 agreement at Magnolia (Socony-Mobil Oil), where there were segregated OCAW locals until 1963, made it possible for 32 Negro high-school graduates to move out of the labor department, and the company subsequently hired ten additional Negro high-school graduates.[48] At Humble in Baytown, which had an independent union at the time, 24 Negroes and 52 Mexican-Americans received temporary promotions, but only six of 130 Negroes tested and three Mexican-Americans received permanent appointments.[49] At Esso in Baton Rouge, 25 Negroes were transferred out of the labor division as a result of a 1955 complaint, though a 1959 layoff reduced this number to 18. In 1959 Esso had 7527 employees, 1200 of whom were Negroes, and in 1959 there were only about 700 Negroes and 5240 employees. Cities Service at Lake Charles had 1814 employees in 1957, 153 of whom were Negroes. In 1962 seven Negroes were reported to have been upgraded at Lake Charles. The PCGC complaint against Union Carbide and Operating Engineers Local 374 resulted in the upgrading of 16 Negroes.[50] No Negroes were upgraded directly as a result of the complaint against Lion Oil at El Dorado because Negroes refused to give up their seniority, as required by the contract, in order to transfer.

Another case resulting in the promotion of Negro employees involved the Celotex Corporation at Merrero, Louisiana. The Celotex case was similar to that of Shell at Houston in the sense that the Negro employees filed a lawsuit as well as a complaint with the PCGC against the company, the OCAW local, and the international.[51] The contract at Celotex contained a nondiscrimination clause, but a system of unwritten seniority established separate lines of progression, making it impossible for Negroes and some whites to bid into higher jobs; it was not necessarily true that Negroes had lower-paying jobs, however, because the highest-paid production worker in the plant at the time of this action was a Negro. The consent decree settling this case provided that unwritten seniority would continue only so long as the worker remained in his present job, and when jobs were changed for any reason the contract term would apply. This settlement, which took place in 1958, resulted in the promotion of 250 of the plant's 750 Negroes (of 1800 total employees) within one year.

There were a number of circumstances making the Celotex settlement relatively satisfactory for the Negro employees: both the company and the international union favored equal job opportunities for Negroes; whites as well as Negroes had been held back by the unwritten seniority system; the Negroes' legal position was strengthened by the federal contract and the nondiscrimination clause in the collective-bargaining agreement; and the Negroes in the bargaining unit formed a club to promote their interests within the union and the plant. The Negro club financed the legal advice and formulated the strategy to get Negroes upgraded.

Conclusions

This review of the postwar developments in the petroleum refining industry, which could be repeated for other industries, suggests several general conclusions concerning the elimination of job segregation.

1. There is obviously an important connection between economic conditions and the speed at which Negro employment opportunities can be improved. In petroleum refining, lowering racial employment barriers produced limited immediate results. (Approximately 553 promotions are attributable more or less directly to this activity in the eleven companies studied, though 250 were Celotex, 124 Sinclair, and 24 of the others were temporary. If we deduct these, there were only about 155 promotions at nine refineries.) And in some cases there appears to have been little change other than those effected immediately after the breakthrough because of declining job opportunities. On the other hand, poor market conditions in the industry undoubtedly made employers more vulnerable to threats of federal contract revocation, which was an important factor in the changes that did take place.

2. Whether reducing the racial employment barriers will produce more jobs, however, would also seem to depend upon the attitudes of management, the white workers, and the union. If management and the union are firm in their efforts to promote Negroes, resistance from white workers will usually be ineffective. The situation at Gulf in Port Arthur, for example, was complicated by the fact that the same local represented workers at Gulf, where there were many

Negroes and a white leadership relatively sympathetic to the Negroes' position, and the Texas Company, where there were fewer Negroes and a strong racist group within the local. At Sinclair, on the other hand, management appears to have taken affirmative action to actively promote Negro employment opportunities, and the union appears to have been a passive force.

3. Whether many Negroes are upgraded after racial barriers are lowered also depends on the particular promotion system. Negroes have better chances to get promoted where plantwide seniority is adopted, but can be blocked by various testing procedures; the nature of the tests is very important, because Negroes generally have been hired for menial jobs and usually have inferior education and training. However, if the tests are objective, and there is no limit on how often or the number of times they may be taken, senior Negroes can move up the line of progression relatively fast, as at Gulf and Celotex. Whether or not Negroes lose seniority when they move out of labor departments is also important, as indicated by the El Dorado case.

4. The petroleum experience also suggests a need for initiative and organization by the Negroes themselves. In every case where Negroes lowered racial employment barriers in this industry, it was through their own organizations, sometimes with the aid of the labor secretary of the NAACP.

5. Finally, these experiences suggest that no single force will usually be sufficient to lower racial employment barriers. In this industry pressures came from a variety of different and complementary sources.

FOOTNOTES

1. This chapter is based on my "Racial Factors Influencing Entry into the Skilled Trades," in Mark Perlman, Ed., *Human Resources in the Urban Economy*, Baltimore: Johns Hopkins University Press for Resources for the Future, 1963, p. 23.
2. For a more thorough discussion of racial employment patterns, see the Appendix: "Negro Employment Patterns."
3. Jacob Seidenberg, *Negroes in the Work Group*, Ithaca, N. Y.: Cornell University, New York State School of Industrial and Labor Relations, Bulletin No. 6, February 1950.
4. Persons concerned with improving the economic status of Negroes frequently stress the Negro's lack of motivation and failure to take advantage of available opportunities. The 1958 report of the Ohio Governor's Advisory Commission on Civil Rights said, for example: ". . . employers, Negroes, educators, and placement personnel repeatedly indicated that the Negro had not taken full advantage of training and educational opportunities and means

should be found to encourage him to motivate him to do so in the future."
See also William E. Amos and Jane Perry, "Negro Youth and Employment
Opportunities," *Journal of Negro Education,* Yearbook No. 32, Fall 1963, p.
358; G. Franklin Edwards, "Marriage and Family Life Among Negroes," in
ibid., p. 451, shows that, in 1960, married females with spouses present was
79.9% for nonwhites and 95.5% for whites (p. 453). Females were head of
21% of nonwhite and 9% of white households (p. 458). Moreover, there was
an average of 4.04 members of households with Negro female heads and 2.93
with white female heads.

5. Median years of schooling completed by nonwhites in 1960 was 8.2 as compared with 6.9 in 1950.

6. 9.7 in 1950 and 10.9 in 1960.

7. The educational distributions for whites and nonwhites according to the 1960
Census were:

Years of Schooling	Whites	Nonwhites
None	2.0%	6.8%
1–4	5.5	20.9
5–6	7.1	14.6
7	6.6	8.4
8	18.4	12.3
High school, 4 years	22.2	12.1
College, 4 years	10.3	3.5

The median education levels of whites and nonwhites for selected Southern
and non-Southern states in 1960 were as follows:

Southern States	Whites	Non-whites	Selected Non-Southern States	Whites	Non-whites
Louisiana	10.5	6.0	Massachusetts	11.6	10.3
Alabama	10.2	6.5	Michigan	11.0	9.1
Georgia	10.3	6.1	Minnesota	10.8	9.9
Florida	11.6	7.0	Iowa	11.3	9.5
Arkansas	9.5	6.5	Indiana	10.9	9.0
Mississippi	11.0	6.0	Connecticut	11.1	9.1
Texas	10.8	8.1	Colorado	12.1	11.2
Kentucky	8.7	8.2	Oregon	11.8	9.9
North Carolina	9.8	7.0	S. Dakota	10.5	8.6
Tennessee	9.0	7.5	Rhode Island	10.0	9.5
South Carolina	10.3	5.9	Pennsylvania	10.3	8.9
Oklahoma	10.7	8.6	Utah	12.2	10.1
Virginia	10.8	7.2	Washington	12.1	10.5
			Wisconsin	10.4	9.0
			Wyoming	12.1	9.3

For discussion of Negro education, see Eunice S. Newton and Earle H. West,
"The Progress of Negro Elementary and Secondary Education," *Journal of
Negro Education,* Yearbook No. 32, Fall 1963, p. 465.

8. L. B. Granger, "Community Factors Affecting Motivation and Achievement

in a Decade of Decision," *Louisiana Education Association Journal,* May–June 1962, p. 4; Naomi Barko, "Dropouts to Nowhere," *Reporter,* March 29, 1962, p. 34.

9. A Connecticut study, for instance, found that only 23% of Negro vocational-technical school graduates had completed high school as compared with 34% of whites. (State of Connecticut, Commission on Civil Rights, *Training of Negroes in the Skilled Trades,* Hartford, Conn., 1954.)

10. Although Negroes have historically had higher rates of unemployment than whites, these unemployment rates reflect in part the Negro's concentration in less-skilled occupations, and his lower seniority because of his more recent commitment to urban occupations. During the 1957–1958 recession, for instance, the unemployment rates for white and nonwhite men rose by about the same amount in the semiskilled occupations, but the unemployment rate for men increased faster for Negroes than whites in the unskilled category. (U. S. Dept. of Labor, Bureau of Labor Statistics, *Notes on the Economic Situation of Negroes in the United States,* August 1959, p. 3.)

11. The rates of unemployment by race for various occupations in 1960 are shown in Appendix, Table 8; however, Gilman concluded that while Negroes "tend to have a disproportionate increase in their aggregate unemployment during troughs of business cycles . . . this greater increase in unemployment is due mainly to their unfavorable occupational distribution." (Harry J. Gilman, "The White/Non-White Unemployment Differential," in Mark Perlman, Ed., *Human Resources in the Urban Economy,* Baltimore: Johns Hopkins Press for Resources for the Future, 1963, p. 102.)

12. U. S. Dept. of Labor, *Manpower Report of the President and A Report on Manpower Requirements, Resources, Utilization, and Training,* March 1963, p. 107.

13. Sumner Slichter, Robert Livernash, and James Healy, *The Impact of Collective Bargaining on Management,* Washington, the Brookings Institution, 1961, p. 69. In 1961, according to the U. S. Bureau of Apprenticeship and Training, there were 155,000 registered apprentices, a decline from 200,000 in 1957. (U. S. Dept. of Labor, Bureau of Apprenticeship and Training, "Trends in Apprentice Registration, 1941–1963," April 1963.)

14. National Manpower Council, *A Policy for Skilled Manpower,* New York: Columbia University Press, 1954, p. 228.

15. The estimates of the proportions to be supplied to various crafts by 1970 at the present rate of apprenticeship training range from a low of 3% for painters and paperhangers and boilermakers to 36% for electricians. *1961 United States Commission on Civil Rights Report,* "Employment," Table 16, p. 232. See also Louis Ruthenburg, "The Crisis in Apprentice Training," *Personnel,* July/August, 1959; U. S. Dept. of Labor, *Our Manpower Implications,* Washington: U. S. Government Printing Office, 1957; and National Manpower Council, *A Policy for Skilled Manpower.* Chapter 9 on public policy discusses recent moves by the federal government to reduce discrimination in apprenticeship training.

16. New York State Commission Against Discrimination, *Apprentices, Skilled Craftsmen and the Negro,* 1960, p. 15.

17. Connecticut Commission on Civil Rights, *Training of Negroes in the Skilled Trades,* Hartford, 1954, p. 56.

18. Report by the District of Columbia Commissioners' Council on Human Relations, 1963.

19. U. S. Commission on Civil Rights, "Reports on Apprenticeship," January 1964, p. 117.

20. *Ibid.,* p. 31.

21. U. S. Senate, *The Nation's Manpower Revolution,* 1963, Part 6, p. 1995.

22. U. S. Commission on Civil Rights, *Reports on Apprenticeship,* p. 41.

23. *Ibid.,* pp. 57–60, 72, 104, 120, and 131.

24. *Ibid.*

25. See Slichter, Livernash, and Healy, *The Impact of Collective Bargaining on Management, op. cit.; Architectural Record,* August 1946, pp. 95–100; *Plastering Industries,* November 1951; *United Association Journal,* May 1952. S. H. Slichter, *Union Policies and Industrial Management,* Washington: The Brookings Institution, 1941, pp. 32–34.

26. Median income for white persons over 14 years of age in 1949 was $2,053 as compared with $973 for nonwhites; in 1959 the medians were $3,024 and $1,502. Thus, although nonwhites gained relative to whites, the nonwhite median was still only about half that of whites. (U. S. Census of Population, 1960, *United States Summary,* "General Social and Economic Characteristics," Table 95.)

27. One management official, sympathetic to the upgrading of Negroes, described a common management view of the use of Negroes in skilled positions: "Negroes, basically and as a group, with only rare exceptions, are not as well trained for higher skills and jobs as whites. They appear to be excellent for work, usually unskilled, that requires stamina and brawn—and little else. They are unreliable and cannot adjust to the demands of a factory." (J. J. Morrow, "American Negroes, A Wasted Resource," *Harvard Business Review,* January–February 1957, p. 69.) A Connecticut study found that management explained the absence of Negroes from skilled positions in that state on the basis of: Negroes are not "by nature" suited for skilled work and are better suited for heavy, unskilled jobs; Negroes do not apply for skilled jobs; Negroes do not possess the skills to do the skilled jobs; they lack education. (Connecticut Commission on Civil Rights, *op. cit.*) A San Francisco study found that employers refused to hire and upgrade Negroes for the following reasons: fear of customer or employee reaction; tradition; and the belief that Negroes are bad credit risks and get involved in heavy debts. About one-third of the San Francisco employers mentioned physical, mental, or social traits that disqualified Negroes for certain jobs, as illustrated by the following statements concerning Negroes: "not orderly—do not have an organized mind," "not intelligent enough to hold higher jobs," "not put in executive training positions because we don't expect them to be and they don't expect to get to be top management," ". . . could not pass the physical examination, especially with regard to venereal disease." "They are not interested in working up because of the grief and responsibility involved. They don't want responsibility." This study concluded that employers who had hired Negroes seemed less prejudiced than those who had not but that there ". . . appeared to be a consensus among some employers that nonwhites lacked motivation for advancement to higher supervisory positions." (Irving Babow and Edward Howden, A Civil Rights Inventory of San Francisco, Part I, *Employment,* Council for Civic Unity of San Francisco, p. 109.) A Birmingham study found that management attributed limited opportunity for Negroes to the following factors: education and training; the inability to use Negroes where they must meet the public; fear of the reaction of white workers (it

was found, however, that where whites dominated the work force before unionization, there tended to be more friction after unions came in); belief that Negroes lack a sense of responsibility; separate rest rooms would have to be installed; Negro workers are "well suited" to the type work they are performing and are more productive than white in jobs requiring a lot of strength, which are repetitive or require intense heat. (Langston T. Hawley, "Negro Employment in the Birmingham Metropolitan Area," Case Study No. 3, in *Selected Studies in Negro Employment in the South,* National Planning Association, Committee of the South, Report No. 6, February 1963.) Noland and Bakke found that Negroes were not hired for skilled jobs because of management's belief that Negroes were not acceptable to white workers, had insufficient training, were careless in work habits and were not self-reliant. (E. William Noland and E. Wight Bakke, *Workers Wanted: A Study of Employer Hiring Policies, Preferences and Practices,* New York, Harper Brothers, 1949, p. 59). They also found that some managements believed that Negroes were "not as capable as whites for production jobs. Their intelligence is believed to be lower and their training less varied and adequate . . . are slow learners . . . unreliable, irresponsible, lazy, overbearing, sensitive, unambitious, restless, and unpersevering." (*Ibid.,* p. 32.) These results were also found in a study by the Urban League in New Orleans and by the New York State Commission Against Discrimination. (Bernard Rosenberg and Penny Chapin, "Management and Minority Groups: A Study of Attitudes and Practices in Hiring and Upgrading," in *Discrimination and Low Incomes,* New York State Commission Against Discrimination, 1949.)

28. In the South Carolina textile industry, for example, employment of white males declined from 62% of the total to 51.8% between 1940 and 1945, while the employment of white females increased their proportion from 34% to 43.1% and Negro males from 3.9% to 5.1%. In all manufacturing in South Carolina, which tends to be dominated by low-wage employment, white males declined 9.7% during these years and white females increased by 8.2% while Negro males increased .2% and Negro females by 1.3%. (Donald Dewey, "4 Studies of Negro Employment in the Upper South," Case Study No. 2 in *Selected Studies of Negro Employment in the South,* pp. 190–194.)

29. Around 1960, for example, when white operating engineers in Virginia threatened to quit if Negroes were hired, they did not do so after the business agent told them they would be replaced by other Negroes.

30. In New Orleans, for example, a food-processing plant formerly hired only whites for certain materials-handling jobs, but introduced Negroes during the war when whites were not available. This action led to strikes by whites, but they were replaced by Negroes and later other whites were hired for the same jobs.

31. Clark Kerr, John T. Dunlop, Frederick Harbison, and Charles Meyers, *Industrialism and Industrial Man,* Cambridge, Mass.: Harvard University Press, 1960, p. 35 (emphasis added).

32. Milton Friedman, *Capitalism and Freedom,* Chicago: University of Chicago Press, 1962, p. 108.

33. On the railroads, for example, the unions have prevented Negroes from being hired as firemen and being promoted to engineering positions. Indeed, the Brotherhood of Locomotive Firemen actually negotiated a contract de-

fining Negroes as "nonpromotable" and sought to force their elimination from railroads. (See footnote 35.)

34. The percentages of Negroes in some of the main building trades for various census years were as follows:

Craft	1950	1940	1930	1920	1910	1900	1890
Bricklayers	10.9%	6.0%	6.9%	8.1%	7.5%	9.0%	6.1%
Carpenters	3.9	3.9	3.5	3.9	4.3	3.7	3.6
Cement finishers	26.2	15.2	15.8	15.4	13.0	10.5	10.3
Electricians	1.0	0.7	0.7	0.6	0.6	NA	NA
Painters	5.2	3.8	3.6	3.2	2.9	2.1	2.0
Plumbers	3.3	2.2	2.0	1.7	1.7	1.2	1.1

Since most of these Negro craftsmen were in the South, and since the strength of building trades unions increased from 1890 to 1920 and declined from 1920 to 1928 and then rose again until 1950, there would appear to be no statistical proof that unions have excluded Negroes from these occupations.

35. See Steele v. L. & N.R.R., 323 U. S. 192; Archibald Cox, "The Duty of Fair Representation," *Villanova Law Review*, January 1957, p. 151; Benjamin Aaron, "Some Aspects of the Union's Duty of Fair Representation," *Ohio State Law Journal*, Winter 1961, p. 39; Wallace Corp. v. NLRB, 323 U. S. 248; Central of Georgia Ry. v. Jones 229 F. 2d 648, Cert. Denied 352 U. S. 848; Richardson v. Texas & New Orleans Ry. Co., 242 F. 2d 230, 77 S. Ct. 230.

36. Leon E. Lunden, "Antidiscrimination Clauses in Major Contracts, 1961," *Monthly Labor Review*, June 1962.

37. See National War Labor Board, Termination Reports, Vol. I, Ch. 12, and Press Release, Office of War Information, Southeastern Region, June 9, 1945.

38. Dewey, "4 Studies of Negro Employment in the Upper South," *op. cit.*, p. 163.

39. This section is based on my "Some Factors Influencing the Upgrading of Negroes in the Southern Petroleum Refining Industry," *Social Forces*, December 1963.

40. For example, the peak employment for both manufacturing and the petroleum refining industry came in 1953 when there were 17.2 million total employees in manufacturing, 13.8 million of whom were classified as production and related workers (that is, excluding salaried workers from the total). In 1958 there were 15.5 million employees in manufacturing, but only 11.7 million production and related workers. In 1953 there were 206,000 employees in petroleum refineries, 142,000 of whom were production and related workers; the comparable figures for 1958 were 192,000 and 121,000. During this period, therefore, total employment in petroleum refineries declined by 6.8% while the number of production and related workers declined by 14.8%; production workers declined from about 69% of the total in 1953 to 63% in 1958. At the same time, production increased by about 9.8% and became more diversified. (*Petroleum Facts and Figures,* American Petroleum Institute, New York, 1959, pp. 110, 420.)

41. A 1957 survey by the Department of Defense revealed that there were 983 Negro workers in 15 non-Southern refineries or 2.8% of total employment, while there were 3129 Negro employees in 8 Southern refineries, or 13.0%

of the total. Negroes constituted 3.1% of the 33,336 workers in 16 refineries surveyed in 1958 and 12.0% of the 25,621 workers in 7 Southern refineries. Almost all Negro employees in the South and the non-South were concentrated in production jobs; there were only 14 Negro white-collar workers in the non-Southern refineries surveyed in 1957 and 15 in 1958, while there were 8 Negroes in this category in the South for both years.

42. In 1960, for instance, 10% of nonwhites and 5.0% of whites in the labor force were unemployed. U. S. Bureau of Labor Statistics, "Special Labor Report," 1960, p. A 40, Table F-5.
43. National War Labor Board, *Termination Reports,* Vol. 1, Ch. 12; and Release of the Office of War Information, Southeastern Region (for the National War Labor Board), June 9, 1945.
44. Syres v. Oil Workers, 223 F. 2d 739, I RRLR 192 (1956).
45. In 1957, for instance, there were 5567 employees at Gulf, 883 of whom were Negroes; in 1958 the total was 5737 and 861 Negroes; and in 1959 there were 4827 employees, 741 of whom were Negroes. All the Negroes in 1959 were classified as skilled or semiskilled, though 40% of them had a "labor" title and over 90% were in the Labor Division. Labor Division wage rates ranged from $2.06 an hour to $2.81, while other rates ranged from $2.06 to $3.36; however, the highest rate in the plant for a Negro was $3.15.
46. National CIO Civil Rights Committee, *Proceedings* of the meeting of October 5, 1954.
47. Cities Service had 1756 employees at Lake Charles in 1953, 138 of whom were Negroes, and 1814 employees in 1957, 153 of whom were Negroes.
48. There were 2452 production workers in 1957, 527 of whom were Negroes; the figures for 1958 were 2402 and 506 respectively.
49. In October 1958 there were 5185 employees at Baytown, 306 of whom were Negroes and 108 of whom were Mexican. In March 1960 there were 4903 employees, 284 of whom were Negroes and 101 of whom were Mexicans.
50. There were 273 Negroes of 2754 employees at Union Carbide in 1957, and 268 Negroes of 2636 employees in 1958.
51. Butler v. Celotex, U. S. District Court, Eastern District of Louisiana, New Orleans Division, Civil Action No. 6978, January 17, 1958.

Appendix—Negro Employment Patterns

The basic pattern of Negro employment has not changed significantly since 1940, but there have been some important trends within various employment categories. As seen in Table A-2 (see p. 167), there was a decline in the proportion of nonwhite males in the relatively less skilled groups from 68.3 per cent in 1940 to 64.4 per cent in 1960; however, these were almost double the white proportions of 38.6 per cent and 33.5 per cent for these years. Table A-4 shows this trend to have continued through 1962 for all nonwhites.

Table A-3 shows the proportion of total nonwhite males to total male employment in each of these categories. The influence of full-employment conditions during the Second World War is demonstrated by the increase in the nonwhite proportion of the total to 9.8 per cent, a proportion which has not subsequently been equaled; nonwhites also increased their proportions of every job category between 1940 and 1944, and declined subsequently, though there was an increase in the proportion of professional, technical, and kindred jobs held by Negroes between 1952 and 1959 and a significant increase in the clerical and kindred categories. There has likewise been a significant decline in the proportion of private household jobs held by nonwhite males. Table A-4 indicates the trend in total (male and female) employment between 1948 and 1962.

Table A-5 gives the number and proportion of Negroes in selected crafts for 1950, and Table A-6 reveals that Negroes held even lower proportions of apprenticeships in various crafts. Table A-7 shows the number of nonwhites in various occupations for 1950 in the United States.

Although the Negro proportions of jobs in the skilled categories are relatively low, they are even lower in the technical fields. In 1950, for example, only 1.1 per cent of male chemists and 0.3 per cent of male technical engineers were Negroes; the proportions for females were 0.2 per cent and 2.3 per cent respectively.

Becker [1] constructed an index of occupational positions of Negro and white males in the North and South by placing Negroes in skilled, semiskilled, and unskilled classifications, estimating the relative income positions in 1939 and multiplying this by the percentages of Negroes and whites in each classification for various years. He concluded from this index that the occupational position of Negroes in the South actually deteriorated between 1910 and 1950; the ratios of Negroes to white "indexes of occupational position" in the South were .67 in 1910, .63 in 1940, and .65 in 1950. The corresponding ratios for the North were .73 in 1910, .74 in 1940, and .77 in 1950. These results caused Becker to conclude "very tentatively" that "almost all the increases in the absolute occupational position of Negroes were caused by forces increasing the position of whites as well" and that there have been "neither striking increases nor striking decreases in discrimination against Negroes . . . during the last four decades."

However, Becker's conclusions are subject to the limitations of any index number. Rayack, for example, objects to Becker's calculations on the ground that the use of 1939 weights of relative income position fails to take into consideration the narrowing of the income spread between skilled and unskilled workers.[2] Since Negroes are concentrated in semiskilled and unskilled occupations, he argues, Becker's use of constant weights underestimates the improvement in the Negro's position. Rayack applies relative income-position indexes for 1939 and 1951 and concludes that Negroes improved their positions relative to whites in the North from .74 in 1940 to .85 in 1950 and in the South from .68 in 1940 to .80 in 1950. It may not be very meaningful, however, to construct different indexes for the North and South because of the influence of population changes. Rayack's more meaningful figures for the United States as a whole found the ratio of Negroes to whites was .68 in 1940, .82 in 1950, and .80 in 1958. The decline in the Negro's relative position since 1948 reflected his higher rate of unemployment.

It should be noted, however, that Rayack and Becker have different purposes. Becker used constant weights in order to abstract from the wage-leveling process that affected whites and nonwhites alike: he was interested in determining changes in discrimination alone, whereas Rayack was interested in the changing conditions of Negroes for whatever reason.

Other evidence from various industries and areas of the country confirms the general pattern established by census data for the whole country. For example, a compliance review survey of defense contractors in 24 standard metropolitan areas in 1957 probably is indicative of the general racial patterns in major manufacturing concerns in the United States. Of the 24 Standard Metropolitan Areas (SMA's) surveyed, 10 were in the South; the Southern firms had 92,136 employees, 13,417 (or 14.6 per cent) of whom were Negroes. The non-Southern metropolitan areas had 430,717 employees, 31,990 (7.4 per cent) of whom were Negroes.

A compliance review survey for defense contractors in 16 non-Southern and 7 Southern automobile plants in 1957, 7 Southern and 11 non-Southern plants in 1958, and 4 Southern and 12 non-Southern plants for 1959 revealed the following:

	1957		1958		1959	
	South	Non-South	South	Non-South	South	Non-South
Total employees	14,825	83,058	11,306	49,606	7,572	30,426
Total Negro employees	495	15,045	424	7,426	335	5,008
Per cent Negro	3.3	18.1	3.8	15.0	4.4	16.5
Negroes salaried	1	129	1	73	1	71
Per cent of total	...	1.0	...	0.7	...	1.8
Negroes hourly	334	14,886	423	7,353	334	4,937
Per cent of total	3.1	21.6	4.6	19.2	5.3	18.8

If these figures are representative of the industry, and they probably are, they support the conclusion that there are very few Negroes in white-collar positions and relatively few in production jobs in the South. Indeed, observations in the South reveal that there were very few Negroes in the automobile industry in other than menial classifications before 1920, though a few have been upgraded in recent years under pressure from Negro organizations and government-contract committees. The only Negro found in a white-collar position in the South by 1959 was at Louisville, Kentucky. Moreover, there were no white-collar workers in the automobile plants surveyed in Baltimore, Cincinnati, Los Angeles, Philadelphia, San Francisco, and St. Louis in 1959; of the 71 Negro white-collar workers in the survey, 41 were in a Chicago plant and 21 in another in the New York area.

The oil-industry compliance surveys for 1957 and 1958 give different results for the North-South comparison. Unlike the automobile industry, a large proportion of petroleum refining is in the South and the Southern refineries are older relatively than Southern automobile plants. As would be expected, therefore, Negroes have a larger proportion of oil-industry jobs in the South than in the non-South, where there are relatively few Negroes. The results of the 1957 and 1958 surveys were as follows:

| | 1957 | | 1958 | |
	South	Non-South	South	Non-South
Total employees	24,124	35,619	19,121	33,336
Total Negro employees	3,129	983	2,281	1,024
Per cent Negro	13.0	2.8	11.9	3.1
Negro white collar	8	14	8	15
Per cent Negro	0.1	0.2	0.3	0.2
Negro production	3,121	969	2,273	1,009
Per cent Negro	17.1	3.5	14.7	14.7

These figures show that there are relatively few Negro white-collar workers in the petroleum-refining industry and that in the South the Negro has not been able to hold his proportion of the jobs in the industry, mainly because Negroes have been concentrated disproportionately in those jobs most subject to technological displacement.

These general conclusions concerning Negro employment patterns have been confirmed by numerous investigations.[3]

Racial employment patterns in the non-South have differed from those of the South in degree, but the general pattern has been essentially the same. Nor is this surprising, since employment opportunities tend to be influenced by family and social relationships and past individual experiences. Moreover, any immigrant group tends to concentrate in narrow occupational categories for ethnic reasons. In the Negro case, however, racial discrimination is a factor in the non-South as well as in the South. Negro supervisors of white workers are rare in the North, but more common than in the South. Although Negroes in the North still occupy a disproportionate number of unskilled and menial jobs, since the beginning of the Second World War it has been increasingly more common for Negroes and whites to work side by side at the same jobs.

Table A-8 shows that nonwhite unemployment rates have been higher than those of whites for every occupational category. We shall also see in Chapter 12 that nonwhite unemployment rates increased relative to whites between 1947 and 1955, but improved slightly relative to the totals between 1956 and 1963.

Our conclusion that there are some jobs for which Negroes have advantages in the South as compared with other areas also holds for the skilled trades generally, as indicated by Table A-9, which shows what happened to the number of nonwhites in various skilled craft categories in the South and non-South between 1950 and 1960. Although nonwhites gained from 2.35 per cent to 3.17 per cent of these crafts in the non-South, the South still had 48.6 per cent of the nation's nonwhite craftsmen. Moreover, though their proportion declined from 8.17 per cent to 8.06 per cent of the total, nonwhites were still much better represented in these crafts in the South than non-South. Nonwhite representation was better in every category in the South, though in the metal-craftsmen category there was a noticeable decline in the nonwhite proportion of the South's total. The decline in nonwhite craft representation in the South between 1950 and 1960 undoubtedly is influenced by migration of Negro craftsmen.[4] Table A-10 indicates that nonwhite representation increased in every category except metal craftsmen, but the increases in every category were greater in the non-South. In the South, moreover, nonwhites increased relative to whites in the foremen, mechanics and repairmen, and construction craftsmen categories, and declined in the others. In the non-South, nonwhites increased faster than whites in every category.

FOOTNOTES

1. Gary Becker, *The Economics of Discrimination,* Chicago: University of Chicago Press, 1959, p. 113.
2. Elton Rayack, "Discrimination and the Occupational Progress of Negroes," *Review of Economics and Statistics,* May 1961.
3. Vivian W. Henderson concluded, concerning the employment situation for Negroes in Nashville, Tennessee, that when Negroes were employed above the unskilled level it was mainly in the Negro community and that 80% of the Negroes in Nashville were in menial, unskilled occupations. He found, further, that there were very few Negroes in manufacturing jobs, that 80% of the unskilled jobs in Nashville were held by Negroes, that Negroes were not employed as managers, clerks, or supervisors in bus companies though Negroes furnish the most lucrative markets for the companies. He noted, however, that Negroes were hired as bus drivers in Nashville in 1960. Most

Nashville Negroes also attended segregated schools and vocational training was available ot them only in jobs they customarily held. The white school offered courses in electronics, IBM, refrigeration, air conditioning, drafting, radio, television, and electronics. The Negro school offered courses in tailoring, bricklaying, cabinetmaking, and diversified occupations to include cook, maid, maintenance, and dietetics. ("Employment Opportunity for Nashville Negroes," Community Conference on Employment Opportunity, Fisk University, April 22–23, 1960).

A New York study of Negro participation in apprenticeship training concluded that "Negroes have not been (and are not) represented in the most minimal way in the New York State apprenticeship programs." This study also found that with only 5.4% of the total work force in New York, Negroes had only 2.9% of the jobs as craftsmen, but the following proportions of unskilled jobs: domestics, 39.8%; service, 14.7%; and laborers, 12.8%. (New York State Commission Against Discrimination, *Apprentices, Skilled Craftsmen and the Negro*, April 1960, pp. 16, 115.)

A Connecticut study found that 92% of the Negroes working for larger employers in that state were in unskilled or semiskilled jobs, and only 4% were in the skilled trades. (H. G. Stetler, "Minority Group Integration by Labor and Management," Connecticut Commission on Civil Rights, 1953, p. 19.) According to another Connecticut survey, ". . . it seems fairly conclusive that Negroes possess decidedly limited opportunities for acquiring training in certain of the highly skilled trades." (Connecticut Commission on Civil Rights, *Training of Negroes in the Skilled Trades*, 1954, p. 56.)

A San Francisco study found that Negroes were concentrated in semiskilled and unskilled jobs, but that even many of these were closed to Negroes and Orientals. With respect to participation in the skilled trades, this study found that "The data on the building trades unions suggests that while there were Negro and Oriental members in a number of them, there remained a serious problem of upgrading, and in a number of unions a problem of admission. While it appears that these skilled crafts were difficult for anyone to enter, the practices of some unions and of many contractors made the problems of training and entry even greater for Negroes than for white workers." (Irving Babow and Edward Howden, A Civil Rights Inventory of San Francisco, Part I, *Employment*, San Francisco: Council for Civic Unity, 1958.)

A St. Louis study found that a high proportion of Negroes were working below their educational levels and that the craftsman was the most underemployed of all. St. Louis Negroes were concentrated in unskilled jobs. (Irwin Sobel, Werner Z. Hirsch, and Harvey C. Harris, *The Negro in the St. Louis Economy*, Urban League of St. Louis, 1954.)

Negroes were concentrated disproportionately in the lower job classifications in companies like International Harvester, which has one of the most equalitarian racial positions of any company in the South. In a study of three Harvester plants in the South, John Hope II found that "Except in one maintenance shop at the Louisville works, the plants have not employed Negro journeymen or journeymen's helpers in the apprenticeable trades, nor have they enrolled Negroes in company sponsored apprentice programs." "3 Southern Plants of International Harvester Company," in *Selected Studies of Negro Employment in the South*, Washington: National Planning Association, 1955.)

In "4 Studies of Negro Employment in the Birmingham Metropolitan Area" (in *Selected Studies of Negro Employment in the South*), Langston Hawley found that a great majority of Negroes were located in unskilled and semi-skilled jobs and in personal and building service occupations and that "For the most part, both the occupations filled by Negroes and the nature of the work required was found to have been remarkably stable since 1939" (p. 247).

William H. Wesson's study of "Negro Employment Practices in the Chattanooga Area" (in *ibid.*) found that 18.3% of the 2276 Negro workers surveyed in that area were in skilled jobs, but that these were mainly in foundry work or in the trowel trades in construction. Wesson found strong regional industry and company biases against using Negroes in higher occupational categories outside these traditional areas.

A Cincinnati study found very small percentages of Negroes in professional or skilled categories. (City of Cincinnati, The Mayor's Friendly Relations Committee, *Racial Discrimination in Employment in the Cincinnati Area,* April 1953.) This study found that Negroes were usually confined to the least desirable types of work, that 60% of casuals were Negroes and that in clerical sales jobs, "whites are 9 times as likely to be placed as Negroes; 5 times as likely to be placed in skilled industrial work; and 6 times as likely in semiskilled work. In service jobs, Negroes are 5 times as likely to be placed as whites, but this reversal of the ratio by no means offsets their low placement rate in longer lasting and generally more desirable jobs" (p. 5). It was also found that in Cincinnati many avenues of training were closed to Negroes regardless of ability.

The "1961 Report of the United States Commission on Civil Rights" concluded that "Although their occupational levels have risen considerably during the past 20 years, Negro workers continue to be concentrated in the less skilled jobs. And it is largely because of this concentration in the ranks of the unskilled and semiskilled, the groups most severely affected by both economic layoffs and technological changes, that Negroes are also disproportionately represented among the unemployed." (*Employment,* p. 153.)

A report by the Ohio Governor's Advisory Commission on Civil Rights (1958) covering employment practices in that state concluded that "While Negroes are able to upgrade from unskilled to skilled occupations in some plants, Negro skilled workers still remain very few in number in a majority of plants" (p. 20). Furthermore, it was found that "Very few plants promote Negroes from factory jobs to supervision, but there are scattered instances of this in most metropolitan communities." (*Ibid.*) Finally, "It is in the apprenticeship field that the suggestion of a pattern of discrimination is most strong with no Negroes enrolled through the state in some programs . . . Negro apprentices are permitted in many industrial unions, although the number of Negro apprentices is extremely small" (pp. 19–20).

Recent studies by the Southern Regional Council in Chattanooga, Atlanta, and Houston confirm the Negro's concentration in low-paying jobs and for discrimination in opportunities for education and training to perpetuate this pattern. See also Walter G. Daniel, "The Relative Employment and Income of American Negroes," *Journal of Negro Education,* Fall 1963, Yearbook No. 32, p. 349; Mathew A. Kessler, "Economic Status of Nonwhite Workers, 1955–1962," *Monthly Labor Review,* July 1963.

4. See Table A-1 for population changes in selected Southern and non-Southern areas between 1950 and 1960.

Appendix Table A-1

Population Changes, Selected Southern and Non-Southern Metropolitan Areas, by Color, 1950 and 1960

Metropolitan Areas	Population, 1960	Per Cent Increase in Population, 1950–1960	Per Cent Nonwhite Population, 1960	Population, 1950	Per Cent Increase in Population, 1940–1950	Per Cent Nonwhite Population, 1950	Per Cent Change in Nonwhite, 1950–1960
South							
Atlanta	1,017,008	46.4	22.8	694,699	29.7	24.7	−1.9
Birmingham	634,864	13.6	34.6	558,928	21.5	37.3	−2.7
Dallas	1,083,601	76.2	14.6	614,799	54.3	13.6	+1.0
Houston	1,243,158	54.1	20.1	806,701	52.5	18.7	+1.4
Louisville	725,139	25.7	11.6	576,900	27.8	11.5	+0.1
Memphis	627,019	30.0	36.4	482,393	34.7	37.4	−1.0
Nashville	399,743	24.2	19.2	321,758	24.1	20.0	−0.8
New Orleans	868,480	26.7	31.0	685,405	24.1	29.3	+1.7
Norfolk-Portsmouth	578,507	29.6	26.4	446,200	72.3	27.5	−1.1
Richmond	408,494	24.5	26.4	328,050	24.7	26.6	−0.2
Southern averages	748,601	37.5		551,583			
Non-South							
Baltimore	1,727,021	29.1	22.2	1,337,373	23.5	19.9	+3.0
Cleveland	1,769,595	20.7	14.5	1,465,511	15.6	10.5	+4.0
Chicago	6,220,913	13.2	14.8	5,495,364	13.9	11.0	+4.8
Cincinnati	1,071,624	18.5	12.1	904,402	14.9	10.6	+1.5
Detroit	3,764,131	24.8	15.1	3,016,197	26.9	12.0	+5.1
Indianapolis	697,567	26.4	14.4	551,777	19.7	11.8	+2.6
Kansas City	1,040,454	27.8	11.4	814,357	18.6	10.8	+0.6
Los Angeles	6,746,356	54.4	8.8	4,367,911	49.8	6.3	+2.5
Philadelphia	4,343,524	18.3	15.7	3,671,048	14.7	13.2	+5.1
Pittsburgh	2,406,301	8.7	6.8	2,213,236	6.3	6.2	+0.6
St. Louis	2,060,614	22.6	14.5	1,681,281	17.4	12.9	+1.6
San Francisco	2,783,355	24.2	12.5	2,240,767	53.3	9.4	+3.1
Washington	1,989,377	35.9	24.9	1,464,089	51.3	23.4	+1.5
Non-South averages	2,816,987	25.3		2,247,947			

Source: U. S. Censuses, 1950 and 1960.

Table A-2

Per Cent Distribution of Employed Males, by Color, 1940–1960

| | Per Cent Distribution | | | | | |
| | Nonwhite | | | White | | |
Occupational Group	1960	1950	1940	1960	1950	1940
Total employed men	100.0	100.0	100.0	100.0	100.0	100.0
Professional, technical, and kindred	3.9	2.2	1.9	11.0	7.9	6.6
Managers, officials, and proprietors, except farm	2.3	2.0	1.6	11.5	11.6	10.6
Clerical and kindred workers	5.0	3.4	1.2	7.1	6.8	6.5
Sales workers	1.5	1.5	1.0	7.4	6.6	6.8
Craftsmen, foremen, and kindred workers	10.2	7.6	4.4	20.5	19.3	15.9
Operatives and kindred workers	23.5	20.8	12.4	19.5	20.0	18.7
Private household	0.7	0.8	2.3	0.1	0.1	0.1
Service, except private household	13.7	12.5	12.3	6.0	4.9	5.2
Laborers, except farm and mine	19.4	23.1	21.3	5.0	0.0	7.0
Other	8.4	1.3	0.6	4.2	1.2	0.7
Total nonfarm	88.5	75.2	58.9	92.1		
Farmers and farm managers	4.4	13.5	21.1	5.6	10.5	14.2
Farm laborers and foremen	8.1	11.3	20.0	2.3	4.4	7.0
Total farm	11.5	24.8	41.1	7.9	14.9	21.2

Source: U. S. Bureau of the Census.

Table A-3

Proportion of Nonwhite to Total Males in Each Occupational Group, 1940–1959 *

Occupational Group	1959	1952	1950	1948	1944	1940
Total employed men	9.2	8.9	8.3	8.4	9.8	9.0
Professional, technical, and kindred	3.0	2.5	2.6	2.6	3.3	3.1
Managers, officials, and proprietors, except farm	1.5	1.6	1.9	1.8	2.1	1.5
Clerical and kindred workers	6.5	3.4 †	2.8 †	2.3 †	2.8 †	1.6
Sales workers	1.8					1.4
Craftsmen, foremen, and kindred workers	4.2	4.0	3.9	3.7	3.6	2.7
Operatives and kindred workers	10.7	10.4	8.5	10.1	10.1	6.1
Private household	37.7	31.6	51.3	53.7	75.2	61.8
Service, except private household	20.6	21.7	21.4	20.7	21.9	17.4
Laborers, except farm and mine	29.5	26.9	21.4	23.6	27.6	21.2
Farmers and farm managers	8.2	10.7	10.5	9.8	11.0	13.1
Farm laborers and foremen	24.0	16.2	19.8	15.8	21.1	22.5

* April of selected years.
† Includes sales, 1944–1952.
Source: U. S. Bureau of the Census.

Table A-4

Employed Persons, by Occupation Group and Color, 1948, 1955, and 1962 *

| | Per Cent Distribution | | | | | |
| | White | | | Nonwhite | | |
Major Occupation Group	1962	1955	1948	1962	1955	1948
Total employed						
Number (thousands)	60.7	56.7	53.4	7.1	6.5	5.9
Per cent	100.0	100.0	100.0	100.0	100.0	100.0
White-collar workers	47.3	42.1	39.1	16.7	12.0	9.0
Professional and technical workers	12.6	9.8	7.2	5.3	3.5	2.4
Managers, officials, and proprietors, except farm	11.9	11.1	11.6	2.6	2.3	2.3
Clerical workers	15.8	14.2	13.6	7.2	4.9	3.3
Sales workers	7.0	6.9	6.7	1.6	1.3	1.1
Blue-collar workers	35.4	39.0	40.5	39.5	41.8	39.7
Craftsmen and foremen	13.6	14.1	14.6	6.0	5.2	5.3
Operatives	17.5	20.2	21.0	19.9	20.9	20.1
Laborers, except farm and mine	4.3	4.7	4.9	13.6	15.8	14.3
Service workers	10.6	9.0	7.9	32.8	31.6	30.3
Private household workers	2.1	1.8	1.5	14.7	14.8	15.6
Other service workers	8.5	7.2	6.4	18.1	16.8	14.7
Farm workers	6.8	9.9	12.4	11.0	14.5	21.0
Farmers and farm managers	4.0	6.0	7.8	2.7	5.0	8.5
Laborers and foremen	2.8	3.9	4.6	8.3	9.5	12.5

* Data for 1948 and 1955 not adjusted to reflect changes in definition of unemployment adopted in 1957.

Note: Because of rounding, sums of individual percentages may not equal 100.

Source: Mathew A. Kessler, "Economic Status of Nonwhite Workers, 1955–1962," *Monthly Labor Review,* July 1963, p. 2.

Table A-5

Male Employment in Selected Crafts, by Race, 1950

Detailed Occupations	Total	White	Negro	Other	White	Negro	Other
						Percentage Distribution	
Boilermakers	34,950	34,140	810	⋯	97.7	2.3	⋯
Brickmasons, stonemasons, tile setters	163,650	145,530	17,910	210	88.9	10.9	0.1
Cabinet makers	71,280	69,480	1,680	120	97.5	2.4	0.1
Carpenters	898,140	861,780	34,860	1,500	96.0	3.9	0.1
Cement finishers	28,200	20,790	7,380	30	73.82	26.17	0.01
Electricians *	307,013	303,429	3,236	348	98.2	1.0	0.8
Machinists	496,320	488,130	7,530	660	98.4	1.5	0.1
Mechanics and repairmen	1,670,370	1,596,450	69,990	3,930	96.6	4.2	0.2
Millwrights	58,980	57,720	1,170	90	97.9	2.0	0.1
Painters	381,150	360,600	19,860	690	94.6	5.2	0.2
Paperhangers	17,760	15,780	1,980	⋯	88.9	11.1	⋯
Plumbers and pipe fitters	271,530	262,940	8,800	210	96.69	3.24	0.07
Roofers and slaters	43,200	40,170	3,000	30	93.0	6.94	0.06
Structural metal workers	64,650	59,940	4,650	60	92.7	7.2	0.1
Sheet metal workers	117,270	116,040	990	240	99.14	0.84	0.2
Tool and die makers	152,940	152,520	420	⋯	99.7	0.3	⋯

* Male and female.

Source: U. S. Bureau of the Census.

Table A-6

Apprentices in Selected Crafts, by Race, 1950

Detailed Occupation	Total	White	Negro	Other	Percentage Distribution		
					White	Negro	Other
Auto mechanics	3,600	3,510	90	…	97.6	2.4	…
Bricklayers	6,510	6,240	270	…	95.9	4.1	…
Carpenters	9,930	9,870	60	…	99.4	0.6	…
Electricians	9,360	9,240	90	30	98.7	1.0	0.3
Machinists and tool-makers	14,550	14,430	60	60	99.2	0.4	0.4
Mechanics	6,720	6,480	210	30	96.4	3.1	0.5
Plumbers and pipe fitters	11,010	10,890	90	30	98.9	0.8	0.3
Building trades (n.e.c.) *	2,690	2,510	150	30	95.1	4.1	0.8
Metal working trades	7,170	7,020	150	…	97.9	2.1	…
Trades not specified	13,440	13,320	90	30	99.1	0.7	0.2

* N.e.c. = "not elsewhere classified."

Source: U. S. Bureau of the Census.

Table A-7

Employed Males in Selected Crafts, by Race and Region, 1950

Craft	United States			South		
	Total	White	Nonwhite	Total	White	Nonwhite
Bakers	101,880	95,460	6,420	18,716	15,214	3,502
Blacksmiths and forgemen	54,240	51,510	2,730	15,494	13,568	1,926
Boilermakers	34,950	34,140	810	9,347	8,956	391
Bricklayers	172,530	154,140	18,390	53,467	39,883	13,584
Carpenters	898,140	861,780	36,360	325,509	297,480	28,029
Compositors and typesetters	160,560	157,620	2,940	29,826	29,026	800
Electricians	302,340	298,920	3,420	79,652	78,300	1,352
Foremen (n.e.c.)	773,100	762,690	10,410	185,697	182,153	3,544
Linemen (telephone, tele-graph, power)	205,230	203,130	2,100	56,126	54,806	1,320
Railroad firemen	53,310	51,180	2,130	14,514	12,690	1,824
Machinists and job setters	520,440	511,890	8,550	84,178	81,875	2,303
Mechanics	1,699,020	1,624,980	74,040	439,324	404,659	34,655
Millwrights	58,980	57,720	1,260	9,002	8,629	373
Molders, metal	57,150	46,650	10,500	8,484	6,877	1,607
Painters, paperhangers, and glaziers	409,290	386,460	22,830	124,253	110,761	13,492
Plasterers and cement finishers	88,380	70,950	17,430	27,413	15,628	11,785
Plumbers and pipefitters	271,530	262,440	9,090	50,655	48,039	2,616
Pressmen (except #6)	47,910	47,220	690	13,988	13,457	531
Stationary engineers	212,580	207,600	4,980	55,286	53,225	2,061
Structural metal workers	48,180	46,680	1,500	12,416	11,676	740
Other	71,730	67,530	4,200	109,716	99,784	9,932
Apprentices (operative)	111,750	109,590	2,160	20,308	19,150	1,158

Table A-8

Unemployment Rates, by Major Occupation, Group, and Color, 1960

	Unemployed as Per Cent of Civilian Labor Force in Category	
Major Occupation Group	White	Nonwhite
Total unemployed	5.0	10.2
Professional, technical, and kindred workers	1.7	2.9
Farmers and farm managers	.3	.5
Managers, officials, and proprietors, except farm	1.3	2.7
Clerical and kindred workers	3.6	7.3
Sales workers	3.6	5.9
Craftsmen, foremen, and kindred workers	5.0	9.6
Operatives and kindred workers	7.5	11.2
Private household workers	3.4	6.6
Service workers, except private household	5.1	9.1
Farm laborers and foremen	4.1	8.2
Laborers, except farm and mine	11.5	15.0

Source: U. S. Department of Labor, Bureau of Labor Statistics, "Special Labor Force Report," from the *Monthly Labor Review*, April 1961, A40, Table F-5.

Nonwhite Male Craft Employment [1]—South [2] and Non-South [3] and Southern Nonwhite Share of Total U. S.[4] Nonwhite Employment— 1950 and 1960

| | SOUTH | | | | Per Cent Nonwhite of South | |
| | Total | | Nonwhite [5] | | | |
	1950	1960	1950	1960	1950	1960
Foremen (n.e.c.) [6]	185,697	277,369	3,544	5,504	1.90	1.98
Mechanics and repairmen [7]	439,312	617,538	34,660	53,051	7.88	8.59
Metal craftsmen [8]	157,671	178,465	9,670	8,153	6.13	4.57
Construction craftsmen [9]	750,027	787,727	76,416	89,552	10.19	11.37
Other craftsmen [10]	259,629	429,503	18,900	28,352	7.28	6.60
Total	1,752,406	2,290,602	143,190	184,612	8.17	8.06

| | NON-SOUTH | | | | Per Cent Nonwhite of Non-South | |
| | Total | | Nonwhite | | | |
	1950	1960	1950	1960	1950	1960
Foremen (n.e.c.)	548,481	815,177	5,768	12,365	1.05	1.52
Mechanics and repairmen	1,180,857	1,568,041	38,194	71,513	3.23	4.56
Metal craftsmen	798,258	919,087	17,295	28,980	2.17	3.15
Construction craftsmen	1,553,677	1,600,813	37,331	47,782	2.40	2.98
Other craftsmen	836,622	1,254,405	17,030	34,732	2.04	2.77
Total	4,917,895	6,157,523	115,618	195,372	2.35	3.17

| | Total | | Per Cent Southern of Total | |
	U. S. 1950	Nonwhite 1960	U. S. 1950	Nonwhite 1960
Foremen (n.e.c.)	9,312	17,869	38.1	30.8
Mechanics and repairmen	72,854	124,564	47.6	42.6
Metal craftsmen	26,965	37,133	35.9	22.0
Construction craftsmen	113,747	137,334	67.2	65.2
Other craftsmen	35,930	63,084	52.6	44.9
Total	258,808	379,808	55.3	48.6

Notes to Table A-9

1 Figures compiled from Census of the Population: 1950, U. S. Department of Commerce, Bureau of the Census, Vol. II, General Social and Economic Characteristics, by State, Table 77—"Detailed Characteristics—Role and Class of Worker of Employed Persons, by Occupation and Sex, for the [each one individually] State and for Standard Metropolitan Areas of 100,000 or More"; 1950 Census of Population; U. S. Department of Commerce, Bureau of the Census, Vol. II—General Social and Economic Characteristics, by State, Table 58—"Occupation Group of Employed Persons by Color and Sex, for the State, Urban and Rural: 1960."

2 South is defined as including Alabama, Arkansas, Delaware, District of Columbia, Florida, Georgia, Kansas, Louisiana, Maryland, Mississippi, North Carolina, Oklahoma, South Carolina, Tennessee, Texas, Virginia, and West Virginia.

3 Non-South is defined as including all other states except Alaska and Hawaii.

4 U. S. is defined as including all states except Alaska and Hawaii.

5 Nonwhite includes Negro, Indian, and Oriental.

6 Same as 1940 census—foremen "not elsewhere classified" (n.e.c.).

7 Same as 1940 census.

8 Includes: blacksmiths, forgemen, hammermen, boilermakers, machinists and job setters, millwrights, molders, tinsmiths, coppersmiths, sheet metal workers, toolmakers, die makers, and setters. 1960 figures also include heat treaters, metal rollers and roller hands which were classified in the 1950 "other" category.

9 Includes: masons, tile setters, carpenters, electricians, painters, paperhangers, plasterers and cement finishers, plumbers and pipefitters, and structural metal workers. Cranemen, hoistmen, and construction machine operators have been substituted in the 1950 figures for the 1960 classification of excavating, grading, and road machine operators. Glaziers and stone cutters, included under "construction" in 1950, are found in the category of "other craftsmen" in 1960.

10 Includes: bakers, compositors and typesetters, locomotive engineers and firemen, pressmen, bookbinders, cabinet makers, engravers, furriers, goldsmiths, inspectors, jewelers, lens grinders and polishers, log and lumber scalers and graders, millers, motion picture projectionists, opticians, piano and organ tuners and repairmen, shoemakers (except in factories), silversmiths, tailors, telegraph and telephone linemen and servicemen, upholsterers, watchmakers, and window dressers. The 1950 figures also include heat treaters, annealers and temperers, metal rollers and roll hands, roofers and slaters, craftsmen and kindred workers (not elsewhere classified), and members of the armed forces, whereas the 1960 figures contain cranemen, derrickmen, electrotypers, glaziers, lithographers, loom fixers, plate printers, stereotypers, stone carvers, and stone cutters.

Table A-10

Percentage Change in Craft Employment, by Category and Race, South,[1] Non-South,[2] and United States,[3] 1950–1960 [4]

SOUTH

	White			Nonwhite [5]		
	1950	1960	1960/ 1950	1950	1960	1960/ 1950
Foremen (n.e.c.) [6]	182,153	271,865	149	3,544	5,504	155
Mechanics and repairmen [7]	404,659	564,487	139	34,660	53,051	153
Metal craftsmen [8]	148,001	170,312	115	9,670	8,153	84
Construction craftsmen [9]	673,611	698,175	104	76,416	89,552	117
Other craftsmen [10]	240,792	401,151	167	18,900	28,352	150
Total	1,649,216	2,105,990	128	143,190	184,612	129

NON-SOUTH

	White			Nonwhite		
Foremen (n.e.c.)	542,713	802,812	148	5,768	12,365	214
Mechanics and repairmen	1,142,663	1,496,528	131	38,194	71,513	187
Metal craftsmen	780,963	890,107	114	17,295	28,980	168
Construction craftsmen	1,516,346	1,553,031	102	37,331	47,782	128
Other craftsmen	819,502	1,219,673	149	17,030	34,732	204
Total	4,802,277	5,962,151	124	115,618	195,372	169

UNITED STATES

	White			Nonwhite		
Foremen (n.e.c.)	724,866	1,074,677	148	9,312	17,869	192
Mechanics and repairmen	1,547,322	2,061,015	133	72,854	124,564	171
Metal craftsmen	928,964	1,060,419	114	26,965	37,133	138
Construction craftsmen	2,189,957	2,251,206	103	113,747	137,334	121
Other craftsmen	1,060,384	1,620,824	153	35,930	63,084	176
Total	6,451,493	8,068,141	125	258,808	379,984	147

[1] (Same as #2, Table A-9.)
[2] (Same as #3, Table A-9.)
[3] Includes figures for all states except Alaska and Hawaii.
[4] (Same as #1, Table A-9.)
[5] (Same as #5, Table A-9.)
[6] (Same as #6, Table A-9.)
[7] (Same as #7, Table A-9.)
[8] (Same as #8, Table A-9.)
[9] (Same as #9, Table A-9.)
[10] (Same as #10, Table A-9.)

CHAPTER 8

Union Racial Problems
in the South

SOUTHERN INDUSTRIAL AND LABOR RELATIONS HAVE BEEN INFLUENCED, as was inevitable, by the racial turmoil after 1950, especially following the Supreme Court's school desegregation decision of 1954. Both unions and employers faced difficult problems. Many national union leaders were afraid that the implementation of equalitarian racial policies would alienate Southern members and potential members. On the other hand, employers are often caught between pressures from Negroes, courts, and the federal government for equal treatment of colored workers and resistance from Southern whites to changing racial employment patterns. This chapter explores some aspects of the racial issue as it affects unions in the South, with emphasis on the reaction of Southern union members to equalitarian racial policies; the segregationist labor organizations formed in the South during the racial turmoil in the wake of the Supreme Court's desegregation decisions; and the effect of racial unrest on union organizing and political activity. In order to carry out these objectives, it will also be necessary to discuss some of the racial experiences of various international unions in the South.[1]

Opposition from Southern Members

Southern unionists have sometimes vigorously opposed efforts by central labor organizations to endorse equalitarian community racial policies. For example, the Chattanooga Central Labor Union was bitterly criticized by segregationist union leaders for endorsing the local school board's plans to comply with the Supreme Court's desegregation decision.[2] The CLU's action was prompted by a 1954 AFL convention resolution endorsing the Supreme Court's decision. Vicious attacks were forthcoming from labor segregationists led by members of the Printing Pressmen and joined by locals of the Switchmen, Carpenters, Plumbers, Machinists, Typographical Union, Stage Hands, Auto Workers (AFL), and International Brotherhood of Electrical Workers; in all, nine affiliated locals and one unaffiliated local opposed the CLU's actions. The CLU and the *Labor World*, the local labor paper, were accused of being under the domineering control of leaders "supporting organizations and sociological theories . . . dedicated to removing the last vestiges of our Southern heritage" and of "selling us out for 30 pieces of our own silver" by contributing union money to the NAACP. Local union leaders were also denounced as "alien Communist lovers and socializers who have had their way for a long time." According to the segregationists, the CLU could not deny "some responsibility for the disgusting integration of Negro and white workers in the labor movement in Tennessee."[3]

As a result of this criticism, some members dropped their subscriptions to the *Labor World*, some locals withdrew from the Central Labor Union, and a special meeting was called to reconsider the central body's support of the school board. This meeting, attended by the largest number of delegates since the 1930's, adopted a resolution which vowed to organize all workers in order to "keep gains of the bargaining table from being taken away by anti-labor legislation," but "because of the highly controversial nature of the issues raised by the Supreme Court's decision on segregation in the public schools, issues which cut across our ranks tending to divide us, it is hereby declared to be the policy of the Chattanooga Central Labor Union henceforth to refrain from involving itself on either side of this issue."[4]

The United Automobile Workers and other national unions likewise have had difficulties implementing equalitarian racial policies in the South. The UAW revoked the charter of a local in Dallas, Texas, in 1952 for refusing to follow the international's racial policies, and it has had considerable difficulty with locals in Memphis and Atlanta. The Memphis International Harvester local was placed under trustee-ship in 1960 after a long series of disputes with the international over racial matters, especially the segregation of drinking and toilet facili-ties at the local's new headquarters. At Harvester, Negro workers have been able to move into a variety of jobs as a result of the firmness on the part of both the company and the international in the face of vigorous opposition from local white members.[5] The Memphis UAW local also defied the international by raising funds for the Little Rock private segregated school organized after public schools were inte-grated. The UAW also has had considerable trouble through the years with its oldest Southern local in Atlanta. Indeed, this local even barred the eight Negro janitors in the plant from membership until forced by the international to admit them in 1946. Even after the Negroes were admitted, however, seating was segregated. In 1962 a Negro who attempted to sit in the white section was hit over the head with a chair by a white member. In 1961 Negroes were up-graded for the first time in the auto plant represented by this local. This gain for the Negroes was partly offset, however, by the loss of twelve jobs from which Negroes were "bumped" by whites after pro-duction lines were integrated.

United Packinghouse Workers (UPWA)

No union operating in the South has followed a more militantly equalitarian racial position than the UPWA. Its members have even gone so far as to strike against racial discrimination and to have non-discrimination clauses included in its contracts, which cover hiring as well as discrimination in conditions of employment and segregated plant facilities. The Packinghouse Workers had an antidiscrimina-tion program under the active direction of an international vice-president.

This relatively militant position has been caused by a number of factors, including a realization by the union's founders that the in-dustry could not be organized unless the large number of Negroes in it were won over; the militant equalitarian position of the Commu-nists, who have been very strong in some of the UPWA's districts; and a realization after 1948 that the union's growth depended on retaining the loyalty of the large and growing proportions of Negro members. A 1949 survey revealed that whites constituted 59 per cent of the union's membership, whereas Negroes represented 34 per cent and Mexicans 7 per cent.[6]

After this survey the UPWA adopted a program to more vigorously implement its racial policies. This invigorated program was based on the conviction that the regular structure of the union should be used to tackle in-plant and internal union problems.

Not all the opposition to the UPWA's racial policies was in the South. In Chicago, after a 1948 strike, some Packinghouse locals became virtually all-Negro as the UPWA got the reputation of being a "Negro" union. Whites in Chicago refused to attend meetings in the Negro section and resisted integrated social affairs.[7] Moreover, stockhandlers' locals in Chicago, St. Joseph, Omaha, and Forth Worth seceded from the UPWA rather than accept Negroes. These stockhandlers, or "wranglers," considered themselves a special breed whose status would be destroyed if they accepted Negroes.

But the most vigorous opposition to the UPWA's efforts undoubtedly came in the South. In Fort Worth attempts to desegregate cafeterias and rest rooms in 1952 were met with mob action and, despite the intervention of top management and UPWA President Ralph Helstein, the company felt it advisable to restore segregation. But just before Christmas 1952, when a strike would have resulted in the loss of holiday pay, facilities were desegregated in accordance with the agreement. Of 1400 workers in the plant, only about fifty withdrew from the union, and segregationists were unsuccessful in defeating the bi-racial slate of officers in the elections following these events. White workers in a Georgia local harassed UPWA representatives, particularly a Negro teacher, so severely that they were unable to conduct a school designed to teach them the benefits of integration. This local seceded from the UPWA and joined the Amalgamated Meat Cutters rather than submit to the UPWA's efforts to desegregate plant facilities.

In 1954 Louisiana UPWA leaders made an effort to get nine sugar locals to withdraw from the Packinghouse Workers partly because of the union's racial policies. The national union was able to avert the secession of five of its largest Louisiana locals with majority Negro memberships by appealing to the union's equalitarian racial position. Four relatively small Louisiana locals withdrew, but only two of these remained out of the UPWA. The others returned when they found it impossible to bargain alone and could find no other national union to take them. Thus, although the race question might have cost the UPWA two small sugar locals with a combined membership of under 200, it made it possible for the national union to retain its largest locals.

Elsewhere in the South, as at Atlanta, Birmingham, and Fort Worth, the UPWA lost some white members who withdrew, leaving the unions with predominantly Negro membership. In District 8 with headquarters in Fort Worth, white leaders who were accused of opposing the UPWA's racial policies were replaced and a Negro was elected district director in May 1954. In District 9, covering Alabama, Georgia, North Carolina, South Carolina, Virginia, Mississippi, Tennessee, and Florida, the district director was accused by the national vice-president in charge of the antidiscrimination policy with violating company policy because he held a segregated dinner. The charges against the district director were withdrawn after an investigation and protest by the CIO Civil Rights Department. The CRC concluded that the charges were politically inspired because of the anti-Communist position of the Atlanta district director, who was not even in town when the segregated dinner was scheduled. However, the charges were sufficiently important to defeat the regional director for reelection in 1954.[8]

The UPWA's opposition to the regional directors at Atlanta and Fort Worth and its opposition to segregation within the CIO caused the Packinghouse Workers to incur the enmity of other CIO unions in the South and contributed to the belief that the UPWA was following the Communist Party tactics of creating racial unrest by pushing racial integration faster than most whites were prepared to go. An event alienating many CIO members in the South was the UPWA's vigorous protest of segregation in Birmingham, Alabama, where the Packinghouse Workers complained of a segregated Political Action Committee dance and banquet in 1953. Because of these segregated affairs, the UPWA's vice-president and director of the Anti-Discrimination Department told the CIO Civil Rights Department that ". . . unless CIO-PAC in Jefferson County shows some indication of fulfilling CIO policy, we shall be forced to withdraw from Jefferson County CIO Council, boycott such Jim Crow PAC activities and refrain from holding union meetings in the CIO City Council Building until all signs of segregation are removed."[9]

However, it is not easy to determine the extent to which the Southern reaction to the UPWA's policies was due to racial prejudice or to a sincere belief that the union's actions were Communist-inspired. There is weighty evidence to support the conclusion that both elements were present. That political factors were involved is suggested in part by the clear evidence of Communist activity in the UPWA during this period.[10]   A UPWA school at the Monteagle, Tennessee, Highlander Folk School in March 1953 convinced many Southern UPWA leaders that the national union's policy was Communist-inspired.   It was announced at this school that the UPWA would support the case of an avowed Communist who had publicly resigned from the party, while claiming her loyalty to it, in order to sign the Taft-Hartley non-Communist affidavit.[11]   The UPWA Executive Board had taken the position that the affidavits should be signed.   A leader of the Southern sugar locals wrote CIO President Walter Reuther on January 4, 1954, that:

Every staff man and officer was told that he must attend the school.   According to the reports of those who did go, this school was nothing but an effort to indoctrinate those who attended in the Communist Party line. Foreign Policy and American programs were criticized and opposed in the same manner as appeared in the Communist Press.   America was blamed for starting the Korean War.   Russia was praised as a peace loving nation. This position was actively supported by the top officers of the U.P.W.A. They said the Korean War was an Imperialistic War and that the United States had no business in it.   They proposed that we remove all foreign military bases and work with Russia for peace.   Also Red China should be admitted to the United Nations as the true representative of the people of China.   A program to wipe out discrimination by force was approved.   At his discussion [a UPWA representative] stated that the Negroes were ready to shed blood to wipe out discrimination.[12]

Therefore, when Livestock Handlers Local 59 in Fort Worth voted overwhelmingly to withdraw from the UPWA, an official declared: "The only issue for it is Communist domination of the international. There is no race issue, except as the Communists have inflamed it to seize control of the international."[13]   The conviction that the UPWA's program was Communist-inspired was further strengthened when an international officer wrote asking for the resignation of UPWA representatives in Texas who had expressed dissatisfaction with the school.[14]

A CIO committee appointed by President Walter Reuther later in 1953 investigated the charges of Communist domination against the UPWA and found that although the top elected officers of the organization were "free from Communist domination or influence, . . . The committee's report did not . . . deal with Communist infiltration and influence in certain local unions and Districts of the Packinghouse workers where it is generally agreed that there does exist Communist influence."[15]

In conclusion, therefore, part of the Southern reaction to the UPWA's equalitarian policies was undoubtedly due to the belief that these charges were Communist-inspired, but was also probably due to the fact that the UPWA was following more equalitarian policies than many other major CIO unions in the region. In race relations as in wages and other matters, interunion comparisons are very important in internal union politics.

Pulp and Paper

The unions in the pulp and paper industry—Pulp, Sulphite and Paper Mill Workers (PSPMW) and the United Papermakers and Paperworkers (UPP)—have maintained segregated locals throughout the South, though there also were some integrated locals. After 1961, moreover, the UPP and the PSPMW merged some of their segregated locals, as we shall see later. There is also some evidence that although these organizations might not in theory have been auxiliaries, they in fact tended to have many of the same features as auxiliary locals. Like the petroleum-refining and tobacco industries, the race problem in the paper industry is restricted mainly to the South because there are relatively few Negroes in this industry outside the South.

In spite of the segregated local unions in the South, the paper union leaders argue that they have greatly improved the economic conditions of Negro workers and therefore resent charges of discrimination. These leaders apparently are unable to understand that in an earlier more paternalistic stage in union race relations, Negroes were more willing to have whites represent them and were not as inclined to protest segregated seniority rosters. Now, however, the ferment in the Negro community has produced demands for full equality.

As in the oil industry, Negroes were commonly hired into labor pools in the pulp and paper industry, whereas whites were hired directly in the operating department. The main difference between Northern and Southern paper mills was that workers in the labor pool (Negroes) did a lot of the work in the South that was done elsewhere by the operators and their helpers. In the paper industry, as in others, the separate seniority rosters were not invented solely to segregate jobs racially, but also were based on the training needs of the companies involved. The fact that Negroes were hired only for menial, dead-end jobs meant that they usually were not as qualified as whites to move into many higher-paying skilled jobs which could not be filled on the basis of seniority alone.

President Kennedy's Committee on Equal Employment Opportunities (PCEEO) caused considerable reaction in the Southern pulp and paper industry during 1962 when it ordered employment in the mills desegregated. The companies apparently were seriously influenced by the PCEEO's threat, because high-ranking company officials supervised job desegregation. Upper management officials met with unions and supervisory employers in order to emphasize the need to integrate in order to keep federal contracts. But some union leaders led protest rallies in an effort to maintain segregation. There were scattered acts of violence, and relations between Negroes and whites within the local unions were strained, but white union leaders and their segregationist allies in the local communities were frustrated in their efforts to avert integration of the mills; about the only advice the White Citizens' Council could offer the protesting union members was "write your Congressmen."

A meeting of 400 segregationists in the high-school auditorium at Springhill, Louisiana, illustrates the feelings of paper union leaders in the deep South. The meeting was called by nine local unions of the huge International Paper mill in Springhill and was attended by members of the Louisiana legislature, White Citizens' Council representatives, and union members; indeed, union leaders said the meeting was open to "all those interested in maintaining our southern traditions."[16] One union leader was quoted as saying that local union leaders had met with the company on August 1, 1962, and had been told that Executive Order 10925 "prohibits the company from using any discretion in hiring employees based on race or color." He told the segregationists that "This executive order is a result of the Anti-God, Anti-Christ Kennedys, Inc."[17] The union leader added that "They may cram it down our throats, but they can't make us agree and like it. Integration is now in Springhill. We don't want trouble and won't agitate trouble, but we are against integration. Our local unions won't be responsible, but we'll stand behind our men."[18] Observers in Springhill report that there was considerable bitterness, but no whites quit their jobs to protest integration. However, very few Negroes were hired the first two years because few Negroes were able to pass the tests introduced when separate lines of progression were abolished. Company officials say the tests were necessary because Negroes must be hired who have the ability to work throughout the mill. Because of limited advancement opportunities by Negroes before integration, little attention had to be given to the qualifications of Negro recruits. On the other hand, Negroes have moved into jobs previously reserved for whites and have been retained in lay-offs according to their seniority. Because of the white unionists' outspoken resistance to integration, the Negroes appear to have lost much of their interest in the union.

United Steelworkers of America (USA)

The steel companies have also followed the tradition of having Negroes concentrated in menial or difficult jobs in the South. Since 1954, however, there has been agitation by Negro members of the USA to integrate these separate lines of progression. At the Sheffield Steel Division of Armco Steel in Houston, for example, there were about 3000 employees, 1300 of whom were Negroes. Around 1954 some Negro workers at Sheffield started agitating for job desegregation, resulting in a contract of May 31, 1956, abolishing separate jobs. Negroes who passed a qualification test could move into line 1 or previously all-white jobs. The Negroes filed suit in the federal district court seeking to have the tests discontinued. The tests were discriminatory, according to the suit, because the whites already in line 1 jobs did not have to pass the tests. However, in a decision that has been quoted in many other cases, the court upheld the tests as a business necessity.[19] By the end of 1957, at least ninety Negro workers had passed the test and forty-five of them had moved into the bottom of the previously all-white line of progression. By 1962 some 180 Negro workers had moved into the line of progression for previously all-white jobs and about 200 of them had passed the test. However, Negroes complained that not many Negroes had moved very far up in line 1 jobs.

Although the Negroes were not satisfied with the results of Sheffield Steel's actions, elsewhere in the South even less job desegregation had taken place by 1962. At Atlantic Steel in Atlanta, for example, a 1953 study found that the 600 Negro workers, of 1600 total employees, were reasonably satisfied with the union. The USA local was described as working out its problems

within the framework of southern tradition and custom, rather than by attempting revolutionary action. It accepts the policies of segregation that are practiced at the plant in deference to southern mores. But it will put the entire resources of the union behind an employee who has been subjected to individual discrimination because of his color, and it works toward expanding job opportunities for Negroes.[20]

Shortly after these words were written, however, Negroes sought outside help to abolish job segregation. The NAACP's labor secretary charged in 1958 that at Atlantic Steel, ". . . because of the operation of separate seniority lines, hundreds of Negro workers suffer dishonest and false job classifications, are limited to some few production and menial job classifications and are denied the right to develop job skills which would permit employment in more desirable production jobs." [21]

In August 1961 the union negotiated a contract providing for the transfer of workers between departments at Atlantic on the basis of seniority, but those who did so lost occupational and departmental seniority. In 1962, therefore, most Negroes remained in low-wage classifications. There were at that time about 1250 employees at Atlantic, one-third of whom were Negroes. Of thirty-two labor grades, Negroes had progressed only to grade 11, which paid $2.65 an hour; the lowest classes paid $2.02 and the highest $4.12. About fifty Negroes are reported to have held jobs higher than class 7, which is the dividing line between skilled and unskilled jobs according to management and union representatives.

As a result of continued dissatisfaction with their progress at Atlantic, thirteen Negro workers filed a petition with the NLRB—through the NAACP—alleging that the local had acquiesced in discriminatory wage rates and had agreed "to a seniority system which perpetuated segregation and confined Negroes to unskilled jobs." Supporting the NLRB regional director, the Board's general counsel ruled that the jobs in question "were in fact different and that the classifications were established by experts on a national basis entirely without regard to the identity of any individuals who occupied the jobs," and that "far from encouraging or even tolerating discriminatory working conditions, the Union had in fact utilized its bargaining strength to the end of eliminating existing disparity." [22] Therefore, in the final action in this case, the NLRB's general counsel sustained the regional director's refusal to issue a complaint against the Steelworkers. [23]

Birmingham is the iron and steel center of the South and fully 40 per cent of the workers there were Negroes in 1951. [24] In Birmingham Negroes worked mainly in "heavy physical work, and simple, repetitive machine operations (also often requiring a high degree of physical exertion and endurance)." [25] Until 1963 the situation in the Birmingham iron and steel industry apparently had changed very little since 1955 when Hawley concluded that if the USA contract were interpreted literally in a particular steel company,

Negro workers would have a complete range of all job opportunities which exist within a given district or area. In practice, however, informal lines of promotion exist and these apparently operate to restrict the Negro worker's job opportunities. . . .

In the majority of firms, then, promotion systems include formal or informal promotion lines. These lines of promotion are commonly established on a color basis, and partly as a result of their operation the Negro shares in promotional opportunities only to a limited extent.[26]

The Steelworkers locals in Birmingham experienced considerable racial tension during the unrest following the 1954 Supreme Court desegregation decision. As in other places, White Citizens' Council members were active in the USA locals. In one Birmingham local, for instance, with about 2500 members, 1000 of whom were Negroes, resolutions were introduced (and defeated) by WCC supporters calling for the local's disaffiliation with the national organization over racial matters. Whites in this local were vigorously opposed to equal job opportunities for Negroes and the labor movement's contributions to the NAACP. This tension caused Negro attendance in local union meetings to decline markedly. Negroes who did attend tended to segregate themselves in union meetings, and social affairs were entirely segregated. Negroes in this local had taken no steps to abolish separate racial lines of progression by the time of the writer's investigations in 1962. Elsewhere, however, the important U. S. Steel subsidiary—the Tennessee Coal and Iron Company—upgraded Negroes in 1963 under pressure from President Kennedy's Committee on Equal Employment Opportunity.

In June 1964, the USA signed a joint nondiscrimination pact with eleven major steel companies (Armco, Bethlehem, Colorado Fuel and Iron, Great Lakes, Inland, Jones and Laughlin, Pittsburgh, Republic, United States Steel, Wheeling, and Youngstown Sheet & Tube) which pledged "continuing action to advance non-discrimination in employment in the steel industry." The unions and the companies previously had signed "Plans for Progress" with the President's Committee on Equal Employment Opportunity. According to the joint agreement signed in June 1964, the union-management Human Relations Committee, established after the 116-day steel strike of 1959–1960 to explore mutual problems, was "presently engaged in intensive joint examination of problems of training and motivation to determine what additional programs may be desirable to enable employes of all races to benefit from the employment and promotional opportunities developing within the operations of the companies." The joint nondiscrimination agreement was an outgrowth of the work of the Human Relations Committee.

We may conclude with an observation concerning the racial policies of the United Steelworkers in general. The activities of USA's formal civil-rights machinery were directed more at community civil-rights programs than at internal union problems. Moreover, as compared with the UAW, the USA had very few Negro international representatives and officials. Reasons suggested for these differences are: the USA was created by the UMW, and follows its paternalistic pattern; Negroes within the USA have agitated less than those in the UAW because they felt that Philip Murray would "look out for" their interests; the Steelworkers were organized later than the UAW, so that by the time the Steelworkers Organizing Committee became an international union, a bureaucracy under Philip Murray was firmly established, whereas there was considerable political ferment within the Auto Workers, in which the Negroes were politically very important, before the Reuther faction established control of the UAW after 1946; the spread between the highest and lowest job classifications in steel is much greater than in autos, creating an additional barrier between whites, who generally have the higher-paying jobs, and the Negroes concentrated in menial occupations.

United Rubber Workers

The rubber industry in the South, like steel, autos, petroleum refining, and others, generally has had Negroes concentrated in lower job classifications or disagreeable job classifications not readily filled by whites. The URW has had some difficulty with its locals at Jackson, Mississippi, Tuscaloosa, Alabama, and Memphis, Tennessee over racial matters.

The most important case involving the URW in the South concerned efforts by the 1200 Negro workers (of 3500 total) at a Memphis rubber plant to abolish the "informal" seniority system. The Negroes complained of discrimination because they were laid off in violation of the formal contract but in accordance with "informal" seniority. When an arbitrator refused to enforce the contract, the Negroes—at the suggestion of a local white leader—filed for an injunction to have the company and the union enforce the contract. The company admitted that the informal seniority system predated the union, but wanted the union to take the initiative in abolishing the system. Union leaders, on the other hand, were willing to shift responsibility to the courts. The parties negotiated a nondiscriminatory contract in 1957 opening jobs to Negroes throughout the plant. The net result of these actions, however, was that Negroes lost more jobs than they gained because more Negroes were "bumped" out of previously Negro jobs than whites out of previously white jobs. This action also caused some tension within the local, causing a biracial slate of officers to be replaced by an all-white slate. However, tension had abated sufficiently by 1959 to permit the election of one Negro on a slate of ten officers.

Tobacco Workers

The Tobacco Workers International Union has been unsuccessful in organizing the huge R. J. Reynolds Tobacco Company, partly because of historical racial conflicts. The importance of Reynolds to the TWIU is indicated by the fact that in 1960 this plant had about 10,000 employees at a time when the TWIU had about 34,000 members. Although other factors also account for the Tobacco Workers' inability to organize Reynolds, a major cause of failure undoubtedly has been the union's lack of support among the Negroes, who constitute about half the plant's employees. Negro employment has been declining at Reynolds, however, and constituted less than 50 per cent in 1962.

Reynolds was organized by the TWIU shortly after the First World War, but lost bargaining rights during the subsequent open-shop period. The plant was organized by the Food, Tobacco and Agricultural and Allied Workers (FTA) between 1944 and 1947. The FTA was supported mainly by Negroes and lost bargaining rights in 1948 after losing a strike which was supported by very few whites. Whites failed to support the FTA partly because its organizers enrolled Negroes first, but also because of its reputation for being a Communist union. The TWIU has subsequently lost several elections due to its failure to get Negro support.

However, the TWIU was also handicapped at Reynolds by other factors, including fear by some TWIU leaders that victory at Reynolds would add enough new members to upset internal political affairs; the union's long history of failure; the company's paternalism; the physical organizing difficulties presented by twenty-eight buildings with thirty-five separate gates; the large number of women workers in the plant; and its maintenance of segregated locals, which turned the militant Winston-Salem Negro community against the TWIU.

Textiles

Many observers believe that community race relations are likely to be "worse" where Negroes constitute larger proportions of the population. In union race relations, however, there has sometimes been more segregationist activity where there were relatively few Negro members. At a multiplant local of the UAW in Atlanta, for example, the greatest anti-Negro feeling was caused by the faction from a plant which had no Negroes; indeed, the Imperial Wizard of the KKK in Georgia was a UAW member from that plant. Similarly, in Port Arthur, Texas, the greatest racial feeling was not in the Gulf Group within Oil, Chemical and Atomic Workers Local 4-23, with many Negroes, but in the Texaco Group of that local with very few. The textile workers in the Piedmont also have vigorously protested the equalitarian racial policies of the American labor movement, even though there are very few Negro workers in the textile industry. For instance, a survey of twenty-three locals of the Textile Workers Union of America in 1959 (which overstates the proportion of Negroes because it intentionally selected several locals with large Negro membership for study), in Georgia, North Carolina, South Carolina, and Tennessee, revealed that of a total of 12,003 union members, only 975 were Negroes; 850 of these Negroes were in five locals. Almost all the Negroes employed in these plants were in maintenance or housekeeping jobs. Eight of the locals had ten or fewer Negro members and four locals had between ten and 100 Negro members (26, 30, 20, and 25 members); only five locals had over 100 Negro members.

The most common experience of these twenty-three locals was that no Negroes attended meetings, especially after the 1954 Supreme Court desegregation decision.[27]

All these locals had had formal protests from members, and sometimes officers, concerning the labor movement's equalitarian racial policies, the most common protest being over the labor movement's contributions of financial aid to the NAACP (at Haw River, N. C., for example, stewards and dues collectors resigned and called for a special protest meeting when they were shown a picture of Walter Reuther making a contribution to the NAACP) and over the AFL-CIO's support of the Supreme Court's desegregation decision. However, apparently only one of the locals, at Clifton, S. C., had had a formal proposal that the local disaffiliate from the national union, and that proposal failed. Textile Workers also were active supporters of organizations like the Ku Klux Klan and the segregationist labor unions discussed later.

The Textile Workers have had two significant incidents involving racial policy. The Front Royal, Va., local supported efforts to form segregated schools after public schools in that city were ordered to desegregate. The private school was conducted in the union hall. The local also attempted to support the private school financially. However, the international union halted these activities by placing the local under trusteeship and its action was upheld by the national convention and a three-member arbitration board which included Arthur J. Goldberg.

In another incident, the TWUA elicited mild protest and a few resignations from Southern members in 1956 when it passed a resolution condemning the White Citizens' Councils as enemies of the workers. Some Southerners walked out of the convention in protest and a few others resigned. In the South the resolution was discussed in almost every local in South Carolina, but delegates to the convention told local members that the TWUA's action was "just a resolution" which Southern delegates had opposed. A local at Spartanburg, S. C., introduced a resolution against the convention's action, but after discussion expunged it from the record. One member withdrew from the Spartanburg local because of the resolution and five withdrew from a local in Columbia. There were also protests from several locals in North Carolina, especially at Draper and Spray, but officers were able to limit resignations in these places to about a dozen. Furthermore, organizers in North Carolina reported that the resolution had no influence at all on their organizing activities in that state. The TWUA's resolution was publicized prominently in newspapers in Greensboro, Winston-Salem, and Leaksville, but according to TWUA representatives the publicity was not antagonistic to the union. Outside the North Carolina-South Carolina area, TWUA members gave little attention to the resolution.

American Federation of Teachers

The American Federation of Teachers (AFT) lost five Southern locals which refused to obey a 1956 convention ultimatum to integrate; the locals had about 4000 members and paid some 30,000 dollars to the AFT annually.[28] About 3000 of these members were in Atlanta and vicinity, and the others were in New Orleans and Chattanooga.

The white local in Atlanta had a long history and was the fourth largest local in the AFT.[29] These losses left the AFT with about 850 Negro members in the South. The relatively small Negro membership was somewhat surprising in view of the fact that Negro locals were theoretically integrated and that an integrated local had been established in Houston, Texas, in 1958.

AFT officials hoped a strong equalitarian racial stand would induce more Negro teachers to join their union. The hope was not realized, apparently because Negro teachers occupy a relatively high status within the Negro community, and, therefore, the element of discontent which is a frequent prerequisite to union organization was absent. Moreover, many Negro teachers join the National Education Association, which has permitted segregated locals and, as a "professional" organization, has had more appeal to Southern teachers than the AFT. However, in 1961 the NEA decided to take measures to eliminate segregated branches in the South.

Segregationist Labor Organizations

The anti-integrationist labor organizations formed in the wake of the Supreme Court's 1954 school desegregation decision created some alarm among national union leaders. One of these segregationist organizations was the United Southern Employees Association (USEA), chartered in North Carolina in 1956. The USEA sought to organize the strikers at the Rock Hill (South Carolina) Printing and Finishing Plant in 1957 and to lead them through a Textile Workers picket line. Subsequently chartered as a corporation in Virginia, Alabama, Florida, Georgia, South Carolina, and North Carolina, the USEA made a strong appeal to employers by encouraging "cooperation and fair dealing," as well as anti-integrationist policies.[30] It also attempted to attract membership through a welfare program, including hospital and pension benefits at a cost to the worker of only 65 cents a month.[31]

A USEA leader told the writer: "The great majority of USEA members are ex-AFL-CIO union members who have quit the AFL-CIO because of [its] race-baiting tactics. . . . We believe that southerners should organize and control their own unions just as we elect our own congressmen from the South to represent us in Congress. We don't need northern rabble rousers to represent us in labor." [32]

The leader of the USEA attempted unsuccessfully to form an alliance with Ku Klux Klan (KKK) organizations in the Piedmont area. Many of the Klan members belonged to the Textile Workers and dropped their KKK membership after they were told that membership in the Klan was tantamount to membership in the USEA. When the USEA criticized the CIO at a Klan meeting, union members protested that they had come to talk about the "colored and white" and not to discuss "our union." The USEA's agitation, together with a newspaper revelation that the KKK had admitted a sixteen-year-old boy, resulted in a decline of Klan membership from about 3000 to around 300 in the Rock Hill, South Carolina, area during 1957.[33]

The USEA's general objectives included organizing all workers in order to drive the AFL-CIO out of the South; improving industry by "increasing the efficiency of the service and by instilling confidence, good will and understanding between our members and their employers[34]; eliminating "communistic" Northern-led unions; promoting the enactment of "laws requiring all advocates of integration to be 'sterilized' so that they will be unable to produce a 'mongrelized offspring'"; "relief and a reversal of the United States Supreme Court 1954 Desegregation decision . . . on the grounds that one of the Justices [Felix Frankfurter] who sat in judgment in that ANTI-SOUTH decision was a former attorney and legal advisor to the N.A.A.C.P."; defeat of liberal candidates for office by splitting Negro-labor alliances where they exist; and the enactment of "right-to-work" laws. The USEA also challenges the view, common in some circles, that racial strife will impede industrialization:

Some of the Wall Street Communist-minded industrialists and some of the Communist-controlled newspapers along with the Communist union leaders are trying to tell the Southern people that industries will not move South unless we accept integration. Of course the propaganda isn't true, because industries continue to move Southward and the most of them moving South is to get away from the Communist union leaders and their brain-washed mongrelized rank and file members who have no respect for law and order, not to mention morals. If their propaganda was true—and the USEA says to hell with any industry or company that will move South only if we Southerners accept the Communist's scheme of integration. All honorable Southerners will accept Hoover Days or go back to the plow before they will yield to the demands of some South-moving industry to ruin our children forever. One badly needed industry that we don't have in the South is a rope factory. We may be needing many ropes before this war is over in order to accommodate the Northern carpetbagger race agitators.[35]

The USEA's doctrinal flexibility is indicated by the fact that the foregoing statement could be issued by the same organization that made the following declaration:

The men and women of the USEA . . . are most earnestly and sincerely dedicated to the cause of freedom, justice and righteousness. With quiet reserve and without emotional heat or excitement, they are of honest convictions, serious of purpose, and tireless in their efforts in behalf of the dignity of the individual to be entrusted with freedom to conduct himself in justice and in righteousness for others, as for himself.[36]

The USEA apparently generated more publicity than collective-bargaining contracts. It was temporarily active in many places but it never succeeded in winning bargaining rights or apparently in establishing permanent labor organizations. It appears to have been limited mainly to the Piedmont, though it is reported to have moved into Birmingham after another segregationist group—the Southern Aircraft Workers (SAW)—failed to win bargaining rights from the UAW at Hayes Aircraft between 1956 and 1958. UAW officials were surprised at SAW's meager support since the vast majority of Hayes workers were strong segregationists and many of the leaders who fought for the UAW at Hayes were the same unionists who had walked out of a union education meeting in North Carolina to protest racial discussions.

An effort was also made to launch a Southern Federation of Labor in Birmingham, July 21, 1956, "to drive the AFL-CIO back North with its notions of integration." However, the meager attendance at these meetings suggested very little support for the SFL. In what was billed as a mass meeting, 135 persons appeared at the afternoon session, including four AFL-CIO observers, four firemen required by the city, a photographer from *Life,* and many curious local union leaders who had no intention of joining the SFL. At the evening meeting, attended by approximately 250 persons, it was announced that the SFL would concentrate on boring from within rather than forming a separate organization. Little has subsequently been heard from the SFL.

Another attempt at a dual labor movement was the Southern Crafts, Inc., headed by a railroad engineer from Birmingham. Southern Crafts was restricted to whites, charged dues of $2 a month, and one of the main reasons the members of this organization withdrew from the AFL-CIO was that they did not "feel that they [could] remain a part of an organization that [would] take its members' money and force integration upon the South." [37]

The Southern Crafts, like USEA, supports laws restricting union security because "THE SUREST WAY to maintain segregation in Alabama and the South for those who earn a living by the sweat of their brow is to preserve our right to work laws." [38] Southern Crafts believes that "without exception, national labor leaders directing the campaign to strike down right to work laws in 17 states, mostly in the South, are bitter enemies of our Southern segregation policy and are working hand-in-glove with the NAACP to uproot it."

Efforts to secure membership figures on Southern Crafts were unsuccessful. It would appear, however, that the organization had very few members even in the Birmingham area.

The Southern States Conference of Union People, formed by a group of Chattanooga unionists, aimed to work from within the regular unions in an effort to educate the AFL-CIO to anti-integrationist policies. The founding committee adopted a resolution which declared that the AFL-CIO was "under the control of labor leaders who are aiding and abetting the mixing of the White and Negro races in our public schools and elsewhere, and . . . have contributed many thousands of dollars to the N.A.A.C.P., an organization dedicated to the elimination of our Southern principle of segregation, and . . . Walter Reuther is a member of the Board of Directors of the N.A.A.C.P., an organization that is Communist influenced and dedicated to destroying our Southern civilization, and . . . ." Because of these things, the SSCUP:

RESOLVED, that (A) to maintain our racial integrity and characteristics, our health, and freedom to choose our associates and the associates of our children in any environments.

(B) [T]o preserve our Constitution States Rights and our status as union people.

(C) [T]o oppose those in our Union movement who have aligned themselves with the radicals and the N.A.A.C.P.

(D) [T]o prevent those radicals from forcing us and our children to comingle with ethnic opposites . . . .

WE, the following members of Union Labor, to implement the aforementioned resolves, join ourselves into a unit to provide a rallying point for all freedom-loving American Unionists who are concerned about the fate of this nation and who desire to maintain the established pattern of life in the South and the integrity of both racial groups which have been living in harmony without outside dictation for many generations.[39]

The Federation for Constitutional Government was organized at Memphis in December 1957 to coordinate the activities of the White Citizens' Councils in twelve Southern states.[40] A leader in the Mississippi WCC movement said that the WCC's were not antilabor but prosegregation and if Mississippi labor was prosegregation, "then we are together." [41] Although the WCC's are not avowedly antilabor, there is no question of their opposition to some national union leaders and especially the CIO before the merger and the AFL-CIO now.

The official paper of the Citizens' Councils of America published a list under the caption "Here is the Enemy!," which included those organizations "appearing in House and Senate committee records as favoring Civil Rights and Anti-South force legislation during 1957 and 1959." Along with the Episcopal Church, other church groups, and civil-rights organizations, this list included the following labor organizations: Amalgamated Meat Cutters' and Butchers (sic) Workmen of North America; AFL-CIO; International Longshoremen's and Warehousemen's Union; International Union of Electrical, Radio and Machine Workers, AFL-CIO; Michigan State AFL-CIO; National Alliance of Postal Workers; New York Hotel Trades Council, AFL-CIO; Textile Workers Union of America, AFL-CIO; Transport Workers Union of America, AFL-CIO; United Automobile, Aircraft and Agricultural Implement Workers; and the United Steelworkers of America, AFL-CIO. The editor suggested, "you file this list for future reference." [42]

Various other groups usually using the names of states' rights associations are related to the Citizens' Councils in personnel and objectives. These groups are also opposed to the racial policies of national labor organizations. A Mississippi states' rights group appealed for support after a statement by Chief Justice Earl Warren that South Carolina had to comply with the Court's desegregation decision and the NAACP's assertion that nothing could be gained in an extended delay in ordering an end to segregation. A "confidential memorandum" from the group referred to

The Communist Party, the Communist-front dominated NAACP, the Committee of One Hundred, the CIO, Americans for Democratic Action (ADA), its Republican counterpart, The Advance, no less than *eighty-seven* named Negro Communist-front organizations, and all other radical left-wing groups are highly organized, liberally financed by misled tax exempt foundations, by the contributions of misguided "liberals" and by the enforced levy of Union dues to be used without any regard for the wishes of the individual union member. . . .
We are twenty years late in beginning an organized fight for our survival. . . . It is perfectly clear at this point in our history that the State will be to a large extent dominated and controlled by the NAACP, even as our government has been to an amazing degree during recent administrations. [43]

Effect of Racial Differences on Organizing

A factor of considerable concern to unions has been the effect of racial conflict on union organizing. Many unions are relatively weak in the South but are under constant pressure to strengthen Southern jurisdictions in order to protect membership elsewhere. This concern for organizing has caused some unions to take measures to appease white segregationists where there were few Negroes, or to cater to Negroes where they constituted sizable elements in the bargaining units.

The AFL-CIO's pro-integration and anti-White Citizens' Council position brought strong reaction from the South, after the Federation's 1956 civil-rights "Progress Report" was widely publicized in that region. AFL-CIO President Meany received an average of 200 protest letters a day from Southern union members. There apparently was an organized campaign to get these letters sent because two-thirds of them began with "I, personally, resent . . . ." That protest was genuinely widespread was confirmed, however, by reports from AFL-CIO representatives and a survey conducted by the Jewish Labor Committee. In his answer to each letter, George Meany explained that he had attacked the White Citizens' Councils because they were controlled by anti-union employers.[44]

The AFL-CIO's reaction to these protests was to adopt a policy position which emphasized no recession from its stated racial policy, but a minimization of public declarations in the South.

Meanwhile, Southern organizing efforts were being countered by anti-union campaigns which stressed trade-union support of integration and financial contributions to the NAACP. The latter charge seems to have been particularly effective with Southerners who were told that joining a union is tantamount to joining the NAACP, an or ganization widely detested by whites in the South. A letter to all employees of the American Hardware Corporation, Clarksdale, Mississippi, from the Coahoma County Chamber of Commerce not only claimed that unions had done nothing to promote the region's industrialization, but that "in practically every instance of industrial expansion into this area and throughout the South, the union of the home plant has threatened to strike to block such a move."

The Coahoma Chamber of Commerce did not restrict its appeal to economic matters, however:

The CIO-AFL [sic] and all of its national leaders have repeatedly stated that they believe in integration of the white and colored races and are supporting the National Association for the Advancement of Colored People with union funds. Do you want your money to be given to the NAACP? If you join a union you can be sure that some of your own money will go directly to it.

The race argument was used against the International Union of Electrical Workers in its election at Sperry Rand Corporation Vickers plant, in Jackson, Mississippi, June 1957. During the election campaign a local paper printed on page one, four columns wide, a picture of IUE's president, James B. Carey, dancing with a Negro woman; this picture was taken in Geneva, Switzerland, and Carey was dancing with a Nigerian union representative's wife. The editorial accompanying the picture said those who favor "whites and Negroes dancing cheek by jowl as 'Brother' Carey is doing should, of course, vote to let the IUE take over control of the Vickers plant and thereby give moral approval of Brother Carey and the company he keeps." [45] The IUE won the election at Vickers, but in September 1957 the same picture helped defeat the union at the NECO Company in Bay Springs, Mississippi.

There were, however, other factors contributing to the IUE's loss at NECO and victory at Vickers. The sexual composition and level of education of the workers in the two plants differed: the Vickers workers were mostly male high-school graduates, whereas the NECO workers were mostly women. Second, the opposition to the union on racial grounds at Vickers was more by the community, especially the strongly segregationist *Jackson Daily News,* and less by the employer, whereas the employer offered the main opposition to the IUE at NECO. Moreover, Vickers is located in a metropolitan area, whereas NECO is in a small rural community of 1302 people; unions generally have more difficulty organizing in rural than urban areas. There were also few alternative sources of employment for any worker at Bay Springs who decided to defy the employer by joining the union, whereas Vickers workers, living in a larger metropolitan area, had other choices. Further, it is probably significant that NECO sold its products mainly to nonunion retailers, and Vickers products were used by employers who frequently dealt with unions. In short, all these factors would have made it much more difficult for the IUE to have organized NECO than Vickers, even if the race issue had not been raised.

Thus, it is not easy to determine the effectiveness of such appeals on union organizing activities. However, the incitement of racial prejudices is probably a minor factor in the spectrum of deep-seated obstacles to union growth that may be observed throughout Southern labor history.[46] As in the R. J. Reynolds Tobacco case, racial factors might be important where nonunion and union forces in a plant are about evenly divided, but has probably been exaggerated as a factor impeding union growth, because workers who are afraid to join unions —or who see no need to do so—frequently use the racial views of the national union or the AFL-CIO as an excuse not to join. If workers are convinced that unions are necessary in their particular situations, they will give little weight to the organization's racial policies in making their decisions to join a union.

This is not to argue, of course, that race conflict in the South has not affected union activities. When unions organized in the South before the Supreme Court's 1954 decision, the race issue was less frequently raised than after 1954, or if it was raised, it could be dismissed by showing Southern union supporters that Negro votes were needed to win the NLRB election or that the economic strength of the organization required colored support. If the opponents of integration persisted in the face of these arguments, and if they were either already segregated or were considered vital to the national union, segregated locals were formed. To be sure, organizers were always conscious of the issue and adopted various strategies to handle their campaigns. Such strategies involved consideration of the relative importance of Negroes and whites in the bargaining unit, whether to use Negro or white organizers in a given situation, which race to organize first, or whether to form segregated or integrated locals. Regardless of the strategy adopted, Negroes would usually segregate themselves in union meetings if segregated locals were not established, and very little subsequent publicity or attention appears to have been given to racial matters. The ferment following the 1954 school desegregation decisions insured that notice would be given to equalitarian policies by segregationists and that discriminatory practices would be attacked by the NAACP and the Negro press.

Although they are generally wary of racial statements, some state labor councils in the South have also started taking bolder stands on racial matters. In March 1960, for example, the North Carolina AFL-CIO unanimously adopted a resolution on the

Negro student groups throughout the South who are demonstrating through the use of peaceful labor techniques such as the picket line, the sit down and the consumer boycott for equal rights to eat in public places.

Therefore be it resolved that this Third Annual Convention of the AFL-CIO express its approval of the efforts of these Negro student groups and express our disapproval of the unwarranted police actions now being carried out in many of these demonstrations as violations of the rights of American citizens to free speech and free assembly.[47]

Some union organizers even reported that civil-rights demonstrations in the South after 1960 have actually helped their organizing efforts. Frank Parker, assistant Southern director for the Retail, Wholesale and Department Store Workers, which has consistently sought to implement its equalitarian policies in the South, reported that the civil-rights demonstrators have caused whites to be more inclined to organize. According to Parker:

Workers have seen these demonstrations and picket-lines involving civil rights and some responded by saying, "If they can get away with it, why can't we?" Of course, this is not new with many Negro workers. They have joined and fought for our union in the past. But the demonstrations have helped to spur them on, to encourage them to look for the union to help them. I would say that in South Georgia in the Macon area, and in South Alabama where we've been organizing, we probably would not have been successful if it hadn't been for the demonstrations in Albany, Georgia . . . some employers use the civil rights agitation against our union, sometimes successfully. . . . Of course, most often this type of attack doesn't help the boss at all.[48]

Organizers from other sections of the South confirm Parker's experiences.[49] This is not to imply, of course, that white workers have embraced the civil-rights cause, they are merely attracted by the methods.

Organizers have noted, however, that although the race issue might not have been a very important factor keeping whites from voting for unions, there is an apparent tendency in some sections of the South for Negroes to give less support to unions than formerly. Until around 1957–1958 unions almost always felt that Negroes would support the union in organizing campaigns. Since then, however, some elections have been lost for lack of Negro support. This is apparently caused by the growing rift between the Negro community and organized labor, reflecting the NAACP's widely publicized attacks on the AFL-CIO and its affiliates after 1958.

We should also emphasize the divergent effects of racial unrest on different kinds of unions. Noncollective-bargaining organizations like the federations and central labor unions are more likely to lose members for racial reasons than local or international unions. This appears to be true because the federations' functions are largely ceremonial, public relations, and political, which do not normally receive the overwhelming support of the locals in a geographic area. In the South, for example, only about half of the locals in a state are usually affiliated with the state AFL-CIO. Locals therefore can and have disaffiliated with the state federations for racial reasons. In Alabama, for example, Governor George C. Wallace has, according to the state labor leaders, encouraged local unions to disaffiliate with the state federation. Locals with about 15,000 members disaffiliated with the state federation (whose total affiliated membership was 60,000 in 1964) between 1962 and 1964.[50]

Political Action

As noted in the USEA case, one of the basic objectives of Southern segregationists has been to break liberal-labor-Negro political alliances. These coalitions have rarely been very strong but often have been effective when the race issue was secondary to joint economic considerations. In other cases, especially in the deep South, union leaders have been afraid of racial alliances, particularly on a statewide basis; in some of these areas labor has been able to accomplish its objectives without the aid of Negro votes, and in others union leaders fear that such coalitions will lead to anti-union legislation.

Segregationists believe that if the number of Negro votes increases to the point at which union leaders are willing to deal with Negro leaders, the balance of power will swing away from segregationist politicians. They consider it important, therefore, to fight unions or bring pressure to bear on union members to support segregation measures and oppose the racial policies of national unions. One effective technique for splitting Negro-labor coalitions is to support prolabor segregationists for public office.

Arkansas furnishes an illustration of the effect of racial conflict on political activity. Governor Orval Faubus was elected in 1956 with Negro and labor support. Late in 1957, however, after much racial tension following the Little Rock school situation, the majority of unionists continued to support Faubus, whereas Negroes obviously were unable to do so. Similar coalitions have been split in Florida and North Carolina when unions supported candidates who were unacceptable to Negroes.

Segregationists have not always succeeded in breaking Negro-labor alliances and defeating "moderates." In 1960, for example, a Negro-labor alliance held together in Tennessee, despite vigorous efforts of segregationists, and provided an overwhelming margin of victory for the late Senator Estes Kefauver in his campaign for reelection. Union leaders attribute Kefauver's victory to hard work by unions, which considered the Tennessee campaign a key contest, and to the fact that the philosophical differences between Senator Kefauver and his conservative opponent gave workers a clear choice. The outcome might have been different if a prolabor segregationist had run against Kefauver. Moreover, in the Tennessee campaign unions emphasized economic and not race issues.

Negro-labor coalitions are being formed in other Southern states, sometimes with the aid of liberals or other minority groups. In Texas, for example, a formal coalition was established between Negro, labor, Mexican-Americans, and liberal groups in 1963. Since Negroes and Mexican-Americans had about 30 per cent of the Texas population in 1960, labor leaders hope that the liberal coalition can gain control of the Texas Democratic Party. This hope is based on the prediction that the growth of the Republican Party in the state (and in the South) will split whites along economic lines, giving a liberal-labor-Negro-Latin coalition the balance of political power. Growing urbanization, increasing union membership, and legislative reapportionment are all expected to increase the power of this coalition. Of course, there is also the assumption that the forces which unite the groups in the coalition are more important than the differences that pull them apart.

Conclusions

In general, the evidence suggests that racial unrest probably has had little effect on union organizing, that surprisingly few locals or members have withdrawn from AFL-CIO unions because of union racial policies, that the segregationist labor organizations have achieved relatively little success in the South, and, aside from considerable embarrassment to national union leaders and internal conflict over external racial matters, the main impact of racial animosity on union activity probably has been to cause some national union leaders to become extremely cautious in pushing equalitarian racial measures in the South. Racial conflict, however, has influenced union political activity—both internally and in governmental politics. The reasons for these conclusions may be partly explained by the following observations.

1. Segregationist labor organizations have been relatively unsuccessful because of inadequate leadership. There seems to have been no case in which a regular union leader has been willing to leave his position to lead one of the racist groups. The experience suggests the improbability of building a labor organization on purely racist principles. This does not imply, however, that union education has persuaded most members to be integrationists; the writer is convinced that the great majority of Southern unionists hold the racial views of their communities. They apparently believe that organizations such as the White Citizens' Councils and the Ku Klux

Klan should attend to racial matters and the union to economic matters. This compartmentalization of thinking probably explains some of the apparently inconsistent dual allegiances to antagonistic organizations. Southern unionists seem to believe that national union leaders understand labor matters but have no real appreciation of local racial problems; they give allegiance to both the WCC-type of organization and to trade unions, because they believe national union leaders are interested mainly in the politico-economic aspects of unionism and will not push integration in the South, a conclusion based on the experiences of most unions in that region.

2. Economic influences encourage union members to continue their allegiance to national unions. The most important unions in the South are craft organizations, railroad brotherhoods, and industrial unions which are associated with strongly organized bases outside the South. Unions often use their power in other areas to force companies with Southern branches to give equal conditions in the South. Southerners who attribute their good conditions to unions will not lightly abandon their jobs or unions over racial matters. Except in rare cases unions which lost Southern locals over race matters alone were really not effective collective-bargaining organizations in the South. Some government-employees unions were in this category, but they will probably become more collective-bargaining organizations since President Kennedy's Executive Order 10988 encouraged bargaining in the government service.

3. The ability of a national union to enforce its racial policies in the South will depend on the relative power of the local and national organizations. Factors involved in this power relation include: whether Southern members' wages are high relative to others in their areas; whether good wages and working conditions are attributed to the union; internal union politics, especially the power of the particular local involved; the organization and numbers of Negroes within the union; the nature of the market and the need for national coordination of wage policy; whether other nationals with more compatible race policies are willing to admit seceding locals; whether the local or the national is certified by the NLRB; the ownership of strike funds and other property; and the ease or difficulty of imposing trusteeships.

National unions will rarely expel locals in the South for violating national racial policies, especially if the national is the certified bargaining agent. The UAW expelled its Dallas local in 1952, but has refused to take similar action against other locals. UAW leaders privately admit that the Dallas expulsion was probably a mistake because it "did not settle anything." The UAW's use of a trusteeship in dealing with its Memphis local was upheld by the Secretary of Labor as valid under the Landrum-Griffin Act. The Textile Workers Union also used a trusteeship to prevent its Front Royal, Virginia, local from giving aid to a private, segregated school formed to avoid the Supreme Court's desegregation decision.

4. Race trouble in the unions seems most likely to occur where there is race trouble in the community, where groups like the Citizens' Councils or the NAACP raise the issue in local union affairs, and where national union leaders make widely publicized integrationist speeches or engage in open integrationist activity. Practices which go unnoticed for years will create trouble if publicized, because publicity frequently causes Southerners to feel compelled to dissociate themselves from the policies of their national leaders. Southern whites frequently break with Southern tradition when they join unions and will rarely risk complete ostracism by becoming identified as integrationists. They, therefore, feel compelled to publicly repudiate equalitarian racial statements and actions by national leaders, especially when challenged by anti-integrationist organizations. For example, Alexandria, Louisiana, union leaders responded to the AFL-CIO Industrial Union Department's support of the Freedom Riders with a public statement:

We would like for the public to know that the union members and the union officials of this area are unalterably opposed to the so-called Freedom Riders. . . .
We want to make it clear that as far as we can determine no union money from the State of Louisiana was contributed to these lawbreakers.

Similar protests were issued by other unions throughout the South, but are likely to be more important for federations than local or national unions.

5. The AFL-CIO racial policy which seems to have developed after the 1959 convention is insistence on compliance with national racial policy. George Meany, for example, has said that equalitarian racial policies will be pushed in the South whether the AFL-CIO organizes a single worker in that region.[51] Some state labor councils have also adopted resolutions supporting equalitarian racial policies; Texas and North Carolina are among those adopting particularly strong statements. These moves apparently reflect the belief that temporizing with racial policy would cost the labor movement more in the end.

6. Racial conflict within the labor movement, following the 1954

Supreme Court school desegregation decision and the merger of the AFL and CIO in 1955, has subsided after reaching a peak about 1957; however, there is much latent feeling that is likely to erupt as a reflection of racial conflict in the larger community. Our analysis suggests, however, that for collective-bargaining unions racial difficulties will usually be exaggerated because they are more newsworthy than peaceful race relations.

FOOTNOTES

1. See my "Union Racial Problems in the South," *Industrial Relations*, May 1962.
2. Resolution passed by the Chattanooga CLU, July 25, 1955.
3. *News-Free Press* (Chattanooga), August 3 and 20, 1955; *Chattanooga Times*, August 21, 1955.
4. Chattanooga CLU, "Statement of Policy on Segregation in the Public Schools," September 12, 1955.
5. See John Hope II, "3 Southern Plants of International Harvester Company," in *Selected Studies of Negro Employment in the South*, Washington, D. C.: National Planning Association, 1953.
6. John Hope II, *Equality of Opportunity, a Union Approach to Fair Employment*, Washington, D. C.: Public Affairs Press, 1956, p. 101.
7. See Theodore V. Purcell, *The Worker Speaks His Mind on Company and Union*, Cambridge, Mass.: Harvard University Press, 1954, pp. 68–73.
8. Material from CIO files, Washington, D. C.
9. Letter from Russell R. Lassley to George L. P. Weaver, director, Civil Rights Committee, CIO, January 10, 1954, in CIO files, Washington, D. C. Copy in writer's possession.
10. See, for example: Statement by Herb March, *Proceedings of the Seventh UPWA Convention*, 1950, p. 226; *Champion*, official organ of District 1, January 1952; UPWA Executive Board meeting, March 13, 1952; *Sub-District News*, official organ of UPWA District 6, June 1950, and Purcell, *op. cit.*, p. 68.
11. Report to the UPWA Executive Board, April 1953, from Russell Lassley and A. T. Stephens, CIO files, Washington, D. C.
12. Letter in CIO files, Washington, D. C. Copy in writer's possession.
13. *Fort Worth Labor News*, May 27, 1954, p. 235.
14. Letter from A. T. Stephens to A. J. Shippey and W. L. McMahon, field representatives, District 8, UPWA, May 28, 1953; Letter to A. T. Stephens from A. J. Shippey, June 2, 1953, in CIO files. Copies in writer's possession.
15. Letter to Ralph Helstein, UPWA president, from Walter Reuther, CIO president, October 30, 1953, in CIO files. Copy in writer's possession.
16. *Springfield Press and News-Journal*, October 10, 1962.
17. *Shreveport Times*, October 13, 1962.
18. *Springhill Press and News-Journal*, October 17, 1962.
19. Whitfield v. United Steelworkers of America, 4 RRLR 128 (1959).
20. Glenn W. Gilman and James W. Sweeney, "Atlantic Steel Company and United Steel Workers," Case Study No. 12, *Causes of Industrial Peace Under*

Collective Bargaining, Washington, D. C.: National Planning Association, November 1953, p. 22.

21. Memo to the writer from Herbert Hill, December 31, 1958.
22. NLRB release, April 9, 1963.
23. Letter to the writer from George A. Leet, associate executive secretary, National Labor Relations Board, March 6, 1964; Letter to Robert L. Carter, general counsel, NAACP, from Stuart Rothman, general counsel, NLRB, April 8, 1963.
24. Langston T. Hawley, "Negro Employment in the Birmingham Metropolitan Area," Case Study No. 3, *Selected Studies of Negro Employment in the South,* Washington, D. C.: National Planning Association, 1955, p. 233.
25. *Ibid.,* p. 235.
26. *Ibid.,* p. 278.
27. Of the 23 locals three were all white, with 78, 225, and 468 members, and the 200 Negroes in one Joint Board were in segregated locals. Information about Negro attendance at two of the locals was unavailable, but of the others, seven reported that Negroes never attended meetings and five reported Negro participation. Another local with 204 members and five Negroes, reported that Negroes were invited to attend both social and business meetings but that they usually did not attend. Another local reported that Negroes took part in both business and social affairs, another said that Negroes attended mass, but not regular meetings, and another said that Negroes were segregated when they attended. Thus, of 21 locals about which information was available, only six reported that Negroes attended meetings.
28. Personal interview, AFM official, Chicago.
29. *Atlantic Journal,* August 24, 1956.
30. USEA, *Independent Trade Union News,* no date.
31. *Charlotte* (N. C.) *Observer,* September 2, 1957.
32. Letter to the writer from Harry W. Brown, president of USEA, June 4, 1959.
33. *Charlotte* (N. C.) *Observer,* September 1, 1957.
34. USEA, *Independent Trade Union News,* no date.
35. USEA leaflet, "Sterilize the Mongrelizers," February 1959.
36. USEA leaflet, "Whose Hidden Hand," 1959.
37. Advertisement published in the public interest by Southern Crafts, Inc., in *South,* June 17, 1957.
38. *Ibid.*
39. Copy in writer's possession.
40. *Chattanooga Times,* July 1, 1956.
41. *Ibid.*
42. *The Citizens' Council,* November 1959.
43. Copy of memorandum in writer's possession.
44. Personal interview AFL-CIO official, Washington, D. C., April 19, 1959.
45. *Jackson* (Miss.) *Daily News,* June 4, 1957, p. 1.
46. For a discussion of these factors, see my "Some Factors Influencing the Growth of Unions in the South," *op. cit.* The NLRB has not prohibited racial arguments, but has "established criteria under which campaign propaganda calculated to overstress and exacerbate racial feelings by irrelevant, inflammatory appeals could be a basis for setting aside an election." (*Twenty-eighth Annual Report of the National Labor Relations Board,* for the Fiscal Year ended June 30, 1963, p. 27; Sewell Mfg. Co. 138 NLRB 66.) But see

Allen-Morrison Sign Co. 138 NLRB 73 (1963), where the Board refused to set an election aside where an employer advised his employees of the union's racial policies.
47. Copy in the writer's possession.
48. RWDSU *Record,* January 12, 1964, p. 9.
49. *Ibid., IUD Bulletin,* February 1964, p. 7.
50. *New York Times,* June 14, 1964.
51. See Chapter 4.

PART **III**

Public Policy

CHAPTER 9

The Fair-Employment Practice and Government-Contract Committees

Introduction

IT IS SIGNIFICANT FOR PUBLIC POLICY THAT, DESPITE YEARS OF HOS-
tile racial discrimination by employers and unions, until the Second
World War American governments generally adopted very few measures to counteract discrimination in employment. Indeed, only twenty
years ago, when Herbert Northrup published his *Organized Labor
and the Negro*,[1] which carefully documented a widespread pattern of
discrimination by unions, there were only the faintest beginnings of
what might be termed "public policy" in this area. Twenty years
later, though, there were a multitude of federal, state, and local
governmental regulations of racial employment relations. By 1964
twenty-four states and numerous localities had passed mandatory fair-
employment laws, and agencies of the federal government had devoted much attention to this problem since 1941, when President

Franklin Roosevelt created the first Committee on Fair Employment Practice (FEPC).

Before we analyze their effects on unions, let us recall some of the main social forces producing these laws, court and administrative decisions, and executive orders. Evidently, the most important of these developments was the Negro's increased power to force political leaders to consider his plight.

This political power was not, however, immediately translated into federal antidiscrimination legislation. Because of the inertia of democratic processes and the inordinate power of senior Southern congressmen and their conservative Northern allies, the federal executive and judiciary have been more willing than the Congress to take action against discrimination in employment. Even so, before the New Deal period Negroes received little help from the federal executive in achieving their objective of general fair-employment practices. After the war even this limited action was nullified by Congress, forcing Presidents Truman, Eisenhower, Kennedy, and Johnson to use relatively impotent executive orders to deal with discrimination. Since these experiences form the background for present policy and elucidate some of the problems involved in changing union racial practices, we shall examine the federal antidiscrimination committees in this chapter. Subsequent chapters will deal with the development of judicial decrees, federal labor-relations regulations, and the state antidiscrimination laws.

President Roosevelt's Committees on Fair-Employment Practice

It is perhaps characteristic of the civil-rights problem in America that the federal government moved to reduce racial employment barriers only under the threat of dramatic demonstrations by Negroes. President Roosevelt issued the executive order creating the first FEPC in August 1941, after A. Philip Randolph organized a movement to lead 50,000 Negroes in a protest march on Washington.[2] That Randolph and his colleagues threatened to take such drastic action undoubtedly reflected the Negro community's sense of outrage at being unable to break racial employment patterns even during war-created labor shortages. This sense of outrage must surely have been intensified by the realization that the nation was preparing for a war against fascism, an ideology based in part on racism.

Besides his role as a Negro community leader, however, Randolph had a more immediate stake in the creation of a federal agency to outlaw discrimination.   As president of the BSCP, he had long been concerned about hostile discrimination against Negroes by railroad unions.   Indeed, Randolph's threatened march on Washington coincided with the formation, under his leadership, of various committees to protect Negro railroad workers, whose jobs were being threatened by the infamous "Southeastern Carriers Agreement" of February 1941.[3]   It is therefore not surprising that the Roosevelt FEP committees (there were two, one lasting from August 1941 to January 1943, and the other from May 1943 to June 1946, but we shall use "FEPC" to mean both committees) should direct much of their attention to racial discrimination on the railroads.

The executive order creating the first FEPC gave the Committee power to "receive and investigate complaints of discrimination" in defense industries and allied work and to "take appropriate steps to redress the grievances it finds to be valid."   But, in spite of this relatively wide jurisdiction (much broader than that of committees created by subsequent presidents), the first FEPC was no match for the combined power of its Southern congressional critics and the railroad unions and employers.   The Committee's railroad hearings met such staunch opposition that they were indefinitely postponed in January 1943 by Paul McNutt, the director of War Manpower, to whose office the FEPC had been transferred.   McNutt's action killed the first FEPC for all practical purposes; it was followed by the resignation of a number of key personnel who could not be replaced because of the Committee's obvious impotence.

The FEPC's advocates did not give up with the demise of the first committee, however, and succeeded in getting a new executive order in June 1943, creating another committee with enlarged powers.   The executive order creating the second committee placed it in the Office of Emergency Management, gave it additional financial support, allowed it to create twelve branch offices, and empowered it to police an antidiscrimination clause to be included in government contracts. This order stated that it was:

the policy of the United States that there shall be no discrimination in the employment of any person in war industries or in Government by reason of race, creed, color or national origin, and . . . it is the duty of all employers, including the several Federal departments and agencies, *and all labor organizations* . . . to eliminate discrimination in regard to hire, tenure, terms or conditions of employment, *or union membership.*[4]   [Emphasis added.]

The second FEPC considered its reestablishment a mandate to continue the railroad investigations.[5]   Since the unions involved (Brotherhood of Locomotive Firemen; Brotherhood of Railway Carmen; Order of Railway Conductors; Brotherhood of Locomotive Engineers; International Association of Machinists; and the International Brotherhood of Boilermakers, Iron Shipbuilders and Helpers of America) boycotted the hearings, counsel for the railroads argued the case for both the companies and the unions. The railroads did not deny discriminating against Negroes but defended their legal right to do so, as well as the unions' right to bar Negroes from membership.

When the FEPC directed them to cease and desist from "discriminatory practices affecting the employment of Negroes," the companies and the unions refused to obey the directive, arguing that the Committee was "wholly without constitutional and legal jurisdiction and power to make and issue the directives and for this reason said directives are without legal effect."

The FEPC answered that its directives were

(1) its judgment as to the specific duties the responding parties are called upon to perform; (2) its instructions and guides as to the manner in which performance is desired. In this sense directives are *directory* only and not mandatory orders. In this connection it should be pointed out that the Committee has never taken the position that it could of itself enforce, or call upon the courts to enforce its directives as other government agencies, expressly authorized by statute to make and issue rules and orders, may do. The Committee has recognized that, aside from the force of public opinion, its ultimate and only sanction, is the disposition of the President to use his good offices or his power to effect compliance with its directives.[6]

A fatal blow was dealt the FEPC when, faced with defiance by the rail unions and employees, it advised President Roosevelt to appoint the so-called Stacy Committee to mediate the dispute.[7] According to Ross:

The setting up of the Stacy Committee was an irretrievable mistake. . . . If I had wanted the railroad cases to expire quietly over the course of the next two years in the hands of the Stacy Committee, no better move could have been made. . . . The mistake was in not realizing that delays and dalliance would take the fire out of this issue unless the President himself, in the first instance, was forced to meet the carriers and the unions face to face and tell them to right the wrong.[8]

In addition to the railway brotherhoods, the FEPC sought to eliminate discrimination by locals of the Boilermakers, the Plumbers, the Street Railway Employees, the Teamsters, the Philadelphia Rapid Transit Employees Union, the Seafarers International Union, the International Brotherhood of Electrical Workers.

Most of the unions simply ignored the Committee or openly defied it. Indeed, even the AFL representative on the FEPC, Frank
Fenton, alternate for William Green, apparently considered it his primary responsibility to defend the unions charged with discrimination;
he argued that discrimination was the private prerogative of the
unions involved. When the Committee found a Chicago local of the
Plumbers guilty of discrimination, for instance, Fenton dissented on
the grounds that the majority "relied much too much on legal thinking and the administrative edict as the ameliorative tools with which
to fashion improved racial and social adjustments." [9] Fenton was
persuaded that the majority had based its case too much on "circum-
stantial evidence," concluding that "People cannot be weaned away
from the formative experience of half a century merely by confronting them with a cold, precise order enjoining not only a change of
economic arrangement, but by implication also habits of mind."

In the Birmingham hearings, Fenton engaged in a debate with
David Sarnoff, also a member of the FEPC, over the right of a Machinists local to refuse the Committee information concerning its
membership requirements on the grounds that this was a secret
which the union could not divulge. Fenton defended the IAM official, but General Sarnoff rejected Fenton's defense on the grounds
that ". . . this Committee would be practicing gross discrimination
if it asked employers for all kinds of information we have been asking employers to furnish and did not inquire of unions the terms and
conditions upon which they accepted or rejected members." [10]

The foregoing is not meant to imply, however, that the FEPC's
efforts to change union racial practices were entirely ineffective, because it was at least partly responsible for getting Negroes employed
in transit companies in Philadelphia and Los Angeles. The Committee was brought into the Philadelphia case in 1941, when Negroes
charged the company and the union with blocking their promotion
to higher jobs; the company said it would promote Negroes if the
union would agree, and the union—the Philadelphia Rapid Transit
Employees Union (PRTEU)—refused to even consider the Negroes'
request, claiming the customary employment practices could not be
changed without management's consent. The FEPC found the union
and the company in violation of the executive order. These findings
were not contested by the company, but the union challenged the
Committee's authority (since the company did not have a government
contract), denied the discrimination charges, and argued that compliance with the FEPC's directives would upset the prevailing seniority system.

However, when the Transport Workers Union (TWU), CIO, which had a publicly announced nondiscrimination program, won bargaining rights for the workers at PRT, the FEPC withdrew from the case. The TWU's victory did not lead to compliance with the FEPC's directives, however, because the PRTEU leaders continued to oppose any efforts to train Negro operators and urged employees to "Call a strike and refuse to teach the Negroes, the public is with you, the CIO sold you out." [11]

The value of different types of power in dealing with such recalcitrants as the PRTEU leaders was demonstrated by the techniques that ultimately settled the strike. Moral pressures from the TWU, newspapers, church and civic groups, who branded the strike as unethical and unpatriotic, apparently made little impression on the strike leaders. But the dispute came to an end when the Army seized the lines and the War Manpower Commission announced that those continuing to strike would be reclassified 1A by the local draft board; the four most prominent strike leaders were arrested, charged with violating the Smith-Connally Act, discharged from the company, and fined $100. The Negroes kept their jobs and one of them was even elected vice-president of the local after the strike ended.[12]

Three days after the cars started rolling again in Philadelphia, the FEPC opened its hearings on the Los Angeles Railway Corporation, where the Street, Electric Railway and Motor Coach Employees, AFL, had collective-bargaining rights. Despite warnings from the union, the company, and city officials that the workers would probably strike if Negroes were hired, the FEPC directive that Negroes be hired was carried out and seventy-four Negroes were working and being upgraded when the FEPC closed the case.[13] The strong measures used to settle the Philadelphia strike undoubtedly made an impression on the Los Angeles workers. Similar cases were pending against the Key System in San Francisco and the Capital Transit Company in Washington when the FEPC's limited power was almost completely destroyed by the end of the war.

The end of the war also reduced the FEPC's power to deal with the Seafarers International Union, AFL, which was accused of restricting Negroes to stewards' jobs. SIU officials refused to cooperate with the FEPC, but were more talkative in the friendlier atmosphere of the Smith Committee hearing, a major purpose of which was to undermine the FEPC.[14] The union's secretary-treasurer told the congressmen how the "starry eyed fellow travelers" of the Recruitment and Manning Organization (RMO) of the War Shipping Administration had interpreted the FEPC's orders in a "dangerous and arbitrary" manner; worse yet, the RMO had taken white boys from American homes and forced them to eat and sleep with Negroes. The union official added: "Our union requires that white seamen shall not be forced to eat and sleep in the same quarters with Negro seamen and vice versa." The congressmen also interrogated RMO officials about their views on the "communistic doctrine of social equality." In spite of the SIU's position, however, the National Maritime Union's experiences with integration and a survey of ships in New York harbor convinced the FEPC officials that opposition to Negro seamen came largely from shore personnel and not from the white seamen themselves.[15]

Unions not only refused to cooperate with the wartime FEPC, but some of them opposed the establishment of a permanent FEPC, particularly if it covered unions. FEPC advocates were convinced that AFL political representatives had lobbied against appropriations for the Committee in 1944; the chairman of the AFL Legislative Policy Committee told the Senate Committee considering the bill that "while it endorses without reservation the policy of nondiscrimination in employment, the Executive Council takes strong exception to the compulsory imposition upon unions of this or any other policy interfering with the self government of labor organizations."[16] However, the 1944 AFL convention adopted a resolution favoring the FEPC and the AFL gave its support to the National Council for a Permanent FEPC. But apprehension concerning the possible impact of the FEPC on AFL unions continued to be sufficient to cause William Green to tell the September 1947 Executive Council meeting that "some sections might embarrass some of our labor organizations because they would be called in and forced to comply with certain regulations and if they failed to comply would be subject to penalties."[17] The Council authorized Green to make an inquiry into the FEP bill and "cause such amendments to be made as may be found necessary to protect our organization in connection with that legislation."

The AFL's worries were in vain, however, because Southerners had sufficient political power to fatally cripple the FEPC and defeat legislation creating a permanent committee. The FEPC was crippled by the 1944 Russell Amendment to an appropriation bill which prohibited the use of funds by the President to pay the expenses of any agency unless Congress appropriated funds for such use.[18]

The failure of the movement for a permanent FEPC caused civil-rights advocates to turn their attention to the passage of state FEP laws, to seek the enforcement of nondiscrimination clauses in government contracts, and to bring legal action against discriminating unions in federal and state courts. These developments will be discussed at length after a brief evaluation of the wartime FEPC.

Conclusions on the FEPC

It is obvious from the foregoing that the FEPC had very limited immediate effects on unions. The Committee's impact was limited mainly by inadequate power to deal with discrimination by powerful labor organizations and their affiliates. The main factor weakening the Committee was congressional opposition, which not only gave moral support to its enemies, but also denied the organization sufficient economic and political power to carry out its functions. The Committee had no power to compel compliance with its orders, or, as is customary with administrative agencies created by Congress, to seek the aid of federal courts in compelling such compliance. In a showdown the Committee had only such power as the President saw fit to give it in that particular case. The President was sometimes willing to give his moral support by personally intervening in a case (as he did with the Boilermakers) but in the face of widespread defiance, this technique could have only limited effect unless we make the unrealistic assumption that President Roosevelt should have become the Committee's full-time director. The crux of the difficulty here, as in so many other racial matters, was that the promotion of minority interests did not take very high priority among the things that the President had to do at that time. As a result of Congress's failure to give it legislative support, the FEPC was never wholly accepted by employers, unions, or the public. Under attack by hostile critics, who questioned its legitimacy because it lacked congressional approval, the Committee was forced to proceed slowly and cautiously.

The FEPC's other problems—such as attracting and retaining a competent staff—relate to its lack of power and therefore low prestige. Congressional opposition not only denied them adequate funds, but also caused the Committee to be widely regarded as a visionary, impractical organization dedicated to integration per se—that is, social as well as economic, despite the FEPC's repeated denial of social objectives.

This is not to argue that the Roosevelt committees had no effect on union racial policies. It must be remembered that the Committee got only the most difficult cases which could not be settled by other agencies. Moreover, the Committee served as a safety valve through which pent-up resentments could be expressed; although about two-thirds of the complaints filed with the Committee proved unfounded, the fact that they could be expressed to an agency of the federal government did much to clear up misunderstandings. Furthermore, the FEPC machinery probably made it possible for some employers and unions who wanted to increase job opportunities for Negroes to use the Committee as an excuse for their actions. The Committee thus became the scapegoat for some unpopular, "messy" decisions. Finally, the Committee contributed to the development of public policy with respect to union racial practices and fair-employment practices generally. The Committee's hearings and orders were indecisive in the short run, but they added their weight to a long stream of moral indictments of racial discrimination that produced the state FEPC laws, court decisions against discrimination, and the government-contract committees.

The following sections will trace the development of the nondiscrimination committees created by Presidents Eisenhower and Kennedy. President Truman's Committee on Government Contract Compliance, created in 1951, did not have much influence on employment and therefore will not be discussed. President Eisenhower's Committee on Government Contracts (PCGC) will receive the bulk of our attention. President Kennedy's Committee on Equal Employment Opportunity—continued by President Johnson—is still in operation and thus cannot be evaluated as completely as the PCGC.

The President's Committee on Government Contracts

The President's Committee on Government Contracts (PCGC) was created by President Eisenhower in 1953 to establish equal employment opportunities for all qualified workers either employed or seeking employment covered by government contracts. In order to achieve this objective, the Committee sought to make it the responsibility of the head of each agency of the federal government to obtain compliance with the nondiscrimination clause in any contract or subcontract entered into or amended by that agency. The Committee transmitted complaints to the contracting agencies and these agencies reported to the PCGC concerning the investigation of those complaints.

As compared with the two FEPC's, subsequent committees have had relatively narrow jurisdictions and unwieldy structures. This is due largely to the crippling effects of the Russell amendment, which restricted the committees' jurisdictions to supervising nondiscrimination clauses in contracts with federal agencies. The agencies themselves are primarily responsible for enforcement of the contracts.

Moreover, since unions are not parties to the contracts, they have not been approached as directly by the contract committees as they were by the wartime FEPC's, which not only had jurisdiction over all essential war industries but unions as well.

There was originally some question concerning the precise acts prohibited by President Eisenhower's executive order, but this was clarified in September 1954 by the stipulation that "The aforesaid provision shall include, but not be limited to, the following: employment, upgrading, demotion or transfer; recruitment or recruitment advertising; layoff or termination; rates of pay or other forms of compensation; and selection for training including apprenticeship."

The PCGC relied upon "education, conciliation, mediation and persuasion" to enforce the nondiscrimination clause, though in 1957 the Committee's chairman, Vice-President Richard Nixon, instructed contracting agencies to take a "firmer approach" where these methods did not "bring about proper results." [19] The Vice-President requested that the agencies consider the past employment records of contractors in awarding contracts and "deny awards, as appropriate, upon determination by your agency of clear and convincing evidence of noncompliance by Government contractors with the standard nondiscrimination clause." [20]

Relations with unions

Since the executive order creating the PCGC made no direct mention of unions, and since unions were not signatories to government contracts, the Committee took the position that it did not have jurisdiction over labor organizations. If the act complained of was attributable entirely to unions, the Committee's usual procedure was to call on PCGC members George Meany and Walter Reuther or their respective alternates Boris Shishkin and George L-P Weaver, to "use their good offices to iron out the difficulties complained of." [21] If the union was jointly charged with the employer, the Committee sought to adjust the discriminatory practice by proceeding against the employer.

In reality, however, it was not as easy to ignore union racial practices as suggested by this formal policy because many aspects of employment are influenced by unions. Indeed, unions sometimes have more control of the employment relationship than employers.

In a *Compliance Guide* issued in October 1958 to contracting agencies, compliance officers were asked to indicate in their reports if discrimination in apprenticeship resulted from union practices [22];

the compliance officer was also told to personally interview "any management or union personnel named in the complaint" [23] and to "bear in mind that in most instances management maintains and insists on the right to hire, promote and otherwise advance its employees," but that these rights might be modified by the collective-bargaining contract. "Should management indicate that the fault lies with the union, or should the union imply that the fault lies with management, the investigator reports the facts as he found them." [24]

Unions were directly or indirectly involved in over 20 per cent of the cases received by the Committee between 1953 and 1956.[25] All these complaints except one, which alleged discrimination against Spanish-Americans by a railroad and railway brotherhood, were for discrimination against Negroes. The specific charges included denial of membership to Negroes, thereby forcing companies to discharge them; refusal by a company to hire a Negro because he could not get in the union; restricting Negroes to certain departments and excluding them from apprenticeship training programs; violation of seniority rights; providing in the contract for separate lines of progression for Negroes and whites; failure of a union to protest seniority violations; refusal to file charges against the company for failing to promote or hire Negroes in categories other than laborers and janitors. Also, a construction local was accused of rejecting an agreement with an international union representative which provided that eight or ten Negroes would be employed on a project; the result was that the Negroes were denied work on the project. Negroes were placed in lower job classifications than called for by the contract; and business agents and stewards were accused of discrimination against Negroes.

We noted in Part 2 some of the PCGC's experiences with unions in the building trades, especially IBEW Locals 38 and 26, and the petroleum-refining unions. A detailed examination of other PCGC experiences with unions is therefore not necessary, but we may note a number of the more important conclusions that seem to flow from a study of the cases involving unions handled by the Committee.

1. The Committee found it practically impossible to carry out its official policy of ignoring unions, because unions in fact controlled employment conditions in some industries. Moreover, employers and unions frequently have tried to shift the responsibility for discrimination to each other.

2. It was not uncommon for Negroes to file complaints with the Committee when they really did not understand the union referral system or, if they did, sought to use the PCGC as a means to circumvent that system in order to get jobs. Sometimes, as in a complaint

against Local 3 of the Operating Engineers, the union claimed to have had a long list of unemployed members and therefore could not take additional members. In another case, Negroes filed a complaint against the St. Louis-San Francisco Railroad alleging the company laid off twenty-two Negroes and filled some jobs with whites having less seniority. These Negroes had been carmen helpers, some of whom had worked as first-class carmen, but none had worked the necessary 1040 hours to get first-class status or seniority. The whites who were retained were first-class carmen, who oiled cars automatically and who could repair freight and passenger cars including electrical and welding work and the servicing of air brakes. The company argued that the complainants could not qualify for this work. Furthermore, the company argued, the white carmen were displaced in other places. And the decision reached by the National Railroad Adjustment Board in Springfield, Missouri, where whites were displaced, was controlling in others. The Charleston Naval Shipyard management told the Committee that many complaints of racial discrimination there were due to a lack of understanding of the promotion system. Negroes sometimes filed charges alleging discrimination in referrals when they had not complied with the union's referring procedures. Finally, in one case, a U. S. senator used the PCGC to get Negro bricklayers hired on a federal office building in his state, though there was in that case no evidence of discrimination. It is entirely possible, of course, to use regular union rules and procedures not discriminatory on their face to bar Negroes. Indeed, this is one of the main problems in proving discrimination in specific cases.

3. The PCGC experience also demonstrated that in some cases employers have preferred Negroes or wanted to hire them on an equal basis with whites but were prevented from doing so by the union. In Philadelphia, for example, investigation revealed that employers wanted to hire Negroes as weighers and checkers, but were prevented from doing so by an International Longshoremen's Association (ILA) local in that city. In one case a company became involved in a dispute with the ILA when it attempted to hire Negro checkers. The dispute was settled when the union agreed that Negroes could work "up to the hook" but all other jobs would have to be filled through the ILA. Management said this agreement was not reached to exclude Negroes from jobs but to permit them to work in jobs not covered by the union. In a Florida case, white workers complained that they had been replaced by a crew of Negro bricklayers; the company involved admitted the action but said the Negroes were more efficient.

4. The Committee was sometimes used by unions to get better jobs for Negroes. For instance, an international union with all-Negro locals in Houston filed charges with the Committee to get jobs for Negroes which were outside the bargaining units. A local union in Cedar Rapids, Iowa, filed charges against a packing company for refusing to hire Negro females as stenographers; the local sent Negro women to apply for work in order to test the company's program and then publicized its efforts in the case. Unions with sizable Negro memberships filed a number of charges against companies alleging discrimination in hiring.

5. A number of complaints filed with the Committee alleged discrimination by reason of segregation or racial employment quotas. For instance, Negroes filed charges with the PCGC against contractors in Savannah alleging a violation of a quota system. The Housing and Home Finance Agency used a quota system to determine the proportion of Negro workers to be employed on construction projects; a presumption of discrimination arose when the number of Negro workers fell below the prescribed quota. A painting contractor used the ratio of ten whites and two Negroes. An investigation in July 1956 revealed that there were two Negroes and sixteen whites, and in June 1956 there were three Negroes and fifteen whites; the PCGC considered this a satisfactory settlement of the complaint. At Knoxville the Negro and white Carpenters locals agreed that Negroes would get 10 per cent of all jobs on an Atomic Energy Commission project. The Negroes complained that this quota was not being observed, but an actual count by the AEC found that Negroes had seventy-one carpenters and five foremen of 501 carpenters. Investigation of a complaint at a shipbuilding company in Mobile revealed that Negroes were not unhappy with the system of job segregation because they felt that this protected their jobs from encroachment by whites. A similar finding was made in the investigation of a complaint against an iron works in Birmingham, where Negroes also held quotas in official union positions. The union business agent admitted that a system of job segregation existed, but insisted that the Negroes preferred the system because it gave them job protection. Quota systems are usually opposed by civil-rights organizations, unions, and employers, but obviously are beneficial to Negroes who do not have any other means to acquire jobs or protect themselves in existing jobs.

It would be dangerous, however, to generalize from these examples. There are many others where Negroes have opposed employment segregation because they felt that it kept them from getting jobs.

6. The PCGC cases also reveal the importance of the fear of white

reaction as a factor making union leaders and employers reluctant to change discriminatory practices. In several cases union leaders refused to support employers in nondiscrimination action for fear they would be voted out by their members. Indeed, there were also a number of cases in which local leaders were voted out for this reason.

7. The PCGC's experience also demonstrated that employers will be more willing to comply with equal job programs, regardless of opposition from the union and white workers, if government contracts are important to them and it appears likely that discrimination will cost them those contracts. It has been observed that employers in the petroleum-refining industry were willing to integrate jobs even in the South partly because of the importance of government contracts at a time of adverse market conditions. On the other hand, the Tennessee Coal and Iron Company (TCI) in Alabama expressed little sympathy for the program and took no action to eliminate separate lines of progression before 1963 partly because there was little pressure from the Negroes to do so, but also because the company's government contracts were relatively insignificant. A TVA investigator thought the company would give up its contract before integrating jobs. In 1963, however, TCI announced the desegregation of lines of progression and the upgrading of "several hundred Negroes" into formerly all-white jobs. Indeed, whites were even reported to be working under Negro supervisors—a rarity indeed in the South. White workers who protested these developments were sent home but usually returned after a few days; good jobs and poor economic conditions lessen the tendency of whites to quit over racial integration. TCI officials announced that these measures were taken mainly because "the Kennedy administration exerted pressure to bring it about." [26] The company and international unions made it clear to local union leaders that they would lose government contracts if discrimination continued. However, the way was paved for these changes by other factors, including the 1962 steel collective-bargaining contract which introduced broader seniority arrangements (Negroes and whites were dissatisfied with the previous system which made it possible for senior men to be laid off while new men were being hired); the increased militancy of Negro civil-rights organizations; and the widespread criticism of TCI's parent United States Steel Company for its failure to exert pressure to improve community race relations in Birmingham. U. S. Steel finally took action in its affiliate but refused to act in the community. The efficacy of stronger measures to eliminate racial discrimination, as compared with PCGC's milder approach, is demonstrated by this case. Moreover, as noted

in Chapter 9, U. S. Steel joined ten other steel companies in signing a joint nondiscrimination contract with the United Steelworkers.

Evaluation of the PCGC

A careful examination of the Committee's record clearly supports the conclusion that the PCGC had a relatively minor impact on unions. The constellation of forces limiting the Committee's power were similar to those frustrating the wartime FEPC. The lack of explicit congressional approval denied it funds for sufficient staff and that power which comes from legitimacy. The difficulties caused by the Russell amendment made it difficult for the Committee to proceed directly against unions, caused heavy reliance on the (perhaps unsympathetic) contracting agencies for enforcement, and introduced an inefficient and complex enforcement structure. In the final analysis, of course, the general attitude projected by the government determines the reaction of contractors to fair-employment programs, and the feeling seems to have been fairly pervasive during the Eisenhower administration that contracts would not be revoked for violations of the nondiscrimination clauses. Even in those cases where complaints were filed and the PCGC sought to reduce discrimination, the Committee seemed willing to settle for very limited corrections. Furthermore, although the Committee took the position that companies could not use the unions' practices to justify their failure to comply with the order, nothing was done to those employers who in fact used the union as an excuse for discrimination.

The PCGC's policy of referring complaints against unions to the AFL-CIO produced only limited results. It is true that George Meany finally broke the color barrier in the Cleveland IBEW local, but this took a long time, resulted in very few Negroes being admitted to the union, and the Negro who brought the case was never admitted. This is not to argue that the Federation and its affiliated national organizations should not be given an opportunity to resolve these cases, but when this is done a definite time limit should be imposed and the cases certainly should not be considered closed simply because they have been referred to the AFL-CIO. Moreover, the Federation's power has been strengthened by federal legislation outlawing discrimination because affiliated unions would probably be more responsive to the AFL-CIO's "suggestions" if failure to comply results in certification of the case to a federal agency.

The PCGC's activities were also limited by the lack of clearly defined spheres of influence between various civil-rights organizations, a problem which was compounded in the PCGC's early days by the uncertainty as to whether the Committee would take cases against unions; the Committee took the position that it had no jurisdiction over unions, but added to the confusion in many quarters by accepting complaints against them. The difficulty with having many civil-rights agencies involved in the same case is that each might be immobilized waiting for the others to act.

The PCGC's effect on unions was also limited by the suspicion that the Committee was more interested in creating political advantage than in solving the problem of racial discrimination. The suspicion of political chicanery probably weakened the willingness of unions to cooperate in the Washington IBEW and other cases.

The foregoing is not to infer that the PCGC had no effect on union racial practices. So far as can be determined, the Committee's greatest effect was in the petroleum-refining industry where the importance of government contracts, the equalitarian position of the international union, and the willingness of Negro workers and the NAACP to organize their resources to abolish racial job segregation contributed to the breakthroughs in that industry. However, the changes effected in petroleum refining were not due so much to the PCGC as to the use of the nondiscrimination clause by other organizations to threaten both the unions and employers.

The President's Committee on Equal Employment Opportunity

President Kennedy's Committee on Equal Employment Opportunity (PCEEO), appointed in March 1961, created a more aggressive impression and took a more direct approach to unions. President Kennedy's executive order gave the PCEEO power to require contractors to submit compliance reports giving information concerning the racial practices of unions dealt with by these contractors. Furthermore, the PCEEO was given the authority to require that contractors provide statements in writing from a labor union

together with supporting information, to the effect that the said labor union's . . . practices and policies do not discriminate on the grounds of race, color, creed, or national origin, and that the labor union or representative will affirmatively cooperate, within the limits of his legal and contractual authority, in the implementation of the policy and provisions of this order or that it consents and agrees that recruitment, employment, and the terms and conditions of employment under the proposed contract shall be in accordance with the purpose and provisions of the order.

The PCEEO was also directed to use its efforts, directly or through other agencies, "to cause any labor union . . . who is or may be engaged in work under government contracts to cooperate with and to comply in the implementation of, the purposes of the order."

In order to accomplish this objective, the Committee was authorized to hold hearings, make recommendations to the President, or to federal, state, or local agencies, "with respect to any such labor organization which in its judgment has failed to cooperate with the Committee, contracting agencies, contractors, or subcontractors in carrying out the purpose of this order."

The PCEEO adopted a program to have unions as well as contractors sign "plans for progress" designed to open employment and promotion opportunities to Negroes. National unions were urged to sign the agreements and to use their influence to get their locals to comply with the purposes of the order. Although the PCEEO has gone further than the PCGC in dealing with unions and employers—it announced in April 1962 that two firms would be ineligible for further government contracts until they ceased discriminating—it is apparent that the PCEEO, like the PCGC, has only limited power over discriminating unions, and therefore had to rely heavily on the voluntary "plans for progress" until the 1964 Civil Rights Act was passed.

Perhaps one of the most significant "plans for progress" inaugurated by the PCEEO involved the Lockheed Aircraft Corporation and the International Association of Machinists (IAM) at Marietta, Georgia. This case was significant not only as a model for the PCEEO, but also because Lockheed and the IAM provide ideal targets for the Committee's activities. At its peak in 1955, Lockheed was one of the largest employers in the South, with 20,000 employees. Moreover, shortly before the "plan for progress" in May 1961, the company was awarded a new one-billion-dollar contract for C-141 jet cargo planes for the Military Air Transport Service. Lockheed was especially vulnerable to the PCEEO's program in 1961, because 90 per cent of the plant's business was done with the Air Force, and business had declined to the point that the company's 1961 employment was only about half of its 1955 peak. It is not surprising, therefore, that management was eager to avoid any difficulty that might cause the loss of federal contracts. Indeed, company officials actually appear to have welcomed the PCEEO's orders to integrate, because it gave them some protection against criticism from the Georgia community.

The IAM also was vulnerable to attacks for racial discrimination because the unions' officers apparently were eager to erase the stigma of a long history of racial discrimination. The Machinists barred Negroes from membership by formal means from 1888, when it was formed in Atlanta, only a few miles from Marietta, until the race bar was removed in 1948.

The official policy of the international union changed during this period, but IAM locals throughout the country, particularly in the South, continued to practice racial discrimination. Some Negroes at the Lockheed Plant in Marietta had sought to eliminate segregated local unions and lines of progression in the plant before 1955, but were stimulated after that date by lay-offs in the aircraft industry and efforts by the NAACP and the National Urban League to eliminate job segregation. Investigations in 1957 revealed that the 1300 (of 18,000 total) Negro employees at Lockheed were restricted to some 30 of the 450 job categories.

One month after the creation of the PCEEO, the NAACP renewed its efforts at Marietta by filing affidavits by thirty-two workers, charging discrimination by the company and the IAM locals.[27] The NAACP alleged a "rigid racial segregation" existed in the plant; though they substantiated many of the complaints, an Air Force investigating team emphasized that Lockheed's employment pattern was far from rigidly segregated. Indeed, some Negroes had moved into white jobs before the agreement between the PCEEO and Lockheed on May 25, 1961,[28] and the international union had attempted to get its Lockheed locals to integrate in 1957.

Not all the resistance to desegregation of the IAM locals at Marietta came from the whites, however, because many Negro unionists were reluctant to merge with the white locals for fear they would lose their representation on the IAM district council and the Lockheed bargaining committee. The situation at Lockheed was confused between 1957 and 1961 by division in the Negroes' ranks; they voted on one occasion to remain segregated and on another to integrate, and there was some question as to which meeting represented the interests of a majority. A compromise was finally worked out in April and May 1961 to make it possible to integrate the locals.[29] The Negro local was combined with the three white locals, but the Negroes retained representation on the bargaining committee and in the district council; this action was taken while the district was under the international's direct supervision because of financial difficulties.

Several changes were also made within the plant in 1961. Negro employment had declined to around 600 from 1400 in 1956 and was still concentrated mainly in the subassembly operations. However, the company advertised for skilled and technical Negro workers in many classifications and enlisted the recruiting aid of the Atlanta Urban League and the Negro schools in the area. The Negroes' lack of education was a major obstacle to job integration and upgrading. Lockheed sought to overcome this disadvantage by creating scholarships for Negroes in various occupations with limited supplies of colored workers. Facilities within the plant were also desegregated, though most Negroes continued to use the rest rooms previously designated for their use. Moreover, the segregated cafeterias were abolished and food was served from mobile canteens. Opposition to integrated drinking fountains was lessened by the use of paper drinking cups.

In addition to the Lockheed case, the PCEEO took other measures which indicated that it would deal more directly with discriminatory unions than had the PCGC. The Committee's compliance procedure noted that "If discriminatory practices are found within labor unions or other employee organizations, the Committee will take such actions, including public hearings, as are deemed necessary to eliminate such practices." [30] In November 1962, 118 international unions, representing over 90 per cent of the AFL-CIO's membership, signed pledges with the PCEEO agreeing to accept all qualified members on a nondiscriminatory basis; to work to ensure equal job opportunities for all workers; to abolish segregated local unions; and to work with management to get antidiscrimination clauses in collective agreements, eliminate discrimination in apprenticeship programs, and abolish segregated facilities in plants.[31] Probably because of pressure from the PCEEO, as well as President Kennedy's instructions for the Justice Department and the NLRB to "take appropriate action against discriminating unions" in the hope that "administrative action and litigation will make unnecessary the enactment of legislation" with respect to union discrimination,[32] several unions adopted programs to eliminate segregated locals in the South. One union is reported to have desegregated its locals in seventeen major cities as a result of the PCEEO pledges.[33] As noted elsewhere, the PCEEO's activities resulted in desegregation in several important industries, including pulp and paper, petroleum refining, and steel, in the South. In June 1964 the PCEEO adopted a new program to attack bias in the construction industry. Working with a special task force of forty men drawn from the staffs of various federal agencies, coordinated by the PCEEO, the Committee held a series of educational conferences throughout the country and sent investigators to check the racial composition of workers on construction sites. During the same month, eleven major steel companies (representing 95 per cent of the nation's steel production) who had previously signed "plans for progress" with the PCEEO, entered into a nondiscrimination agreement with the Steelworkers union (USA). Designed to implement the spirit as well as the letter of nondiscrimination provisions in existing contracts, the USA and the companies pledged continued efforts to build positive support for equal job opportunities by management and workers.

The angry mood of the Negro community, symbolized by the growth of "black nationalism," racial clashes, the increasing militancy of previously "moderate" organizations, and the increased tempo of racial demonstrations in the spring and summer of 1963, gave a new urgency to the PCEEO's antidiscrimination activities, resulting in several significant developments. In June 1963 President Kennedy announced that all federal projects would be reviewed for discriminatory activity and Secretary of Labor Wirtz warned that unions could not be used by employers as excuses for discrimination: he emphasized that "contracts will be cancelled or they will not be let." [34] Also in June, union leaders agreed to a five-point program calling for: the creation of a top-level AFL-CIO committee to concentrate on the elimination of discrimination in thirty or forty major cities; union support for biracial committees to be established throughout the country; labor support for voter registration drives in order to get more procivil-rights congressmen; placing more Negroes in responsible union positions; and union support for social legislation. [35] This agreement was followed by an announcement from the presidents of eighteen building-trades unions that a program would be adopted to eliminate discrimination in apprenticeship training, admission to membership, and referrals. These unions tacitly admitted discrimination, but defended their unions by saying that the charges against them "indicates a serious lack of knowledge of the facts," [36] and announcing that they would resist any government effort to determine qualifications for admission to their unions or trades. Early in July the powerful United Brotherhood of Carpenters (UBCJ) ordered an end to segregated locals and the elimination of discrimination in referrals, admission policies, and apprenticeship training. The Carpenters' Executive Board attempted to excuse their previous policy on segregated locals by declaring: "We have decided that to be consistent our brotherhood cannot maintain segregation at the request of the same minority groups who are justifiably anxious to wipe out all segregation." [37]

In September 1963 the PCEEO issued rules for the implementation of a policy, under an executive order announced in June, of banning discrimination in federally assisted construction projects. This program could have far-reaching effects. Like the nondiscrimination clauses in government contracts, it is administered by the federal agencies and departments involved.   The PCEEO's rules provide that applicants for federal grants, loans, insurance, or guarantees must agree to require contractors and subcontractors to sign an equal-employment opportunity pledge committing contractors not to discriminate and to take "affirmative action" to ensure equal job opportunities.[38]   The pledge also requires the contractor to send notification of the employer's commitment to each labor union with which he has an agreement.   And contractors are required to provide periodic compliance reports and to submit to reviews by the government agencies.

Federal apprenticeship standards

The PCEEO has also given much attention to the problem of racial discrimination in apprenticeship training.   This is so because many civil-rights leaders consider apprenticeship to be the key to upgrading Negroes into the skilled trades.   The PCEEO's attention also was called to apprenticeship programs because of widespread criticism of the federal Bureau of Apprenticeship and Training (BAT) for either refusing to eliminate discrimination in this area or for actually participating in that discrimination.   In 1961, for example, the U. S. Commission on Civil Rights concluded that: [39]

Apprenticeship training could be an important means of fulfilling the increasing demand for skilled workmen and of helping minority groups emerge from their traditionally low economic status.   However, present apprenticeship training programs are not training even enough craftsmen to replace those who retire, and Negroes constitute a disproportionately small minority of the inadequate number of workers being trained.

The nationwide paucity of participation by Negroes in apprenticeship training programs is caused by lack of qualified applicants and also by discriminatory practices of both labor organizations and employers, who control admission to such programs.

As the craft unions generally control admission to apprenticeship training programs, racial discrimination policies also operate to exclude Negroes from these programs.

The Commission recommended that federal assistance to apprenticeship training be expanded, but that ". . . as a condition of Federal assistance, all such programs be administered on a nondiscriminatory, nonsegregated basis." [40]

The Bureau of Apprenticeship and Training came in for criticism because of the natural assumption that it could have done something to make federally assisted programs available to Negroes. Before 1961, however, BAT took the position that its duties were largely promotional and that it therefore had no power to prevent discrimination in apprenticeship training.[41]   Indeed, the Bureau's director even indicated to a Special Subcommittee of the House Committee on Education and Labor that he did not want the power to eliminate discrimination in apprenticeship training.[42]   The congressional hearings also focused attention on what appeared to be racial discrimination by BAT itself, leading to a recommendation by the PCEEO to the Secretary of Labor that BAT's director be required to "take affirmative action within 30 days to recruit members of minority groups into the program of the Bureau." [43]   At the same time it was announced by an assistant secretary of labor that BAT had been instructed to include a nondiscrimination clause in the new apprenticeship agreements with all firms doing work for the federal government and that selection without regard to race be made one of the nine standards for registered apprenticeship programs.

In a press release June 6, 1963, Secretary of Labor Wirtz outlined the following "standards" to be used as guidance in carrying out a nondiscrimination policy in apprenticeship training:

1. The selection of apprentices on the basis of merit alone, in accordance with objective standards which permit review, after full and fair opportunity for application; provided that, where there are established special applicant preference practices, arrangements will be made which will permit the selection of a significant number of any qualified applicants who would otherwise be improperly discriminated against;
2. The taking of whatever steps are necessary, in acting upon application lists developed prior to this time, to offset the effect of previous practices under which discriminatory patterns of employment have resulted; and
3. Nondiscrimination in all phases of apprenticeship and employment during apprenticeship after selections are made.[44]

These standards were supposed to have been implemented by an interpretive circular to BAT's staff on July 17, 1963,[45] which provided for the deregistration of all apprenticeship programs which did not contain the new standards, but opposition from the building trades delayed the implementation of this order.   In August 1963, the Plumbers Union and a number of other organizations concerned with apprenticeship training in that industry (National Joint Plumbing Apprenticeship Committee, the National Association of Plumbing-Heating-Cooling Contractors, the National Joint Steamfitter-Pipefitter Apprenticeship Committee, the National Joint Sprinkler Fitting Committee, and the National Automatic Sprinkler and Fire Control Association, Inc.) approved a joint statement expressing unwillingness to comply with BAT's July apprenticeship standards. The building-trades unions, fearing a loss of control of the labor supplies which give them their economic power, sought to avoid the new rules by direct attacks and by creating a counterplan drawn up by the Construction Industry Joint Conference (CIJC) which created a Joint Committee on Equal Employment Opportunity under the chairmanship of Professor John T. Dunlop. The CIJC recommendations to local joint apprenticeship committees, announced in September 1963, included: the inclusion of a nondiscrimination clause as a part of apprenticeship standards; selection of apprentices solely on the basis of qualifications without regard to race, creed, color, or national origin; the determination of qualifications on such objective measures as age, education, physical ability, and aptitude tests, or fair and impartial interviews to determine qualities such as interest, character, cooperativeness, judgment, and similar factors where these were considered necessary in the selection of applicants; the construction of new lists where present lists do not meet the standards of nondiscrimination; an appeals procedure for aggrieved applicants which should include a board made up of representatives of labor, management, and the public.[46]

The attacks from the building trades caused the Department of Labor to issue new standards in October 1963, which met some of the unions' major criticisms. The unions' chief public complaint was that the Labor Department was attempting to establish a racial quota system for apprentices. The main offending words in the standards were "the taking of whatever steps are necessary . . . to offset" in the second standard; "remove" was therefore substituted for "offset." The earlier standards also provided that apprenticeship lists based on merit systems prior to the adoption of those standards "must be disregarded to the extent necessary to provide opportunities for current selection of qualified members of racial and ethnic minority groups for a significant number of positions." "Significant number" was also interpreted to mean the adoption of a quota system, though Secretary of Labor Wirtz repeatedly denied any intention of imposing a racial quota on the industry. The October USDL standards therefore deleted the offending phrase and provided that where the apprenticeship program was not based on qualifications, application lists must be "opened to the extent necessary to provide current opportunities for selection of qualified members of racial and ethnic minority groups." The July standards provided that where applicant lists were not based on merit systems, equal opportunity for minorities could be demonstrated by reserving "a significant number of positions for qualified members of racial and ethnic minority groups." The October USDL standards substituted for this standard the requirement that "an alternative equal opportunity plan" be adopted subject to the Department's approval.

Even these modified apprenticeship standards failed to satisfy the building-trades unions, however, and the implementation of the new apprenticeship standards was again postponed. Building-trades leaders not only objected to the implication that Negroes were to be given preferential treatment to overcome the products of past discrimination, but also were reluctant to follow a suggestion that civil-rights organizations be notified of apprenticeship vacancies and that relatives could no longer receive preference. A statement by Peter Schoemann, president of the powerful Plumbers and Pipefitters union is perhaps characteristic of the thinking of the building-trades unions on this matter. Schoemann charged the Department of Labor with "bureaucratic entrapment" and said the new standards smack of "angelic objectivity." [47] While professing to support President Kennedy's nondiscrimination program, Schoemann argued that the complaint procedure adopted by BAT would unnecessarily interfere with the work of the local apprenticeship committees. He added that the new standards were a more detailed control of hiring practices than the PCEEO's regulations, which concern themselves with charges of discrimination and not details of the hiring process. Schoemann's main complaint was the proposal to revise application lists "to remove the effects of previous practices under which the discriminatory patterns of employment may have resulted." This, the Plumbers' president argued, runs counter to the "free enterprise system." In what has become a standard defense by building-trades unionists, Schoemann resented the implication that the absence of Negroes from apprenticeship programs resulted from discrimination. "It 'just may have resulted,'" he argued, "from the fact that no minority group member had enough interest and inclination and initiative to apply." Schoemann also has suggested that "someone" is trying to reform the building trades by abolishing the sponsorship systems which favor relatives or friends or existing members. In an amazingly candid statement, the Plumbers' president felt that this was contrary to the American system:

. . . sponsorship and favoritism are phenomena of American political and business life. Indeed, one may wonder whether they are not necessarily inherent in a free democratic society, in which men derive much of their motivation from a desire to accomplish something for their families and friends, and where they have a free choice of selection of people, in government or private employment.

He concluded:

Until American society as a whole accepts generally the proposition that employment and promotion should be based exclusively on merit, if indeed it ever will or ever should accept such a proposition, the United Association [of Journeymen and Apprentices of the Plumbing and Pipefitting Industry of the United States and Canada] will neither endorse nor support any effort by the federal government to regulate out of existence systems and practices of sponsorship in the selection of apprentices.

Peter Schoemann's declaration illustrates vividly an attitude among building-trades unions which makes it very difficult to alter their practices.

As a result of opposition from the building trades, the October apprenticeship standards were again revised before they were made effective on January 17, 1964, though the original standards remained virtually unchanged. The new rules permitted selection of apprentices on the basis of (1) qualifications based on objective standards, (2) any manner in which equality of opportunity can be demonstrated, (3) or any manner that assures equality of opportunity to the satisfaction of the BAT. Equality can be shown by the racial composition of the work force, though the rules disclaim any intention of establishing specific quotas.

Apprenticeship programs that do not meet these standards may be deregistered, which means that employers in these programs could not pay apprentice wages on federal projects, might lose draft deferment for these apprentices, and apprentices would lose the accreditation status that goes with federal registration. These are obviously weak penalties where employers and unions are recalcitrant, as appears likely in some building trades. Indeed, one of the reasons for the Labor Department's long delay in implementing the rules was the realization that in the absence of stronger penalties the decertification of an apprenticeship program is not a very effective remedy. It is also for this reason that the PCEEO was considering declaring employers ineligible for government contracts if the Labor Department rules their apprenticeship programs discriminatory. This, of course, would increase BAT's power over apprenticeship training, a power which it obviously has not welcomed. BAT officials and the building-trades unions complain that the new apprenticeship regulations have destroyed the previous cooperative relationship that existed between them, making BAT a police agency. Civil-rights leaders, on the other hand, feel that this change was long overdue because the previous relationship either encouraged or did little to reduce racial discrimination.

Evaluation of the PCEEO

It is, of course, too early to gauge the impact of the PCEEO's operations on union racial practices. The Committee has been attacked by the NAACP's labor secretary for having provided only "symbolic breakthroughs" on the technical and professional level, but "very little real change for the Negro industrial worker." [48] Moreover, the United States Commission on Civil Rights (USCCR) noted in 1961 that the PCEEO had "taken steps to overcome obstacles encountered by [the PCGC]," but much more was required, including reaffirming that "when Government contractors completely delegate to labor organizations the power of hiring, or of determining admission to apprenticeship training programs or other terms and conditions of employment, they will be held responsible for discriminatory acts of the unions." In a report two years later, the USCCR noted some progress along these lines,[49] particularly the Programs for Fair Progress. Although these pledges are "relatively meaningless in terms of legal obligation since the signatory internationals have no power to compel compliance by their member locals, [they] do commit the AFL-CIO and the internationals to full cooperation" with the PCEEO.[50] Moreover, field interviews by the writer suggest that employers and unions feel that the PCEEO has made a strong effort to enforce its nondiscrimination program. This undoubtedly accounts for the extent to which at least formal measures have been made to end job and union discrimination in the South.

The denial of federal contracts where the Department of Labor decides discrimination exists in apprenticeship programs would be a potent threat, though the writer is persuaded that not many Negroes, or whites, will acquire skills through apprenticeship training unless such programs are greatly expanded and other measures are taken to ensure a high level of employment. As presently constituted, apprenticeship training, though important in some trades, has been greatly exaggerated as a possible source of jobs for Negroes.

The PCEEO has had some difficulty proceeding directly against unions because they are not parties to government contracts, but the value of the Committee's indirect effects should not be underestimated.

Experience demonstrates that unions will not long deny membership to Negroes if the employer hires them under the threat of cancellation of government contracts.

The PCEEO has also suffered the same limitations as its predecessors of being created by executive order and not by Congress, but this defect was remedied by the passage of the 1964 Civil Rights Act, providing a permanent agency and directly prohibiting discrimination by unions as well as employers. Passage of this Act will not automatically result in an end to discrimination, but it can be predicted that Negro political power, the vulnerability of the federal government to moral pressures, the persistence of Negro leaders, and the pervasiveness and importance of government contracts will make the newly created Committee on Equal Employment Opportunity an important agency for changing union racial practices.

Finally, the PCEEO's "Plans for Progress" have caused some controversy among civil-rights experts. The plans are criticized for relying on "voluntarism," which has not proved effective in these cases. Proponents, on the other hand, point out that the plans apply to unions and firms not covered by government contracts, making it possible for the PCEEO to expand its scope. Similarly, the "Recommended Apprenticeship Standards and Procedures" of the Construction Industry Joint Conference Joint Committee on Equal Employment Opportunity apply to all apprenticeship programs, whereas BAT's regulations apply only to those that are registered—about half of the total. Moreover, through either the threat of legislation or revocation of contracts, the plans for progress have been relatively successful in producing jobs for Negroes. It was reported, for example, that in three months firms signing the plans added 60,000 employees, 15,000 of whom were Negroes.[51] The demonstrations in New York in the summer of 1963 probably produced less than 200 jobs.

The Civil Rights Act of 1964

Although it is still too early to evaluate its impact on unions, because much depends upon how the Act is administered and interpreted, we should at least note some of the more important provisions of the Civil Rights Act of 1964 as they pertain to unions. Title VII of that Act deals with discrimination in employment and makes it an unlawful employment practice for a labor organization

(1) to exclude or to expel from its membership, or otherwise to discriminate against, any individual because of his race, color, religion, sex, or national origin;

(2) to limit, segregate, or classify its membership, or to classify or fail or refuse to refer for employment any individual, in any way which would deprive or tend to deprive any individual of employment opportunities, or would limit such employment opportunities or otherwise adversely affect his status as an employee or as an applicant for employment, because of such individual's race, color, religion, sex, or national origin; or

(3) to cause or attempt to cause an employer to discriminate against an individual in violation of this section.

The Act also makes it unlawful for employers or unions to discriminate in apprenticeship and other training programs.

The Civil Rights Act creates an Equal Employment Opportunity Commission (EEOC) of five members (no more than two from either major political party). The EEOC has power to receive complaints of racial discrimination, to attempt to settle these complaints through informal "conference, conciliation, and persuasion," and, if such measures fail, a civil action may be brought in federal district court by the aggrieved party. The district court may also issue an injunction against the discriminating party. The U. S. Attorney General is empowered to bring civil action whenever "he has reasonable cause to believe that any person or group of persons is engaged in a practice of resistance to the full enjoyment of any of the rights secured" by Title VII. If the Attorney General certifies that a case brought by an aggrieved individual is in the public interest, the court may permit him to intervene in the private civil suit. If the court's order in the civil action is not obeyed, the EEOC is authorized to "commence proceedings to compel compliance with such orders."

The Civil Rights Act does not supersede the state FEP laws unless those laws permit or require acts made unlawful by the Civil Rights Act. Indeed, the federal law specifically prohibits the filing of a complaint with the EEOC until

sixty days after proceedings have been commenced under the State or local law, unless such proceedings have been earlier terminated, provided that such sixty-day period shall be extended to one hundred and twenty days during the first year after the effective date of such State or local law.

If a charge is filed with the Commission concerning an unlawful practice occurring in a state or local area with an antidiscrimination law, the EEOC is required to "notify the appropriate State or local officials and, upon request, afford them a reasonable time . . . to act under such State or local law to remedy the practice alleged."

Any attempt to compare the relative merits of relief from the EEOC and the National Labor Relations Board (NLRB) must be purely speculative at this juncture. Much depends on how the Civil Rights Act is interpreted and administered as well as whether it is upheld in the federal courts. Moreover, it still remains to be seen whether the Supreme Court will uphold the *Hughes Tool* doctrine, discussed in the following chapter, giving the NLRB the power to declare racial discrimination an unfair labor practice. With all the uncertainties in the EEOC procedures, however, an aggrieved individual would probably be able to get faster relief through the NLRB. In addition, the NLRB has immediate power to handle all cases over which it has jurisdiction, whereas the Civil Rights Act exempts unions with fewer than 25 members after three years, with fewer than 75 members after two years, or with fewer than 100 members after one year. If the *Hughes Tool* doctrine is not sustained, however, the Board's power would be limited to revoking or denying certification. An uncertified union is vulnerable to raids by other unions and cannot file unfair labor-practice charges against employers, but these are relatively unimportant to many of the strong craft unions which have the most discriminatory reputations.

FOOTNOTES

1. New York: Harper, 1944.
2. See Herbert Garfinkle, *When Negroes March*, Glencoe, Ill.: The Free Press, 1959.
3. Mimeographed news release, n.d., Citizen's Committee to Save Colored Locomotive Firemen's Jobs. See Chapter 10 for further discussion of the Southeastern Carriers agreement.
4. Executive Order No. 9346, May 27, 1943, emphasis added.
5. Malcolm Ross, *All Manner of Men*, New York: Reynal and Hitchcock, 1948, p. 123; for additional information on the railway hearings, see U. S. Congress, House, Special Committee to Investigate Executive Agencies, 78th Congress, 1st and 2d Sessions, *Hearings on House Resolution 102*, Washington, 1944; Louis Ruchames, *Race, Jobs, and Politics*, New York: Columbia University Press, 1953, Ch. 4.
6. *Hearings on H. R. 102, op. cit.*, p. 85.
7. Ross, *op. cit.*, p. 132.
8. *Ibid.*
9. Dissenting opinion of Frank P. Fenton, in *Hearings*, Committee on Fair Employment Practices, April 4, 1942.
10. FEPC, "Birmingham Hearings," June 18, 1942 (typewritten transcript), p. 125.
11. Joseph E. Weckler and Robert E. Weaver, *Negro Platform Workers*, Chicago: American Council on Race Relations, 1945, p. 12.

12. Information on the Philadelphia transit case was taken from: Weckler and Weaver, *ibid.*; Ruchames, *op. cit.*, Ch. 7; FEPC, *Final Report* and *Chronological Summary of Developments in Philadelphia Transportation Company and PRT Employees Union Cases*; Herbert C. Bergstrom and Glen Everett, *The FEPC Faces a Crisis: The Philadelphia Strike*, American Friends Service Committee and the Friends Committee on National Legislation, Philadelphia and Washington, 1944; and Ross, *op. cit.*

13. FEPC, *Final Report*, p. 15.

14. *Hearings on H. R. 102*, 78th Congress, 1st and 2d Sessions, Part 2.

15. FEPC, *Final Report*, p. 22.

16. Letter from W. C. Hushing to Dennis Chavez, September 7, 1944, *Hearings on S. 2048*, pp. 194–195, cited by L. C. Kesselman, *The Social Politics of FEPC*, Chapel Hill: University of North Carolina, 1948, p. 146.

17. AFL *Executive Council Minutes*, September 8–13, 1947, p. 113.

18. Act of June 27, 1944, 58 Stat. 387, Independent Offices Appropriations Act of 1945, 31 USC 696.

19. Letter from Vice-President Nixon to all contracting agencies, May 4, 1957.

20. *Ibid.*

21. Letter to the writer from Dr. Jacob Seidenberg, formerly executive director of the PCGC; and personal interview January 2, 1959.

22. P. 23.

23. P. 34.

24. P. 37.

25. Tabulated from PCGC complaints.

26. *New York Times*, October 25, 1963.

27. PCEEO Newsletter No. 1, June 19, 1961.

28. See U. S. Air Force Report on Lockheed Marietta Plant, released by PCEEO, May 25, 1961.

29. *Dallas Morning News* and *Houston Post*, May 3, 1961.

30. PCEEO pamphlet, "Equality in Job Opportunity," n.d.

31. *New York Times*, November 26, 1962.

32. *IUD Bulletin*, March 1963.

33. *Wall Street Journal*, November 9, 1962.

34. *New York Times*, June 5, 1963.

35. *AFL-CIO News*, June 15, 1963.

36. *New York Times*, June 22, 1963.

37. *New York Times*, June 2, 1963.

38. *New York Times*, September 7, 1963.

39. *1961 Report of the U. S. Commission on Civil Rights*, "Employment," pp. 104–111.

40. *Ibid.*, p. 162.

41. U. S. Department of Labor, Bureau of Apprenticeship and Training, *The National Apprenticeship Program*, 1962.

42. U. S. Congress, 87th, 1st Session, House of Representatives, Committee on Education and Labor, *Special Subcommittee Hearings on H. R. 8219.*

43. U. S. Commission on Civil Rights, *Reports on Apprenticeship Training*, January 1964, p. 7, n. 17.

44. U. S. Department of Labor press release, June 6, 1963; Circular 64-7, July 17, 1963.

45. Circular 64-7, July 17, 1963.

46. *AFL-CIO News*, September 28, 1963; *New York Times*, September 24, 1963;

Construction Industry Joint Conference, Joint Committee on Equal Employment Opportunity, Statement, August 9, 1963, and "Recommended Apprenticeship Standards and Procedures," September 20, 1963.

47. Quoted by John Herling, "Union Chief Raps Apprenticeship Standards," *Report on Labor,* November 13, 1963.
48. *New York Times,* January 2, 1964.
49. *Reports on Apprenticeship,* January 1964, p. 13.
50. *Ibid.*
51. See statement by Otis E. Finley, Jr., in *The Nation's Manpower Revolution,* Hearings before the Subcommittee on Employment and Manpower of the Committee on Labor and Public Welfare, U. S. Senate, 82nd Congress, 1st Session, Part 6, p. 1926, 1963.

CHAPTER 10

The Duty of Fair Representation, the Courts, and the NLRB

The Duty of Fair Representation

Introduction and basis for the duty

A BASIC DILEMMA IS CREATED BY THE FACT THAT DISCRIMINATING unions derive some of their power from the federal government. When a union wins a representation election, supervised by either the National Mediation Board (NMB) for railroad or airline workers or the National Labor Relations Board (NLRB) for those in other industries affecting commerce, that union is certified as exclusive bargaining agent for the workers in that unit by an agency of the federal government. It therefore becomes questionable whether unions certified by the NMB or the NLRB can continue their discriminatory practices; alternatively, it becomes questionable whether legislation permitting such discrimination violates the guarantees of the Fifth Amendment of the U. S. Constitution.

In view of the long history of racial discrimination by railroad unions, it is not surprising that the first test of the legality of racial discrimination by a certified union involved the Brotherhood of Locomotive Firemen and Enginemen (BLF). When the job of shoveling coal into engines was hot, dirty, and of low prestige, it was generally regarded as "Negro work," but when diesel engines and other technological changes made the jobs more attractive, whites sought to displace Negroes as firemen. Moreover, with the growth of unions on the railroads during the First World War—when the federal government encouraged collective bargaining—the BLF and other railroad labor organizations insisted that seniority govern in promotions and the choice of jobs. If seniority had been strictly observed, however, Negroes would have been promoted to engineers, which would have been unthinkable because engineering was "white" work. The BLF and the Brotherhood of Locomotive Engineers (BLE) got around this sticky problem by refusing to admit Negroes to membership and defining them as "unpromotable." But this was not entirely satisfactory to the whites. It was still necessary for engineers to acquire experience as firemen and a large proportion of the firemen were Negroes who had acquired considerable seniority because they could not be promoted. The unions faced the dilemma of promoting Negroes, doing away with the treasured seniority system, or attempting to remove Negroes from the roads; they chose the latter. Thus, the net result of unionization was a great decline in the proportion of Negro firemen on the railroads. In 1910, before unions became established in the industry, 6.8 per cent of all firemen in the United States (5188 of 76,381) and 41.6 per cent of Southern firemen (4897 of 11,782) were Negroes; by 1950 Negro firemen had been reduced to just under 4 per cent (2130 of 53,310).[1] Moreover, almost all of these Negro firemen were in the South; for example, in 1957 there was not one Negro fireman on nineteen railroads operating in New Jersey and New York.[2]

In the late 1920's the BLF entered into an agreement with the carriers stipulating that two-thirds of the available jobs would be given to "nonpromotable" (Negro) firemen and one-third to "promotable" (white) firemen.[3] This arrangement continued with local modifications in the percentages until 1941. Since there were still too many Negro firemen to suit the BLF, in 1941 the union and twenty-one railroads worked out the "Southeastern Carriers Agreement" which established a quota system limiting the number of Negro firemen that could be employed to 50 per cent in each class of service in each seniority district. According to this agreement, no new jobs could be filled by Negroes until this proportion was attained, and no Negroes could be assigned to jobs they did not already hold. This agreement led to the Steele case, which established the basic legal doctrine of union race relations.

Steele was in the passenger pool of the Louisville and Nashville Railroad, with three other Negroes and one white employee, until April 1941 when the jobs held by the Negroes were declared vacant and filled with four whites, all junior to the Negroes whom they replaced. Steele was laid off for sixteen days and then assigned to a less desirable job than the passenger service from which he had been removed. On January 3, 1942, after suit was filed in the Alabama state courts against the BLF and the railroad, Steele was reassigned to passenger service; the Negro firemen resorted to the courts only after their appeals to the BLF and the company went unheeded. The Alabama Supreme Court ruled that the Negroes' complaint stated no cause of action because the BLF had been elected to represent all of the members of the craft or class and had authority either to create or to destroy the rights of members of that craft. The Alabama Court apparently felt that the Negro firemen exhausted their legal rights when they were allowed to vote for or against the BLF. It therefore held that neither the BLF nor the railroad violated any of the Negroes' rights by negotiating the contracts which discriminated against them.

Now the Wagner or National Labor Relations Act [which is still the basic labor-relations law in the United States, though it has been amended by the Taft-Hartley or Labor-Management Relations Act (1947) and the Landrum-Griffin or Labor Management Reporting and Disclosure Act (1959); the National Labor Relations Act as amended will hereinafter be referred as the NLRA] and the Railway Labor Act (RLA) give labor organizations the exclusive power to represent workers in appropriate bargaining units, whether or not those workers are members of the union. For instance, Section 9 of the NLRA provides: "Representatives designated or selected for the purposes of collective bargaining by the majority of the employees in a unit appropriate for such purposes, shall be the exclusive representative of all employees in such unit. . . ." Section 2 of the RLA contains a similar provision. This means that the NLRA and the RLA deprive workers of the right to bargain as individuals and give the bargaining representative exclusive power to make agreements regulating their wages, hours, and working conditions. If, therefore, the RLA gave the BLF this power without any statutory duty to represent all members of the bargaining unit fairly, constitutional questions arose. The U. S. Supreme Court, in reversing the Alabama Supreme Court in the Steele case, raised these constitutional questions in the following manner: [4]

For the representative is clothed with power not unlike that of a legislature which is subject to constitutional limitations on its power to deny, restrict, destroy or discriminate against the rights of those for whom it legislates and which is also under an affirmative constitutional duty equally to protect those rights. If the Railway Labor Act purports to impose on petitioner [Steele] and the other Negro members of the craft the legal duty to comply with the terms of a contract whereby the representative has discriminatorily restricted their employment for the benefit and advantage of the Brotherhood's own members, we must decide the constitutional questions which petitioner raises in his pleading.

The Court was not persuaded, however, that the constitutional question had to be raised in this case because it thought:

. . . that Congress, in enacting the Railway Labor Act and authorizing a labor union, chosen by a majority of a craft, to represent the craft, did not intend to confer plenary power upon the union to sacrifice, for the benefit of its members, rights on the minority of the craft, without imposing on it any duty to protect the minority. . . .
We think that the Railway Labor Act imposes upon the statutory representative of a craft at least as exacting a duty to protect equally the interest of the members of the craft as the Constitution imposes upon a legislature to give equal protection to the interests of those for whom it legislates. Congress has seen fit to clothe the bargaining representative with powers comparable to those possessed by a legislative body to create and restrict the rights of those whom it represents . . . but it also imposed on the representative a corresponding duty. We hold that the language of the Act, . . . expresses the aim of Congress to impose on the bargaining representative . . . the duty to exercise fairly the power conferred upon it in behalf of all those for whom it acts, without hostile discrimination against them.

Justice Murphy was not satisfied with the way the majority opinion sidestepped the constitutional question in this case. He agreed that the constitutionality of the RLA could be saved only by interpreting the Act as requiring the duty of fair representation, but, in a concurring opinion, he expressed some skepticism of the basis on which the majority interpreted the RLA. He thought that any construction of the Act "under the guise of congressional authority, to allow the cloak of racism surrounding the actions of the Brotherhood in refusing membership to Negroes and in entering into and enforcing agreements discriminating against them" would make the Act unconstitutional.

Applicability to unions covered by the NLRA

As we have noted, the duty of fair representation applies to unions acting as bargaining representatives under the NLRA as well as under the RLA. Indeed, in 1943, a year before the Steele decision, the National Labor Relations Board (NLRB), which administers the NLRA, applied the same interpretation to that duty as used by the Supreme Court in Steele,[5] and by the National Mediation Board in railroad cases prior to the Steele decision.[6] Furthermore, in the Wallace case, decided the same day as Steele (December 18, 1944), the Supreme Court upheld the Board's interpretation of the NLRA as requiring the duty of fair representation.[7] The Wallace case did not involve racial discrimination, but in another 1943 case,[8] the Board required equal treatment of all employees in a bargaining unit covered by the certification irrespective of race or color. The Board had also interpreted the NLRA as requiring equal treatment of members of the bargaining unit in the 1945 Larus Brothers Case, in which it held:

This Board has no express authority to remedy undemocratic practices within the structure of union organizations, but we have conceived it to be our duty under the statute to see to it that any organization certified under Section 9(c) as the bargaining representative acted as a genuine representative of all of the employees in the bargaining unit.[9]

Most of the court cases arising under the duty of fair representation have involved unions on the railroads, probably because aggrieved minorities have some administrative relief under the NLRA, since discrimination is an unfair labor practice if it involves hiring or tenure or terms of employment, whereas under the RLA the aggrieved employee's only remedy is to file suit alleging a violation of the duty of fair representation.[10] The NLRB, however, has limited power to prevent racial discrimination and has interpreted its power rather narrowly, forcing Negroes to resort to federal courts for relief in some cases. In the Syres case, for instance, Negro workers at the Gulf Refinery in Port Arthur, Texas, brought suit against Local 23 of the Oil Workers International Union to prevent that organization from entering into a contract restricting Negro employees to the Labor Division. The Negroes brought suit in federal court because their attorney had been unable to get the NLRB to entertain a similar complaint.[11] The federal district court dismissed the Negroes' complaint for lack of jurisdiction because, it argued, the duty of fair representation was imposed on the union by state and not federal law. The court of appeals sustained the dismissal, but the U. S. Supreme

Court granted *certiorari* and, without hearing arguments on the merits or receiving briefs, reversed the lower court, citing the Steele decision.[12]

There is some question as to whether the duty of fair representation applies to unions which have not been certified as exclusive bargaining agents under the RLA or the NLRA. The Supreme Court's reasoning in Steele leads one to believe that the duty applies because a labor union "assumes to act as the statutory representative." An alternative interpretation might be that unions are covered by the RLA and the NLRA whether they have been certified as bargaining agents or not and that the duty of fair representation thus applies to all unions in interstate commerce.

Employer's liability

Not only does the duty of fair representation apply to unions covered by the NLRA as well as the Railway Labor Act, but some courts also have ruled employers are jointly liable for the enforcement of that duty. In Jones v. Central of Georgia,[13] for example, a group of Negroes represented by the Brotherhood of Railroad Trainmen (BRT), which excluded Negroes by constitutional provision until 1960, sued the union and the company for restricting Negroes to certain jobs.

The federal district court awarded damages and granted an injunction restraining the enforcement of the discriminatory provision. The union and the company appealed this decision, and the Negroes appealed the application of the Alabama statute of limitations to the damages award. The U. S. Court of Appeals for the Fifth Circuit upheld the lower Court on all points.

The significance of the Central of Georgia decision for our purposes was the Court's ruling that the company was jointly liable with the union for the latter's violation of the duty of fair representation. The Court reasoned that the company knew, or should have known, that the union had violated its legal obligation; therefore, the discriminatory provision was illegal and the contract should have been read as if it did not exist. This means that the employer violated the contract by not giving the Negro yardmen the pay and job assignments to which they were entitled by the other provisions of the contract.[14] The Court held that the railroad not only had to pay vicarious wages for one year, but also had to give equal employment opportunity to Negro and white workers in the future.

The following year, 1957, in the Richardson case,[15] a federal district court held that the Texas and Pacific Railway was jointly liable for damages on the same basis as the Central of Georgia:

> It takes two parties to reach an agreement, and both have a legal obligation not to make or enforce an agreement or discriminatory employment practice which they either know, or should know, is unlawful. Unless financial responsibility for a joint breach of such duty is required from both sides of the bargaining table, the statutory policy implied under Steele will be impracticable of enforcement. . . .
>
> The Railroad may not have been the Brotherhood's keeper for bargaining purposes, but we think that, under the allegations of this complaint, it may be required to respond in damages for breach of its own duty not to join in causing or perpetuating a violation of the Act and that policy which it is supposed to effectuate.

The doctrine laid down in the Central of Georgia decision could go a long way toward eliminating discriminatory provisions of contracts. How effective this doctrine may be could depend on whether it applies to discrimination that is not specifically embodied in contracts and whether the doctrine is upheld by the U. S. Supreme Court.[16] In the Steele case, the Supreme Court implied some liability on the employers' part when it said that the railroad was not "bound by or entitled to take the benefit of a contract which the bargaining representative is prohibited by statute from making." [17] The doctrine would presumably apply to discrimination not specifically included in a contract since the duty of fair representation does not require that discrimination be embodied in the contract. In the Dillard case, for instance, the Fourth Circuit Court of Appeals ruled: "It is the unlawful use of power vested in the union . . . which gives rise to the jurisdiction of the court to afford relief, not the particular form which such abuse takes." [18]

Acts prohibited by the duty of fair representation

The federal courts have ruled that a wide range of practices are forbidden under the duty of fair representation. The Steele decision held that unions could not seek the removal of Negroes from their jobs. The courts have also ruled that unions cannot do any of the following: deny equal promotion opportunities to Negroes [19]; fail to protest the discriminatory discharge of Negro workers [20]; block the promotion of Negroes [21]; relegate Negroes to certain kinds of jobs where they are frozen from promotion by departmental or other forms of seniority [22]; eliminate Negroes by requiring them to take tests, the failure of which would result in discharge [23]; limit a Negro to only one employer during a six-month period [24]; discriminate against Negroes in wage rates, hiring, discharge, lay-offs, and job assignments.[25] Moreover, the duty of fair representation imposes on the union the obligation to use its bargaining power to *remove* discrimination by the employer in violation of a contract.[26]

Opinion is divided, however, on whether the union is required to bargain to remove discrimination that existed *before* it acquired bargaining rights or to resist employer discrimination not included in the contract. Cox argues that the duty of fair representation does not impose upon unions "the affirmative obligation of making reasonable efforts to abolish racial discrimination." [27] However, the writer is inclined to agree with Sovern that though proof that unions had not resisted sufficiently an employer's long-standing discrimination "would be nearly impossible," [28] the clear intent of court decisions is to impose this duty upon unions. Sovern also argues that job applicants, as well as union members and nonmembers, are protected by the duty of fair representation.

Some questions raised by the duty

Jurisdiction of the federal courts. One of the first questions that had to be established was the jurisdiction of the federal courts in such cases. Jurisdiction was important because the federal courts were likely to invalidate racial discrimination that would have been allowed by state courts in the South, where most of the cases originated. Moreover, federal courts were likely to invalidate discriminatory actions which were specifically allowed—if not actively encouraged—by the National Railroad Adjustment Board (NRAB), the National Mediation Board (NMB), and the National Labor Relations Board (NLRB). The NRAB, for instance, is supposed to handle cases arising out of the interpretation and application of agreements between unions and employers covered by the Railway Labor Act, and in most of the racial cases involving the duty of fair representation the lower courts held that the cases should have been heard by the NRAB before coming to the courts. Moreover, as in Steele, the state courts sometimes held that the Negroes exhausted their legal rights when they voted for or against particular unions in representation cases.

Because of the clear failure of both the NRAB and the NMB to protect the interests of Negro workers, or, indeed, because those agencies aided unions in their discriminatory practices, the U. S. Supreme Court was called upon to reject this reasoning in almost every one of the major cases considered above. In the Steele case, for instance, the Court pointed out that the Adjustment Board had "consistently declined in more than 400 cases to entertain grievance complaints by individual members of a craft represented by a labor organization." [29] Further, since unions selected the members of the NRAB and prescribed the rules under which it operated, "the Negro firemen would be required to appear before a group which is in large part chosen by the respondents against whom their real complaint is made." And, since the unions and the carriers are empowered by the Act to select regional boards of adjustment, "for the purpose of adjusting disputes of the type which may be brought before the Adjustment Board . . . We cannot say that a hearing, if available, before either of these tribunals would constitute an adequate administrative remedy." [30] The Court concluded, therefore, that in the absence of judicial review, the right of fair representation would be meaningless because the plaintiffs could not expect justice from the NRAB.

The Supreme Court seems to have been exasperated by the lower courts' repeated dismissal of cases involving violation of the duty of fair representation when it declared in the Graham case:

> If, in spite of the Virginian, Steele, and Tunstall cases . . . there remains any illusion that . . . the federal courts are powerless to enforce these rights, we dispel it now. The District Court has jurisdiction to enforce by injunction petitioner's rights to nondiscriminatory representation by their statutory representative. [31]

Despite this emphatic statement, inferior courts continued to dismiss such cases for lack of jurisdiction. [32]

The use of tests which might be discriminatory. A question that assumes increasing importance as segregated seniority rosters are abolished is whether employers and unions may agree on tests that block the promotion of Negroes. After the Steele decision, the BLF sought to require Negroes to take the same tests required of white firemen before they could be promoted to engineer and to require the removal of all firemen who failed to pass the tests. The federal district court for the District of Columbia enjoined the enforcement of this "forced promotion" contract in the Palmer case, [33] but the Virginia federal district court, in the Rolax case, denied a similar injunction because the Negroes refused to take the same tests given to whites (since failure would have resulted in their dismissal). The district court ruled in Rolax: "When offered absolute equality with the white firemen they [the Negro firemen] seek and obtain an injunction preventing the Brotherhood from entering into a contract to effect that object, contending that the Brotherhood is not acting in good faith." [34] The Court of Appeals for the Fourth Circuit disagreed with the reasoning of the Virginia district court, because "To say that the forced promotion order put all firemen on an equal basis is to shut one's eyes to the real situation which existed and to allow the Brotherhood to make a cruel use of its bargaining power to get rid of the helpless minority whose rights the courts have been attempting to protect." [35]

Other practices that were allowed by the courts in the Whitfield and Washington cases carry greater potential for restricting Negroes in certain job categories. In the Whitfield case,[36] decided by the Court of Appeals for the Fifth Circuit in 1959, Negro members of an integrated local brought an action for a declaratory judgment, an injunction, and damages against the white officers of their Houston, Texas, local of the Steelworkers and the Sheffield Steel Company, charging that a contract entered into by the company and the union discriminated against them through the use of separate lines of progression in promotion. The company and the union had eliminated the separate lines of seniority, one skilled (line 1) and the other unskilled (line 2), by allowing Negroes to move from line 2 to line 1 on the basis of a written qualification test. The Negro plaintiffs argued that this was discriminatory because the qualification test had not been required of white workers already in line 1; they also complained that Negroes starting in line 1 would have to start at the bottom, thereby requiring some of them to take a wage cut. The whites who were in line 1 had not taken the test, but had been subjected to screening and probationary requirements; in the future, however, both Negroes and whites would be required to take the test. The labor pool, which was now composed of both Negro and white employees, would be tapped under the 1956 agreement complained of to fill jobs in line 1 after qualified workers in line 2 had been given an opportunity to bid on them. The Court of Appeals upheld the contract provisions as being based on skills—a business necessity—and not on racial discrimination. The Court was persuaded that this was "an honest attempt to solve a difficult problem" and would not substitute its judgment for that of the parties, who it said "had attempted to abolish discrimination from now on."

Negro leaders have expressed some concern that this technique, which has been relied on by the NLRB and courts in other cases, might make it possible for unions and employers legally to discriminate against colored workers, especially where the tests are based on subjective factors. Although this will undoubtedly be a problem, the tests have the merit of overcoming the white workers' fears that a large number of senior Negroes will block their advancement; and, if the tests are fairly administered, this procedure might meet the objections of employers to promotion of Negroes to better-paying jobs. It could also make it possible to continue to concentrate Negroes into low-paying jobs if the employer intentionally hires Negroes he believes will be unable to pass the tests.

There is also some concern that standard tests used to select employees might inadvertently discriminate against Negroes. In March 1964, for example, a hearing examiner for the Illinois FEP Commission ordered the Motorola Co. to stop administering a general-ability test to job applicants because it discriminated against "the hitherto culturally deprived and the disadvantaged groups." The company appealed the decision to the full Illinois FEPC.

When the Negroes are represented by another union. Most of the cases dealing with the duty of fair representation involve Negroes who are either in the bargaining unit represented by a union which will not admit them to membership or are members of the bargaining unit and the union. The question arises, however, as to the applicability of the doctrine when the Negroes discriminated against are represented by another union. Such an issue was involved in the Howard case.[37] Long before the First World War, the St. Louis-San Francisco Railroad assigned Negro porters some head-end braking duties, which also were performed by white brakemen at substantially higher wages. During the First World War, the U. S. Railroad Administration gave Negro and white railroad workers equal wages for the same work. In 1921, when the railroads were returned to private control, the Negroes were reclassified to train porters with sizable wage cuts, even though their work remained unchanged and most of their time consisted virtually of the same work and responsibility as the white brakemen. In March 1928 the Brotherhood of Railroad Trainmen, with the aid of the National Mediation Board, entered into a contract providing that in the future only white men would be hired in train, engine, or yard service. After extended conflict all during the Second World War, involving pressure by the BRT to prevent the use of train porters to perform brakemen's duties, the carrier signed a contract in March 1946 under a strike threat, which stipulated that porters would not be used for brakemen's work. This would have required the carrier to discharge Negroes because there was not enough porter work to warrant their retention. After the Negroes appealed to the BRT, the carrier, the NMB, and the NRAB, they filed suit in the Howard case. In 1949, when the BRT was threatened with a four-million-dollar damage suit, the contract limiting employment in train, engine, or yard service was annulled.

A basic difference between the facts in the Howard and Steele cases must be emphasized: in Steele, the Negroes were members of the firemen class, whereas in Howard they were members of a separate class, porters, represented by a different union, the Brotherhood of Sleeping Car Porters. The district court held, for this reason, that the dispute should be settled by the administrative machinery set up by the Railway Labor Act, and, if the actions of these agencies violated the Steele doctrine, the Negroes would then have a justifiable cause of action. But the U. S. Supreme Court held that the BRT had breached its statutory duty within the meaning of the Steele doctrine. The Court held that the union could not use the power granted by the RLA to destroy the Negro workers' jobs in order to give them to whites. The Supreme Court also denied the argument advanced by the carrier and the BRT that this was a jurisdictional dispute to be decided within the administrative framework established by the Railway Labor Act, contending that the dispute involved the validity of the contract and not its interpretation.[38]

The conclusion reached by the majority of the Supreme Court in the Howard case has been questioned by some authorities as unwarranted extension of the Steele doctrine.[39] Cox offers alternative theories, but suggests that "Probably the Howard case should be limited to its peculiar facts." [40]

If we cut through the words, it seems to make little difference whether we call the Negro brakemen "train porters" or some other name so long as they did brakemen's work. In this respect, and by the BRT's own admission, the Negroes were doing brakemen's work over which the Brotherhood claimed exclusive jurisdiction. It must also be considered that the "train porters" were applicants for membership in the BRT as brakemen. The opponents of the Howard decision place great weight in the fact that the Negro brakemen were members of another union, but nothing in the RLA of the NLRA prohibits minority members from forming a competing union—all the law does is to deny the minorities any bargaining rights until they become majorities. In addition, using a job description for a brakeman, it seems reasonable to argue that in this case the Negroes were members of that bargaining unit and were classified as porters mainly because of their race. It seems clear, on this basis, that the facts bring the Howard case within the purview of the Steele doctrine.

The only way that the contrary could be argued is to assume that these Negro brakemen were train porters because they could not get in the BRT!

The right to union membership. The theory that unions are voluntary associations like fraternities, churches, and civic clubs seems to be firmly entrenched in the American legal system, but the theory is at least rendered questionable by the duty of fair representation, to say nothing of the economic facts of life. It is instructive, therefore, to look at the development of legal doctrine and opinion on the union's right to exclude Negroes from membership.

The U. S. Supreme Court ruled in the Steele case that the Railway Labor Act "does not deny to such bargaining labor organization the right to determine eligibility to its membership." [41] Moreover, the Conference Committee Report on the Taft-Hartley Act specifically permitted both segregated unions and restrictions on union membership,[42] and the Act itself does not "impair the right of a labor organization to prescribe its own rules with respect to the acquisition or retention of membership therein. . . ." [43]

Similarly, even before the Taft-Hartley amendments, the NLRB consistently disclaimed authority to require unions to admit Negroes to membership, in spite of its unanimous ruling in 1943 that "We entertain grave doubt whether a union which denies membership to employees on the basis of race, may nevertheless bargain as the exclusive representative in an appropriate unit composed in part of members of the excluded race." [44] Indeed, the Board went so far in the 1945 General Motors case as to indicate that racial discrimination by a union might lead to the dismissal of its petitions for a representation election.[45] However, the Board refused to follow this line of thought to its logical conclusion, probably because of congressional hostility to making racial discrimination an unfair labor practice and because until the passage of the Taft-Hartley Act in 1947 the Board did not have authority to issue orders against Unions.[46]

Following the U. S. Supreme Court's 1954 decision against segregation in the public schools, many Negroes thought that the time was ripe to have the same doctrine applied to unions. Accordingly, a group of Negro firemen brought suit in the Oliphant case [47] in which they argued that it was impossible for them to get the fair representation to which they were entitled under the Railway Labor Act and the Fifth Amendment as long as the BLF refused to admit them to membership. The colored firemen believed that racial exclusion from the statutory bargaining agent denied them the same equal protection that the states were declared to have denied Negro children in the school cases. In fact, they argued that they had a stronger case because

> . . . the enforced inequality of racial segregation is far clearer in the labor area than in education. In finding segregated schooling inherently unequal, the Supreme Court emphasized the resulting psychological and social barriers for Negroes. The inequalities involved here are even more obvious; appellants do not sue for the right to non-segregated instruction, but for the right to participate with their fellow workers in the meetings and elections at which their most vital and fundamental rights are determined—the hours of labor, wages, retirement age, runs, assignments—all the working conditions bargained with the employers. If the Fifth Amendment precludes segregation and exclusion of Negroes in public education, it necessarily precludes segregation and exclusion of Negro firemen from the election of those who exercise statutory bargaining power on their behalf and from participation in the statutory bargaining process whereby their employment rights are determined.[48]

The BLF defended its exclusionist policies by arguing that the union was a private association and had complete freedom to determine membership eligibility, that it would do Negroes no good to get in the BLF because members did not determine the policies of that organization (!), and that the Negroes misconstrued their remedies under the Steele doctrine. On the last point, the BLF argued that if Negroes were discriminated against, they should seek court decrees alleging the union's violation of its duty of fair representation.

The Ohio federal district court denied the Negro firemen the relief requested on the grounds that the specific acts complained of, though having adverse effects on colored firemen, applied to "all who come within the terms of the [collective bargaining] rule involved," so "this court cannot state definitely that this Brotherhood adopted these practices for the purpose of discrimination against the Negroes."[49]

The district court ruled that the real question was not whether the Negro firemen had been discriminated against by the specific acts complained of, but whether the plaintiffs' ineligibility for membership in the union was responsible for the discrimination that they alleged and was therefore federal action that violated the Fifth Amendment. On the first point, the court held: "There can be no real assurance that membership in the defendant would prevent discrimination, since it is my opinion under the evidence here that the effective discrimination is by the railroad employer, rather than by the brotherhood, and the railroad employers are not parties to the action." The Court added that it could

. . . feel that a situation is unjust and may need some remedial action, but unless upon sound equitable principles relief can be granted, the remedy does not lie with the courts. Certainly voluntary action by the defendant or *Congressional legislation present the only corrective where a manifest inequality exists.* . . . To compel by judicial mandate membership in voluntary organizations where the Congress has knowingly and expressly permitted the bargaining agent to prescribe its own qualifications for membership would be usurping the legislative function. [Emphasis added.]

The United States Supreme Court denied *certiorari* with the following order: "In view of the abstract context in which the questions sought to be raised are presented by this record, the petition for *certiorari* to the United States Court of Appeals for the Sixth Circuit is denied." [50]

The Oliphant decision is in keeping with most court decisions, but there are a number of legal authorities who argue that the "voluntary associated doctrine should not be applied to unions." [51] As Summers put it: "To exclude a man from a club may be to deny him pleasant dinner companionship, but to exclude a worker from a union may be to deny him the right to eat." [52] A study group report published in 1961 by the Committee for Economic Development argued that the guarantee of the "right of entry" into labor unions was a major omission from the "Bill of Rights" of the Landrum-Griffin Act. [53] The report argued that

Without this additional right, the guarantees assured by the law became meaningless for many individual workers who never get the opportunities to avail themselves of these guarantees. . . . Unions should be open to all qualified persons regardless of race, creed, color, national origin, political beliefs, or family ties. Employers have an equal responsibility to see to it that an individual is not denied equal access to job opportunities for which he may be qualified. Unions permitting or imposing such discriminatory barriers should not be entitled to certification as an exclusive bargaining agent.

Similarly, the 1961 report of the U. S. Civil Rights Commission observed that the refusal by Congress, the courts, and the NLRB

to consider exclusion from union membership as failure to provide "fair representation" . . . seems inconsistent with the requirement of fair representation. Unions exercise control over the fate of a worker through negotiation and administration of collective bargaining contracts. . . . It is difficult to conceive how an employee can be fairly represented by a union that does not permit him a voice in its decision.[54]

The "voluntary association" doctrine does not mean, however, that unions cannot be required by law to admit Negroes. It also has been established that labor organizations cannot enforce union security provisions against Negroes denied equal membership in the unions.[55] Both the Railway Labor Act and the National Labor Relations Act provide that union-shop agreements do not apply to employees "to whom membership is not available upon the same terms and conditions as are generally applicable to any other members, or to members who are denied membership for any reason other than the failure to tender dues, initiation fees, and certain assessments uniformly required of members."

Since the lack of congressional action is so important in these cases, before leaving this section we might note some of the attempts to amend the NLRA and the RLA to prevent certification of unions for racial discrimination. When the Railway Labor Act was being amended in 1951, Senator Jenner's motion to amend the Act to prevent racial discrimination by refusing certification as exclusive bargaining agent to unions that barred Negroes from membership was tabled.[56] Both the House and Senate made it perfectly clear that they did not intend to interfere with the "voluntary association" doctrine when amending the Act to permit the union shop. However, Senator Lehman insisted that it be made equally clear that Negroes would not lose their jobs where there were union-shop agreements and Negroes were not admitted to the unions on equal terms.[57] A similar guarantee was placed in the Taft-Hartley Act. Senator Taft explained: "Let us take the case of unions which prohibit the admission of Negroes to membership. If they prohibit the admission of Negroes to membership, they may continue to do so; but representatives of the union cannot go to the employer and say, 'You have got to fire this man because he is not a member of our union.' " [58]

During the debates on the Landrum-Griffin bill in 1959, Congressman Powell attempted to amend the so-called "Bill of Rights" in title I to provide: "Except that no labor organization shall . . . refuse membership, segregate, or expel any person on the grounds of race, religion, color, sex, or national origin." [59] Congressman Landrum, co-author of the bill, opposed the Powell amendment, declaring: "We do not seek in this legislation, in no way, no shape, no guise, to tell the labor unions of this country whom they shall admit to their unions." [60] Although the Powell amendment was defeated, observers think it arguable that section 101(a)(1) of that Act gives qualified employees who are denied admission to unions on an equal basis as other employees "equal rights and privileges within such organization to nominate candidates, to vote in elections and referendums . . . to attend membership meetings, and to participate in the deliberations and voting upon the business of such meetings, subject to reasonable rules and regulations in such organization's constitution and bylaws." [61] Those who argue that employees in a bargaining unit who are denied membership in a union representing that unit are entitled to these benefits rest their case on the Act's definition of "member" to include "any person who has fulfilled the requirements for membership in such organization, and who neither has voluntarily withdrawn from membership nor has been expelled or suspended from membership after appropriate proceedings consistent with lawful provisions of the Constitution and bylaws of such organization." [62] The right of rejected nonmembers to these benefits of union membership is seen by some to be conveyed by the Act's declarations of findings, purpose, and policy, which makes no mention of "union members" and speaks only of "employees." [63] However, in view of the debate on the Powell amendment and Congress's repeated refusal to prohibit membership discrimination by unions, we must agree with Aaron when he says:

Despite these faint glimmers of hope, however, the chances of qualified employees who are unfairly denied union membership securing the right to share equally in the normal rights and benefits of membership must still be considered as remote. [64]

Thus, the Landrum-Griffin Act probably provided no right to union membership, but it did contain some guarantees which might make it possible for Negroes to gain equal treatment within a union if they are accepted as members, though the rights guaranteed in the Act's so-called "Bill of Rights" were rendered less effective by the requirement that the individual discriminated against bring civil action for enforcement. [65] Furthermore, the Act's trusteeship provisions can probably be used by international unions to require the admission of Negroes from excluded locals. [66]

The Effects of the Federal Courts on Union Racial Practices

The federal courts' ability to alter union racial practices is derived from their power to interpret the constitutionality of an act and to impose duties that are compatible with constitutional requirements, to issue injunctions, award damages, and interpret contract and other legal violations.

Injunctions

The injunction occupies an important place in the legal history of the labor movement because of its effectiveness as a weapon to curtail the activities of unions. What commended the injunction to those who wanted to check unions was the rapidity with which temporary court orders could be secured and the sweeping prohibitions in their language, since they were frequently written by company lawyers. Continuing the forbidden action after a restraining order or injunction was issued "brought down on the heads of the offenders the vengeance of the court through the exercise of its contempt power, unrelieved by the tender mercies of a jury. Hence, strikes, picket lines and boycotts were easily broken up almost before they were begun." [67] The injunction was such an onerous anti-union weapon that labor organizations marshalled their political forces against it and were finally able to get it curtailed by the Norris-LaGuardia Act in 1932.

It was established in the Steele case, however, that Norris-La-Guardia's prohibitions on the use of federal injunctions in labor disputes did not apply to cases of racial discrimination, or apparently to other cases where workers were injured by the union's breach of the duty of fair representation. In the Graham case, for example, the union argued that an injunction could not be issued until the provisions of the Norris-LaGuardia Act had been met. The Supreme Court's answer was that if, in spite of its many decisions to the contrary,

. . . there remains any illusion that under the Norris-LaGuardia Act the federal courts are powerless to enforce these rights, we dispel it now. The District Court has jurisdiction to enforce by injunction petitioner's rights to nondiscriminatory representative.[68]

The Court's reasoning in this case was that the Norris-LaGuardia Act was designed to protect the workers' interests, so to prohibit the use of the injunction when a union had violated the rights of Negro workers "would indeed be to 'turn the blade inward.' " [69] The legal rationale for this decision is not clear, but probably rests on the assumption that conflicts between the union and members of the bargaining unit do not fall within the statutory definition of "labor disputes." This seems to be a justifiable theory because the term "labor disputes" more properly applies to conflicts between unions and management than between members of the bargaining unit.[70]

Injunctions are powerful weapons to protect the interests of minority members of the bargaining unit because these orders can be in force while the legal issues are being settled. In the Hunter case, for instance, an injunction was used for this purpose.[71] The Hunter dispute grew out of a conflict between the Brotherhood of Railroad Trainmen, the company, the NRAB, and Negro porter-brakemen on the Santa Fe as to whether the Negroes would be allowed to keep the braking jobs that they had held as a class since about 1900. In 1942 the NRAB granted the work to the brakemen in a case originating in 1939, and in 1944 a temporary restraining order was issued by the federal district court enjoining the displacement of train porters; additional temporary injunctions were entered in 1948 and 1952. In 1958 the court entered a final decree, ordering the redetermination of the basic dispute by the Adjustment Board. The contention that kept this issue alive for about twenty years was whether the NRAB gave proper notice of the original hearing because of its failure to notify Negro porter-brakemen and the Sleeping Car Porters, which sometimes represented porters but did not in this case. During this entire time, however, injunctions were in force which made it possible for the porter-brakemen to keep their jobs; the court issued a new injunction forbidding the displacement of the porter-brakemen until the NRAB opened its files and disposed of the case.

Damages

The award of damages, another power possessed by the courts in these cases, would be very effective if damages could readily be assessed and could be designed to deter transgressors. The problem of assessment is not too difficult where the contract alters preexisting rights, in which case the amount of damages is the difference between actual earnings and the amount that they would have been under the previous arrangement.[72] But in other cases it is not as easy to determine the damages actually suffered.

Some of the problems involving damage suits for racial discrimination by unions were revealed in the Clark and Syres cases. In the Clark case,[73] the company and the union were charged with violating Negro plaintiffs' rights by withholding from them the same opportunities to qualify for and occupy the position of car retarder operator as were afforded white brakemen. The question of damages was complicated by several factors: this was a class action, praying for all Negroes in the class, whereas damages must be awarded on an individual basis; the difficulty in determining whether or not the plaintiff would have been promoted if he had not been discriminated against; and the problem involved in establishing the time periods and amounts involved. None of the Negroes in the Clark case ever qualified for retarder operator; some of them applied and were given opportunities to qualify but failed, whereas another retired before being given the opportunity to qualify. The court decided that the worker who had retired could have passed the examination and learned the higher-paying job if he had been given an opportunity. According to the judge, "This plaintiff testified as a witness and impressed the court as an alert and very intelligent person. . . . I am not too strongly impressed with the argument that the position of car retarder operator is one of great difficulty requiring exceptional aptitude." However, the court found it impossible to calculate damages; a theoretical formula would have been the difference between the amount this worker earned as a brakeman and what he would have earned as a car retarder, but the many variables determining a railroad worker's earnings rendered the calculation of this amount impossible. The court made a "fair estimate" of $1800. Compensatory damages could not be established for the other workers, but all of the plaintiffs were awarded $1000 punitive damages for the invasion of their legal rights and $750 as part of the costs to be applied on plaintiffs' counsel fees.

The Syres case presented even greater difficulties in determining damages.[74] This case arose out of a discriminatory contract negotiated in 1954 by a local of the Oil Workers in Port Arthur after the Negro and white locals amalgamated. Since Negroes were in the minority, they lost their representation on the bargaining committee following the amalgamation. The Negroes filed suit against the white union to enjoin the enforcement of the discriminatory contract. The case went to the Supreme Court after lower courts dismissed it for lack of jurisdiction; the Supreme Court established federal jurisdiction[75] and remanded the case for further hearing. By the time the case was heard again, however, a new contract had been negotiated (in 1956) which was not alleged to be discriminatory. The district court thereupon dismissed the case as moot except for the money damages suffered under the previous contract.

The Negro plaintiffs asked for $150,000 damages. They based their request on the

. . . difference between the average wage in the Operating Mechanical Division and that of the Labor Division, said average being the total of all salary items in either division, divided by the number of salary items in either division, times forty (40) (hour work week), times the number of weeks the contract of April 17, 1954, was in force, multiplied by the number of men that would have received such vacancies but for the contract of April 17, 1954.

The sum came to $11,000,580.80; the plaintiffs asked for $150,000 because they had not expected the discriminatory contract to be in force long enough to amount to the larger figure.

Plaintiffs appealed after the jury rendered an adverse verdict and the Court of Appeals sustained the lower court, holding that there was no proof of any actual damages and noting that none of the plaintiffs had applied for jobs in the other division. The appeals court ruled that the violation of the Negroes' rights would have been enjoined if the 1954 contract were still in force and that:

Damages may sometimes be recovered in a class action, but where the damages, if recovered, would be in different amount to separate individuals, the persons entitled thereto must be made parties or interveners before the damages can be awarded.

Lawsuits are probably more valuable as threats to unions than anything else, a factor enhanced by the uncertainty as to their outcome. This has undoubtedly been a factor deterring unions in the making of discriminatory contracts; in the Syres case, the nondiscriminatory contract was not due entirely to the pressure from the damage suit, but there can be little doubt that this was a consideration.

Conclusions

Although court action is frequently the only course open to the worker whose rights have been violated, several factors limit its effectiveness. First, court cases take too long to offer effective relief. Second, the outcome of such cases is too uncertain, not entirely because of the lack of clarity as to legal principle, but also because of the difficulties in establishing appropriate damages. Third, courts, as well as administrative bodies, have received insufficient power from Congress to handle these problems; if the court or board strikes out on its own, in view of the clear legislative history of these laws, it is likely to be undermined by its shaky legal position. Fourth, court cases are too expensive to afford effective remedies to Negroes each time their rights are violated. In view of these difficulties, therefore, there is a clear need for effective administrative relief for aggrieved minorities.

The Effect of the NLRB on Union Racial Practices

It is clear that the duty of fair representation applies to unions certified under the National Labor Relations Act as well as the Railway Labor Act, but it is not clear how much authority the NLRB has to prevent racial discrimination. The Board has consistently ruled that certified bargaining agents may not discriminate against members of the bargaining unit on a racial basis, but the Taft-Hartley Act is silent on how aggrieved workers can enforce this duty, and the legislative history of the Act made no mention of the Steele doctrine.[76] Probably the most effective way to redress such complaints is to file a private lawsuit alleging violation of the duty of fair representation, as was done in the Syres and Whitfield cases. It is at least arguable, however, that the aggrieved workers should be able to get the same relief from the Board as they can get from the federal courts, since both the courts and the Board require the same duty and the U. S. Supreme Court has upheld the Board's right to require that duty.

The Board does have the power to revoke certification of a union for violating its duty of fair representation, and to enforce the union-security and unfair labor-practice provisions of the Act.

Decertification

The Board had frequently threatened but until the 1964 *Hughes Tool* decision, discussed below, had never actually used its power to decertify a union for violating its duty of fair representation in a racial case. The first time the NLRB revoked certification of a union for failing to represent fairly was not on a strictly racial basis. In the 1953 *Hughes Tool* case [77] the Board held, at the urging of the International Association of Machinists, that the duty of fair representation was violated when an all-white Independent Metal Workers' union in Houston, Texas, charged nonmembers $15 to process grievances and $400 to carry cases to arbitration. The NLRB also ruled that Tobacco Workers International Union Local 219 violated its statutory duty by having a Negro auxiliary covered by a check-off and union-security provisions. The union voluntarily relinquished certification and the contract expired, relieving the Board of its duty to revoke certification, which it claims it would have done; however, the Board required the union to file a new petition in the name of both the white and Negro locals if it wanted to be certified.[78]

In another case, Local 211 of the Steamfitters voluntarily relinquished certification after the Teamsters challenged the local's right to represent a bargaining unit because it discriminated against Negroes.[79] Race was not mentioned in the report of this case, but the NLRB ruled that the hearing officer "found as a fact that Pipefitters Local 211 has failed to perform its full statutory duty under the certification of March 4, 1953, to represent all employees equally and without discrimination, and he therefore recommended that the Board enter an order rescinding and revoking the certification of Pipefitters Local 211. . . ."[80]

Although the Board clearly has the power to decertify—or, at least, that power can reasonably be inferred from the NLRA—its power to refuse certification is less clear. Refusal to certify would infer that a history of discrimination justified an assumption that the union will continue to discriminate. This assumption is not always justified, but an argument can be made for it on the ground that it would take too long to determine whether a union would discriminate.[81] However, the writer is inclined to believe that refusal to certify is an improper remedy. Unions should be given a chance to prove that they will not discriminate, though unions with discriminatory records should be watched more carefully than others. It would not always be practical to judge a given local by the practices of the other locals or the parent international. Moreover, in refusing to certify, the Board would have to be very specific about the discriminatory acts to be prohibited because some discrimination exists in every union.

It should also be noted that the NLRB has consistently refused to permit the exclusion of Negroes from bargaining units or to entertain petitions from joint bargaining agents which would not admit units composed of Negroes.[82] However, the Board does permit unions which exclude Negroes from membership to stand for election in units containing Negroes.

The NLRB traditionally has also taken a much narrower view of its obligations to prevent racial discrimination than have the federal courts. Though it "entertained grave doubts" that exclusionist unions could represent Negroes fairly, the Board, like the courts, refused to require that unions admit Negroes to membership in order to satisfy that duty. Furthermore, the Board has taken a more limited view than the courts of things that violate the duty of fair representation. In 1956, for example, the Board ruled that the NLRA was not violated when Negroes were restricted to the lowest job categories.[83] Courts, on the other hand, have usually held such practices in violation of duty of fair representation.[84]

Moreover, the general counsel ruled that a union did not violate its duty of fair representation when it failed to protest a company rule which restricted Negroes to certain job categories since "Discrimination because of race does not fall within the scope of the Act. The union did not violate the Act by its failure to raise a question as to the company's disputed practice, such an assertion would constitute an unwarranted extension of the . . . Act."[85]   In contrast, the U. S. Supreme Court in Conley v. Gibson [86] held that the duty of fair representation included the duty to protest actions by a company which discriminated against Negroes by discharging them. We must note, however, that this particular aspect of the duty of fair representation does not seem to be very important where there is no duty by the employer not to discriminate. As a general rule, in the absence of a nondiscrimination law or clause in the contract, the right to private employment without discrimination on the basis of race is not one protected by the Constitution or common law,[87] so the union can protest, but it is questionable that it has a legal right to *compel* the employer not to discriminate unless he violates the contract.[88]

Union security provisions

The legal proscriptions on union security have influenced union racial practices because even the most discriminatory union usually will change its ways rather than give up closed or union-shop arrangements. As discussed earlier, the courts and the NLRB have ruled that the union shop is incompatible with the closed union. The Taft-Hartley Act prohibits the closed shop and stipulates that employers are not justified in discharging workers under union-security provision if membership is not available to those workers on the same conditions as other employees.

The legality of union hiring halls, which have facilitated discrimination by the building trades, seagoing unions, and other organizations of casual workers, was called into question by the anticlosed-shop provision of Taft-Hartley. Observers have generally agreed that hiring halls serve useful functions for employers and employees, though it is also clear that this arrangement gives unions great power to discriminate against nonmembers. The NLRB sought to avoid this dilemma by holding, in the Mountain Pacific case, that the hiring hall was illegal per se unless certain conditions were established to insure that nonmembers were not discriminated against.[89]   The Mountain Pacific arrangement was specifically permitted in the Conference Report on the Landrum-Griffin Act,[90] but the U. S. Supreme Court ruled in 1960 that the NLRB did not have the authority to outlaw the hiring hall in the absence of discernible evidence that the union discriminated against nonmembers.[91]   As it stands, therefore, the hiring hall cannot be used to discriminate against nonmembers and thus could conceivably be used by Negro workers who are barred from membership as a means of getting referred to jobs.   The effectiveness of this procedure, however, would be modified by the employer's right to refuse to hire colored workers.   But in some situations the use of union hiring halls by Negro draftsmen barred from membership could serve to clarify the source of discrimination and get jobs for colored workers where employers are willing to hire Negro workers, or are forced to do so.

Unfair labor practices

In addition to its power to decertify a discriminating union and to refuse to permit the exclusion of Negroes from appropriate bargaining units, the NLRB has prohibited discrimination which was incidental to unfair labor practices—though its action in these cases has usually been against employers and not unions.   In the hiring-hall cases, for instance, racial discrimination is just one form of discrimination practiced against nonmembers, but the Board might be used to correct such actions.   There have been other cases where race was specifically involved as incidental to an unfair labor practice.[92]

The Hughes Tool Case of 1964

The *Hughes Tool* decision,[93] handed down by the NLRB the same day President Johnson signed the Civil Rights Act of 1964, raises some important questions and, if sustained in the federal courts, could have important consequences for union racial practices.   Specifically reversing the NLRB's previous position, the Board ruled for the first time that a violation of the duty of fair representation is also an unfair labor practice.   Previously, the NLRB had interpreted its authority in such cases as limited to the relatively weak penalty of revoking a union's certification, and by holding that a discriminatory contract would not bar a representation election.[94]   But if the union's violation of the duty of fair representation is also an unfair labor practice, the Board can issue cease and desist orders enforceable in the federal courts.   The *Hughes Tool* theory would in effect give the aggrieved person an administrative remedy for the duty of fair representation, making it no longer necessary for him to seek relief in the courts.

The *Hughes Tool* case involved a complaint by a Negro, Ivory Davis, who charged that an independent white local union in Houston, Texas, had committed an unfair labor practice because it negotiated a contract which discriminated against him on racial grounds. Davis was a member of an independent Negro local which was jointly certified with the white local by the NLRB. However, the Negro local had refused to ratify a contract which restricted the apprenticeship program to whites. Davis was denied participation in the apprenticeship program and filed a grievance against the employer. But the white local refused to prosecute his grievance.

A majority of the NLRB upheld the trial examiner's contention that the white local had committed an unfair labor practice "by its failure to entertain in any fashion or to consider the grievance filed by an employee in the bargaining unit, Ivory Davis, and by its outright rejection of Davis' grievance for reasons of race. . . ." The majority ruled that the white local had violated the following provisions of Section 8(b) of the NLRA which make it an unfair labor practice for unions

(1) to restrain or coerce (A) employees in the exercise of the rights guaranteed in section 7: *Provided,* that this paragraph shall not impair the right of a labor organization to prescribe its own rules with respect to the acquisition or retention of membership therein; . . .
(2) to cause or attempt to cause an employer to discriminate against an employee in violation of subsection (a)(3) or to discriminate against an employee with respect to whom membership in such organization has been denied or terminated on some ground other than his failure to tender the periodic dues and the initiation fees uniformly required as a condition of acquiring or retaining membership;
(3) to refuse to bargain collectively with an employer . . .

Section 7 guarantees workers the right to organize and bargain collectively through representatives of their own choosing (or to refrain from such activity). Subsection (a)(3) makes it an unfair labor practice for an employer "by discrimination in regard to hire or tenure to encourage or discourage membership in any labor organization."

With respect to the representation case, which is the traditional provision upon which the duty of fair representation rests, the Board ruled that the joint certification of the independent locals "be rescinded because the certified organizations executed contracts based on race and administered the contracts so as to perpetuate racial discrimination in employment." However, two of the Board's five members refused to join the majority in taking the additional step of "overturning an outmoded and fallacious doctrine which the Board established long ago." The majority ruled that the certification of the locals should be rescinded because they

discriminated on the basis of race in determining eligibility for full and equal membership and segregated their members on the basis of race . . . we hereby expressly overrule [previous NLRB cases] insofar as such cases hold that unions which exclude employees from membership on racial grounds may obtain or retain certified status under the Act.

In justifying this departure from previous doctrine, the majority argued that it acted under authority from the 1947 Taft-Hartley Act, which for the first time prohibited unfair labor practices of unions. The majority reasoned that most of the cases involving the duty of fair representation arose under the Railway Labor Act (RLA). Although the RLA contains provisions similar to the unfair labor practices in the NLRA, the courts had ruled in each of the railroad cases that the federal courts had jurisdiction because the aggrieved Negroes had no administrative remedy under the RLA. When, therefore, the NLRB held that the Wagner Act imposed the duty of fair representation on unions, it did so under the provisions of the representation election provisions of Section 9, because before the Taft-Hartley amendments the Board did not have authority to issue orders against labor unions. However, according to the *Hughes Tool* majority, the Taft-Hartley unfair labor-practice amendments gave aggrieved individuals administrative relief for racial discrimination by unions.

Two of the Board's five members agreed with the majority that the white local had committed an unfair labor practice in violation of Section 8(b)(1)(A) by refusing to process Ivory Davis's grievance because he was not a member of the white local, but they rejected the majority's argument that a violation of the duty of fair representation was an unfair labor practice. The minority based its position on the legislative history of the NLRA and the specific refusals by Congress to give the Board power to deal with racial cases. Moreover, according to the minority, the Board's decision was unwise because it went beyond the Act's primary purposes of protecting "the organizational rights of employees" and leaving the parties a "wide latitude in their negotiations, unrestricted by a governmental power to regulate the substantive solution of their differences."

The minority also argued that the 8(b)(2) and 8(b)(3) charges were not properly before the Board because of procedural irregularities which had denied the independent union the right to respond to these charges. Moreover, the minority reasoned that 8(b)(2) outlaws only discrimination which is related to "union membership, loyalty, and the acknowledgement of union authority or the performance of union obligations." Section 8(b)(3) was not applicable, according to the minority, because it pertains mainly to bargaining between unions and employers and not between unions and employees.

A review of past court decisions, the legislative history of the NLRA, and the language of the RLA and the NLRA seem to support the conclusion that the NLRB's decision is tenable with respect to the representation case but untenable with respect to the unfair labor practices case. This conclusion is not based on a belief that racial discrimination should not be an unfair labor practice, but on the assumption that, as the NLRA stood at the time of the NLRB's decision, racial discrimination per se was not an unfair labor practice. As noted earlier, racial discrimination is an unfair labor practice where it is incidental to a practice which is clearly prohibited by Section 8. There seems to be little doubt that the discrimination stipulated in the NLRA refers to discrimination because of union membership or the lack of it and not because of race. Moreover, Section 8(b)(1) specifically provides that "this paragraph does not impair the right of a labor organization to prescribe its own rules with respect to the acquisition or retention of membership therein." The Civil Rights Act of 1964 denies unions the right to discriminate in membership on racial grounds, but the NLRA does not.

The majority's reasoning concerning the differences between the NLRA and RLA also is unconvincing. Though the Supreme Court recently left open the question of whether a breach of the duty of fair representation violated Section 8(b)(1)(A),[95] we noted in the *Syres* case that the Court applied the duty of fair representation equally to the RLA and the NLRA under the similar representation provisions of the two acts. Moreover, we also noted that even after the Taft-Hartley Act the courts have taken jurisdiction in other cases involving the duty of fair representation which were not railroad cases; the *Whitfield* case, for example, was in the steel industry.[96] That more nonrailroad cases did not arise under the duty of fair representation doctrine is probably due to the fact that the most hostile forms of discrimination occurred on the railroads. The railroad contracts frequently were intentionally discriminatory whereas those in other industries rarely contained specific discriminatory provisions. Indeed, outside the railroad industries Negroes have been able to sue for violation of specific nondiscrimination clauses in contracts, to file suits with the government contract committees (which hesitated to take jurisdiction over the railroad brotherhoods), or to file charges under state or local antidiscrimination laws. Moreover, the aggrieved Negroes could usually solicit the aid of the AFL-CIO or its affiliated international unions whereas the railroad brotherhoods were themselves responsible for discrimination in many cases. The Board rests its decision on the fact that Negroes had no administrative relief under the RLA, but, although the courts did rule that the aggrieved Negroes had not had effective administrative relief under the RLA, it is not clear whether this was because of the provisions of the Act itself or because the railway labor boards refused to protect the Negroes' interests.

FOOTNOTES

1. U. S. Bureau of the Census, 14th Census of the United States, Vol. IV, Population, p. 353; 1950 Population Census Report, P-D, No. 1B, Vol. IV, p. 1, C.B. p. 29.
2. N. Y. State Commission Against Discrimination, *Railroad Employment in New York and New Jersey,* 1957, p. 5. 1910 and 1950 figures from *U. S. Census of Occupations,* 1910 and 1950.
3. BLF v. Tunstall, 136 F. 2d 289 (1944).
4. Steele v. Louisville and Nashville R. Co., 65 S. Ct. 226 (1944).
5. Wallace Corporation 50 NLRB 138 (1943).
6. See: 13 LRRM 712.
7. Wallace Corp. v. NLRB, 323 U. S. 248 (1944).
8. In the Matter of Bethlehem-Alameda Shipyard, Inc., 53 NLRB 999 (1943).
9. Larus & Bros., 62 NLRB 1095 (1945).
10. Archibald Cox, "The Duty of Fair Representation," *Villanova Law Review,* January 1957, p. 151.
11. Personal interview with Roberson L. King, attorney for the Negroes in Syres, Houston, Texas, June 7, 1962.
12. 350 U. S. 892, reversing 223 F. 2d 739 (5th Cir., 1955).
13. 229 F. 2d 648 (5th Cir.) cert. denied, 352 U. S. 848 (1956).
14. See also Richardson v. Texas and New Orleans R.R. Co., 242 F. 2d 230 (1957).
15. 242 F. 2d 230.
16. See also Clark v. Norfolk and Western Ry. Co., U. S. Dist. Ct., Western Dist., Virginia, May 5, 1958, Civil No. 689; III RRLR 988 (1958).
17. At this writing, April 1964, the Supreme Court has not ruled on the legality of that aspect of the Central of Georgia decision holding employers jointly liable for the duty of fair representation, though the Court refused to review other aspects of the case (77 S. Ct. 57). The company apparently decided not to appeal that part of the decision. The Central of Georgia Railroad hired some Negro firemen in 1959 for the first time in many years, but it is not known what influence the Court's decision had on this move.
18. Dillard v. Chesapeake and O. Ry., 199 F. 2d 951 (1956).
19. Dillard v. Chesapeake and O. Ry., 199 F. 2d 951; 136 F. Supp. 689; I *Race Relations Law Reporter* 389 (1956).

20. Conley v. Gibson, 355 U. S. 41, 33 L.C. 71,077 (1957).
21. Richardson v. Texas and New Orleans Ry. Co., 242 F. 2d 230 (1957); Steele v. L. & N.R.R., 323 U. S. 192 (1944).
22. Syres v. Oil Workers, 35 U. S. 892, reversing 223 F. 2d 739; I *Race Relations Law Reporter* 20 (1956); Clark v. Norfolk and Western Ry. Co., III *Race Relations Law Reporter* 988 (1959); Jones v. Central of Georgia, F. 2d 648, I *Race Relations Law Reporter* 558 (1956).
23. Salvant v. L. & N.R.R., 83 F. Supp. 391 (1950); Rolax v. Atlantic Coast Line R.R., 186 F. 2d 478 (1950); BLF v. Palmer, 178 F. 2d 723 (1950).
24. Blue v. Shaefer, 33 LRRM 2852 (1957).
25. Cox, *op. cit.*, p. 159.
26. Conley v. Gibson, 355 U. S. 41 (1957).
27. Cox, *op. cit.*, pp. 151, 156.
28. Michael I. Sovern, "The National Labor Relations Act and Racial Discrimination," *Columbia Law Review*, April 1962, p. 582.
29. 15 LRRM 714 (1944).
30. *Ibid.*
31. 338 U. S. 240.
32. See Richardson v. Texas and New Orleans R.R., I RRLR 561, reversed by 242 F. 2d 230 (1957); Conley v. Gibson, 78 S. Ct. 99 (1957); Syres v. Oil Workers, 223 F. 2d 739, reversed by 350 U. S. 892 (1956).
33. BLF v. Palmer, 178 F. 2d 723 (1950).
34. Rolax v. Atlantic Coast Line R.R., 186 F. 2d 592 (1950).
35. 186 F. 2d 473 (1950).
36. Whitfield v. United Steel Workers of America, Local No. 2308, IV *RRLR* 122 (1959).
37. Howard v. St. Louis-S. F. Ry., 191 F. 2d 442 (1953); *Wisconsin Law Review*, May 1953, p. 529.
38. 343 U. S. 774 (1953).
39. "Judicial Regulations of the Railway Brotherhood's Discriminatory Practices," *Wisconsin Law Review*, May 1953, p. 516.
40. Cox, *op. cit.*, p. 158.
41. 65 S. Ct. 226.
42. House of Representatives 510, 80th Congress, 1st Session, pp. 41, 60.
43. Sec. 8(b)(1).
44. Bethlehem-Alameda Shipyard, Inc., 53 NLRB 999 (1943).
45. 62 NLRB 427.
46. NLRB, *Tenth Annual Report*, 1945, p. 18.
47. 262 F. 2d (1958).
48. Oliphant v. BLF, Brief for the Appellants in the U. S. Ct. of Appeals for the Sixth Circuit, No. 12,387.
49. Oliphant v. BLF; 156 F. Supp. 89; II *RRLR* 1128 (1959).
50. 79 S. Ct. 648.
51. Ross v. Ebert, 32 *Labor Cases* 70, 627, 82 NW 2d 315 (1957).
52. Clyde M. Summers, "The Right to Join a Union," *Columbia Law Review*, January 1947, p. 42.
53. Committee for Economic Development, *The Public Interest in National Labor Policy*, New York: The Committee for Economic Development, 1961, p. 150.
54. U. S. Commission on Civil Rights, *Employment*, Washington, D. C.: U. S. Govt. Printing Office, Book 3, p. 146.
55. James v. Mariship, 25 Calif. 2d 721; Wallace Corp. v. NLRB, 323 U. S. 248.

56. 81st Congress, 2d Session, *Congressional Record,* pp. 16536, 16537, and 16541.
57. *Ibid.*
58. "Remarks of Senator Taft," 93 *Congressional Record* 4193 (1947).
59. "Remarks of Congressman Powell," 105 *Congressional Record* 15721 (1959).
60. "Remarks of Congressman Landrum," 105 *Congressional Record* 15724 (1959).
61. Benjamin Aaron, "The Labor-Management Reporting and Disclosure Act of 1959," *Harvard Law Review,* 851 (1960).
62. See Benjamin Aaron, "Some Aspects of the Union's Duty of Fair Representation," *Ohio State Law Journal,* Winter 1961, p. 39.
63. See Richard A. Givens, "The Enfranchisement of Employees Arbitrarily Rejected for Union Membership," *Labor Law Journal,* November 1960, p. 809.
64. "Some Aspects of the Union's Duty of Fair Representation," p. 45.
65. See *New York Times,* April 23, 1950, and April 26, 1959.
66. See V *Race Relations Law Reporter* 926 (1960).
67. Charles O. Gregory, *Labor and the Law,* second revised edition, New York: Norton, 1958, p. 99.
68. 338 U. S. 240.
69. *Ibid.,* 237.
70. For a contrary view, see Cox, *op. cit.,* p. 175.
71. Hunter v. Atchison, Topeka & Santa Fe Ry., U. S. Dist. Ct., Northern District, Illinois, August 8, 1959; III *RRLR* 996.
72. See Rolax v. Atlantic Coast Line, 186 F. 2d 473 (1950).
73. III *RRLR* 998 (1958).
74. Syres v. Oil Workers, 257 F. 2d 479 (1958).
75. 350 U. S. 892.
76. See Cox, *op. cit.,* p. 172.
77. 104 NLRB No. 33; 32 LRRM 1010 (1953).
78. Larus and Bros., 62 NLRB 1085 (1945).
79. Case No. 39-RC-854 (1955).
80. Case No. 39-RC-572, Oct. 12 (1955).
81. See Sovern, *op. cit.,* pp. 596–597.
82. Larus & Bros., 62 NLRB 1082 (1944).
83. Case No. K-311 (1956); 37 LRRM 1457.
84. Syres v. Oil Workers, 76 S. Ct. 152 (1956).
85. NLRB General Council Administrative Ruling, Case No. 1057, 35 LRRM 1130 (1954).
86. 78 S. Ct. 99; II *RRLR* 1093 (1957).
87. Jones v. American President Lines, 40 LRRM 2035 (1959).
88. See also Central of Georgia v. Jones, 229 F. 2d 648, 650 where Circuit Judge Brown declared "the Brotherhood had, to be sure, the profound obligation fully and earnestly to bargain to prevent and, where necessary, remove discriminations." (Cox doubts the soundness of this reasoning; see *op. cit.,* p. 176.)
89. Mountain Pacific Chapter of the Associated General Contractors, Inc., 119 NLRB No. 126A (1958).
90. U. S. House of Representatives, 86th Congress, 1st Session, *Conference Report on the Labor-Management Reporting and Disclosure Act of 1959,* Report No. 1147, p. 41.

91. Teamsters Local 357 v. NLRB 42 LC 16,888; see also Richard Harvey Siegel, "The Demise of the Mountain Pacific Doctrine: Teamsters Local No. 357 v. NLRB," *Labor Law Journal,* June 1961.
92. NLRB Hearings, Intermediate Report, "Peninsula Tile and Terrazzo Co." (12-CA-486).
93. Independent Metal Workers Union and Hughes Tool Co., Case No. 23-CB-429; United Steelworkers and Independent Metal Workers, Case No. 23-RC-1758, Feb. 26, 1963, p. 12; 147 NLRB No. 166 (1964).
94. Pioneer Bus Co. and Transport Workers, 140 NLRB 54 (1963).
95. Humphrey v. Moore, 375 U. S. 335 (1964).
96. IV *RRLR* 122 (1959).

CHAPTER 11

State Fair-Employment
Practice Laws

Introduction

SINCE THE SECOND WORLD WAR ENFORCEABLE FAIR-EMPLOYMENT
practice (FEP) laws have been passed in twenty-four states and
many municipalities.[1]   By 1964 these laws covered virtually the entire
nonwhite population outside the South and prohibited discrimination
by employers and employment agencies as well as unions.[2]   The laws
are usually administered by commissioners, who are part-time officials
in every state except New York.   The powers relating to the adjustment of complaints are fairly uniform and include: (1) the power to
receive, investigate and pass upon complaints alleging discrimination
in employment; (2) where investigation reveals probable cause for
crediting the allegations, the duty to eliminate these practices by
conference, conciliation, and persuasion; (3) the power to conduct
public hearings, subpoena witnesses, compel their attendance, ad-
minister oaths, take testimony of any person under oath, and to require the production of any books or papers relating to matters be-

fore the commissions; (4) the power to seek court orders enforcing subpoenas and cease and desist orders; (5) the power to undertake studies of discrimination and publish the results.

The commissions' budgets and staffs are much less uniform than the provisions of the laws under which they operate. Observers generally agree that New York is the best financed of the state agencies. Considered relative to population, the only other fair-employment commission approaching the budget and staff of New York is the Philadelphia Commission on Human Relations.

Aside from some details, there is likewise much uniformity of procedure among the commissions. Except in Ohio, Rhode Island, and Philadelphia, complaints of discrimination must be restricted to discrimination against the persons filing the complaints. Since New York's law has been the model for other agencies, the complaint procedures in that state are typical of others. In New York, after the complaint has been duly registered with the Commission, it is investigated by a field representative, who submits a written report to an investigating commissioner assigned to the case. If the commissioner determines that probable cause exists to warrant an allegation, he is required to "immediately endeavor to eliminate the unlawful discriminatory practice complained of by conference, conciliation and persuasion." [3] The commissioner utilizes this conciliation conference to work out an agreement eliminating patterns of discrimination even when the specific charge cannot be proved. If the case is settled at this stage, a stipulation is signed by the parties. There will probably be periodic reviews by field representatives, however, to see if discriminatory practices have been corrected. The great majority of cases are settled by conciliation; if not, they are ordered to public hearing before the other commissioners where the entire case is reviewed. If cases are not settled during the public hearing, the Commission can issue cease and desist orders enforceable in state courts. That the New York Commission has used the public hearing only sparingly is indicated by the fact that it ordered only twenty-nine cases to public hearing of over 3000 cases in which "probable cause" was found between 1945 and 1960. However, other cases were settled only after a threat of public hearing. Most respondents seemed very reluctant to sustain the unfavorable publicity involved in public hearings. In New York the Commission does not have the power to initiate complaints, but does conduct "informal investigations" and studies of employment patterns where there are suggestions of discrimination. It is also possible, moreover, for the New York attorney general to file complaints with the Commission.

Experience with Unions

Before examining the various commissions' efforts to eliminate racial discrimination by unions, we should note that labor organizations have played a prominent role in the legislative effort which resulted in the passage of fair-employment laws. In almost every state, unions were prominent in the passage of these laws, and in states like California, Michigan, Pennsylvania, and New York the unions were probably the decisive forces causing the laws to be passed. And union leaders have actively served on the commissions in several states (Michigan, Pennsylvania, and Washington, for example). Furthermore, in keeping with its equalitarian civil-rights policies, the AFL-CIO strongly favored the passage of the 1964 Civil Rights Act, which President George Meany publicly stated was needed to help organized labor eliminate racial discrimination in its own ranks.[4]

In view of this record of support by organized labor, it may seem paradoxical that some of the most intransigent respondents before the state commissions have been unions. This paradox is more apparent than real, however, because the cases of hostile discrimination have been restricted to a relatively small proportion of the total labor movement. The unions that have actively supported fair-employment legislation are primarily politically oriented organizations, with a large stake in winning Negro support for their political objectives. And the union leaders who are encouraging and participating in the commissions' activities are mainly industrial union or federation leaders whose organizations rarely exclude Negroes from membership.

Unions have provided the commissions with some of their most difficult cases, but there have been relatively few cases against unions —generally less than 10 per cent of all compliance activity. Table 11-1 gives the complaints filed with the New York Commission between 1945 and 1962; it will be noted that complaints against unions constituted just over 8 per cent of the total, and from a quantitative standpoint the New York experience is typical.[5]

There are a number of reasons for the relative paucity of cases against unions. The fewness of discriminating unions in the North where the laws exist is surely an important factor. Moreover, those who have the strongest cases frequently will not file complaints for reasons of apathy, fear of retaliation, or desire to avoid embarrassment. In addition, most agencies, in processing complaints against discrim-

Table 11-1

Complaints Filed by Alleged Discriminatory Act, New York, 1945–1962

Act	1962		1945–1962	
	Number	Per Cent	Number	Per Cent
Total	1,171	100.0	9,733	100.0
Employment				
Refusal to employ	235	20.0	3,365	34.6
Dismissal from employment	154	13.2	1,732	17.8
Forced retirement	. . .	0.0	9	0.1
Conditions of employment	113	9.6	1,054	10.8
Employment agency referral	48	4.1	493	5.1
Union membership withheld	5	0.4	138	1.4
Conditions of union membership	39	3.3	504	5.2
Other union discrimination	2	0.2	101	1.0
Unlawful inquiry or specification	4	0.3	207	2.1
Abetting discrimination	11	0.9	122	1.3
Total	611	52.2	7,725	79.4
Public Accommodations				
Total	141	12.0	899	9.2
Other				
Education	2	0.2	27	0.3
Obstructing political nomination	. . .	. . .	8	0.1
Total	2	0.2	35	0.4

Source: New York State Commission for Human Rights, *Annual Report,* 1962, p. 13.

inating unions, have displayed a marked reluctance to undertake vigorous and sustained compliance efforts in such cases because the structure of the unions is such as to make it difficult for union leaders to compel compliance by their members. Thus, achieving compliance is inherently more difficult with discriminatory unions than with employers, where only management's acquiescence is necessary to effect compliance. Because they deal directly with the public, employers are also probably more vulnerable than unions to adverse publicity.

The railroad unions

In view of the long history of discrimination by railroad unions, it is not surprising that the case which tested the constitutionality of the first FEP law involved a railroad union. The union, the Railway Mail Association (RMA), successfully defended its right to bar Negroes from membership (on the grounds that it was a voluntary association) when that organization was prosecuted under a 1940 New York state law prohibiting racial discrimination by collective-bargaining organizations.[6] The RMA attempted to use the same defense for its discriminatory practices before the New York Commission Against Discrimination (SCAD, established in 1945), but this time the U. S. Supreme Court could see "no constitutional basis for the contention that a state cannot protect workers from exclusion solely on the basis of race, color or creed by an organization, functioning under the protection of the state which holds itself out to represent the general business needs of employees."[7]

SCAD also took action against several railroad unions with racial bars in their constitutions and caused them to either eliminate their formal racial restrictions or make them inoperative in New York. After being investigated by SCAD, the following unions removed their color bars on the dates indicated: Maintenance of Way Employees, 1946; Railway Yardmasters of North America, 1946; Railway and Steamship Clerks, 1947; Switchmen's Union of North America, 1947; Airline Dispatchers Association, 1946; Blacksmiths and Boilermakers, 1947; and the International Association of Machinists, 1948. SCAD investigated the Airline Pilots Association and the Wire Weavers Protective Association, but both of these organizations had dropped their restrictive provisions before the New York law was passed. The following organizations made their discriminatory clauses inoperative in New York: the Brotherhood of Locomotive Firemen and Enginemen; National Rural Letter Carriers Association; Brotherhood of Locomotive Engineers; Order of Railroad Telegraphers; Brotherhood of Railway Carmen; Order of Railway Conductors; Railway Mail Association; National Association of Letter Carriers.

The most obstinate of these organizations was the BLE, whose Grand Chief Engineer wrote SCAD on February 11, 1946:

This organization stands on its constitutional rights to determine by its rules and laws enacted by delegates to a constituted convention who have authority under the laws governing its membership and to determine for itself whom it shall accept for membership.

On October 10, 1947, a month before he used his authority to waive the race bar in New York, the Grand Chief told SCAD:

We are of the opinion that your Commission does not understand that whether a person is admitted depends upon the will of the members in the respective subdivisions to which such a person makes application. And, it may interest you to know that included among members of the B. of L.E. are full blooded Indians, Mexicans, half-breeds, etc.

Furthermore, the section of our laws to which your Commission objects has been in our Statutes for many, many years and we do not have any official record of any person having been denied membership because of race, religion, creed or color.

SCAD reported on January 13, 1948, that "progress has been made in wiping out discriminatory practices in more than 30 unions with a total membership of 750,000" and that only the BLE had refused to cooperate with the Commission.

Despite these formal changes, however, Negroes apparently continued to be barred from the railroads in New York and New Jersey. A joint study by SCAD and the New Jersey Division Against Discrimination (DAD) in 1957 found that there were very few employment opportunities for Negroes in those states; according to the study, "By the irony of history, Negroes in the South had greater opportunities for employment in operating departments of the railroads than those in the North."[8] The DAD also had a number of complaints that railroad locals excluded Negroes.

Auxiliary and segregated locals

In addition to racial exclusion, a number of cases have been filed with the commissions against unions for maintaining segregated and auxiliary locals. As noted in Chapter 5, the Brotherhood of Railway and Steamship Clerks (BRSC) abolished its auxiliaries in 1947 after being investigated by SCAD. The BRSC, however, was charged with maintaining segregated locals after the auxiliaries were abolished. But even though they violated the New York law, segregated BRSC lodges continued for a number of reasons: (1) white members of local lodges could bar Negroes with three blackballs; (2) Negro and white locals recruited their own memberships; (3) in one case the financial secretary of the Negro lodge handled all applications and referred Negroes and whites to the respective Negro and white locals. (But after SCAD suggested that the Negro and white lodges merge, the BRSC locals stamped all applications with "New York Lodges 783, 975, and 6118 have concurrent jurisdiction. You may apply to either."); (4) since BRSC lodges were organized on occupational bases, some were segregated because of segregated hiring patterns.

In spite of lengthy negotiations with the BRSC, SCAD could not effect the merger of these segregated lodges or get the whites to accept a Negro member. A complaint was filed in January 1957, and by April the Commission decided that there was sufficient evidence to support the claim and gave the union until the "first of next year to effect the consummation of an effective plan to change the segregated pattern." But in September 1958 SCAD held a compliance review and found the locals still segregated; and the white local had no plan to change its practices. SCAD did not bring action to compel a merger but told the union that it could not enforce the union shop against Negroes who were denied membership in the white local if they applied. As a result, a 1961 review by the Commission revealed that thirty Negroes had been accepted by the white lodge.[9]

The International Longshoremen's Association had one segregated local in New York until June 1959 when it merged with Tony Anastasia's Local 1814.[10] Members of a predominantly Negro ILA local in New Jersey were permitted to work at the Bayway terminal after a complaint against a predominantly white ILA local was filed with the DAD. Investigation revealed, however, that the Negro local had complete control of jobs with another company.

As noted in Chapter 5, the American Federation of Musicians has had segregated locals for many years, and Negroes have frequently resisted desegregation. When, for instance, the Connecticut Commission investigated a complaint against a white AFM local, it found that the local could not admit Negroes without the Negro local's consent. The Commission succeeded in getting the Negro into the white local but was unsuccessful in effecting a merger. In Massachusetts a Negro musician thought his chances of getting a job with the Boston Symphony would be improved if he could get into the AFM local in Boston, but the president of the white local said he could accept the Negro's application only if he got a waiver of jurisdiction from the Negro local. The executive board of the Negro local objected to the white local taking in colored members, though both locals already had some Negro and white members. The Commission decided in this case that the unions could remain segregated but that members of either race could join either union. The Ohio Commission ordered six AFM locals in that state to integrate by January 1, 1961, though only the Columbus locals were willing to carry out its order. Other segregated locals were located in Youngstown, Dayton, Toledo, Columbus, Cleveland, and Cincinnati. The white locals of Dayton, Youngstown, and Cleveland had four, one, and two Negro members respectively in 1961. With so much discrimination by other unions, the Negro musicians argued, it seemed unreasonable for the Commission to bring action against the AFM. The locals at Youngstown said they would jointly reject merger because their counsel said their practices were not unlawful. A Columbus merger agreement was accepted, and at Cleveland both the Negro and white locals refused to discuss integration but asked the Commission for an extension to attempt a solution. The white locals at Cincinnati and Toledo proposed merger plans which were rejected by the Negroes, and both locals refused to merge "under existing conditions" at Dayton.

The California FEP Commission effected the merger of the Negro and white locals in San Francisco on April 1, 1960. Opposition by the colored leaders was overcome by an agreement to give two Negroes jobs in the merged local and to place a third Negro on the local's executive board.

Building trades

The FEP experience confirms the existence of intransigent discrimination by some building-trades unions. The first cases to reach public hearing in Connecticut involved the refusal of IBEW Local 35 in Hartford to admit two qualified Negro electricians to membership. As noted in Chapter 5, the Connecticut Civil Rights Commission ordered Local 35 to admit the Negroes, and upon appeal by the union the Commission's order was upheld by the Connecticut Superior Court and the Supreme Court of Errors.[11] Local 35's membership voted to reject the Negroes, but finally accepted them after being fined $2000 and $500 for each week that it remained in contempt.[12] The Cleveland Community Relations Board was not as successful with IBEW Local 38, but the local finally accepted Negroes in 1957 under a threat of expulsion by the AFL-CIO.

The publicity given the vigorous defense of discriminatory practices by IBEW locals in places like Hartford and Cleveland [13] caused civil-rights organizations to carefully scrutinize complaints against locals of that union because of a general assumption that all IBEW locals discriminate. However, SCAD's experiences with the New York IBEW locals show that this assumption is not always valid. SCAD representatives admitted that they investigated IBEW Local 3 with unusual care because of the publicity given the Local 38 (Cleveland) case, but were unable to find probable cause to credit a specific complaint. At the suggestion of a NAACP representative, the Commission kept the case against Local 3 open by finding "other evidence of discrimination" because the union's application blank asked for "place of birth." But the union removed this question in September 1956.

Investigation of Local 3's racial practices disclosed a number of Negro members. Of 30,000 members in 1956 in all classifications, the local claimed some 2000 Negro members and many others among the 1800 working in the city on temporary permits. Investigation in 1961, however, revealed that the local had only about thirty Negro members in the construction and marine division, and that of these only eight were in construction and the other twenty-two were in "repair and maintenance"; the latter classification carried a lower hourly rate than construction electricians. None of the Negro journeymen had served apprenticeships and some of them had been brought into the union because of pressure from the Negro community during organizing drives. Although few Negroes had been admitted to Local 3's apprenticeship program before that time, under the terms of its February 1962 contract with the New York electrical contractors, the union agreed to take in 1000 more apprentices in return for the twenty-five-hour week and other contract benefits. The union's president made a special effort to recruit qualified Negro apprentices through the Urban League, the NAACP, and other agencies, asking them to send qualified Negro applicants.[14] Perhaps the Local 3's relatively unusual (for an IBEW local) conduct can be partly explained by its desire to organize Negro members in the industrial division or perhaps it is because the president of Local 3 is also president of the New York Central Labor Union and realizes that his position in the labor movement would be damaged by a discriminatory record.

The Michigan FEP Commission had three complaints against IBEW Local 58 in 1957 alleging discrimination in admissions to the construction division and to the apprenticeship program. Investigation revealed that the 4000 member local had had one Negro in the construction division, and, as at Hartford, the union's attorney argued that the case might be beyond the purview of the FEP Commission because the local's system discriminated against Negroes and whites alike. Characteristically, union politics was an important factor in the Detroit case because the local business agent was afraid that he would be voted out if he agreed to admit Negroes, even under pressure from the FEPC; the Commission therefore granted his request for a ninety-day delay until after the local's forthcoming elections.

After this period, and after further negotiations with the Commission, the complainant and seven other Negroes were admitted to the union.

The apprenticeship question proved less amenable to solution.[15] The local business agent was afraid that the Commission's actions would cause the local to lose control over admission to the trade and on one occasion even suggested that it might be better to abolish the apprenticeship system than to submit to the Commission's orders to admit two Negro applicants to the program. The question was complicated because the Detroit local had about 500 applications each year for between sixty and seventy-five positions; about two years were required for the successful applicant to enter the program after filing his application. After the Michigan Commission assured the local that it would not force it to give special treatment to Negroes but merely insisted that all applicants be treated alike, the union agreed to interview two Negroes for apprenticeship positions and waive the usual sponsorship requirements. One of the Negro applicants refused to cooperate with either the local union or the Commission; the other was interviewed, but by the end of 1961 had not been admitted to the apprenticeship program.

Thus, the cases were similar in some respects, but the Detroit IBEW local proved much less recalcitrant than its Cleveland counterpart. Undoubtedly, the adverse publicity given the Cleveland case and the pressures brought to bear on that local from a variety of sources convinced the Detroit electricians that cooperation with the Commission was the wiser course.

The Wisconsin FEPC's experience with the Milwaukee Bricklayers local demonstrates the value of giving the commissions power to enforce their decisions in courts, but is not necessarily typical of the racial practices of that international union.[16] Two Negroes filed complaints with the Wisconsin Industrial Commission alleging that Milwaukee Bricklayers Local 8 had refused to admit them to membership because of their race. Shortly before the Local 8 case, the Commission had successfully prosecuted a Plasterers and Cement Masons local in a Wisconsin circuit court for discriminating against a Negro applicant.[17] In February 1955, therefore, when the industrial commission ordered the Milwaukee Bricklayers to admit two Negro applicants, it assumed that it had the power to enforce its decisions. But the Wisconsin Supreme Court upheld the right of the Milwaukee Bricklayers local to exclude Negroes.[18] The union did not deny discrimination in this case, but argued that neither the Wisconsin FEP law nor the state's constitution required it to admit Negroes to membership. The Court ruled that the Commission did not have authority to enforce its decisions because "Investigation, publicity, and a commission recommendation are what the statute provides in consequence of racial discrimination practiced by an employer or a union. We grant that it is cold comfort to applicants but it is all the Legislature saw fit to provide." Like the U. S. Supreme Court, the Wisconsin Supreme Court ruled that in the absence of enforceable statutes, the Negroes had no constitutional right to membership in the union because labor organizations were voluntary associations.

Partly as a result of this case, the Wisconsin legislature strengthened the FEP law by giving the Industrial Commission power to enforce its decisions in court, but provided a rather ambiguous paragraph to the effect that if an order of the Commission proved "unenforceable against a labor organization in which membership is a privilege, the employer with whom such a labor organization has an all-union shop agreement shall not be held accountable under this chapter, when such employer is not responsible for the discrimination." [19]

Within three months after the FEP act was strengthened, the Milwaukee Bricklayers admitted the two Negroes to membership. The local alleged that the Negroes could not be accepted because they did not have the vouchers required for membership, but it relented when faced with the threat of prosecution under the stronger Wisconsin FEP law, the urging of the international union, and adverse publicity.

Negroes have filed a number of complaints against building-trades unions alleging discrimination in job assignments. Sometimes the charges were difficult to substantiate because of general discrimination by the union leaders involved, sometimes in favor of a particular clique within the locals. There were also strong suggestions that some building-trades unions discriminated against Negroes by giving them temporary work permits, which were more profitable to locals than membership dues, or the fees for which were pocketed by the business agents.

Investigation of several complaints against the Hod Carriers and Common Laborers (HCL) revealed that although many Negroes were working under the unions' jurisdictions, there sometimes were discriminatory job assignments and unequal representation in union leadership positions. For instance, investigation of twenty-two complaints by eighteen men against the Detroit HCL local disclosed that the union had between 3500 and 4000 members, about three-fourths of whom were Negroes, though the main officers were white and only three of the twelve business agents were Negroes. This complaint alleged that business agents discriminated against Negroes by requiring them to use the formal referral system, whereas whites were hired directly on the job through informal means. There were also charges of favoritism and "kickbacks" to both the white and Negro business agents. The Commission found that discrimination probably existed in this case, not all of which was racial. In a 1958 consent agreement, the local's president and business manager denied discrimination but agreed to replace the old referral system with an open registration list and make other changes which would eliminate discrimination.[20] This agreement did not end charges of discrimination, however,[21] and with the aid of a Negro labor organization the Negroes within the local elected a Negro president in February 1960. The new president campaigned on the basis of no discrimination of any kind.[22]

Some of the charges against building-trades unions have alleged that labor organizations discriminated by imposing different standards of admission for Negroes than whites. When the tests apply to Negroes and whites alike, the commissions have usually dismissed the complaints, as was the case when the Massachusetts Commission concluded that a Bricklayers local was justified in excluding a Negro who failed a test uniformly given as a condition of membership. In Pennsylvania, on the other hand, a complainant learned that only Negroes were given tests for admission to a Painters local. When the complainant, who was very light complexioned, asked a white Painters official about the test required for membership, he was assured that he would have no difficulty, but that any Negro who took the test would have trouble. The complainant was admitted after these facts were discovered and after investigation by the Commission revealed that the Painters previously had attempted to establish a segregated local for Negroes. This union subsequently started actively seeking Negro members through such organizations as the Urban League, and in the summer of 1959 there were over twenty Negroes in the district council.

In March 1964 the New York State Commission on Human Rights (CHR) handed down an unprecedented decision against Local 28 of the Sheet Metal Workers (SMW). The CHR found Local 28 guilty of having barred Negroes from membership and ordered the local to open its rolls to the complainant. The local was also ordered to invalidate its waiting list containing 900 names and to adopt a new procedure for selecting apprentices based on objective written standards approved by the State Industrial Commission. The CHR required the local to end its father-son relationship and to cease requiring that applicants be sponsored by members of the local. The Commission's decision was also unprecedented because it took into consideration the historic pattern of discrimination by the local and its parent international organization. The local was accused of automatically excluding Negroes for the seventy-six years of its existence and the international of having had a constitutional race bar until 1946. It appears, however, that the international did not exclude Negroes entirely but restricted them to auxiliary locals.

In August 1964 Justice Jacob Markowitz of the New York Supreme Court upheld the CHR's ruling in the SMW Local 28 case and, in what could be a very important precedent, handed down a decision requiring the local to end its nepotism and accept an apprenticeship system with objective admissions standards approved by the court. The decision by Judge Markowitz embodied an agreement by Local 28 that, "in order to be fair to minority groups," application fees would be set at $10. The agreement also provided that only two years of high school would be required between 1965 and 1966. For 1967–1968 it was stipulated that three years of high school would be required, but that thereafter applicants must be high-school graduates.

On September 1, 1964, a law became effective in New York which sought to end nepotism in all joint employer-union apprenticeship programs registered with the state. This law sets objective standards for admission to apprenticeship programs and provides for review of these programs by the State Labor Department. At their August 1964 convention in New York City, members of the New York State Building and Construction Trades Council criticized the new law and Judge Markowitz's decision in the SMW Local 28 case. Some delegates to the convention resented the charge that only relatives could get into the building trades, but others defended nepotism as fair on the grounds that union members had paid for and built up the apprentice programs. The New York unions had originally caused the apprenticeship law to be defeated in the legislature, but were forced to reverse their position after a storm of protest from civil-rights leaders and officials of unions like the International Ladies' Garment Workers Union.

Longshoremen

There have also been a number of charges of discrimination against the International Longshoremen's Association in Philadelphia, New York, and New Jersey, and against a local of the International Longshoremen and Warehousemen's Union in Portland, Oregon. These charges against the Longshoremen have come from a number of sources. When the New York State Crime Commission investigated the waterfront between December 1952 and January 1953, it concluded that "'the shape-up' method of employment of longshoremen was not only degrading and vicious to human beings but fostered corruption."[23] As a result of public hearings, the New York-New Jersey Waterfront Commission Compact of June 25, 1953, sought to eliminate the general shape-up by establishing employment centers throughout the Port of New York.

NAACP Labor Secretary Herbert Hill charged in 1959 that despite these changes, "the 'shape-up' remains the basic vehicle through which longshoremen secure employment on the docks of the New York Waterfront."[24] Moreover, Hill argued, the continuation of the "shape-up" was "a result of collusion between the ILA and the management of steamship lines and stevedore companies." Finally, Hill charged, "fears of reprisals and threats of intimidation" prevented Negro longshoremen from personally testifying to the discrimination which they faced. "Unfortunately," he added, "the traditions of violence on the waterfront gives credibility to their fears."

The Urban League of Greater New York (ULGNY) was also convinced that the "shape-up" with "all its evils still exists," "that favoritism is still practiced widely by hiring agents," and that the ILA and the employers were in collusion to discriminate against Negroes.[25] Specifically, the League charged that the only Negroes with relatively permanent employment on the waterfront were in gangs performing the most "arduous and least desirable work." Moreover, the League claimed, Negroes who were "experienced, skilled and licensed by the Waterfront Commission, made the shape daily, but were refused employment. . . . Hundreds of casual longshoremen were hired, but Negro longshoremen were repeatedly ignored during the shape-up." The ULGNY was critical of SCAD for not using its subpoena powers to get evidence of discrimination against Negro longshoremen, and recommended "setting up a priority system based on the length of service and work records," which, it argued, would eliminate "the existing arbitrary and discriminating system of selecting employees."

In its investigations of these and other charges, SCAD found probable cause in only one instance. In that case, a checkers' local vigorously denied that SCAD had proved racial discrimination, but agreed to admit three Negroes after a threat of public hearing.[26] However, the union failed to comply fully with the agreement settling this case, and it became necessary for the New York Commission to seek a court order requiring compliance. Faced with prosecution for contempt of court, the checkers' local took in a group of applicants which included four Negroes. The local also amended its constitution, deleting the so-called "closed books" clause which prohibited the admission of any new member; eliminating the clause restricting membership to applicants under forty years of age; and amending its procedures for processing applicants to require consideration on a nondiscriminatory basis, though over one-third of the membership could still block an applicant.[27]

A 1957 complaint by ten men charged the ILA and the companies with collusion to pass over Negroes in employment. The complainants specifically alleged discrimination on the luxury piers along the west side of Manhattan. However, SCAD's efforts to follow up on these complaints proved frustrating. Attempts to contact the ten men were fruitless as letters from field representatives went unanswered. The Commission finally arranged a conference with four of the complainants; of the others, one had died after a foot injury, one was no longer working as a longshoreman, and one had been admitted to a gang. The four men who met with the Commission could give no specific examples of discrimination. Indeed, one of them had been a longshoreman since 1911, and said that he could work anywhere on the waterfront. The replies from the other three suggested that they were more interested in enlisting SCAD's aid in getting jobs than in having it investigate charges of racial discrimination.

Many factors undoubtedly account for the absence of verifiable complaints against the ILA in spite of the numerous general charges of discrimination made against the organization. The fear of reprisals has apparently deterred many Negroes from filing complaints, but perhaps the complicated hiring arrangements on the waterfront have made it difficult to prove discrimination and have been misunderstood by Negroes who assumed that they were being discriminated against because of the smaller proportion of Negro longshoremen who have permanent employment. These hiring patterns are due partly to the fact that Negroes have not been on the waterfront as long as whites. In fact, there is a rough correlation between the control of good piers and the ethnic stratification of the work force. Before 1880, 95 per cent of New York longshoremen were Irish and the other 5 per cent were Germans and Scandinavians.[28] Italians and some Negroes were used as strikebreakers in 1887, and Italians continued to gain relative to other ethnic groups until they represented about one-third of the total in 1912 and predominated after the First World War, by which time many of the Irish had moved to better jobs elsewhere. These developments caused some of the ILA's locals to be made up entirely of particular ethnic or language groups. The best piers were monopolized by the strongest group or the one that came on the docks first; these choice positions were apparently maintained against all comers, white or black, and sometimes by physical force. The shape-up facilitated the control of jobs by each group; control was also perpetuated by amicism and nepotism. This system was not opposed by employers, who gained a surplus labor supply thereby, and foremen, gang leaders, and union delegates favored the shape-up because it gave them control over scarce jobs. Once these forces became institutionalized they were extremely difficult to change.

Nor was this system changed very much by the establishment of the employment centers, because preference was still given to men who had been attached to particular piers and gangs, and there remained many more applicants than jobs. SCAD and other civil-rights organizations became concerned that Negroes would be permanently frozen out of longshoring jobs by the 1958 General Cargo Agreement, which attempted to stabilize and regularize waterfront employment. The question of seniority and equalizing the earnings of the so-called "extra gangs" was submitted to Professor Vernon Jensen of Cornell University for arbitration after the parties failed to reach an agreement. The Jensen award followed the past practices of the port for the most part, establishing a system of priorities which gave preference to men who had been attached to particular piers.[29]

Since Negroes were concentrated disproportionately in the casual group forced to report to the hiring halls daily for work,[30] the Jensen award caused some frustration for civil-rights agencies interested in getting jobs for Negroes. SCAD therefore held a conference with the president of ILA and the chairman of the New York Shipping Association to discuss the discriminatory pattern of employment on the waterfront and the "very strong suggestions which the Commission had received from various quarters that an effect of the Jensen Arbitration Award would be to continue and perpetuate the asserted existing pattern of discrimination."[31] Although SCAD warned the union and the employer that nothing in the Jensen award would limit the Commission's usual procedures to eliminate discrimination and issue its usual findings and orders, it was obvious that the racial employment pattern on the New York waterfront could not be changed by SCAD's techniques in the absence of some rapid and unforeseen turnover of employment.

Breweries

Several FEP commissions and civil-rights organizations have long sought to change the racial employment pattern in the brewery industry. This industry has come to the attention of groups attempting to increase employment opportunities for Negroes because Negroes hold very few of the permanent jobs in the industry. A 1951 study by the National Urban League found fewer than 500 Negro brewery workers in the United States, and that "Among those employed, the number covered by labor union contracts was negligible—fewer than twenty-five production workers in Northern and Western brewing centers, and less than 100 in several auxiliary unions in Texas and Louisiana." [32]   More surprising still, a 1949 SCAD study found only one Negro production worker in New York breweries. [33]   The employment pattern in the brewery industry can be explained by other factors, but there is ample evidence of discrimination by affiliates of the two unions with jurisdiction in this industry—the International Brotherhood of Teamsters and the International Union of United Brewery, Flour, Cereal, Soft Drink, and Distillery Workers. In spite of the nondiscrimination clause in the Brewery Workers' constitution, Kerns concluded "that there is not only discrimination, but a rather hostile attitude toward any efforts designed to integrate Negroes in the unions." [34]   It is not clear, however, whether the union officials' hostility resulted from racial prejudices or to the fear that civil-rights agencies would interfere with long-established seniority rights of union members.

Technological change and declining employment have also influenced the unions' attitudes toward the admission of Negroes to the brewery industry. Of the 1100 breweries in the United States, only 177 survived prohibition, and technological change subsequently reduced the demand for manpower in the industry at a time when declining per capita consumption reduced the demand for beer. These secular and technological problems were compounded by the seasonal nature of the industry, which has a busy season between April and October. Thus, the absence of Negroes from breweries can be explained partly by the fact that the industry was unionized when there were very few Negroes in the beer-production centers, and partly because the declining demand for labor has limited the opportunities for Negroes to break into the industry. In many places the union has been primarily an in-group, fighting to conserve the limited amount of employment available.

The barriers to Negroes in New York breweries were strengthened in 1949 when the Brewery Workers and the New York Brewery industry adopted an agreement to stabilize employment by creating certain seniority groupings. Groups I and II had seniority and union membership, whereas Group III was made up of casuals, who were required to complete 165 days employment in the same department of a brewery, uninterrupted by a lay-off of more than six consecutive months, in order to gain Group II status.   Since Negroes were concentrated in Group III, and since only one Negro had acquired permanent status in a New York brewery by 1949, civil-rights agencies suspected a conspiracy to prevent Negroes from acquiring seniority, a suspicion that was strengthened in February 1952 when the rule for acquiring Group II status was stiffened to require 250 days with one employer, uninterrupted by a lay-off of over one consecutive month.

The 1952 rule made it extremely difficult to acquire seniority status because a worker who had accumulated as much as 249 days could lose all of this and be required to start over because of a month's lay-off after the busy season.   It was also possible that a worker would get the required days, but with different employers, in which case they could not count.   Group III workers got their jobs by "shaping" at the union halls (controlled by the Teamsters after the Brewery Workers lost bargaining rights in 1953), so it was naturally suspected that Group III workers, who were not members of the union, were referred to jobs in such a way as to make it impossible for them to meet the requirements of Group II status.

It is against this background that we must understand the agitation by various Negro organizations to gain more jobs for Negroes in the brewery industry in New York.   Since beer is easily boycotted, a number of Negro groups in various cities, particularly New York and Chicago, had used this technique, or the threat of it, to attempt to get jobs for Negroes   The Urban League of Greater New York (ULGNY) and the United African Nationalist Movement (UANM) started boycotts in New York for this purpose in 1951.   The UANM's argument was that the boycotted company, which was popular in Negro communities, should hire Negroes in proportion to the number of jobs their beer drinking created.   The UANM's strategy included pickets, publicity, and encouraging Negroes to "shape up" at the union halls.   Charges were also filed with SCAD against both the companies and the union.   The ULGNY's demands, on the other hand, included a quota system to absorb at least 100 people in seniority jobs during the season.   The League's plan provided that the first three people hired in each department of each brewery would be Negroes, but SCAD vetoed this plan as discrimination against whites.

The first group of complaints against the breweries and the unions in 1953 revealed no clear and definite examples of racial discrimination, though there were strong inferences that it existed.   SCAD's figures show that, of those who had 100 days toward Group II status in the fall of 1953, 23 per cent of the whites and 8 per cent of the

Negroes made Group II status by 1954. These cases were settled by an agreement whereby the hiring procedure was regularized in such a way as to make it easier to detect discrimination. A registration system was adopted from which referrals were made, though exceptions were allowed where employers required men with special qualifications. Moreover, those men who were nearing Group II status were given privileges to permit them to be referred ahead of others.

In spite of these reforms, however, charges of racial discrimination continued and SCAD held new hearings on this industry in 1955. It was alleged that the IBT officials would wait until senior whites arrived in the hall before making referrals, and that Negroes were sent to less desirable jobs. As a result of these hearings, SCAD, the employers, and three IBT locals entered into a consent decree to give nineteen Negroes Group II status. Fourteen of these Negroes were within the jurisdiction of Local 1345, which argued that SCAD had not proved racial discrimination and that the Negroes were in fact being given preferential treatment over whites with more seniority. SCAD officials admitted that these Negroes had not met the contract requirements for Group II status, but argued that they would have it if they had not been discriminated against in the past. Local 1345 finally agreed to the stipulation in order to avoid further litigation; in spite of resentment among whites in Group III, who felt that they were being discriminated against, the union relented, according to its attorney, not because SCAD had proved its case but for "social advancement." [35]

In conclusion, the agitation to get brewery jobs for Negroes produced union membership for thirty-five Negroes by 1955, compared with only one before 1953. Moreover, by the middle of 1954, 128 Negroes had at one time or another been employed as production workers in the New York industry and a more systematic referral system which could be easily checked had been established.

An important public-policy question arising from the waterfront and brewery experiences is whether unions and employers should be allowed to adopt rules by collective bargaining which conserve the available jobs for a particular group. A related question concerns the propriety of an FEP commission voiding such a system to promote the interests of minorities ahead of whites in the same seniority classifications. In the brewery case, SCAD brought pressure to bear on the unions to circumvent the contractual system, though it refused to do this in the waterfront case. These cases also raise the question of the legitimacy of the use of quotas to compensate Negroes for past discrimination.

Hotels and restaurants

A number of complaints charged discrimination against Negroes in hotels and restaurants, a casual industry where Negroes have traditionally been concentrated. A complaint with the California FEP Commission against the bartenders in San Francisco, alleging the exclusion of Negroes from certain areas, not only resulted in a Negro bartender being hired, but also caused the union to change its practices. The Culinary Workers Union in Los Angeles was charged with discrimination against Negro women, but this union changed its practices while the investigation was underway. A Michigan local of the Hotel and Restaurant Employees (HRE) was accused of discriminating against Negro waitresses, though as a result of this complaint the union adopted a nondiscrimination resolution at its annual convention in June 1959. A rather thorough examination was conducted of HRE locals in Philadelphia because of the history of racial discrimination in those unions. Indeed, until the Philadelphia Commission on Human Relations held its hearings in 1959–1960, Waiters and Waitresses Local 302 had a contract with the Restaurant Association which stipulated:

There shall be no change from male to female employees or vice-versa, or from white to colored employees or vice-versa unless there is a vacancy created by transfer, dismissal or voluntary quit of a then employed employee, and the consent of the union in such case shall first have been received by the employer. The union's decision in this regard shall be conclusive and it shall not be subject to arbitration.

The Philadelphia FEP Commission conducted an intensive investigation of the hotel and restaurant industry which revealed that: employers and unions frequently blamed each other for discrimination; Waiters and Waitresses Local 301 did not refer Negroes to places where they were not specifically requested; Bartenders Local 115 accepted and filled job orders specifying race; several locals discriminated in referring only white employees to jobs on the so-called "banquet wheel," used to provide employment for unemployed members; Local 301 maintained racially segregated offices; and the Bartenders had a pattern of all-Negro or all-white employment, with 85 per cent of the establishments all-white. As a result of the Philadelphia Commission investigations, unions and employers took action to promote more equal job opportunities for Negroes. Though information concerning the extent to which the patterns have changed is not available, it is known that a number of employers altered their practices and either hired more Negroes or hired them for the first time.

Conclusions on FEP experience with unions

1. The commissions have succeeded in changing the formal racial practices of a number of unions, especially on the railroads, and have succeeded in directly obtaining admission of hundreds of workers who were formerly excluded from membership in labor organizations. Moreover, the commissions have aided in the regularization of many referral systems, making it more difficult for these to be used as vehicles for discrimination. In addition, the FEP laws undoubtedly have been used by some union leaders as excuses to make equalitarian changes that were not considered politically feasible before the laws were passed. The FEP laws are important symbols registering prevailing moral sentiment, so forces within a union favoring equalitarian racial policies are strengthened considerably by having a law on their side. Moreover, the commissions have found that the labor movement's formal equalitarian policies help them enforce the law. One New York SCAD commissioner told the writer:

We have not always had the cooperation of local union officers, who are much more likely than employers to tell us to go to Hell, but we have always had the cooperation of state federation leaders and international union officers in dealing with their affiliates. This is easily accomplished when we can say to top officials, "because of your unions policy on this matter I am asking your help in overcoming this violation not only of state law but of trade union law."

2. In spite of these positive accomplishments, however, the evidence suggests that the commissions have not changed the basic employment patterns in most unionized industries. There are many reasons for this, including: (*a*) in dealing with unions, the commissions rely heavily on conciliation, persuasion, and the threat of public hearing, though it is generally conceded that recalcitrant local unions are less responsive to these tactics than employers. (*b*) However, there were other factors complicating the commissions' operations, including internal union politics, nepotism, amicism, the natural intractability of employment patterns, declining economic opportunities in many of the industries where Negroes are concentrated or where they are attempting to get jobs, the natural slowness of the case method in proving racial discrimination, the fewness of verifiable complaints

against unions in most of the states, the complicated hiring arrangements in most of the casual occupations, and the autonomy of many local unions.

3. Finally, the FEP cases raise a number of difficult questions for public policy. (*a*) Effective collective bargaining requires that the parties should be given as much freedom as possible to make their own rules. At a time of declining employment opportunities in many industries, it is particularly important that unions and employers be encouraged to make arrangements to stabilize and regularize employment. But when these arrangements also have the effect of freezing the existing racial employment patterns, as in the brewery and longshore cases, should they be permitted?

(*b*) Although unions have been given the right to make their own internal rules, should they be allowed to exclude Negroes from membership through such internal procedures as blackballing an applicant for membership?

(*c*) It is recognized that unions have a legitimate interest in regularizing employment in an industry, but should those unions that have a vested interest in reducing the labor supply be permitted to determine the number of workers to be trained in an industry, or should such control in fact be vested in a tripartite agency?

(*d*) These cases also raise the question of who is legally responsible for employment when a union hiring hall is used. The commissions' experience demonstrates that the effective way to eliminate "buckpassing" is to jointly charge both the employer and the union.

FOOTNOTES

1. The twenty-four state laws in the chronological order of their enactment are: New York and New Jersey (1945), Massachusetts (1946), Connecticut (1947), New Mexico, Oregon, Rhode Island, and Washington (1949), Alaska (1953), Michigan, Minnesota, and Pennsylvania (1955), Colorado and Wisconsin (1957), California and Ohio (1959), Delaware (1960), Illinois, Kansas, and Missouri (1961), Indiana, Hawaii, Iowa, and Vermont (1963). In addition, Idaho, Arizona, Utah, and Nebraska have laws making discrimination a misdemeanor and Nevada has a law which is not enforceable. No laws existed in the South, but in 1964 West Virginia, Kentucky, and Oklahoma had set up commissions to consider the adoption of antidiscrimination laws.
2. New York State Law Against Discrimination, Section 296.1.
3. *Ibid.*, paragraph 297.
4. Statement of George Meany, president, AFL-CIO, in Hearings before the Special Subcommittee on Labor of the Committee on Education and Labor,

House of Representatives, 87th Congress, 2d Session, January 24, 1962, Part II, pp. 985–995.

5. The experiences of some of the other FEP commissions with unions were as follows:

The Connecticut Commission had 23 cases against unions between May 15, 1947, and October 1, 1958, representing about 3% of the total cases handled during this period. In 9 of the 12 cases brought by the Commission itself, clauses in the railroad brotherhoods' constitutions restricting membership to whites were either removed or made inoperative in Connecticut. Three of the other 11 cases involved segregated locals; in one of these cases, a Negro was admitted to a "white" local of the Musicians and unsuccessful efforts were made to merge the Negro and white locals. In another individual complaint, an Electrical Workers' local was forced to admit two Negro electricians. The other six Connecticut cases were filed by union members alleging discrimination in the conditions of membership; no evidence was found to support the charge that a union blocked the promotion of a minority worker in one case, or that unions discriminated in job referrals in two cases; in another case a worker was reinstated to his job and in his local after he was discharged for filing a complaint against a construction company; a Jewish worker was admitted to a local union after he complained that a local refused to honor his transfer because of his religion; finally, the Commission found no evidence to support the allegation that a union refused to refer a worker because of his nationality.

The Michigan FEP law became effective in 1956, and received a total of 960 complaints by January 1959. Unions were respondents in 7.3% of the cases. The following figures show the types of discrimination alleged against unions in the cases filed through December 16, 1958:

Failure to represent	12
Admission to membership	6
Membership conditions	2
Failure to refer	43
Other (hiring cases)	1

The cases were disposed of as follows:

Adjusted	36
Dismissed	14
Withdrawn	3
Pending	11

The Michigan Commission, like others established after 1950, had more complaints against unions involving referrals than any other cause.

The Oregon FEP Commission had a total of 116 cases between 1949 and 1954; 22 of these, or about 20% of the total, were against 10 separate locals. Discrimination was found and corrected in 14 of these cases. Nine cases involved one local railway brotherhood "which resisted repeated efforts to secure compliance with the law through conference, conciliation and persuasion." It was only after a public hearing and the issuance of a cease and desist order by the commissioner of labor that discriminatory practices were eliminated by this union. (State of Oregon, Bureau of Labor, "Five Years of Progress Under Oregon's Fair Employment Practice Act," 1954, p. 5.)

The Oregon Commission had 50 complaints between October 1957 and October 1958, five of which were against unions.

The Washington FEP Commission had a total of 357 formal complaints between June 1949 and December 31, 1957, 24 of which were against unions (6.7%) during this period, 11 of 182 informal complaints (6.0%) filed with the Commission were against unions. (Washington State Board Against Discrimination Annual Report, 1958.)

The Minnesota law became effective July 1, 1955, and by December 1, 1957, two cases, representing 4% of all complaints, had been filed against unions.

The Pennsylvania FEPC was established in 1956, and between March 1, 1956 and March 1, 1959, 531 cases had been filed, 13 of which were against unions (2.4%). Of the 13 union cases, 8 were dismissed, one for lack of jurisdiction and 7 because no evidence of discrimination was found.

The Philadelphia and Pittsburgh FEP commissions have had more experience with unions than the state organization. In Philadelphia, where a commission was established in 1951, 108 complaints, representing 6% of the total, had been filed against unions by October 28, 1958. These 108 cases were disposed of as follows:

Discrimination found and adjusted	15.0%
No evidence of discrimination found	65.0%
Complaint dropped for lack of jurisdiction	4.5%
No evidence of discrimination found, satisfactory adjustment achieved	9.0%
Complaint withdrawn by complainant	29.0%
Cases still in process, 10-28-58	4.5%

The union experience may be compared with the following percentage distribution of all cases handled through December 1957:

Discrimination found and adjusted	30%
Unlawful practice not established	61%
No jurisdiction	3%
Withdrawn	5%

Of the cases filed with the Pittsburgh Commission between April 1, 1953, and August 31, 1955, 11.1% were against unions. Eight of these complaints, representing 4.2% of the cases filed with the Commission, alleged denial of membership, and four, representing 2.1% of the cases, alleged discrimination in referrals. The Pittsburgh Commission found no justification in 28% of the union cases, probable cause in 46%, and in 13% no provable cause was found to credit the specific complaint, but the respondents were found to be guilty of other discriminatory actions.

For a more detailed discussion of the general effects of state antidiscrimination laws, see Paul H. Norgren and Samuel E. Hill, with the assistance of F. Ray Marshall, *Toward Fair Employment*, New York: Columbia University Press, 1964.

6. N. Y. Session Laws, 1940, c. 9(1); Railway Mail Association v. Murphy, New York Supreme Court, Albany County, November 4, 1943.

7. Railway Mail Assn. v. Corsi, 326 U. S. 88 (1946).

8. N. Y. SCAD, "Railroad Employment in New York and New Jersey," A Joint Study by the New York SCAD and the N. J. DAD, 1957.

9. Letter to the writer from Milton Rosenberg, director, Division of Employment Discrimination, N. Y. State Commission for Human Rights, July 24, 1962.

10. *New York Times,* June 23, 1959, p. 20.

11. 18 Conn. Supplement, 125–127; *Connecticut Law Journal,* October 7, 1953, p. 2; IBEW Local 35 v. Commission on Civil Rights, Connecticut Supreme Court of Errors, October Term, 1953.

12. IBEW Local 35 v. Commission on Civil Rights, Superior Court, Hartford County, Conn., File No. 90352, March 25, 1954.

13. See Chapter 5.

14. See Chapter 5.

15. See Chapter 10.

16. See Chapter 5.

17. Blue v. Schafer, 25 Labor Cases, Wisconsin Circuit Court, Milwaukee County, 1954.

18. Ross v. Ebert, 32 Labor Cases, 70; 82 N.W. (2d) (315).

19. Wisconsin Statutes, "Fair Employment," 111.36 (3).

20. Michigan FEPC press release, July 24, 1958.

21. *Detroit Free Press,* August 20, 21, 1959.

22. *Ibid.,* February 4, 1960.

23. Waterfront Commission of New York Harbor, *Annual Report,* 1953–1954.

24. Statement at Press Conference, New York City, 9-14-59.

25. Waterfront Committee of the Urban League of Greater New York, "An Indictment of the 'Shape-up' Hiring System in the Port of New York which fosters racial and individual discrimination," June 1959.

26. 4 *Race Relations Law Reporter* 804, 1959.

27. N. Y. Commission for Human Relations, *Annual Report,* 1962, pp. 20–21.

28. The Citizen's Waterfront Committee, "The New York Waterfront," 1946.

29. "In the Matter of Arbitration between International Longshoremen's Assn.-Independent, and Affiliated Locals in the Port of New York, and New York Shipping Association, November 5, 1958."

30. In 1959, for instance, a knowledgeable observer reported that of approximately 25,000 longshoremen in the Port of New York, 6000 were Negroes and Puerto Ricans, about 1300 of whom were permanent employees, largely in permanent fruit and paper unloading gangs. The other Negroes and Puerto Ricans reported to the Waterfront Commission's hiring halls for work. Approximately 16,000 of the 19,000 whites were in permanent gangs or more or less permanently attached to some company, pier, or position.

31. Letter from Elmer A. Carter to Alexander P. Chopin and Capt. William Bradley, March 4, 1959.

32. J. Harvey Kerns, *The Negro in the Brewing Industry,* New York: National Urban League, 1951, p. 48.

33. Gladys Engel Lang, "Discrimination in the Hiring Hall: Case Study of the Pressures to Promote Integration in New York's Brewery Industry," Ch. 7, in *Discrimination and Low Incomes,* State of New York, Interdepartmental Committee on Low Incomes and State Commission Against Discrimination, November 1957 (mimeo), p. 2.

34. *Op. cit.,* p. 42.

35. 36 LRRM 163 (1955).

CHAPTER 12

Concluding Observations

ALTHOUGH THE COMPLEXITY AND EMOTIONAL NATURE OF UNION racial practices and the natural perils involved in predictions make these comments highly tentative, I feel an obligation to conclude this study with some general observations concerning the Negro and organized labor. In order to place my observations in proper perspective, however, it is necessary to reemphasize that this was not intended to be a survey of union racial practices. Since I have focused on the problems of discrimination by unions, I probably have not adequately reflected the positive things done by unions to improve the Negro's position.[1] My basic objective has not been to condemn or praise unions or civil-rights organizations but to understand their inner workings. In particular, I have sought to uncover the basic factors tending to perpetuate or change union racial practices. It is for this reason that I have selected particular practices for examination instead of attempting an exhaustive survey. I am well aware of the limitations imposed by this approach, but it is hoped that by eliciting debate that will correct my errors and offset my bias, this book will lead to a better understanding of a very important problem.

Not only do emotions cause various organizations—both civil rights and labor—to exaggerate their positions and erect obfuscating symbols, but personal bias undoubtedly obscured my own vision in spite of my attempt to take a detached view. Since I cannot completely escape from my prejudices, perhaps misunderstanding will be minimized if I clarify my position with respect to Negro employment problems and unions.

Discrimination and Negro Employment Patterns

Discrimination in employment is morally and economically wrong. Morally wrong, because it unjustly impedes the fullest expression of the individual human personalities of Negroes. Economically wrong, because it deprives the nation of the most efficient use of human resources. Discrimination thus does moral and economic damage to whites as well as nonwhites.

Clearly, however, the Negro's occupational disadvantages are not entirely caused by racial discrimination, but also by historical and cultural patterns which are themselves only partly the result of discrimination. It follows that the elimination of racial discrimination would not cause the Negro to have complete equality in employment opportunities. An important function of public policy therefore must be to create a framework within which Negroes can overcome these historical handicaps. Legislation such as the 1964 Civil Rights law can prevent some overt acts of discrimination and establish a framework within which Negroes can move toward more equal employment opportunities, but the law's critics and defenders agree that legislation cannot solve the problem. If by solution we mean equal-employment patterns, truly heroic efforts will be required by the Negro community and by white employers and union leaders. The Negro community has a major responsibility to understand the need for increased education, training, and competence as racial barriers are lowered. But since this is a chicken-and-egg problem, and since whites have major responsibility for employment, unions and employers will also have to understand the need to assist and encourage Negroes in their efforts.

One of the continuing controversies for the next few years undoubtedly will involve the question of preferential treatment to overcome the Negro's past disadvantages. The fact that the Civil Rights Act of 1964 *does not require* preferential treatment, but presumably *permits* it, does little to ease the controversy. Whatever the merits of arguments for or against *preferential* treatment, it seems safe to conclude that Negroes are, and will continue to be, given *special* treatment because of the pressures being exerted, and likely to be exerted, by civil-rights groups and because many employers, government officials, and union leaders feel that this is the right thing to do. Although preferential treatment has few defenders (it is not likely to be supported by the NLRB or the Equal Employment Opportunity Commission established by the Civil Rights Act of 1964), in the past it seems to have been the natural reaction of many employers, unions, and government officials in cases of racial conflict. Such conflicts over jobs and union offices frequently have been settled either through quota systems or other special arrangements to allocate positions to Negroes. These arrangements are based on the assumption that racial prejudice and discrimination make it unlikely that Negroes would get jobs or union offices in the absence of such special measures. Racial quota systems have been used in casual occupations where employment is not normally based on seniority like the Southern building-construction and longshoring industries. In these cases, Negroes sometimes have had enough economic power to force unions to give them a proportion of the jobs. Quotas have also been sanctioned by federal agencies to insure Negro employment on public-works projects in the South. It is difficult to see how racial employment quota systems designed to overcome discrimination could be considered "preferential" treatment for Negroes.

Of course, the reason most employers, unions, and government officials publicly oppose preferential treatment for Negroes is because it might deprive whites of their rights and therefore would be discrimination in reverse. Union leaders fear preferential hiring will destroy seniority, which is a vital right to most unions and their members. Furthermore, quota systems might discriminate against Negroes and whites. But special programs for Negroes need not take the form of quota systems and need not deprive whites of existing rights. It would not be preferential treatment, for example, for unions and employers to make special efforts to recruit qualified Negroes or to help them acquire training; this would merely extend to Negroes benefits which whites already enjoy. Negroes are even given *preference* in some cases without altering the preexisting rights of whites. For example, if a Negro and a white applicant were about equally qualified, it would be preferential treatment if the Negro were hired in order to demonstrate to the Negro community (or government agencies) that the campany had lowered its racial barriers. Some employers believe this kind of preferential treatment has been expected of them by the federal contract committees. But what most critics of preferential treatment apparently have in mind is the practice of hiring or upgrading Negroes regardless of their seniority or qualifications when more senior or qualified whites are eligible. Preferential treatment which displaces whites or ignores the qualifications of Negroes or whites understandably leads to racial unrest. Preferential treatment which destroys the preexisting rights of whites is based on the theory (in my judgment, mistaken) that whites as a race are collectively responsible for the disadvantages suffered by Negroes and that whites therefore should be penalized in order to compensate Negroes for their historically conditioned disadvantages. It seems to me to be just as unfair to hold all whites responsible for the Negroes' conditions as it is to consider all Negroes inferior to all whites.

Although there are some special measures that can be taken to improve the economic opportunities of Negroes, the most effective programs are likely to be those which help all disadvantaged workers who are similarly situated, regardless of race. Indeed, at this juncture, when there are numerous antidiscrimination programs in operation, the most effective measures to better the Negro's lot are those which would improve the education and training of all low-income groups and combat unemployment. These programs not only would reduce the Negroes' frustrations and bitterness, but also would lessen white resistance to the Negro's advancement.

Training is important because the supply of qualified Negro workers has been a crucial factor in changing racial employment and union membership patterns. The supply of qualified Negroes is particularly important in the major Northern cities where the racial barriers of strong craft unions have been breached since 1950. And the inadequate supply of qualified applicants for occupations from which Negroes have been barred in the South is likely to be an important impediment to improving the Negro's job opportunities under the provisions of the Civil Rights Act of 1964. Furthermore, a good way to test the effectiveness of the AFL-CIO's program to get its affiliates to voluntarily comply with the Civil Rights Act would be to confront unions with qualified applicants.

Measures to combat unemployment are very important because the great increase in unemployment among Negroes since 1953 undoubtedly has been one of the main causes of the increased intensity of racial unrest. And one of the main factors responsible for the disappointing changes in racial employment patterns as racial barriers are lowered has undoubtedly been declining employment opportunities in the industries and occupations where Negroes have been concentrated. The deterioration in the nonwhite employment picture since 1953 is indicated by the following unemployment rates:

	White	Nonwhite
1953	2.3%	4.1%
1954	4.5	8.9
1955	3.6	7.9
1956	3.3	7.5
1957	3.9	8.0
1958	6.1	12.6
1959	4.9	10.7
1960	5.0	10.2
1961	6.0	12.5
1962	4.9	11.0
1963	5.1	10.9

Source: Mathew A. Kessler, "Economic Status of Nonwhite Workers, 1955–62," *Monthly Labor Review,* July 1963; and the U. S. Bureau of Labor Statistics.

If the nation could achieve the so-called "interim" overall unemployment rate of around 4 per cent, suggested by the Johnson Administration and the Council of Economic Advisers (which was the rate between 1955 and 1957), the Negro unemployment rate could be reduced to perhaps 7.5 per cent and the white rate to perhaps 3.5 per cent. If the unemployment rate could be sustained at 4 per cent, the gap between the Negro and white unemployment rates could be narrowed, as it was during and immediately after the Second World War. In every year between 1955 and 1963, for example, the nonwhite unemployment rate was over twice the white rate, but in no year between 1947 and 1954 was the nonwhite rate twice that of whites. To a very significant extent, therefore, what has happened is not so much a deterioration in the Negro's economic position because of increased discrimination. Discrimination—by unions and in the larger society—has declined markedly since 1940 and significantly since 1960. However, technological change and depressed economic conditions have eroded the Negro's overall economic condition relative to whites faster than it has been improved through migration out of agriculture, falling racial barriers, and improved training and education. The median family income of nonwhites had advanced to 56.8 per cent of whites at its postwar relative high in 1952, but was only 51.2 per cent in 1958 and 54.4 per cent in 1961. In order to maintain even these relative positions, however, nonwhites have had to have a larger number of wage earners per family than whites. The relative civilian labor-force participation rate in 1962 was 60.0 per cent for nonwhites and 56.1 per cent for whites. Significantly, the nonwhite male participation rate (76.4 per cent) was *lower* than the white male rate (78.6 per cent), but the nonwhite female rate (45.6 per cent) was much higher than the white female rate (35.6 per cent). The participation rates for both nonwhite males and females was higher in 1948 (84.8 and 44.4 per cent) than the rates for whites (84.2 and 30.6 per cent).[2] These statistics tend to support the argument that at least some of the unrest in Negro communities is attributable to the deterioration in the economic opportunities of Negro males.

Although the nonwhite unemployment rates have been about twice those of whites, the following figures show that nonwhite unemployment rates improved slightly relative to the totals between 1956 and 1963:

	Ratio of Unemployment in Each Group to National Unemployment Rate		Percentage of Total Unemployment in Each Group	
	White	Nonwhite	White	Nonwhite
1956	.87	1.98	78.5	21.5
1959	.88	1.95	78.8	21.2
1962	.87	1.97	78.1	21.9
1963	.89	1.91	78.8	21.2

Source: R. A. Gordon, "Has Structural Unemployment Worsened," *Industrial Relations*, May 1964, p. 71.

These figures suggest that the *increases* in nonwhite unemployment rates since 1956 are due mainly to increases in the general level of unemployment.

The Role of Unions

So much for my attitudes concerning Negro employment problems. My basic position with respect to organized labor rests on the assumption, which seems to me to be strongly supported by the historical record, that unions and collective bargaining make important contributions to a free society. Collective bargaining contributes to a free society by permitting a decentralized nongovernmental process whereby workers and employers can jointly formulate and enforce rules governing wages, hours, and working conditions. Moreover, free unions, by giving expression to the interests of workers in general, serve the socially useful function of regulating workers' protests and contributing to the formation of that consensus among groups necessary to a free, pluralistic society. I consider it highly significant that free unions and collective bargaining have never been permitted in a totalitarian society and that communism rarely if ever gains much support from workers in countries with strong trade-union movements.

With respect to unions and public policy, I believe that the main function of a union should be to represent its members. It is therefore unreasonable to expect union leaders to jeopardize their positions in order to carry out desirable public policies—whether it be in racial or purely economic matters. Governments should, through understanding the structures and policies of unions and the motives of their leaders, adopt measures that will encourage unions to comply with the public interest, but should always be prepared to compel such compliance. Voluntary compliance can effect changes beyond the reach of the law and is less likely to create resentment among union leaders and their constituents. But since unions are democratic organizations, union leaders are in much better position to gain compliance with public policy if they can demonstrate to their followers that the failure of voluntary action will lead to legal enforcement.

But should unions concern themselves with civil-rights matters? There can be little question that it is the proper function of a union to see to it that the workers it represents are not discriminated against in employment on such irrelevant grounds as race. Justice also requires that unions admit to membership all those they represent except where there are justifiable trade-union reasons for denying union membership.

Should unions involve themselves in civil-rights activity that is outside the realm of employment? It seems to me that as defenders of a democratic society unions have an obligation to work for the basic elements of democracy. Indeed, unions have a vested interest in preserving a free society. It is not entirely coincidental, of course, that the same forces which seek to defeat unions also seek to deprive Negroes of their basic rights as citizens. It is for this reason that unions must seek to promote the basic civil rights of all citizens. Of course, the question of special civil-rights legislation—like open housing or school integration laws—creates some difficult problems for unions. Some unions with what are considered to be good racial records, like the United Mine Workers, have paid very little attention to general civil-rights matters. Moreover, in the South it is almost certain that unions would weaken themselves at the federation level if they pushed general civil-rights legislation. This means, of course, that unions would possibly sacrifice some of their power to secure trade-union and economic legislation if they pushed civil-rights matters. Our analysis of the Southern reaction to equalitarian racial policies by international unions and the AFL-CIO suggests, however, that unions will have less to fear from Southern members if they use their collective-bargaining power to promote economic equality for Negroes. Whatever one's value judgments, however, whether unions will involve themselves in general civil-rights questions depends, as we shall argue later, on the effects of such involvement on the basic objectives of the unions and their leaders.

If the foregoing evaluations have any bases in reality, it follows that the relationship between Negroes and unions has important implications for the whole society. Continued widening of the schism between these groups could impair the functioning of unions and civil-rights organizations. If my understanding of the reasons for the Negro-union split is correct, conflict between these groups will probably continue but will not result in a complete break. It is highly unlikely, for example, that the Negro-union relationship will revert to what it was before the New Deal period. The conflict probably will continue because practices that are discriminatory or that appear to be discriminatory will be difficult to overcome, particularly in some of the craft unions and at the local level. Moreover, even with complete agreement between Negro and labor leaders over objectives, there will be differences in the priority assigned those objectives, the methods of their attainment, and the appraisals of the progress that has already been made. Union leaders are likely to emphasize the progress that has been made whereas Negroes are more likely to look at the distance they still have to go. Unions also will understandably place more emphasis on internal cohesion and the achievement of union objectives than they will on general civil-rights objectives and overcoming discrimination in their own ranks. However, the overall conflict between unions and the Negro community probably will be diminished by the steady decline in discrimination by unions. And discrimination probably will decline because of external pressures on unions from governments and civil-rights groups, and internal pressures from Negroes and those white union leaders who see that discrimination damages the entire labor movement. The priority of the race issue within the labor movement has been raised because these pressures make it increasingly obvious to union leaders that continued discrimination and further widening of the Negro-labor split will subject unions to increasing regulation and loss of support from the general public.

The net effect of the racial demonstrations in major Northern cities during the summers of 1963 and 1964 probably will be to improve relations between national union leaders and more moderate civil-rights organizations like the NAACP and the Urban League. These demonstrations, and the Civil Rights Act, probably strengthened the equalitarian forces within the trade-union movement. Moreover, the attacks on the building trades probably led to a better understanding of the whole problem of union racial practices. The fewness of applicants who came forward in New York in the summer of 1963, in spite of intensive recruiting efforts among Negroes and Puerto Ricans, undoubtedly increased the Negro community's awareness that the fewness of Negroes in the skilled trades was not caused entirely by racial discrimination. The fewness of qualified Negro and Puerto Rican applicants also probably lessened union members' fears that more liberal admission policies would cause them to be flooded with new members to the detriment of union standards. Finally, by producing the so-called white "backlash" against the civil-rights movement and conservative opposition to the Civil Rights Act, and by highlighting extremist influence in the civil-rights movement, these demonstrations apparently brought union leaders and the more moderate civil-rights groups closer together.

Although there are several other possibilities, the Negro-labor alliance is likely to be an increasingly important political force in the South, particularly in those areas where the Republican party grows and splits the white vote along economic lines. Unions are also likely to be strengthened in the South as that region continues to industrialize and as Supreme Court decisions and mounting Negro voter registrations increase the political power of urban areas where unions have their greatest strength and where ever larger proportions of Negroes will live. There is a possibility, however, that racial factors will continue to unite whites, making Negroes a permanent minority with little other than local political power. If this happens, there is a real prospect that demonstrations and racial violence will continue, in which case these will be the vehicles to force concessions from whites. Moreover, in the long run, if racial matters take lower priority than economic interests with middle-class Negroes, the Negro vote will become more conservative and will itself split along economic lines.

There are also some other factors which will continue to divide Negroes and unions. Some of the current differences between these groups stem from misunderstandings and mutual suspicions which will persist because they have become institutionalized as a part of the ideologies of Negro and labor groups. Union leaders under attack from civil-rights groups are likely to consider the latter to be more interested in publicity and perpetuating their movements than in resolving basic differences. These union leaders are also likely to feel that Negroes are mainly interested in getting jobs which unions have fought through the years to improve and which present members want to preserve for themselves and their relatives. Moreover, these leaders argue, Negroes want to get *their* (union members') *jobs* whether they are qualified for them or not. These unionists are therefore likely to discount the importance of discrimination as a factor keeping Negroes out of jobs and to insist that discrimination be proved on a case-by-case method. Another cause of suspicion is a belief, apparently held by a minority of union leaders, that the civil-rights movement is part of a general conspiracy by "left-wing extremists" or misinformed intellectuals to discredit conservative unions. Moreover, it is a standard craft-union defense that racial discrimination by unions has been greatly exaggerated and that discrimination in employment is mainly the responsibility of employers and not unions. Given this complex of attitudes, leaders of unions with the greatest reputations for discrimination are likely to accept Negroes only grudgingly and under great pressure from within the labor movement and from civil-rights groups and the government. Moreover, since discrimination violates basic trade-union ideology, union leaders at every level are likely to exacerbate Negro-union relations by their extreme sensitivity to criticism on this point. At the same time, however, this sensitivity is a force conditioning union leaders for change. Finally, union leaders are likely to contribute to a continuation of Negro-labor differences by their failure to understand the nature of the civil-rights movement. There has been a perceptible tendency, for example, for some union leaders to think in terms of the kind of racial climate existing in the 1920's. The realities of the present situation, however, have a way of disabusing top union leaders of these attitudes.

For their part, many civil-rights leaders misunderstand the nature of the labor movement and exaggerate the extent of racial discrimination. They are likely to overestimate the labor movement's power to solve its own problems and to feel that discrimination is the main reason for the Negroes' unequal status in places where inadequate training, education, and seniority really account for the Negroes' position. There is an understandable tendency for Negroes to underestimate the importance of ability and training in acquiring new jobs. Moreover, civil-rights leaders are likely to suspect that unions are mainly interested in "window dressing" by enunciating equalitarian civil-rights policies which they have no intention of implementing. To a large extent, of course, this criticism is justified, particularly at the national and local union level. But it is not surprising that a movement should desire a favorable public image and that its goals do not describe its practices. The proper criterion by which to judge organizations is not the gap between their objectives and their goals but the extent to which they are exerting themselves to close the gap.

But, it might be asked, does not the evidence show that AFL-CIO leaders are insincere in their civil-rights policies because they have dealt more vigorously with the other main problems of the postwar period—communism and corruption—than they have dealt with the civil-rights problem? The CIO expelled unions for being communist-dominated and the AFL-CIO expelled unions for corruption.[3] But no unions have been expelled because of their racial bars. Indeed, the AFL-CIO even admitted two unions with race bars in their constitutions. Nevertheless, experience would seem to justify the arguments used by the AFL-CIO's leaders in admitting these unions and refusing to expel others. They have argued that the communist and corruption problems were at the leadership level, so the federations had no alternative other than to expel these unions and hope that their members would oust their leaders. The civil-rights problem, on the other hand, is a membership and not a leadership problem, and little would appear to be gained by expulsion, particularly where the union's leaders appeared to be sincerely interested in overcoming discrimination in the organization's ranks. Outside the federation, the race bars would probably have been retained much longer because the organizations would not have been subject to the pressures of the AFL-CIO's leaders and its constitution. The fact that the Locomotive Firemen and the Railroad Trainmen, both AFL-CIO affiliates, removed their racial bars while the independent Conductors and Engineers retained theirs would seem to suggest the validity of the Executive Council's position.

Employer policies are also likely to be important influences on the relationship between unions and Negroes. In this respect, employers can be expected to add their weight to the pressures for equal treatment of Negroes. Indeed, because they have more power vis-a-vis the general public, and because companies are not democratic organizations, business leaders can exert more influence on race relations than unions. Moreover, employers have little motive for discrimination where laws, unions, and other pressures require equal wages and where Negroes can no longer be relied upon to be anti-union or support employer political interests. To a very limited extent, employers have benefited by the Negro-labor split since the AFL-CIO merger and have gained a little political support from Negroes in some areas. But the basic pro-union, pro-Democratic Party relationship established during the New Deal period does not seem to have been disrupted very much by the differences between the AFL-CIO and the Negro community. Indeed, most civil-rights leaders acknowledge their debt to the labor movement for the civil-rights legislation that has been passed since the Second World War. Moreover, the interests of unions and Negroes are likely to be very similar with respect to economic legislation. Thus, employers can expect to gain very little from attempting to widen the Negro-labor split. In fact, whatever their political activities, it is obvious to most unionized employers that they have a great deal to lose by racial turmoil within their plants.

Employers would also appear to have few status motives for opposing Negro equality. Negroes are not likely to challenge management positions to a significant extent any time soon. Employers might lose community prestige in some cases by integration policies, but the climate of race relations is such that they can usually give justifiable reasons for equalitarian policies. Indeed, in the very logic of their positions employers have little to gain from discrimination. If plants are integrated, not only can workers be selected on the basis of their abilities, but expensive duplication of facilities within plants can be avoided. In the past those employers who have wanted to have rational personnel policies have been prevented from doing so by legal requirements or fear of retaliation from whites. When employers were subject to no outside pressures to integrate, they rarely risked these adverse reactions. But now that the civil-rights movement has broadened and become more intense, and pressures are being exerted on employers by governments and civil-rights groups, management not only has the motive to adopt equalitarian racial policies but it also can shift the blame for doing so to the government or to racial demonstrators.

I do not mean to imply that many employers in the South strongly desire to take equalitarian policies for moral reasons. Many employers are prejudiced and as a group they strongly resent the pressures being put on them by governments and civil-rights organizations. However, as I shall argue with respect to unions, these attitudes are less important than the power situations confronting business leaders. And those power situations are likely to require employers to take equalitarian measures. The extent to which employers respond to these pressures will be determined by such factors as the importance to them of government contracts, the strength of the union, whether they identify with their communities and thus fear that racial strife will interfere with community economic development, whether their products are easily boycotted, the geographic location of their markets, the importance of Negro customers, the fear of white-consumer reaction, and whether their competitors adopt similar policies. The evidence suggests that many of the nation's major companies are currently reconsidering their racial employment policies and are adopting equal employment programs. Moreover, in many Southern communities business groups were decisive in reducing racial strife before the Civil Rights Law of 1964 and are leading the efforts to gain compliance with that law.

The Trends in Union Racial Practices

So much for the general relationships between Negroes, unions, and employers. Let me next review briefly some of the major trends in union racial practices and then attempt to outline the major factors responsible for those trends. We have seen that, although the rate of change has been disappointing to most civil-rights advocates, the trend in union racial practices has been toward the equalitarian end of the spectrum. The number of unions with formal race bars has been reduced to two and these are outside the AFL-CIO. Informal racial barriers are still important, but they have been greatly reduced since 1930. Indeed, there have been some important breakthroughs in craft unions in several major cities outside the South since the AFL-CIO merger in 1956. Moreover, racial auxiliary locals have been virtually abolished and few new segregated locals have been established since the Second World War. There has also been a decline in informal segregation within the labor movement in the South, but voluntary segregation by Negroes within union meetings is still common. However, even in the South Negroes and whites meet together with little difficulty whereas integrated union meetings were rare in 1930. The power of Negroes within the labor movement has increased greatly. In 1930 there were probably no more than 56,000 Negro union members as contrasted with between 1.5 and 2 million today. Negroes also occupy official positions at every level in the trade-union movement. These Negroes have formed organizations within the labor movement to protect and promote their interests and at least eighteen international unions have or have had Negroes on their executive boards. Two Negroes were elected to the AFL-CIO Executive Council. Moreover, racial wage differentials have been virtually eliminated in unionized plants and several important Southern industries have desegregated their seniority rosters. Major industries in the North desegregated their lines of progression during the Second World War. We have also noted that in spite of differences between the Negro community and organized labor, Negro-union relations are much closer than they were in 1930. The AFL-CIO adopted a much more equalitarian racial program than any of its predecessor federations and many AFL-CIO affiliates have strong equalitarian programs.

In short, union racial practices have become much more equalitarian and the whole level of the debate between Negroes and unions has changed. In 1930 the main problems were formal exclusion, segregated and auxiliary locals, racial wage differentials, and the use of Negro strikebreakers. In 1964 the main problem areas were exclusion by some craft unions and their apprenticeship programs, overcoming Negro and white resistance to desegregated locals, and the election of Negroes to leadership positions. And the changed importance of the race issue within the labor movement made it fairly obvious in 1964 that much more attention would continue to be devoted to these problems than had been given to the more serious forms of discrimination in 1930.

Factors Influencing Union Racial Practices

Before we summarize the main factors that have changed or perpetuated union racial practices, we must emphasize the need to qualify our generalizations. It is not true, for example, that all craft unions are more discriminatory than all industrial unions or that all unions in the South discriminate more than unions outside the South. Industrial locals have also discriminated against Negroes. The important difference, of course, is the nature of the union and its power to discriminate. Craft unions are more discriminatory generally than industrial unions because local craft unions have the power to control the labor supply and because they enhance their power by restricting the supply of labor. We have noted, however, that there is likely to be a conflict on this point between local and international craft unions because the latter gain strength by expanding, not restricting, membership. Moreover, the craft local probably is more likely than the industrial local to be controlled by its membership.[4] For one thing, craft locals are likely to be more important to their members because they control jobs. In addition, the nature of the market is likely to require industrial unions to be more centralized. As a generalization, however, craft unions are more discriminatory than industrial locals. This does not mean, of course, that craft union members are more prejudiced than industrial union members. It simply means that craft unionists have more opportunities to discriminate as well as more power to do so. The fact that various forms of discrimination are not randomly distributed throughout the labor movement suggests that this is not entirely a moral problem and should caution us to look for other causes.

Likewise, we have noted that some unions in the South have had more equalitarian policies than non-Southern locals of the same internationals. Again, however, this does not mean that Southerners in those locals are less prejudiced than non-Southerners in unions barring Negroes from membership. The main explanation is probably that there are more Negro craftsmen in the South. For example, Bricklayers and Longshoremen locals have been able to bar Negroes from membership in the North because there were relatively few Negroes in these crafts. In the South, on the other hand, Negroes were too numerous to permit effective unionization without admitting the Negroes to integrated or segregated locals. As a rule, however, since unions tend to reflect their environments and since racial segregation has been much more rigid in the South, Southern unions are more likely than their Northern counterparts to practice racial discrimination.

Although it is necessary to qualify our generalizations as well as to avoid the common assumption that discrimination can be explained entirely by prejudice, our understanding of this problem nevertheless is enhanced by such simplification.

For conceptual purposes, therefore, the factors influencing union racial practices may be divided into general and specific causes, though there are obvious mutual relationships between these levels of causation. The general factors establish the framework within which specific union racial practices are determined. Our analysis suggests, for example, that general economic conditions are important because equalitarian racial practices are most likely when labor shortages give employers incentives to hire Negroes and relax some of the white workers' basic motives for restricting the Negro's employment opportunities. Sustained full employment would also increase the supply of Negro workers in various job categories because colored youths would have greater incentives to seek training if they knew jobs were available to them.

Furthermore, measures taken to improve the operation of the labor market by increasing job knowledge and promoting rational selection and promotion policies will tend to reduce racial employment barriers. Indeed, one of the likely results of the continuing conflict over racial discrimination in employment will undoubtedly be to improve the operation of the labor market by reducing nepotism and amicism in the selection, promotion, transfer, and referral of employees. Antidiscrimination policies also will increase the use of objective testing procedures in the selection and upgrading of personnel. Finally, emphasis on inadequate training and employment opportunities for minority youth has focused attention on the general inadequacies of training and labor-market information in this country.

Another general factor conditioning union racial practices is race relations in the larger community. We have demonstrated that the evolution of race relations is reflected in the attitudes of union members. The current militant mood of the Negro community causes racial matters to assume higher priority in the community as well as within unions.

Political arrangements in the larger community also condition the practices of unions. We have noted that the increased political power of the Negro community is a factor causing the federal government and various state governments to take measures to eradicate discrimination in unions. The steady increase in civil-rights legislation since the beginning of the Second World War reflects the increasing political power of the Negro community.

Within the framework imposed by such general economic, social, and political forces, specific union racial practices will be determined by the structure, power, and objectives of unions, the motives and attitudes of union leaders, and the power relations between union leaders and members, civil-rights groups, employers, and governments. We assume at the outset that as a generalization union leaders are mainly interested in keeping their jobs and that their racial practices will be determined by that motive. We further assume that union racial policies rarely change without some pressure for change. Few union leaders will go out of their way to look for trouble because they usually feel that they have enough already. I also assume the attitudes of union leaders to be relatively unimportant as determinants of specific practices. However, since attitudes determine the extent to which union leaders will strain at the power limitations in which they find themselves, the importance of attitudes as determinants of practices will depend on the strength of the union leader and the freedom of action permitted by the pressures he must reconcile in order to retain his position. Attitudes also are probably more important determinants of such union political activities as the support of civil-rights legislation than they are of collective bargaining and internal union matters.

Our analysis of union racial practices demonstrated that different kinds of unions have different objectives and are therefore vulnerable to different kinds of pressures. Federations like the AFL-CIO or state labor councils, for example, are more vulnerable than either national or local unions to moral pressures (public hearings, publicity). This is because federations are primarily political organizations, are more conspicuous, and operate to a significant extent by appealing to the general public for support. Moral threats are not very effective against many local craft unions because they have narrow political and social objectives, do not deal with the general public, and are mainly economic organizations. Our discussion of public policy demonstrated that these unions are more likely to respond to fines and threats to their control of the supply of labor. Nationals are more likely than locals to respond to moral pressures, but whether they respond will depend on the importance of the moral pressures to their basic objectives. Nevertheless, moral pressures are likely to be very effective against all kinds of unions in the long run. This is true because in the short run issues are usually decided on the basis of the economic or political interests of the parties immediately involved. But parties not immediately involved will normally be influenced by moral considerations. And in the long run these third parties can take action (influencing public officials, serving on juries, honoring picket lines or boycotts, encouraging friends to join or not to join a particular union) which will ultimately influence the organization's policies.

Union structure is important to an understanding of union policies because it determines the extent to which different parts of the union hierarchy can influence each other. It is for this reason that moral pressures against the AFL-CIO are likely in the short run to have very little influence on discriminating locals. The AFL-CIO has little other than moral power to use against its international or local affiliates. We also noted that the power of the state federation over the local is very weak. However, the power relationship between the local and its parent international is much more important. The international usually has more control over local unions than the AFL-CIO has over the internationals. The local-international relationship will be determined by such factors as: the effect of a particular practice on the international's objectives as interpreted by its leaders and as it influences their official positions; the strength of the forces compelling the union to adopt equalitarian policies; the availability of alternatives for the local, especially whether the local can survive as an independent of whether there is a rival union to which it can turn; whether the employer will support the international; the dues structure and financial strength of the international; the economic importance of the local to its members; constitutional provisions with respect to the ownership of the local's property if it secedes; labor-market conditions; the ease or difficulty of imposing trusteeships or expelling local unions; and the effectiveness of the international's education program.

Expulsion and union education programs are probably of very limited importance in changing a local union's practices. Most international unions are interested in gaining, not losing, members, and there seems to be a strong consensus among collective-bargaining unions that expulsion is "not the answer" to enforcing compliance with an international's racial policies. We noted, however, that trusteeships are likely to be more important. Unions will also use education as a means of attempting to get local leaders and members to comply with its policies, but union education probably is too limited and affects too few members to have much value in offsetting those environmental factors which determine attitudes and practices.

Labor-market forces are very important in the international-local relationship and in conditioning the racial practices of local unions. Particularly important factors include the supply of Negro workers, the scope of bargaining, technological change, and employer preferences. Of these, the strongest force overcoming discrimination by local craft unions is probably the number of qualified Negroes in a trade; this factor influences and is influenced by the other major factors influencing unions.

The scope of bargaining is important because organizations with local bargains are more likely to discriminate than organizations with national bargains. Moreover, national bargaining arrangements strengthen the international union relative to its locals because of the need for national coordination of wages or other contract provisions. The international will also be strengthened if it, rather than the local, is certified as bargaining agent by the NLRB. Since workers will almost never risk good jobs for racial reasons, the international will be strengthened if wages established by its national agreement are higher than prevailing wages in a local area.

Since Negroes have been concentrated disproportionately in jobs likely to be eliminated by technological change, this has been an important factor determining the supply of Negro workers. Negroes have been displaced whenever innovations abolish jobs or make them more attractive to whites. Racial trouble frequently has started when unemployment rises and whites start moving into jobs held by Negroes or senior Negroes are laid off while junior whites are retained.

The ease or difficulty of learning the trade will also be important. If the trade is relatively easy to learn, or Negroes can learn it in trade schools, the armed forces, or by "picking it up," the union will have difficulty excluding Negroes or will face deteriorating economic conditions. In the plumbing and electrical industries, for example, where apprenticeships are important, it is relatively difficult for Negroes to learn the trade because there are few colored craftsmen and until recently whites had rarely taken Negro apprentices or trainees. One of the reasons Negro bricklayers, cement finishers, and plasterers have been able to perpetuate themselves in the South is that there is a sizable number of Negroes who will teach these trades to others. Moreover, the techniques used in these trades are relatively stable, so white craftsmen cannot monopolize the newer techniques in order to exclude Negroes. Negroes have also been allowed to retain some jobs which were difficult to perform or had other undesirable features.

The employers' preferences for Negro or white labor also perpetuate racial job patterns. This preference is influenced by stereotypes concerning whether Negroes can do certain kinds of work, have higher rates of turnover or absenteeism, are subject to more wage garnishments, and the like. Employers in the South have traditionally preferred Negroes for some kinds of work, particularly some undesirable jobs which whites were likely to leave as other alternatives became available. Negroes have been more dependable for these jobs because they were frozen into them by fewer alternatives than are available to whites. Before the 1930's employers sometimes preferred Negroes to whites as a means of defeating union organizing, but changes during the New Deal period reduced the importance of this factor. Employer preferences also are affected by the uncertainties as to the reaction of white workers and the supply of Negroes with the necessary skills if employers are boycotted. Boycotts against employers will rarely be attempted in stable industrial jobs; in construction work, on the other hand, it is a simple matter for workers who change jobs frequently to boycott a particular employer. The main white-worker reaction in industrial jobs has been the racial protest strike. However, these strikes have become much less common since the Second World War, especially where both the employer and the international union oppose the striking white workers. Moreover, the necessity that Negroes accept lower wages in order to overcome the employers' preferences for whites in the better jobs has also declined markedly since the Second World War.

The operation of these forces may be illustrated by reviewing the factors responsible for perpetuating or changing union racial practices in the American labor movement. We have already discussed the reasons why craft unions and those in the South are more likely to exclude Negroes than industrial unions or those outside the South. Other considerations include: (1) because of the egalitarian trend in race relations, those unions that are older seem more likely to exclude than newer unions; (2) some unions originally were fraternal organizations at a time when it was not considered proper to have fraternal relations with Negroes; (3) in some cases employers determine hiring policies and therefore decide whether Negroes will be hired; (4) whites are likely to attempt to exclude Negroes from certain status jobs like airline pilots, stock wranglers, locomotive engineers, and white-collar and supervisory jobs; and (5) exclusion is sometimes directed against all except a particular nationality or family group, in which case Negroes are discriminated against along with all except members of the favored group.

The forces that caused unions to abandon exclusion, or to do it by more subtle means, included: expansion of Negro employment in jurisdictions covered by these unions, especially during periods of labor shortages; competition between unions for Negro votes in representation elections; embarrassment of exclusionist union leaders at conventions and in the press by criticism from Negro and white union leaders; action by such governmental agencies as the wartime and state FEP committees; and fear of loss of exclusive bargaining rights, union security provisions, or other legal privileges under the Railway Labor or National Labor Relations acts.

Programs and strategies to change union racial practices in specific cases have been adopted and implemented by Negro union members or workers, civil-rights organizations, government agencies, and internal union civil-rights agencies. The disadvantaged Negroes usually constitute the most important catalyst for change. We noted that union discrimination frequently was overcome only after the Negroes who were the victims of discrimination organized for political purposes, to take legal action, to vote in representation, or to take other action against unions or their leaders. Negro workers usually have been aided by the NAACP, the National Urban League, the Jewish Labor Committee, or some other outside agency or individual. The NAACP, through its labor secretary, has been particularly active in giving publicity to union discrimination and assisting Negroes in filing complaints with various governmental agencies. The Urban League has usually operated with less publicity and has served a very valuable research and advisory role in this field. Because of the structure of the labor movement, the AFL-CIO and the various internal union civil-rights organizations have had rather limited roles as initiators of action to abolish discrimination, but they have served to settle complaints, to educate union leaders and members in the civil-rights field, and to represent organized labor in the civil-rights movement. However, it seems fairly conclusive that the AFL-CIO does not have the power to eradicate discrimination within the ranks of organized labor without the aid of outside forces.

We noted in Part 2 of this study that these forces rarely operated in isolation and rarely produced a complete change in union practices, but that there was an evolution through various patterns which unions seem to have copied from each other. When unions would not accept Negroes employed in their jurisdictions, a pattern emerged whereby the excluding union would have Negroes in its jurisdiction organized directly by the AFL or some other international union, an arrangement which proved unsatisfactory to the union (which could not collect dues) and the Negroes (who were inadequately represented); Negroes were consequently admitted to auxiliary locals controlled by whites; the auxiliary local was then eroded by various legal pressures making it unlawful for the union to have union-security provisions covering workers who were not accorded full membership privileges. The auxiliaries were then transformed into segregated locals with at least the theoretical right to govern their own affairs. After the Second World War, segregated locals came under increasing attack because of the Negro community's opposition to segregation in all its forms. The state FEP commissions and the Kennedy and Johnson administrations also took action against segregated locals. In industrial plants the segregated seniority roster was the most common form of discrimination and this too has been attacked by a variety of agencies since the Second World War. Moreover, informal exclusion, discrimination in referral systems, and discrimination in apprenticeship and other training programs have come under increasing attack in the postwar period.

FOOTNOTES

1. For a discussion which "accentuates the positive" with respect to union racial practices, see Harry Fleischman and James Rorty, *We Open the Gates: Labor's Fight for Equality,* New York: National Labor Service, September 1958.
2. Mathew A. Kessler, "Economic Status of Nonwhite Workers, 1955–1962," *Monthly Labor Review,* July 1963, Table 7.
3. For a discussion of this experience, see Lloyd Ulman, "Unionism and Collective Bargaining in the Modern Period," in Seymour Harris, Ed., *American Economic History,* New York: McGraw-Hill, 1961, pp. 459–467.
4. George Strauss, "Control by the Membership in Building Trades Unions," in Walter Galenson and Seymour Lipset, Eds., *Labor and Trade Unionism,* New York: Wiley, 1960, p. 282.

Index

DATE DUE

JUL 6 '69	JAN 8 '81		
MAR 4 '70	FEB 9 '81		
	APR 30 '89		
FEB 14 '71			
APR 14 '71			
APR 23 '71			
MAY 9 '71			
MAY 20 '71			
NOV 12 '72			
E H			
NOV 14 '73			
H 3			
MAY 24 '77			
MAY 9 '77			
MAY 23 '78			
MAY '79			PRINTED IN U.S.A.